CADOGAN

Catherine Day

North of
Irelar

D1120591

Cadogan Guides
11 Hills Place, London W1R 1AH, UK
e-mail: becky.kendall@morrispub.co.uk

Distributed in North America by
The Globe Pequot Press
246 Goose Lane, PO Box 480, Guilford
Connecticut 06437–0480

First published 1995
Updated 2000 by Cameron Wilson
Copyright © Catharina Day 1995, 2000
Illustrations © Marcus Patton 1995

Book and cover design by Animage
Cover photographs by John Ferro Sims (*front*) and Travel
Library (*back*)
Maps © Cadogan Guides, drawn by Map Creation Ltd

Editorial Director: Vicki Ingle
Series Editor: Linda McQueen

Editor: Dominique Shead
Updater: Cameron Wilson
Indexer: Caroline Wilding
Production: Rupert Wheeler Book Production Services

A catalogue record for this book is available from the
British Library
ISBN 1–86011–970–0
Printed and bound by Cambridge University Press

Please Note

The author and publishers have
made every effort to ensure the
accuracy of the information in the
book at the time of going to
press. However, they cannot
accept any responsibility for any
loss, injury or inconvenience
resulting from the use of information contained in this guide.

Please Help Us Keep This Guide Up to Date

Every effort has been made to ensure the accuracy of the information in this book at the time
of going to press. However, practical details such
as opening hours, travel information, standards
in hotels and restaurants and, in particular,
prices are liable to change.

We would be delighted to receive any comments
concerning existing entries or omissions. Writers
of the best and most helpful letters will receive a
copy of the Cadogan Guide of their choice.

About the Author

Catharina Day comes from a long-established Irish family. She was born in Kenya but moved to County Donegal as a small child. She attended Derry High School before travelling to a convent boarding school, and then University in England. She was married in County Donegal and visits frequently with her husband and four children from her home in Scotland. She has compiled an anthology of Irish literature.

Acknowledgements

Numerous people have helped me compile this book, and to them I wish to say many thanks. It would take pages to mention all but a few by name for through my researches on the guide I have met lots of delightful people who have given me an insight into their locality. In particular I would like to thank Bord Fáilte and the Northern Ireland Tourist Board who have always been extremely generous with information, advice and goodwill. My family have over the years been very supportive and a great help. My mother has been an enthusiastic gatherer of information and her wide general knowledge has been invaluable. My sister Angelique has been a great help, and my husband Simon has helped me in countless ways, acting as my agent, and trying out hotels and restaurants on his business trips to Ireland. I am indebted to the late Araminta Swiney who advised me on what to leave out, Flora Armstrong for her initial help with South Ulster and Co. Armagh, John Colclough who recommended eating out and places to stay, and Fergus Hanna Bell, Dr B. M. Walker, Marcus Patton, Richard Gordon and Sean Rafferty for their general help and advice. Finally, thanks to Cameron Wilson and Dominique Shead, and to Paula Levy who first gave me the opportunity to explore and write about this lovely country.

To my mother

About the Updater

Cameron Wilson was born in Sydney in 1965 and still calls Australia home, at least some of the time. Having spent six years wandering the world with a guitar and a backpack, he settled in to a Communications Studies degree at Murdoch University in Perth, Western Australia, and began pestering newspaper editors with travel stories and photos. Currently based in London where he complains a lot about the weather, Cameron is a freelance travel writer and editor, and has contributed to several other guide books as well as newspapers in Britain and Australia.

Updater's Acknowledgements

Thanks to Marc and Cecile, the cheeriest hitch-hikers a fellow could pick up—and who also earned their stripes as navigators and travel buddies. Several of the folks at Northern Ireland's tourist information offices were helpful above and beyond the call—notably staff at Newcastle, Armagh City and Derry. As always, the people of Northern Ireland have my undying admiration for their humour and charity in the face of difficult times, and most of all for their healthy disrespect towards politicians on all sides. My sincere wishes for a much brighter future.

Contents

Blake's bar,
Enniskillen

Introduction

Do you think of the 'Troubles' when Ulster is mentioned? Most people do. This is a great pity, for this beautiful part of Ireland is not a grim, dispirited place. It has always brimmed with energy, and has been reinvigorated by progress towards a lasting peace. Ulster folk are a resilient and resourceful people, as a study of their history and industrial activity reveals, and their endurance of 30 years of violence proves. Those who in the past were adventurous enough to visit Ulster always returned full of praise for the countryside, the artistic life, the wit, friendliness and warmth of the people.

Maybe you are confused about what geographical or political terrain Ulster covers? The labels 'Ulster', 'the Province', 'the six counties', 'Northern Ireland' and 'the North' are used as synonymous by people who do not come from Ireland. Within Ireland they have different political nuances. In this guide, 'Ulster' is used in its cultural and historical sense, as one of the four ancient provinces of Ireland, and so it includes the Republic of Ireland counties of Cavan, Donegal and Monaghan. The other six—Antrim, Armagh, Down, Fermanagh, Londonderry and Tyrone—are known officially by the title 'the Province of Northern Ireland', and are part of the United Kingdom. In spite of the borders and politics, there is an inherent unity between the people of the nine counties of Ulster. They are every bit as 'Irish' as the people of Munster—although some would undoubtedly describe themselves as Ulstermen first.

When you are speaking of the six British-ruled counties, whether in Dublin, London, Belfast or Letterkenny, the most politically neutral term is 'the North'. Unionists talk of 'the Province'. Nationalists talk of 'the six counties'.

The North you will see today has suffered hugely from the 30 years of the Troubles. This has paradoxically brought about planned and attractive public housing and public buildings for the most part. The countryside is as beautiful as (and perhaps more accessible than) anywhere else in Ireland, because of the development of forest parks and the guardianship of bodies such as the British National Trust. The North is also different because it was industrialized during the 19th century and so endured the more ugly stages of capitalist development. Co. Donegal, Co. Monaghan and Co. Cavan are still largely free of the suburban sprawl, networks of power-lines and dual carriageways which are predominant in the North.

The North and the South, as the two states are referred to, co-operate in many areas, especially the arts and tourism. A major example of this co-operation has been the re-opening of the 19th-century Ballinamore and Ballyconnell canal that links the Shannon and Fermanagh lake system. It fell into disuse over a hundred years ago, and its restoration was funded by both governments, the EU and the International Fund for Ireland.

The Ulster border, which has shifted around since historical records began in the 7th century, has meant much through the ages: *Cú Chulainn*, the Hound of Ulster, was perhaps its most famous guard when he defended it against the host of Ireland during the epic battles of the Brown Bull of Cooley. It is interesting to contemplate how myth and history support each other over this enmity between North and South. Irish archaeologists have concluded that a great earthen wall was built two thousand years ago to separate Ulster (*Ulaidhster*—Land of the Ulstermen) from much of the South of Ireland. It consisted of two pairs of double ramparts, the largest of which was 90ft (27m) wide, 18ft (5.5m) high and 1½ miles (2.8km) long, and formed part of a defensive border along the line of the upper reaches of the Shannon River. It is thought that the wall was built by tribal rulers in central Ireland as a defence against the warlike tribes of Ulster to prevent two of the major fords across the Shannon, at Drumsna and Carrick in County Leitrim, being used by the Northern invaders. The Drumsna wall cuts off a loop of the Shannon and is broken only by an entrance complex which formed a huge gateway into tribal territory—probably the Kingdom of Connacht. Another earthwork, built in the 3rd or 2nd century BC and known as the Black Pig's Dyke, stretches intermittently from Donegal Bay to the Dorsey and Newry Marshes in the east. This time the defence was built by the Ulstermen against the Southerners. It is likely that the two earthworks reflect different stages in the armed conflict between these two major prehistoric tribal groupings. It may even be that the legendary Connacht Queen Maeve or *Medb* built the Carrick and Drumsna defences during the great battles over the Brown Bull of Cooley.

Myth and history is often used as a political weapon in Ulster. Some experts on the Irish race maintain that in ancient times the North was full of Picts and the South full of Milesians—a Celtic tribe from Spain whose invasion is recorded in the ancient manuscript the *Lebor Gabala* or *Book of Invasions*. They probably arrived around 200 BC. What is more sure is that later, in the 17th century, Ulster was the most systematically planted province, because of its continued fierce resistance to the English. Thus the hardy Scots were introduced into the province to provide a loyal garrison.

The sign of Ulster is the Red Hand. This symbol is the result of the race for the overlordship of Ulster between the Gaelic MacDonnells and the Norman de Burghs, in the 12th century. The first to reach land would take the prize and, as the two contestants struggled through the shallows off the Antrim coast, MacDonnell, fearing that de Burgh, who was leading the race, would win, cut off his own hand and threw it on to the strand where it lay covered in blood. Thus the symbol of this fair land is oddly prophetic of the many bloody struggles for its conquest.

The two great clans of the west are descended from the sons of the great high king of Ireland, Niall of the Nine Hostages (AD 379–405). Their names were Conal and Eoghan and they gave their name to districts in this part of the province, Tyrconnell and Tyrone. When Brian Boru, the great high king of the 11th century, instituted surnames in Ireland, the followers and descendants of Conal and Eoghan took the names O'Donnell and O'Neill respectively, and it was they who rebelled against English rule.

With your head full of myths, legend and literature, travel with stout shoes, a warm jersey, an ear tuned in to history and an eye focused on beauty. There is no such thing as a tiresome hot journey in Ulster. The climate is good and damp, and the sunshine, when it comes, intensifies the already beautiful colours of the landscape. The minor roads are usually empty and traffic jams are still an exception. Do not rush, for if you do the charm of the countryside and its people will pass you by. The largest concentration of houses and cars is in the lively city of Belfast (although much of its Victorian and Edwardian charm has been sadly destroyed by the development of car parks, roads, and above all the bombing campaigns of the Troubles). The prosperous suburbs and housing estates which reach well into Co. Down and Co. Antrim are similar to the urban sprawl increasing everywhere in western Europe, but they are easy to escape from. A short distance away is the beauty of the Antrim glens and coastline, the tranquillity of the lakelands of Counties Cavan, Monaghan and Fermanagh, and the mountains and lakes of Donegal.

Wherever you go in Ulster, it is possible to stay in friendly, hospitable B&Bs or tranquil country houses where the proportions and the furnishings of the rooms are redolent of a more gracious age. Not only is the food delicious, and made from the freshest seafood, local meat, game and vegetables, you will also often find well-chosen wines and, of course, decent whiskey and beer. The owners and staff of these places are keen to help with any request you have, whether it's finding the origins of your great-granny, or directing you to the best fishing, golf, beaches, and sites of historical interest.

The way the Irish speak is another pleasure in store for you. In Ulster you will find a race who can express themselves with great character, humour and exactness. Those dry archaeological and historical facts suddenly become much more fascinating when you can ask for the local version of events, and hear for yourself the wonderful stories which make up history.

When you are in Ireland, the irritations and annoyances which accompany one through everyday life disappear, and the desire for a good day's tramp in the mountains, a spot of fishing, or a good read before a warm fire become realities. However, it is important not to stick rigidly to a scheme, for nothing in Ireland can be planned right down to the last detail.

Guide to the Guide

The guide begins with a comprehensive **Travel** section, followed by the **Practical A–Z** packed with information that will help you get the best from your visit, including advice on where to stay and eat, shopping, sports and leisure activities. There's a short section on **History** from pagan times to the present day which outlines the main events and problems that constitute the complex Ireland of today; this is followed by a brief résumé of the **religious** background and a selection of the country's most famous saints. The next section, **Topics**, covers a variety of subjects including a piece on Irish linen, music, how to trace your ancestors, and a feature specifically on the gardens of Ulster.

Ulster is made up of the six counties that constitute Northern Ireland—Fermanagh, Tyrone, Londonderry, Antrim, Down and Armagh—and Donegal, Cavan and Monaghan, which are part of the Republic of Ireland. Each chapter consists of a gazetteer of the whole county with lots of local history and anecdotal knowledge together with descriptions and details of the places of interest. Practical lists of transport facilities, tourist information centres, festivals and sports and leisure activities for each county are given at the beginning of each chapter, with shopping, suggestions of places to stay and eat, as well as entertainment possibilities, at the end.

At the end of the book there are features on **Old Gods and Heroes**; ancient sites and early architecture (with a glossary of terms); an essay on **language**; a **chronology** of events; a recommended **further reading** list; and a comprehensive **index**.

Travel

Getting There

From Europe

British Airways, British Midland, Air City, Jersey European Airways, easyJet and **KLM** run regular flights to the north of Ireland from the UK, Paris and Amsterdam.

The main airport is **Belfast International** (Belfast Aldergrove), but Belfast also has another, smaller airport called Belfast City. There are also flights to **Londonderry/Derry** (Eglinton Airport) and **Enniskillen**.

Belfast International serves connections from Birmingham, Bristol, Cardiff, East Midlands, Edinburgh, Glasgow, Leeds/Bradford, Manchester and Newcastle-upon-Tyne. Belfast City Airport serves flights from Birmingham, Blackpool, Edinburgh, Exeter, Glasgow, the Isle of Man, Leeds/Bradford, London (Luton), Manchester, Newcastle-upon-Tyne and Teeside. Eglinton is served by direct flights from Glasgow and Manchester.

A full-price British Midlands return from Belfast to London can cost over £200. However, prices start from around £75, and vary according to your date and time of departure. EasyJet (for example) offer some early morning mid-week flights one-way to Belfast for £18.

There are no direct flights between **Dublin** and **Belfast** but the train service is very efficient, or you can hire a car at the airport and drive north. It is about 100 miles between the two cities, much of which is motorway.

From the USA and Canada

Aer Lingus operates direct flights to Belfast from New York and Boston. However, depending on your broader travel plans, you may find that the best deal is still to fly via London. For charter companies that operate flights to Belfast from New York, Florida and Toronto, look for the advertisements in the travel pages of the major newspapers.

You can fly direct to Dublin from Atlanta, Boston, Chicago, Montreal and New York. The main transatlantic carriers flying direct to Ireland are Delta Air Lines and Aer Lingus, who have flights into Dublin, Shannon, Cork, Galway, Sligo and Kerry from Newark, New Jersey.

Transport from the Airports

There is a regular **airbus** service into Belfast from Belfast International (£5 single), and a regular **train** service from Belfast City Airport to Belfast Central Station. For Derry from Belfast International Airport it is quickest to take a **taxi** to Antrim railway station (six trains to Derry per day). The 10-minute drive costs an exorbitant £6 or so, but you can spread the cost by sharing the taxi with other travellers. Derry City's airport bus drops you at Foyle Street, just below the city centre.

By Boat

The **ferries** from the British west coast tend to cross the Irish Sea in the shortest distance possible: from the points along the coasts of Wales and Scotland which stretch out furthest towards the east coast of Ireland. Which port and crossing you choose will depend on where you are starting from, and where you wish to go—which is not quite such an obvious statement as it may seem. The main crossings are as follows: Fishguard and Pembroke in South Wales serve Rosslare Harbour (near Wexford) and southeast Ireland. Holyhead, off Anglesey in north Wales, takes passengers to Dublin and the neighbouring port of Dun Laoghaire, in the centre of the east coast. This route is also served by a high-speed **catamaran** which crosses the Irish Sea in 1hr 50mins. The two main ports in the north of Ireland are Belfast and nearby Larne, served by ferries and the Sea Cat taking the short crossing from Cairnryan and neighbouring Stranraer in southwest Scotland, and by ferries taking the much longer journey from Liverpool.

All the ferry ports are well connected to bus and rail transport (*see* pp.3–5), and all the ferry services have drive-on/drive-off facilities for car drivers.

Prices depend very much on the time of year and the length of the crossing. Price structures also relate to how long you intend to stay and, if you are taking your car, the number of passengers and so forth. To give you some idea of costs, here are a few examples. Figures quoted are for 1 adult, 2 adults and a car or 4 adults and a car. The upper and lower estimates are for high and low season respectively. With P&O, crossing from Cairnryan to Larne, passengers pay £25 to £30 each way; cars cost from £150 to £200 each way including 2 adults; but there are also special fares for trips outside peak travel times. On Stena Line's service between Fishguard and Rosslare in the Republic, passengers pay £22 to £32 each way; cars cost £95 to £175 each way, but this price includes up to four people travelling with the car. The Sealink Catamaran costs approximately £10 more for passengers and £30 more for a car. Passenger fares for children are approximately half the adult fare.

Ferry Services

To the North of Ireland from Great Britain

Stena Line ✆ (0990) 707070:

> **Stranraer–Larne**, 8 sailings daily, all year (excluding 25–26 Dec and 1 Jan), 3hrs.

P & O European Ferries, ✆ (0990) 980777:

> **Cairnryan–Larne**, 6 sailings daily, all year, 2¼hrs.

Norse Irish Ferries, ✆ (0151) 944 1010:

> **Liverpool–Belfast**, 1 per day, all year, 11hrs.

Seacat, ✆ (0990) 523523:

> **Stranraer–Belfast**, 5 sailings daily, all year, 1½hrs.
>
> **Troon–Belfast**, daily, all year, 2hrs.

To the Republic from Great Britain

Irish Ferries, ✆ (0990) 171717:

> **Holyhead–Dublin**, 2 sailings daily, 3½ hrs
>
> **Pembroke–Rosslare**, 2 sailings daily, 4¼hrs.

Stena Line, ✆ (0990) 707070:

Holyhead–Dun Laoghaire, 4 sailings daily, 3½hrs;
2 catamaran sailings daily, 2hrs.

Fishguard–Rosslare, 2 sailings daily, 3½hrs;
3 catamaran sailings daily, 1½.

Isle of Man Steam Packet Company, ✆ (0151) 236 3411:

The Isle of Man Steam Packet Company run a seasonal service to and from the Isle of Man:

Isle of Man–Belfast, mid-May–mid-Sept, 5hrs;
Sea Cat, 2hrs 40mins.

Note that at some peak times of the year—Easter, Christmas and around the April and October bank holidays—and on all sailings from Liverpool, the number of passengers on certain crossings is controlled. All non-motorist passengers must have a 'sailing control ticket' to board the ship at these times. This can be obtained when you book your crossing or, if you change your booking or have an open ticket, from the ferry offices. It is worth checking whether you need a control ticket before you start your journey.

By Train

All the car ferries crossing back and forth between England and Ireland are scheduled to link up with the **British Rail InterCity trains** which go frequently and speedily from London to Fishguard, Liverpool, Holyhead and Stranraer. You can buy your **ticket** at any British Rail station or booking office; credit card bookings can be made on the telephone; enquiries ✆ (0345) 484950 or with **Northern Ireland Railways** in Belfast ✆ (028) 9089 9411. There are free **seat reservations** on all direct train services to and from the ports. You can get couchettes on the night trains, but when it is not crowded it is possible to have a comfortable snooze by stretching out along the seats.

London (Euston) to Belfast via Liverpool is about 16hrs; and London (Euston) to Belfast via Stranraer and Larne takes about 13hrs. Of course there are numerous other train routes connecting with the ferry ports. Adult single fares for London to Belfast, £45–£60. Trains go to all destinations from Belfast Central Station, East Bridge Street, except for Larne Harbour for the boat train (and ferry), for which you want Yorkgate Rail Station, ✆ (028) 9074 1700. A Rail-link bus runs frequently between the stations, Mon–Sat, 7.15am–8.45pm. Outside these hours buses take you either to Oxford Street bus station or City Hall.

By Bus

Travelling by bus/ferry to the north of Ireland is quite an endurance, with lots of stops through England and Ireland to pick up other travellers. The main advantage is that it is cheap and gets you straight to destinations all over the province, so there's no need for further buses, trains or taxis. The major bus companies are National Express, ✆ (020) 7730 8235, and Ulsterbus in Belfast, ✆ (028) 9033 7002. National Express buses leave London from Victoria coach station. It is important to note that Belfast has two main bus stations: Europa Centre, Glengall Street and Oxford Street near the main rail station. Check before leaving that you are going to the right one.

London to Belfast takes 13 hours, travelling overnight via Stranraer, and costs £32 single, £48 return.

Tour Operators

Special-interest Holidays

There are a large number of tour companies offering all manner of enticing holidays. The Northern Ireland Tourist Board have lists of the main operators, which are published in their brochures. Alternatively, contact your travel agent.

Travellers who want holidays with a special focus—ancestor-hunting, angling, bird-watching, farm and country, gastronomy, gardens, golf, horse-riding, painting, sailing, or a mixture of these—are particularly well catered for. Oideas Gael, Glencolmcille, Co. Donegal, offer a workshop-type course in **Irish culture and language**, including folklore, singing, storytelling, set dancing and local history; ✆ (073) 30248 (Donegal).

Holidays based around **arts and crafts** courses (weaving, patchwork and painting) can be organized through Ardress Craft Centre, Kesh, Co. Fermanagh, ✆ (028) 6863 1267.

John Nicholas Colclough also runs fascinating, informative **tours** anywhere in Ireland. He will tailor an itinerary to suit you, organize a car with a guide/driver, and superb accommodation ranging from the traditional farmhouse to the grandest castle. His tours can take in gardens, genealogy, ghosts, gourmet meals, and sites of historical importance. He will act as guide himself—and you cannot find anyone more engaging and informative. He is prepared to investigate any obscure angle on Ireland that you may wish to pursue. Contact Colclough Tours, 71 Waterloo Road, Dublin 4, ✆ (01) 668 6463.

Entry Formalities

Passports and Visas

Entry formalities are exactly as they are for entry to the United Kingdom. UK citizens do not need any sort of visa for either the Republic or the North, but it is as well to carry proof of identity, since, if you are stopped in a security check, quick identification will speed the process. **US** and **Canadian** as well as **Australian/NZ** citizens require a passport, but no visa.

Citizens of **European Union** (EU) countries need a full passport for entry into Northern Ireland and if you want to cross into the Republic.

Passports and visas may be required for visitors of countries not included in the above. Check with the Northern Ireland Tourist Board or with the visa departments of the Irish or British embassies. In any case, entry regulations are liable to change, so check before you leave.

Customs

There is no limit on goods brought between the UK and Northern Ireland but visitors from anywhere else are subject to restrictions on the quantities of certain goods. These apply to cigarettes and other tobacco products, alcoholic drinks, perfume and gifts and other new goods. The regulations are labyrinthine, since they differ according to whether or not you are resident in the EU, and whether or not the goods were bought in EU countries. Furthermore, EU residents have to take into account two separate structures, one for goods bought in duty-free shops in the EU, and another for goods bought, tax-paid, in an EU country.

To ensure that you have up-to-date information, it is better that you refer to the tourist offices, airlines and ferry services. However, the **customs regulations** are standard, and, provided that you are seventeen years old or more, you can be sure of being allowed to import at least 200 cigarettes, 50 cigars, one litre of spirits or two litres of wine and 50 grams of perfume; depending on where you live and where you bought your goods, you may be able to import rather more than this.

Dog- and cat-owners may like to know that they can bring their pet to the north of Ireland and take it across the border to the Republic, provided that it comes directly from Britain, the Channel Islands or the Isle of Man, and has lived there for at least six months.

For residents of EU countries, the usual EU regulations apply regarding what you can bring into your home country. Again, this depends on whether the goods have been bought in Northern Ireland itself, tax-paid, or in a duty-free shop. Note that you cannot bring fresh meat, vegetables or plants into the UK.

Residents of the USA may each take home $400 worth of foreign goods without attracting duty, including the tobacco and alcohol allowance. Canadians can bring home $300-worth of goods in a year, plus their tobacco and alcohol allowances.

You can claim back the **Value Added Tax** (VAT) on goods purchased in Northern Ireland and the Republic and exported by you, unless you are a UK citizen, provided that you export them within two months of purchase and their total value exceeds £50 (or £102 if you are resident in another EU country). The VAT rate is 17½% in Northern Ireland and approx 21% in the Republic. You will need a **Cashback voucher** stamped by the shop; this must be stamped by Customs before you leave Ireland. You can present the stamped vouchers at the Cashback desk at Belfast, Shannon or Dublin airports and obtain a refund there and then, or you can claim the refund by post after your return.

Getting Around

By Train

Rail travel in Northern Ireland is run by **Northern Ireland Railways** (NIR), with three main routes: north to Derry via Ballymena; east to Bangor along the shores of Belfast Lough; and south to Dublin via Newry. This system is fully integrated with the CIE services of the Republic, and lines between Belfast and Dublin are operated jointly by NIR and CIE. It takes two hours to reach Dublin on the Belfast–Dublin non-stop express, and there are six trains a day (three on Sundays). The fare is £13 day-return and £20 for two days or more. For further information about rail travel in the north of Ireland, contact the InterCity Travel Centre, Belfast, ✆ (028) 9023 0671; or the Travel and Information Centre, Central Station, Belfast, ✆ (028) 9089 9411.

Special Rail Tickets

Rail runabout tickets giving 7 days' unlimited travel can be bought at main railway stations. The **Emerald Card** offers unlimited travel throughout Northern Ireland and the Republic on both trains and buses: an 8-day adult ticket costs £105, children (under 16) £53; a 15-day ticket costs £180, £90 for children. The **Brit/Ireland Pass** is a money-saving package which combines rail travel in Britain and Ireland with a round-trip crossing of the Irish Sea by Stena Sealink. It can only be purchased in your country of origin. Contact:

England: British Rail, ✆ (0171) 928 5100.

Australia: Thomas Cook, ✆ (2) 248 6100, or National Australia Travel, ✆ (2) 215 7127.

New Zealand: Thomas Cook, ✆ (9) 379 6800, or Gulliver's Pacific Travel, ✆ (9) 307 1801.

South Africa: World Travel Agency, ✆ (11) 297234.

For **steam train enthusiasts** there are plenty of places where you can travel on one as more and more narrow-gauge line is opened up. The Northern Irish Tourist Board publishes a comprehensive guide to steam trains and railways which covers the whole of Ireland.

By Bus

The **bus service** throughout Ulster is efficient and goes to the most remote places. The main companies are **Ulsterbus**, ✆ (028) 9033 3000, in Northern Ireland and **Irish Bus** (or *Bus Eireann*), ✆ (01) 836 6111, run by CIE, in the Republic.

Ulsterbus runs frequent services to all parts of the north of Ireland. You can pick up timetables at any Ulster bus station, or the tourist office in Belfast. There are two main bus stations in Belfast, the Ulsterbus head office at Great Victoria Street (also known as the Europa Bus Centre, Glengall Street), and the Oxford Street bus station; information number for both stations: ✆ (028) 9033 3000. The Citybus service operates in Belfast only, ✆ (028) 9024 6485. There are a number of day and half-day coach tours on offer from the Europa Bus Centre to various places of interest such as Fermanagh Lakeland, Causeway Coast, The Mournes, Armagh City, and the Glens of Antrim.

Special Bus Tickets

For concessionary tickets applying to both bus and rail, *see* the 'Special Rail Tickets' section, above. Ulsterbus offers **Freedom of Northern Ireland Tickets**: one-day ticket £13, seven-day tickets, £35; these can be purchased from Ulsterbus depots. For further details of special fares and bus excursions, see *On the Move*, published by the Northern Ireland Tourist Office.

By Car

To explore the north of Ireland with minimum effort and maximum freedom, bring a car. If you fill it up with people who share the ferry and petrol costs, it won't be too expensive. Buy a detailed **road map** and, if you have time, choose a minor road and just meander. It is along these little lanes that the secret life of the country continues undisturbed. The black and red cows still chew by the wayside whilst the herdsman, usually an old man or a child, salutes you with an upward nod. Nearby is the farmstead cluttered with bits of old machinery and a cheerful sense of makeshift, where everything is kept to be used again: an old front door will stop a gap in the hedge; old baths serve as cattle troughs; clucking hens roost on the old haycart—next year it might be bought by the tinkers, who will varnish it up to adorn some suburban garden. You will come upon castles, and the ruins of the small, circular buildings called *clochans*, still breathing with memories, tumbled even further by the local farmer in search of stone; and there are views of those many hills which have never reached the pages of any guidebook. If your car **breaks down** you will always be able to find a mechanic to give you a hand; whether it's late at night or on a Sunday, just ask someone. He or she will sweep you up in a wave of sympathy and send messengers off in all directions to find you someone with a reputation for mechanical genius. If it is some small and common part that has let you down, he will either have it or do something that will get you by until you come to a proper garage. One thing you will notice is that the Irish have a completely different attitude to machinery from most nationalities. In England, if you break down, it is an occasion for embarrassment; everybody rushes by hardly noticing you or pretending not to. In Ireland, if your car has broken down the next passing car will probably stop, and the problem will be readily taken on and discussed with great enjoyment. The Irish can laugh at the occasional failure of material affairs.

Facts and Formalities for Car Drivers

You **drive on the left** throughout Ireland (when you are not driving in the middle of the road). **Petrol stations** stay open until around eight in the evenings, and the village ones are open after Mass on Sundays. If you are desperate for petrol and every station seems closed, you can usually knock on the door and ask somebody to start the pumps for you. It's well worth keeping an eye on the the price of petrol, as it varies between the two states, and the exchange rate can have a bearing on price. At the time of writing, a litre of petrol was 58p in the Republic and 72p in the north; effectively 20p per litre cheaper to buy petrol in the Republic. The **speed limits** are the same as in the UK—70mph (112kph) on dual carriageways, 60mph (100kph) on country roads, 40mph (60kph) in built-up areas and 30mph (50kph) in towns; in the Republic it is 60mph (100kph) on all roads and 30mph or 40mph (50kph or 60kph) through the villages and towns. Drivers and front-seat passengers must always wear a **seat belt**—it is illegal not to. Children under 12 should travel in the back. There are strict drink-driving laws in the North and in the Republic, and the police will use a breathalyzer test if they suspect that you are driving under the influence of alcohol.

There are some excellent **motoring maps**: Bartholomew's ¼-inch, obtainable from the AA and Bord Fáilte, gives good details of minor roads. Scenic routes are signposted and marked on the Bord Fáilte map. Place names on signposts in the Republic are usually given in English and in Irish; in the places where Irish only is used, a good map will be useful. The old white signposts give distances in miles; the new green ones give distances in kilometres; as a general rule, distances are posted in kilometres in the Republic, in miles in the North. All other traffic signs are more or less the same as the standard European ones.

Residents of Northern Ireland, Great Britain and the Republic of Ireland using private cars and motorcycles may cross the borders with very little formality. A **full, up-to-date licence** is all you need. Under EU regulations, private motor insurers will provide the minimum legal cover required in all EU countries, although they may need to be told before you travel. Always carry the **vehicle registration book**. If you have hired a car, be sure to tell the rental company if you intend to cross borders, and that you have all the necessary papers; the rental company should also deal with all the insurance headaches.

AA (Automobile Association) offices will usually give you details of the necessary formalities if you are not clear about anything. Their number in the Republic is (01) 677 9481, in the North (0990) 989989; for breakdown service call ✆ (0800) 887766.

Parking: The universal blue P sign directs you to car parking or a lay-by. There are car parks in most towns, generally inexpensive or free, and it's as well to use them. You can generally park on the street but look out for control zone areas in some towns which are indicated by pink or yellow signs 'Control Zone. No Parking.' In Belfast, meter parking is limited to the south side of the city behind the City Hall and around St Anne's Cathedral on the north side. You can find free street parking up towards Queen's University and the Ulster Museum and there are plenty of car parks throughout the city.

Car Hire Operators

In Northern Ireland Avis, Hertz and Europcar all operate from both Belfast's airports, but it may be less expensive to hire a car from their city centre branches. Local firms (see phone book) can offer even better deals. These are only some of the big ones who will meet you at the airports and the ferry ports:

    Avis Rent-A-Car Ltd, Belfast, ✆ (028) 9024 0404,
    Budget Rent-a-Car, Belfast, ✆ (028) 9023 0700,
    Europcar, Belfast International Airport, ✆ (028) 9442 3444,
    Hertz Rent-A-Car, Belfast, ✆ (0990) 996699

Renting a car in the north of Ireland is not cheap whoever you rent it from. You might be able to bargain slightly if business is slack. Prices range from about £180 to £250 for a standard family car for a week, including insurance, unlimited mileage and VAT. Remember always to check the total cost, as insurance and VAT are often added to the quoted price. You must be at least 23yrs (21 with some companies) to rent a car and have held a valid driving licence for at least 2 years. Some companies won't rent to drivers over 70yrs. Look out also for fly-drive or rail-sail-drive packages offered by some of the airlines and ferry companies: these usually represent major savings. The car hire company will organize insurance, but do check this. If you do not take extra collision-damage waiver insurance you could be liable for extensive damages.

By Taxi

You can find taxis at main railway stations and airports. In Belfast, the taxi ranks for cabs with meters are at both rail stations, both bus stations and City Hall. They are London-type black cabs and have a yellow disc on the windscreen. Other taxis may not have meters so ask the fare to your destination before setting off. Hotels are happy to order taxis for you.

By Bicycle

The north of Ireland is one of the pleasantest places to cycle in. The roads are uncrowded, there are still lots of birds and animals that live around the hedgerows, and there is relatively little pollution. In between the delicious whiffs of gorse or honeysuckle will come strong manure smells! You can bring your bicycle free on the ferry, or you can rent one. The Tourist Board produces a leaflet on cycling (*Information Bulletin 3*), which lists tours, routes, and events for cyclists, plus a number of cycle hire companies. Prices begin at about £7 per day, £30 per week, with a deposit of about £40. You can also hire bikes at some of the youth hostels; contact YHANI, ☎ Belfast (028) 9032 4733. Note that bicycles hired in Northern Ireland cannot be taken into the Republic.

On Foot

Hitch-hiking is probably not a very fast or satisfactory way of getting around. You might find that people will not pick you up because years of the Troubles have made them cautious, although the ceasefire may have made people more relaxed about stopping. As ever, women simply should never hitch alone.

Practical A–Z

Children

If you are travelling with children you will find that bed and breakfast establishments will welcome them. Many have family rooms with four or five beds, and charge a reduced price for children. Most supply cots and high chairs, and offer a baby-sitting service, but always check beforehand. Some farm and country houses keep a donkey or pony, and have swings and a play area set up for children.

Irish people love children, and are very tolerant of seeing and hearing them in bars and eating places during the daytime. They will offer children's menus at a cheaper price and generally be helpful, but they will not be so tolerant if you turn up with them for dinner at night. If you are contemplating staying in some of the smart country house hotels which are full of precious antiques, etc., please check that it is a suitable place for children beforehand. The many national monuments, heritage centres, gardens and parks usually charge much less for children or offer a good value family ticket.

Climate

The north of Ireland lies on the path of the North Atlantic cyclones, which makes the climate mild, equable and moist. Rainfall is heaviest in the high western coastal areas, where it averages over 80ins (203cm) a year. On the east coast, rainfall averages between 30 and 40ins (76 and 101cm). Rain here is a blessing, yet from the reputation it has both at home and abroad you might imagine it was a curse. It keeps the fields and trees that famous lush green, and the high level of water vapour in the air gives the region a sleepy quality and softens the colours of the landscape. The winds from the east increase the haziness and mute the colours, but these are nearly always followed by winds from the northwest which bring clearer air and sunshine. So the clouds begin to drift and shafts of changing light touch the land. Nearly every drizzly day has this gleam of sunshine, which is why the Irish are always very optimistic about the weather. The Gulf Stream in the Atlantic means that there are never extremes of cold or hot.

Snow is not common, and is seldom severe. The spring tends to be relatively dry, especially after the blustery winds of March, and the crisp colours and freshness of autumn only degenerates into the cold and damp of winter in late December. You can hope for at least six hours of sunshine a day during May, June, July and August.

Average Temperatures

January	4°C (39°F)	– 7°C (45°F)
July/August	14°C (57°F)	– 24°C (75°F)

Disabled Travellers

The Northern Ireland Tourist Board and Bord Fáilte show that Ireland has made considerable efforts to help handicapped travellers, and both of these tourist boards have produced useful booklets containing advice. Particularly commended is *The Disabled Tourist in Northern Ireland*, published by the NITB and distributed free. It lists hotels, guesthouses and restaurants, what to see and where to shop, based on suggestions by individual disabled people. It also gives telephone numbers, so that you can check facilities beforehand. Bord Fáilte has a similar publication, updated annually, called *Accommodation for the Disabled*.

In Britain, RADAR (Royal Association for Disability and Rehabilitation), Unit 12, 250 City Road, London EC1V 8AF, ✆ (020) 7250 3222, is an excellent source of advice, and publishes its own fact sheets on holiday planning, accommodation and so forth, and fuller guides for the disabled traveller for the UK and abroad. The Holiday Care Service, Imperial Building, Victoria Road, Horley, Surrey RH6 7PZ, ✆ (01293) 774535, offers advice for all travellers with special needs.

Electricity

The current is 220 volts AC, so you should bring an adaptor if you have any American appliances. Wall sockets take the standard British-style three-pin (flat) fused plugs, or two-pin (round) plugs. If you are worried, there are good travellers' adaptors on the market which can usually cope with most socket-and-plug combinations that you are liable to encounter abroad.

Embassies and Consulates

US Consulate (Belfast), 14 Queen's Street, Belfast BT1 6EG, ✆ (028) 9032 8239.
Canadian High Commission, 38 Grosvenor St, London W1, ✆ (020) 7629 9492.
Australian High Commission, Australia House, Strand, London, WC2 B4L, ✆ (020) 7379 4334.
New Zealand High Commission, New Zealand House, 80 Haymarket, London SW1Y 4TQ, ✆ (020) 7930 8422.

Fishing

Ulster has a wealth of lakes, rivers and tributaries, and fine sport can be had in all areas. Seasons vary, as they do in the south, and costs are not high.

Lough Erne is well known for quality in all types of fishing. The upper water is mostly for coarse fish, while the lower holds salmon and trout as well. The River Foyle and its tributaries, some running into Lough Foyle, have good runs of salmon and sea trout. The River Bann divides into two; the lower drains Lough Neagh and is famous for its salmon-fishing, but the lower beats are expensive. The Upper Bann rises in the Mountains of Mourne and fish run later. The popularity of sea-fishing has grown immensely in recent years. Twenty-four species of sea-fish are caught regularly. The main centres where boats can be hired are Moville in Co. Donegal; Portrush, Glenarm, Larne and Whitehead in Co. Antrim; and Bangor and Donaghadee in Co. Down.

Rod licences, which are issued by the Fisheries Conservancy Board (FCB) or the Foyle Fisheries Commission (FFC), cost £15.50 for 14 days. Permission to fish from the owner of the water—often the Department of Agriculture, which is the ultimate authority for fisheries in the north—takes the form of a permit. The '8-day general game permit' costs £14.50 or you can buy a daily one at £8.50. Angling clubs which own waters not held by the Department issue daily tickets costing £4. Ghillies charge about £50 per day. There are many different kinds of permits and licences and the Northern Ireland Tourist Office at 59 North Street, Belfast, ✆ (028) 9024 6609, has a limited selection. For full details of what is available contact the Fisheries on ✆ (028) 9052 2157. **Licences** for fishing in the Republic can be divided into four categories: **game**, for salmon and sea trout (migratory); **trout** (non-migratory); **coarse**, for perch, roach, rudd, bream, tench, and pike; and **sea-fishing**. Visitors require a licence for the first. A general licence covering all salmon and sea trout costs IR£15 for 21 days, or IR£20 for a season, or IR£4 a day. It is possible to purchase individual or composite licences from Bord Fáilte offices in your country of residence. In the Republic, they can be bought from any Tourist or Fisheries Board office, from all government-run fisheries, and many tackle shops.

For general information, the Lakeland Visitors' Centre, Enniskillen, ✆ (028) 6632 3110, is very helpful. Tackle shops throughout the Province issue permits and tickets for, or information on, angling clubs. (Thanks to Peter O'Reilly for his help with updating this section.)

Food and Drink

Eating Out

Eating out in the north of Ireland can be a memorable experience, if the chef gets it right. The basic ingredients are the best in the world: succulent beef, lamb, salmon, seafood, ham, butter, cream, eggs and wonderful **bread**—which is often home-made, and varies from crumbly nutty-tasting wheaten bread to moist white soda bread, crispy scones, potato bread and barm brack, a rich fruity loaf traditionally eaten at Hallowe'en. Irish **potatoes** are light and floury, best when just off the stalk, and crisp carrots and cabbages are sold in every grocery shop, often bought in from local farms. If you stay in a country house hotel, the walled garden will probably produce exotic vegetables and fruit.

The history of Ireland has quite a lot to do with the down-side of cooking: overcooked food, few vegetables, and too many synthetic cakes. The landless peasants had to survive mostly on potatoes, milk and the occasional bit of bacon, so there is little traditional 'cuisine'. **Fish** was until recently regarded as 'penance food', to be eaten only on Fridays. Local people talk with amusement of those who eat oysters or mussels, and most of the fine seafood harvested from the seaweed-fringed loughs and the open sea goes straight to France, where it appears on the starched linen table-cloths of the best restaurants. But do not despair if you love fat oysters or fresh salmon, because they can always be got, either in the bars, the newer restaurants, or straight from the fisherman. Remember, everything in Ireland works on a personal basis. Start your enquiries for any sort of local delicacy at the post office, grocer or butcher, or in the pub.

Since the relative prosperity of the 1960s, many people in Ireland like to eat **meat**: you cannot fail to notice the number of butchers or 'fleshers' in every town. Steak appears on every menu, and if you are staying in a simple Irish farmhouse, huge lamb chops with a minty sauce, Irish stew made from the best end of mutton neck, onions and potatoes, and bacon and cabbage casserole baked in the oven are delicious possibilities; and fish is becoming more and more readily available.

The standard of **restaurants** is getting much better. This is especially true of those that are run by people from the Continent, many of whom set up here because of the beauty of the country and the raw ingredients. There are Irish cooks, too, who combine the local specialities and traditional recipes with ingredients and cooking methods from other cultures. Still, eating out can be a massive disappointment, and it is wise to go to only those establishments which have been recommended, and to book ahead if you've set your heart on a particular restaurant. Too many places still serve up musty and watery vegetables, overcooked meat, frozen fish, and salads of the limp-lettuce-and-coleslaw variety. Also, eating out is not cheap, unless you have a pub lunch. Some restaurants offer a tourist menu, but on the whole these establishments offer good value rather than good cooking.

To get around the serious problem of eating cheaply, fill up on the huge breakfasts provided by the bed and breakfast places. If the lady of the house also cooks high tea or supper for her guests, take advantage of that as well. The food she produces is usually delicious and very good value. Irish people love their food, and are generous with it: huge portions are normal in the home and often in restaurants. It is a sign of inhospitality to give a poor meal. Bakeries usually sell tea, coffee and soft drinks along with fresh apple pie, doughnuts, cakes and sausage rolls. Roadside cafés serve the usual menu of hamburgers, chicken 'n' chips, etc. Many of the big towns have Chinese restaurants, pizza places and fish and chips. Vegetarians will find an increasing number of restaurants in Belfast and the larger towns that cater specifically for their needs. Certainly, vegetarians will find that, even where no special menu exists, people are generally keen to provide suitable fare. If you are staying in a country house, you should telephone in advance to let them know you are vegetarian. You can sample the many delicious cheeses of Ireland by finding a good deli or wholefood shop, buying some bread and salad and taking yourself off for a picnic in some wonderfully scenic place. If it is drizzling, warm yourself up afterwards with a glass of Irish coffee in the local pub.

A variety of good eating places are listed at the end of each county chapter. Do bear in mind that proprietors and places change, so it is always best to telephone before you arrive. The establishments are categorized in the following cost brackets:

luxury

Over £40. These restaurants include creative and delicious cooking from fine ingredients. They are often in the dining-rooms of rather stately country houses or castles, where the silver and crystal sparkle and you are surrounded by fine pictures and furniture. Or they may be smart, fashionable places in the cities.

expensive

Over £20 a head, excluding wine. Restaurants in this category are similar to those in the luxury bracket, with an emphasis on well-cooked vegetables and traditional ingredients. Again, many country house hotels come under this category, as do seafood restaurants around the coast and city establishments. Lunch in expensive places is often a very reasonably priced set meal, so ask about it if you do not want to fork out for dinner.

moderate

£10–20 a head, excluding wine. The quality of the food may be as good as the more expensive places, but the atmosphere is informal and, perhaps, a little less stylish.

inexpensive

Under £10 a head, excluding wine. This category includes bar food, lunchtime places and cafés. You can usually be sure of good home-made soup and one simple course.

Most restaurants do lunch and dinner but do check before you go. A few do only dinner and Sunday lunches. Some country places only open for the weekend during the winter months. Cafés and snack places are not usually open in the evening for meals. Service is usually included in the bill at all restaurants. In the country towns you may find it difficult to pay by credit card. Check this out before you order your meal! If there is no liquor licence of any sort, the manager is usually quite happy to let you bring in your own wine or beer, if you ask. (The publicans have a monopoly on licences and many restaurants cannot get them without having to fulfil ludicrous requirements for space-planning.)

Drink

'The only cure for drinking is to drink more', so goes the Irish proverb. Organizations such as the Pioneers exist to wean the masses off 'the drink'—alcohol costs an arm and a leg, what with the taxes and the publican's cut; nevertheless, an Irish bar can be one of the most convivial places in the world. The delicious liquor, the cosy snugs and the general hubbub of excited conversation, which in the evening might easily spark into a piece of impromptu singing, makes the business of taking a drink very pleasant. Pubs can also be as quiet as a grave, especially in the late afternoon when a few men nod over their pints, and an air of contemplation pervades.

Guinness

You are bound to have been lured into trying Guinness by the persuasive advertisements you see all over Europe, for the export trade is thriving; but the place to get a real taste of the creamy dark liquor is in an Irish bar. It is at its most delicious in and around Dublin, where it is made. Guinness does not travel well, especially on Irish roads. It is said to get its special flavour from the murky waters of the River Liffey. The quality of taste once it has left the brewery depends on how well the publican looks after it and cleans the pipe from the barrel, so it varies from bar to bar. If it's obvious that you are a tourist, your Guinness may be decorated with a shamrock drawn on its frothy head They've finally managed to get Guinness into a can—by all accounts it's very good but it's apparently important that it's drunk chilled (bottled draught no longer exists). If you are feeling adventurous, try something called black velvet—a mixture of Guinness and champagne.

bars

The old-fashioned serious drinking bar with high counter and engraved glass window, frosted so that the outside world couldn't intrude, is gradually disappearing. It used to be a male preserve. Farmers on a trip into town can be heard bewailing the weather or recounting the latest in cattle, land prices or gossip. What the inns have lost in character they compensate for, to a degree, with comfort. The bar of the local hotel is the place to find the priest when he is off-duty. Another favourite drinking establishment is the grocery shop which is also a bar, where you ask for a taxi/plumber/undertaker, only to find that the publican or his brother combine all these talents with great panache.

whiskey

Whiskey has been drunk in Ireland for more than five hundred years and the word itself is derived from *uisge beatha*, the Irish for water of life. It is made from malted barley with a small proportion of wheat, oats and occasionally a pinch of rye. There are several brands; Bushmills is the best in the north and Jameson's and Paddy are the best made in the south.

Irish coffee

Irish coffee is a wonderful combination of contrasts: hot and cold, black and white, and very intoxicating. It was first dreamed up in County Limerick earlier this century. It's made with a double measure of Irish whiskey, one tablespoon of double cream, one cup of strong, hot black coffee, and a heaped tablespoon of sugar. To make it, first warm a stemmed whiskey glass. Put in the sugar and enough hot coffee to dissolve the sugar. Stir well. Add the Irish whiskey and fill the glass and pour the cream slowly over a spoon. Do not stir the cream into the coffee; it should float on top. The hot whiskey-laced coffee is drunk through the cold cream.

Poteen (pronounced 'pot-cheen') is illicit whiskey, traditionally made from potatoes, although nowadays it is often made from grain. Tucked away in the countryside are stills which no longer bubble away over a turf fire, but on a Calor gas stove. Poteen is pretty disgusting stuff unless you get a very good brew, and it probably kills off a lot of brain cells, so it's much better to stick to the legal liquid.

licensing hours

Public houses are open Mon–Sat 11.30am–11pm, and they are closed on Sundays. You can always get a drink on Sundays at a hotel, though you are supposed to justify it by having a meal as well if you are not staying there. If you do get into a conversation in a bar, a certain etiquette is followed: men always buy everybody in your group a drink, taking it in turn to buy a round; women will find they are seldom allowed to! Both sexes offer their cigarettes around when having one. If there are ten in your group you will find yourself drunk from social necessity and out of pocket as well!

Golf

With the possible exception of Scotland, Ireland can boast more courses per head of population than any other country in the world. As with Scotland, quality is in no way diminished by quantity and, in common with the rest of the British Isles, the greatest courses are situated at the seaside. As host to the British Open Championship, names like St Andrews, Muirfield and Royal Birkdale are famous around the world. The likes of Portmarnock, Mount Juliet and Royal Portrush suffer nothing by comparison. But they are just the tip of Ireland's golfing iceberg, and no discerning golfer's experience is complete without a taste or two of what's littered around the shores.

South of Belfast and close to the border with the Republic, **Royal County Down Golf Course** at Newcastle is quite possibly the best links course in the world. Scenically stunning and lying right at the base of the Mountains of Mourne, literally where 'they sweep down to the sea', Newcastle is at its visual best in summer when the broom, so dangerous for the errant golfer, is in full bloom.

Up on the northern coast and within a short distance of the Giant's Causeway is **Royal Portrush**, the only Irish course ever to have hosted the Open Championship. Lacking perhaps Newcastle's visual charm, it is nevertheless a great test and only the most competent should tackle it on anything other than a calm day.

While there, don't ignore the **Valley Course**, which partially lies between Portrush and the sea. In fact, an entertaining few days can be spent in the Portrush and Portstewart area, for there are no less than five courses within a mile (1.6km) or so of one another.

Across Loch Foyle to the West, **Ballyliffin Golf Club** is well worth a visit. Set amid daunting sand hills and surrounded by the Atlantic on three sides, the course is nevertheless inland in character. Continuing westward across Lough Swilly, **Portsalon** and **Rosapenna** are a pair of courses from the last century that still test the games and equipment of the modern giants. That, allied to the stunning views of the rugged Donegal coastline, makes for a very special golfing treat.

The relatively new linksland, **Donegal Golf Course** at Murvagh, is a splendid challenge, measuring over 7,000 yards (6400m) off the back. Whatever your standard you'll find something to enjoy. With facilities getting ever more crowded around the major cities of the world, Ireland offers golf as it used to be—the ability to get on a course in the hours of daylight, and green fees that are not going to break the bank.

A couple of words of advice. If you are thinking of a golfing holiday, some of the courses do get busy in summer and it is always advisable to check with clubs in advance and, where necessary, get a confirmed tee time. Also, every travelling golfer should carry a handicap certificate as proof of competence. Trolleys are for hire at most clubs and quite a few will be able to lay on caddies if ordered in advance. Golf carts are not yet a feature of Irish golf and are not encouraged. One or two courses will permit their use with a medical certificate, but you will have to provide the cart!

Many thanks to Bruce Critchley, one of television's golf commentators, for this guide to courses in Ulster.

Here is a selection of golf courses in the north of Ireland, and contact numbers. Both the Northern Irish Tourist Board and Bord Fáilte publish a comprehensive list:

Co. Donegal: Bundoran Golf Club, Bundoran, ✆ (072) 41302. Donegal Golf Club, Murvagh, ✆ (073) 34054; Portsalon Golf Club, Portsalon, ✆ (074) 59459; Rosapenna Golf Club, Downings, ✆ (074) 55301; Ballyliffin Golf Club, Carndonagh, ✆ (077) 76119; Letterkenny Golf Club, Letterkenny, ✆ (074) 21150; Narin & Portnoo, Narin, ✆ (075) 45107.

Co. Cavan: County Cavan Golf Club, Cavan, ✆ (049) 31283; Slieve Russell Golf Club, Ballyconnell, ✆ (049) 26444.

Co. Monaghan: Rossmore Golf Club, Cootehill Park, ✆ (047) 81316; Nuremore Golf Club, Carrickmacross, ✆ (042) 64016.

Co. Down: Ardglass Golf Club, Ardglass, ✆ (028) 4484 1219; Bangor Golf Club, Bangor, ✆ (028) 9127 0922; Clandeboye Golf Club, Newtownards, ✆ (028) 9127 1767; Royal Belfast Golf Club, Holywood, ✆ (028) 9042 8165; Royal County Down Golf Club, Newcastle, ✆ (028) 4372 3314.

Co. Antrim: Royal Portrush, Portrush, ✆ (028) 7082 3335; Lisburn Golf Club, Lisburn, ✆ (028) 9267 7216; Ballymena Golf Club, Ballymena, ✆ (028) 2586 1487; Ballycastle Golf Club, Ballycastle, ✆ (028) 2076 2536.

Co. Armagh: County Armagh Golf Club, Armagh, ✆ (028) 3752 5864; Portadown Golf Club, Portadown, ✆ (028) 3835 5356; Lurgan Golf Club, Lurgan, ✆ (028) 3832 1068.

Co. Londonderry: City of Derry Golf Club, ✆ (028) 7131 1496; Portstewart Golf Club, Portstewart, ✆ (028) 7083 2601; Castlerock Golf Club, Castlerock, ✆ (028) 7084 8314.

Co. Fermanagh: Enniskillen Golf Club, Enniskillen, ✆ (028) 36625 250; Castle Hume Golf Club, Castle Hume, ✆ (028) 6632 7077.

Co. Tyrone: Dungannon Golf Club, Dungannon, ✆ (028) 8792 2098; Killymoon Golf Club, Cookstown, ✆ (028) 3876 3460; Omagh Golf Club, Omagh, ✆ (028) 8224 3160.

midges

Toads and adders are said to have fled from Ireland at the sound of St Patrick's bell tolling from the top of Croagh Patrick mountain; unfortunately, the voracious midges of the west coast did not take their cue. They are very persistent on warm summer evenings, so remember to arm yourself with insect repellent of some sort (plenty of choice in the chemists if you forget). Wasps, hornets and horseflies also emerge in summer.

beasts

If you decide to have a picnic in some inviting green field, just check that there is not a bull in it first. High-spirited bullocks can be just as alarming; they come rushing up to have a good look and playfully knock you over in the process.

sea

A major hazard can be strong currents in the sea. One beach may be perfectly safe for bathing, and the one beside it positively dangerous. Always check with locals before you swim. There are lifeguards on most of the resort beaches.

walkers

Walkers who intend to go through bog and mountainous country be warned that, even though it looks dry enough on the road, once into the heather and moss you will soon sink into waterlogged ground. Wear stout boots (brogues) and bring at least an extra jersey. Sudden mists and rain can descend, and you can get very cold. Mountain rescue teams only operate in the main mountain areas, so if you do disappear into a mountain range, leave word locally as to where you plan to go, or put a note on your car. During the shooting season (grouse and snipe from August to 3 January, duck from September to 31 January, and pheasant from 1 November to 1 January), be careful of wandering into stray shot on the hilly slopes or in marshy places.

motorists

As a general rule always lock your car, and, if you're in a town or city, leave it in an authorized car park. Do not leave luggage or valuables in the car.

emergencies

As mentioned above, if you do find yourself in trouble in the north of Ireland, you will find no shortage of sympathetic help. If you fall ill, have an accident or are the victim of some crime, people will rush to your aid. Whether they bring quite the help you need is another matter. If in doubt, get the advice of your hotel, the local tourist office, or the police. In serious cases (medical or legal), contact your embassy or consulate (*see* p.13). Try to keep your head: in the case of medical treatment, take your insurance documents, inform the people treating you of your insurance cover, and make sure you keep all receipts (or at least get someone reliable to do this for you).

The emergency telephone number (to call any of the emergency services) is ✆ 999.

Insurance

general

The best advice is, always insure your holiday, and do so as soon as you book your ticket. Standard travel insurance packages issued by the major insurance companies cover a broad range of risks, including cancellation due to unforeseen circumstances, transport delays caused by strikes or foul weather, loss or theft of baggage, medical insurance and compensation for injury or death. The cost of insurance may seem substantial, but it is negligible when compared to almost any claim, should misfortune befall you. That said, it is worth checking to see whether any of your existing insurance schemes cover travel risks: certain British household insurance schemes, for example, include limited travel cover.

medical

Do remember that if you need medical or dental treatment you will be expected to pay for the treatment yourself, and then claim back the costs from your insurance company. This, of course, may not be something you can discuss on the operating table. *In extremis* the international emergency services offered by companies such as Europ Assistance or Travel Assistance International, which are often incorporated into travel insurance packages, demonstrate their blessings. For all kinds of medical care, citizens of EU countries as well as Australian/NZ citizens can benefit from the mutual agreements that exist between EU member countries.

claims

Remember that to make a claim for loss or theft of baggage you will need evidence that you have reported the loss to the police. Check your insurance details for the documentation required of you by the insurance company in such circumstances. It is, by the way, useful to have more than one copy of your insurance policy—if your baggage is stolen, the document may go with it.

Money

currency

Sterling is the currency used in the six counties that make up Northern Ireland, but in the rest of Ulster—Donegal, Monaghan and Cavan—the Irish punt is the currency. Since the Republic joined the European Monetary System, the Irish pound (IR£) and the English pound (UK£) are no longer worth the same. The difference fluctuates, usually to the detriment of the Irish pound or punt (pronounced 'poont'); at the time of writing, the UK£ was worth 15% more than the IR£.

Shopkeepers in Northern Ireland do not accept the Irish punt but those in the Republic generally accept sterling. Both currencies use the pound as the basic unit, divided into 100 pence. There are coins for the pence in both currencies; and £1 and IR£1 coins. There are notes of £5, £10, £20, £50 in both currencies, and a IR£100 note.

There is no restriction on the amount of foreign or Irish currency brought into the Republic, but you must not leave with more than IR£100 cash, in denominations of IR£20 or less, although any uncashed traveller's cheques may be taken out. There are various *bureaux de change* where you can change money, and most major hotels also provide this service, but these are unlikely to offer as good an exchange rate as the banks. There is an exchange counter at Belfast International Airport for international flights open between 7am and 8pm. Visitors from outside the UK will need to change both sterling and punt.

traveller's cheques

Traveller's cheques and Eurocheques are widely accepted. Leading credit and charge cards (MasterCard/Access, Visa, American Express and Diner's Club) are accepted in most major hotels and restaurants, but do check this beforehand.

banks

All small towns have at least one bank. Banks are open Mon–Fri, 10–12.30 and 1.30–4, and in Belfast and Londonderry they do not close for lunch.

tipping

Tipping is not really a general habit, except in taxis and in eating places where there is table service. Taxi-drivers will expect to be tipped at a rate of about 10 per cent of the fare; porters and doormen 50p or so. There is no tipping in pubs, but in hotel bars where you are served by a waiter it is usual to leave a small tip.

A service charge of 12 per cent, sometimes 15 per cent, is usually raised automatically on hotel and restaurant bills. Where this is not the case, a tip of this magnitude would be in order, if the service merits it.

Museums and Galleries

Most museums and galleries, etc. are either free or charge a small admission price of between IR£1.50 and IR£4. This is indicated throughout the book by '*adm*'; any museum whose admission charge is above IR£5 is indicated as '*adm exp*'. Specific opening hours are given with each museum; note that the last admissions are generally a half-hour or more before closing time.

Newspapers

The most widely read morning newspapers in Ulster are the *Belfast Newsletter*, which has a Unionist slant, and *The Irish Times*; all the UK newspapers are widely available. The only evening paper, the *Belfast Telegraph*, is middle-of-the-road.

Packing

Whatever you do, come to Ulster expecting rain—gumboots, umbrellas, raincoats, etc. are essential, unless you want to stay inside reading a book all day. Once you get out into the rain it is never as bad as it looks, and the clouds begin to clear as you appear. Bring warm jerseys, trousers, woollen socks, and gloves for autumn, winter and early spring. The best thing to do is to expect the cold and wet and then get a pleasant surprise when it's sunny and hot—so don't forget to sneak in a few T-shirts just in case. Sometimes the sun shines furiously in March and April and you end up with a very convincing tan.

If you like walking, bring a pair of fairly stout shoes—trainers end up bedraggled and let the water in. Fishing rods and swimsuits are worth packing, if you think you may have cause to regret leaving them behind. Bring a sleeping bag inner-sheet if you plan to stay at youth hostels. If you plan to stay in bed-and-breakfast accommodation, take your own towels, as those traditionally supplied tend to be on the mean side.

You will be amazed at what the village shop sells: anything from pots and pans to the finest French wines, and maybe some fresh salmon trout if you are lucky. In the Republic you can be sure of finding a shop open until 10 o'clock in the evening and on Sundays as well. The chemists are also well stocked so that headache pills, camera films, contraceptives etc. are easily obtainable.

Post Offices

Letterboxes are red in Northern Ireland and green in the Republic. As you would expect, you use British stamps from the six counties and Irish stamps from the rest of Ireland.

If you do not have a fixed address while you're in Ulster, letters can be sent poste restante to any post office and picked up when you produce proof of your identity. If after three months they are gathering dust in the corner of the post office, they will be sent back to the sender. There is a post office in every village, which is usually the telephone exchange as well and a hive of activity. The post office should be open 9–5 on weekdays, 9–1 on Saturdays, and closed on Sundays and public holidays. Sub-post offices close on one day a week at 1pm.

Public Holidays

New Year's Day	1 January
St Patrick's Day	Republic only, 17 March
Good Friday	(widely observed as a holiday, but not an official one)
Easter Monday	
May Day	1st May/early May N. Ireland
Spring Holiday	N. Ireland only, end May
June Holiday	Republic only, first Monday in June
12 July	N. Ireland only
August Holiday	Republic only, first Monday in August
Summer Holiday	N. Ireland only, end August
October Holiday	Republic only, last Monday in October
Christmas Day	25 December
Boxing Day/St Stephen's Day	26 December

Sailing

The coastline is uniquely beautiful, with diverse conditions and landscapes. The waters are never crowded, and the shoreline is completely unspoilt. On one of those sublimely beautiful evenings when the light touches each hill and field with an exquisite clarity, you will think yourself amongst the most privileged in the world. And if you want a bit of 'craic', there are many splendid bars and restaurants to be visited in the sheltered harbours. But the peace and calm of the sky, the land and the sea in the many inlets is deceptive, for the open seas in the northwest can be rough and treacherous, exposed as they are to the North Atlantic. A journey around the whole coastline should only be attempted by experienced sailors. If you do not have your own yacht, it is possible to charter a variety of craft; whilst if it is your ambition to learn to sail, there are several small and friendly schools.

Ireland has a long sailing tradition, with more than 125 yacht and sailing clubs around the country. Many of these clubs preserve their original clubhouses, and emanate a feeling of tradition and comfort. Visitors are made very welcome, and are encouraged to use the club facilities. Those who wish to eat on board can buy wonderful bread, cheese and other high-quality groceries from the local shops. Seafood can be bought from the trawlers fishing the waters around you. And it is possible to find good food and entertainment in local bars and restaurants. In the north is the glorious coastline of Donegal. You need to be an experienced sailor to sail in these waters, for the charts are outdated and inaccurate, whilst the currents and shallows are sometimes treacherous, and there are few facilities for sailors. More wonderful sailing can be had on Strangford and Carlingford Loughs in County Down, and around the Antrim Coast.

Galway hookers

The most traditional form of sailing boat is the Galway hooker, with its black sails. Galway hookers used to be a familiar sight, transporting turf and other goods between the islands, but by the 1970s they had almost disappeared. Happily, a few sailors discovered what great sport can be had with hooker-racing—you can see these races at summer regattas in the west of Ireland—and the craft of making the hooker is slowly reviving.

bringing your own yacht

There is no tax or duty if you bring in your own yacht for a holiday; a special sticker is issued by customs officials on arrival. Mariners should apply to the harbour master of all ports in which they wish to anchor. On arrival at the first port of entry, the flag 'Q' should be shown. Contact should then be made with the local customs official or with a *garda* (civil guard) who will be pleased to assist. Fees are very reasonable in marinas and harbours. It is illegal to land any animals without a special licence from the Department of Agriculture, but this does not apply to pet dogs which come from Great Britain.

information

Information on yachting facilities, sailing schools and charter companies can be had from the House of Sport, Upper Malone Road, Belfast, ✆ (028) 9038 1222.

useful media

The Irish Cruising Club publishes *Sailing Directions* which covers the entire coast of Ireland, and includes details of the coast, sketch plans of harbours, tidal information and information about port facilities. The *Directions* come in two volumes—one for the south and west at IR£30, and one for the north and east, price IR£27. Available from most Irish booksellers. Also recommended: *Sailing Around Ireland* by Wallace Clark (Batsford), and *Islands of Ireland* by D. McCormick (Osprey, 1977). The BBC issues gale warnings and shipping forecasts on Radio 4.

Shopping

Shopping is the most relaxing pastime because nobody ever makes you feel that you have to buy anything, so you can browse to your heart's content. Good design and high-quality craftsmanship make for goods which will last you for a lifetime, and delight the senses. Some of the best things to take home are Irish linen, handloomed tweed, Aran sweaters, pottery, glass and modern Irish silver. These you can find easily in the craft centres which have been set up all over the country. If you see something you like at any of the craft shops and centres, buy it then and there because you are not likely to see it again in another shop. These craft items are not cheap because of the artistry and labour involved, but you can find bargains at china, crystal and linen factory shops if you are prepared to seek them out.

The main goodies to take home with you are described in detail below. More fleeting pleasures, which you can share with your friends back home, are smoked salmon, cheese, wheaten bread, home-cured bacon, and whiskey.

opening hours

Shops are open 9.30–5.30, Mon–Sat. Craft shops in scenic areas are usually open on Sundays as well, especially if they combine as tea shops. In some towns there is an early-closing day when businesses close at 1pm. This is normally a Wednesday, although it may be a different day in some areas. You can be sure that if one town has shut down, its neighbour will be busy, and open for business. Large shopping centres which operate on the outskirts of town are unaffected by early closing.

Weights and Measures

1 kilogram	=	2.205 lb	1 lb	=	0.45 kilograms
1 litre	=	1.76 Imperial pints	1 Imperial pint	=	0.56 litres
	=	2.11 US pints	1 US pint	=	0.47 litres
1 centimetre	=	0.39 inches	1 Imperial gallon	=	4.54 litres
1 metre	=	39.37 inches	1 US gallon	=	3.78 litres
	=	3.28 feet	1 foot	=	0.305 metres
1 kilometre	=	0.621 miles	1 mile	=	1.609 kilometres
1 hectare	=	2.47 acres	1 acre	=	0.404 hectares

Irish Specialities

Irish lace is one of the lightest and most precious of all the specialities you can pack in your suitcase, and you find it in Carrickmacross, County Monaghan. Some smart shops also stock it, but it is fun to go around the convents and co-operatives where the lace is made. Carrickmacross lace from the Lace Cooperative, Carrickmacross, © (042) 62506. In Carrickmacross the nuns design lawn appliqué on a background of net. In Limerick the lace is worked completely in thread on the finest Brussels net.

Tweed is a wonderful fabric. Not only does it keep you warm in winter, but it also lets your skin 'breathe' and it is useful most of the year round if you live in northern climes and are not addicted to central heating. It is hand-woven from sheep's wool, and the Irish have got not only the texture and tension of the cloth right, but also the speckled, natural colours of the countryside.

Donegal tweed is particularly attractive, and in every subtle shade under the sun. It is available all over County Donegal but a particularly wide selection is available from Magees, The

Diamond, Donegal Town, ✆ (073) 21100; and McNutts, The Harbour, Downings, ✆ (074) 55324. Both shops also stock sports jackets and wonderfully stylish coats for women. If you explore around Ardara you will still find thick, naturally dyed tweed. You can also find **bainin** (pronounced 'bawneen'), an undyed tweed which is often used for upholstery.

Hand-knitted sweaters. Make sure you buy one which has the hand-knitted label on it; it makes the whole difference when you are buying an Aran. These are made out of tough wool, lightly coated in animal oils, so they are water-resistant and keep you as warm as toast. You can get them in natural white or various colours, and the pattern differs quite a bit. In the past the wives of the fishermen used to have a family pattern so that they could identify anyone who had drowned. These knits come in a variety of styles; they stretch after being worn a while and last for years. It is possible to buy original and attractive hand-knitted clothing in craft shops all over the north of Ireland, although Donegal has the greatest variety and generally cheaper prices on knitwear than elsewhere.

Linen. Ulster is still famous for its linen, although the blue fields of rippling flax flowers are no more. You can buy excellent linen tea cloths and fine linen sheets in Belfast. Hand-embroidered handkerchiefs and tablecloths in Co. Donegal.

Glass. Waterford Crystal is world-famous for its quality and design. All imperfect pieces are smashed, so you cannot buy cheap seconds. Shops will pack and mail glass overseas for you. It is still possible to buy old Waterford glass, which has a blackish tint to it, in antique shops—but it is very costly. Attractive crystal glass can be bought at the factories in Co. Cavan and Co. Tyrone.

Pottery and china. Talented potters work in rural communities all over the country, and one of the best places to find their work for sale is at IDA centres. Craft shops also usually carry the local potters' work. Belleek pottery in Fermanagh produces another very individual type of china. The pottery has been established since the 18th century and the pieces are typically of a lustrous creamy glaze decorated with shamrocks and flowers. Contact the Factory Shop, Belleek, ✆ (028) 6865 8501.

Woven baskets. All over Ireland you can buy baskets made of willow or rush in different shapes and sizes: bread baskets, turfholders, place mats and St Brigid Crosses—charms against evil.

Food and drink. Soda, wheaten and potato bread are found all over the country. Take home some Sheelin Bakery wheaten mix or the freshly made loaves, which are delicious. Smoked salmon is also a speciality and is widely available. Farmhouse cheese in every shape, size and texture can be bought from the producer and from wholefood shops and delicatessens. Irish whiskey (note the 'e', which is the Irish way of spelling it) is slightly sweeter than Scotch. Try Bushmills, Paddy's, Powers and Jameson's. All these brands are available in off-licences throughout the country. Cork gin is considered to have a delicious tang of juniper, far superior to the English brand of Gordon's. Popular liqueurs are Irish Mist, which contains whiskey and honey; Tullamore Dew; and Bailey's Irish Cream. Definitely worth trying if you like sweet and tasty things, Black Bush is a liqueur whiskey.

adventure sports

The Sports Council can give you contact numbers and addresses for any sporting activity in the state. Contact the Sports Council for Northern Ireland House of Sport, Upper Malone Road, Belfast, BT9 5LA, ✆ (028) 9038 1222.

For addresses in the Republic contact the Association for Adventure Sport (AFAS), House of Sport, Longmile Road, Dublin 12, ✆ (01) 450 9845.

beagling

This is an athletic sport in which you follow the hounds on foot until they pick up the scent of a hare, then you usually have to start running. The hare is always a good match for the hounds when it is on home ground. You do not need any special clothes or skill and visitors are welcome. They meet in the winter, and often on Sundays. The tourist boards (NITB and Bord Fáilte) have a list of beagle hunt clubs.

bird-watching

You can still hear the corncrake amongst the fields of Rathlin Island, or the choughs calling from the rocky headlands. Walking along the coastal mudflats in winter, you will very likely see whooper swans.

There are numerous bird sanctuaries all over Ulster. For details contact the RSPB, Belvoir Park Forest, Belfast 8, ✆ (028) 9049 1547, or the National Trust (NI), Rowallane, Saintfield, Co. Down, BT24 7LH, ✆ (028) 9051 0721. For bird sanctuaries in the Republic, write to the Wildlife Service, Office of Public Works, 51 St Stephen's Green, Dublin 2, ✆ (01) 661 3111. You can also contact any of the above organizations and the Irish Wild Bird Conservancy, Rutledge House, 8 Longford Place, Monkstown, Co. Dublin, ✆ (01) 280 4322, for details of organized field trips.

canoeing

This is an exciting and compelling way to tour around Ulster and you can always camp by the waterside as long as you get permission from the owner.

For details of the many rivers and waterways, sea canoeing and tuition, write to the Sports Council, The House of Sport, Upper Malone Road, Belfast, BT9 5LA, ✆ (028) 9038 1222, or the AFAS, House of Sport, Longmile Road, Dublin 12, ✆ (01) 450 9845.

caving

This activity has become more organized recently with the establishment of the Speleological Union of Ireland. The caving possibilities in the Cavan/Fermanagh area are numerous. For information, contact: AFAS (address above).

cruising the inland waterways

This is an unforgettable and exciting way to travel around the country. The main areas are the River Shannon, which is navigable from Lough Key to Killaloe; the River Erne, which has two huge island-studded lakes and is navigable for more than 50 miles (80km) from Belturbet to the little village of Belleek (which makes exquisite china). The two are now linked due to the recent restoration and opening of the Shannon-Erne Waterway. Along the waterways you pass tumbledown castles, abbeys, beautiful flowers, birds and peaceful, lush scenery. In the evening you can moor up your boat for a meal and a jar and listen to some good traditional music. There are festivals and boat rallies, but they only happen for a couple of days a year, so if it's peace and quiet you want, don't worry.

The **Erne waterway** is beautifully wooded with nature reserves and little islands amongst which to meander. In all, Lough Erne covers 300 square miles (777sq km) of water. Cruiser hire companies operate around the lakes. Contact the Erne Charter Boat Association through Fermanagh Tourism, Enniskillen, ✆ (028) 6632 3110. Now that the Shannon Erne waterway is open, it is possible to navigate 300km of waterways. You can rent either for one way or return. Contact Erincurrach Cruising, Blaney, Enniskillen, ✆ (028) 6664 1507/6664 1737.

There are several companies offering luxury cabin cruisers for self-drive hire, ranging from two to eight berths. All are fitted with fridges, gas cookers, hot water and showers; most have central heating. A dinghy, charts, binoculars and safety equipment are included on the river and lough routes. Groceries and stores can be ordered in advance and collected when you arrive. You have to be over 21 to be skipper, and the controls must be understood by at least two people, but no licence is necessary. You get an hour of tuition, or more if you need it. The average price for a six-berth cruiser for one week ranges from £600 in April to about £1,500 in July/August. Ask for details from your travel agent, or the nearest tourist office. You will find that there are excellent pubs and restaurants catering for the needs of the cruisers; ask at the local tourist office.

hang-gliding

Ulster is a hang-glider's paradise: the wind blows from the sea or from the flat central plains. Most of the hills are bare of power-lines and trees, and the famous turf provides soft landings. Contact the Northern Ireland Hang-gliding Club, 43 Ransevyn Park, Whitehead, BT38 9LY, Co. Antrim, ✆ (028) 9337 3439. Also contact the Sports Council for Northern Ireland. Flying in the 26 counties is controlled by the Irish Hang-Gliding Association. Contact: AFAS House of Sport, Longmile Rd, Dublin 12, ✆ (01) 450 9845.

hunting

This is a popular sport all over the country. Any visitors are welcomed by the various hunts, and it is not very expensive. Ask the NITB or the Irish Tourist Board (Bord Fáilte) for a list, or the local riding centre for details. The hunting **season** starts in October and ends in March, with meets starting in the mid-morning. Stables for the hire of a horse for the day's hunting can usually be found through the local hunt secretary (although you must be experienced), and costs about £60. The cap fee varies from £30 to £70 per day.

hurling

This is to the Irish what cricket is to the English. Fifteen men with hurleys thrash away at a leather ball and combine neat footwork in perfect combination with the stick-work. Hurling and Gaelic football are promoted by the Gaelic Athletic Association and played with an exhilarating and unbelievably deft skill. When it is played well it can be beautiful to watch and occasionally extremely dangerous. Look in local newspapers for details of matches.

mountaineering and hill-walking

The mountains and hill areas are not high (few peaks are over 3,000ft/915m), but they are rugged, varied, beautiful and unspoilt. There are quartz peaks, ridges of sandstone, bog-covered domes, and cliff-edged limestone plateaux. Excellent walking trails have been or are in the process of being developed at the moment. General advice, information and a list of hill-walking and rock-climbing clubs can be obtained from the Sports Council for Northern Ireland, House of Sport, Upper Malone Road, Belfast BT9 5LA, ✆ (028) 9038 1222, or the Mountaineering Council of Ireland, Association for Adventure Sports (AFAS), House of Sport, Long Mile Road, Dublin 12, ✆ (01) 450 9845. They can also send you a full list of guides. Tourist offices throughout the country stock hill-walking information sheets for individual areas.

The Ordnance Survey ½-inch-to-1-mile maps and a compass are essentials for serious walkers. Please remember there are very few tracks on the mountains, and always let your hotel know where you are climbing or walking, or leave a note in your car, just in case you have an accident. Mountain rescue in the six counties is co-ordinated by the Royal Ulster Constabulary and by the Garda (police) in the Republic. There are mountain rescue teams in the main mountain areas. For climbing in the Mourne Mountains, contact the Tullymore Mountain Centre, Bryansford, Nr Newcastle, Co. Down, ✆ (028) 4372 2158; or House of Sport, Upper Malone Road, Belfast, ✆ (028) 90381222, which will book courses for you.

riding holidays

The country is really opening up for horse-riders, with many new residential schools and companies offering pony-trekking holidays. The people's natural love of horses is being put to good use, and the areas of beauty where you can ride include empty beaches that stretch for miles, heathery valleys, forests, empty country roads and loughside tracks. Accommodation and food are arranged for you. Full details from the Northern Ireland Tourist Board, 59 North Street, Belfast BT1 1NB, ✆ (028) 9024 6609, and Bord Fáilte, PO Box 273, Dublin 8, ✆ (01) 284 4768.

sub-aqua

Ireland's oceans are surprisingly warm and clear because they are right in the path of the Gulf Stream, so it would be very difficult to find a better place for underwater swimming or diving. The underwater flora and fauna is vast and varied, and you are always bumping into shoals of fish. *Subsea* is the official journal of the Irish Underwater Council, which publishes information about the affiliated clubs, articles on diving, etc. Write to the Irish Underwater Council, Haigh Terrace, Dun Laoghaire, ✆ (01) 284 4601. Centres for experienced divers and equipment hire are in Co. Donegal and Co. Down. Ask for the relevant fact sheet in any tourist office.

By the way, it is illegal to take shellfish from the sea.

surfing

Owing to the geographical position of Ireland great swells endlessly pound the west coast, producing waves comparable to those in California. Thus the northwest coastline is ideal for surfing when the beach, tide and wind conditions are right. Many of the beaches in Co. Donegal are considered first-rate for breakers. As hire centres are not numerous, it is best to bring your own board and wetsuit; although you can occasionally hire them from hotels and adventure sports centres.

All those interested in the huge Atlantic swell should contact the Irish Surfing Association, Tirchonaill Street, Donegal Town, Co. Donegal, ✆ (072) 21053.

swimming and beaches

There are lovely beaches (also called strands) wherever the sea meets the land. If you wish to go sea-bathing (it can be surprisingly warm because of the Gulf Stream), bear in mind that swimming is not a regulated sport, and that there are lifeguards only on the most popular beaches, if at all. Be aware of the possibility of a strong undertow or current, and ask locally about the safety of beaches.

walking

The Ulster Way: The attraction of this well-marked trail is that you can pick a short stretch and walk for a day, or one of the five main sections and walk for a week; or, if you have plenty of time and energy, walk the entire circuit of six counties—Armagh, Antrim, Down, Fermanagh, Londonderry and Tyrone—which is 566 miles (1,070km) and will take about a month. The Way takes in beautiful coastal scenery as well as wild mountain stretches and quiet farming country. You can get a list of B&B accommodation which is en route or only a few miles off the trail.

The Northern Ireland Tourist Board (NITB) Belfast stocks this, as well as the 1:250,000 Ireland Holiday map (1 inch:4 miles), cost £4, published by the Ordnance Survey (OSNI). This map gives a good overall view of the Ulster Way. You will also need the 1:50,000 (1¼ inch:1 mile) OSNI Discovery series costing £4 per sheet for the actual walk, also stocked by the NITB and bookshops. Master maps of the Ulster Way can be perused at the Sports Council, Home of Sport, Upper Malone Road, Belfast BT9 5L, ✆ (028) 9038 1222. A good preparatory read is Paddy Dillon's *The Complete Ulster Way Walks*, £9.99.

Telephones

For the six counties that make up Northern Ireland, codes are as in mainland UK dialling. To call the UK from the Republic, the code is 00 44 and then the number, dropping the first 0. Similarly to call the Republic from the UK dial 00 353 followed by the area code minus the first 0. Please note too that new area codes and prefixes are to be introduced for Northern Ireland from September 2000, so if you have trouble calling, it may be worth checking that you have the correct code and prefix.

It is more expensive to telephone during working hours than outside them. For example, at the time of writing a call to Britain from the Republic costs 9p per minute, but after 6pm and at weekends and on public holidays the charge is 5p per minute. For direct-dial transatlantic calls the standard rate is about 29p per minute, with reduced rates after 6pm of 22p and economy rates of 19p a minute.

Note that if you telephone from your hotel you are liable to be charged much more than the standard rate.

Ireland shares the same time zone as Great Britain, and follows the same pattern of seasonal adjustment in the summer (i.e. Greenwich Mean Time plus one hour, from the end of March to the end of October).

Toilets

Loos—public ones, labelled in Irish: *Fir* (men) and *Mna* (women)—are usually in a pretty bad way. Nobody minds if you slip into a lounge bar or hotel to go to the loo, though it's a good excuse to stop for a drink as well.

Tourist Information

Ireland is served by two separate tourist boards: **Bord Fáilte** (or the Irish Tourist Board) in the Republic, and the **Northern Ireland Tourist Board.**

The Northern Ireland Tourist Board

The people who work for the Northern Ireland Tourist Board (NITB) are friendly, helpful and humorous and very proud of their bit of Ireland. The Head Office is at 59 North Street, Belfast, BT1 2DS, ✆ (028) 9024 6609, ✉ (028) 9024 0960.

There are over 30 local tourist offices in Northern Ireland. All of them will give you details of what is on in the province: sports festivals, arts, bus tours, accommodation, etc. Many of them are open only during the tourist season, but the following are open all year. (For a full list, contact the NITB Head Office.)

Northern Ireland

Antrim, ✆ (028) 9446 5156.

Armagh, ✆ (028) 3752 7808.

Ballycastle, ✆ (028) 2076 2024.

Ballymena, ✆ (028) 2566 0300.

Bangor, ✆ (028) 9127 0069.

Carnlough, ✆ (028) 2888 5236.

Carrickfergus, ✆ (028) 9336 6455.

Cookstown, ✆ (028) 3876 6727.

Cushendall, ✆ (028) 2177 1180.

Derry, ✆ (028) 7126 7284.

Downpatrick, ✆ (028) 4461 2233.

Enniskillen, ✆ (028) 6632 3110.

Fivemiletown, ✆ (028) 8952 1409.

Giant's Causeway, ✆ (028) 2073 1855.

Kilkeel, ✆ (028) 4176 2525.

Larne, ✆ (028) 2826 0088.

Limavady, ✆ (028) 7772 2226.

Magherafelt, ✆ (028) 7963 2151.

Newcastle, ✆ (028) 4372 2222.

Omagh, ✆ (028) 8224 7831.

Portadown, ✆ (028) 3835 3260.

Portrush, ✆ (028) 7082 3333.

Website, *www.ni-tourism.com*

the Republic

Dublin, Tourist Information Office, 16 Nassau Street, Dublin 2, ✆ (01) 679 1977, ✉ (01) 679 1863.

Great Britain

London, NITB, 1 Lower Regent Street, London SW1, ✆ (020) 7766 9920.

Glasgow, NITB, 135 Buchanan St, Glasgow, G1 2JA, ✆ (0141) 204 4454, ✉ (0141) 204 4033.

USA, NITB, 555 5th Ave, New York, NY 10176, ℰ (212) 922 0101, free-call 1800 326 0036, ✆ (212) 922 0099.

elsewhere in the world

Australia, Level 5, 36 Carrington Street, Sydney 2000, ℰ (02) 9299 6177.

Northern Ireland Tourist Board publications are distributed overseas by the British Tourist Authority, which maintains offices in many countries. Consult the telephone directory.

Bord Fáilte

Like their Northern Irish counterparts, the people who work for Bord Fáilte would get you to the moon if they could—should you ask for it. They will do anything to help and organize whatever is practicable; and if they do not know the answer to something, they can always refer you to someone who does.The Head Office in Dublin is at Baggot Street Bridge, Dublin 2, ℰ (01) 676 5871, ✆ (01) 602 4100. For general postal enquiries write to Bord Fáilte, PO Box 273, Dublin 8. Website: *www.ireland.travel.ie*

the rest of Ulster

Cavan, ℰ (049) 31942; **Donegal,** ℰ (073) 21148; **Letterkenny,** ℰ (074) 21160; **Monaghan,** ℰ (047) 81122.

Northern Ireland

Belfast, 53 Castle Street, Belfast B1 1GH, ℰ (028) 9032 7888, ✆ (028) 9024 0201.

Derry, 44 Foyle Street, Derry BT48 6PW, ℰ (028) 7136 9501.

Great Britain

London, 150 New Bond Street, London W1Y 0AQ, ℰ (020) 7493 3201 ✆ (020) 7493 9065; also at 1 Lower Regent Street, London SW1.

North America

USA, 345 Park Avenue, New York, NY 10154, ℰ (212) 418 0800, ✆ (212) 371 9059.

Canada, 160 Bloor Street East, Suite 1150, Toronto, Ontario, M4W 1BN, ℰ (416) 929 2777, ✆ (416) 929 6783.

Australia and New Zealand

Australia, Level 5, 36 Carrington St, Sydney, NSW 2000, ℰ (02) 9299 6177.

New Zealand, 2nd Floor, Dingwall Buildiing, 87 Queen St, PO Box 279, Auckland 1, ℰ (09) 379 3708.

Where to Stay

Whether you are a traveller with plenty of loot to spend, or one who is intent on lodging as cheaply as possible, there is plenty of choice. Places to stay range from romantic castles, graceful country mansions, cosy farmhouses, smart city hotels and hostels which, although spartan, are clean and well-run. Many of these hostels have double or family rooms, are independently owned and require no membership cards.

At the end of each county chapter there is a list of recommended accommodation, divided into price categories which are explained below. With this list as a guide, it is possible to avoid the many modern and ugly hotels where bland comfort is doled out for huge prices, and to avoid shabby motels and the musty bed-and-breakfast establishments. Some counties are favoured with many desirable hotels and B&Bs, whilst a few are meagrely served. If that is the case where you are, your best bet for a pleasant stay is to stick to farmhouse accommodation, which is usually very adequate.

One thing you can be sure of is that the Irish are amongst the friendliest people in Europe, and when they open their doors to visitors they give a great welcome. The many unexpected kindnesses and the personal service that you will experience will contribute immeasurably to your visit. The countryside is beautiful, and there are many sights to see, but what adds enjoyment and richness, above all, is the pleasant conversation and humour of the people.

Prices

The Northern Ireland Tourist Board and Bord Fáilte register and grade hotels and guest houses, and they divide the many B&B businesses into Farm, Town and Country Houses. All of this is very useful, but, apart from indicating the variety of services available and the cost, you really do not get much idea of the atmosphere and style of the place. The establishments listed in this book are described and categorized according to price, and include a variety of lodgings ranging from a luxurious castle to a simple farmhouse—all have something very special to offer a visitor. This may be the architecture, the garden, the food, the atmosphere and the chat, or simply the beauty of the surrounding countryside. The most expensive offer high standards of luxury, and the cheapest ones are clean and comfortable. Most are family-owned, with a few bedrooms, and none fits into a uniform classification, but they are all welcoming and unique places to stay. The price categories are of necessity quite loosely based, and some of the more expensive establishments do weekend deals which are very good value. Please, always check prices and terms when making a booking. Rates are quoted in sterling—the value of which at the time of writing is 15 per cent greater than the punt.

luxury

B&B from £80 per person. You can expect top-quality lodgings with style and opulence. Furnishings will include priceless antiques, whilst the facilities and service provide every modern convenience you could wish for. Some of the Grade A* hotels in the cities fall into this category, but there are also delightful castles and mansions set in exquisite grounds.

expensive

From £50 B&B per person. All the bedrooms have their own bathroom, direct-dial telephone, central heating, TV and the other paraphernalia of modern living, but they have something else as well—charm, eccentricity, and a feeling of mellow comfort. They are places where you might sleep in a graceful four-poster hung with rich cloth, and wake up to the sort of hospitality where the smell of coffee is just a prelude to a delicious cooked breakfast, and the sharp sweet taste of homemade jam on Irish wheaten bread.

moderate

From £30 to £50 B&B per person. Although not as luxurious, most of these places have private bathrooms and an extremely high standard of cooking and service. Again, they have a wonderful atmosphere combined with attractive décor which is sometimes more atmospheric for its touch of age.

From £10 to £30 B&B per person. Pretty whitewashed farmhouses, Georgian manses, rectories, old manor houses, modern bungalows and fine town houses come under this heading. They are very good value, and you will get marvellous plain cooking. Only some of the bedrooms will have en suite facilities, and some will not have central heating, but there will be perfectly good bathrooms close by and washbasins in the room.

Reservations

The Northern Ireland Tourist Board and Bord Fáilte can be of immense help when you are making a reservation or trying to decide where to stay. You can make a reservation direct with the premises, or use the NITB and Irish Tourist Board offices in Great Britain and Northern Ireland who operate a booking service. Offices in other countries operate an enquiry service only. Northern Irish tourist offices and Bord Fáilte throughout the country will make a reservation for the price of a telephone call. They will only book you into registered and approved lodgings, and a 10 per cent deposit is payable. Make sure that you book early for the peak months of June, July and August. At other times of the year it is usually quite all right to book on the morning of the day you wish to stay. However, the excellent lodgings soon get known by word of mouth, so they are always more likely to be booked up in advance.

Literature

The Northern Ireland Tourist Board stocks plenty of booklets on various types of accommodation, including a comprehensive list of accommodation called *Where to Stay in Northern Ireland*, price £4.99. *The Hidden Ireland Guide, Friendly Homes of Ireland*, Ireland's *Blue Book*, and *Elegant Ireland* all have a few recommendations in Ulster, as does the *Good Hotel Guide*. The Bord Fáilte tourist offices keep a similar stock of booklets covering all types of accommodation, camping and self-catering; their comprehensive list is called *Accommodation Guide*, price IR£5.00.

The Northern Ireland Tourist Board (NITB) and Bord Fáilte register and grade hotels into five categories: **A*** stands for the most luxuriously equipped bedrooms and public rooms with night service, a very high standard of food and plenty of choice. Most bedrooms have their own bath and suites are available—the sort of place where delicious snacks are automatically served with your cocktails. This grading includes baronial mansions set in exquisite grounds or the rather plush anonymity of some of the city hotels. **A** grade stands for a luxury hotel which doesn't have quite so many items on the *table d'hôte*, nor does it have night service; but the food is just as good and the atmosphere less restrained. **B*** grade stands for well-furnished and comfortable; some rooms have a bath, cooking is good and plain. **B** and **C** grades are clean, comfortable but limited, **B** offering more in the line of bathrooms and food. All graded hotels have heating and hot and cold water in the bedrooms. The prices of hotels vary enormously, no matter what grade they are, and the grading takes no account of atmosphere and charm. Many of the most delightful and hospitable country houses come under grades B or C, whilst some of the grade A hotels are very dull. All graded Northern Irish hotels are listed in the *Where to Stay* guide, and those in the Republic are listed in Bord Fáilte *Guest Accommodation* booklet and in the *Be Our Guest* booklet.

Guest Houses

These are usually properties which have become too large and expensive to maintain as private houses. The minimum number of bedrooms is five. The grade **A** houses are just as good as their hotel equivalent, as are those lower down the scale, although the atmosphere is completely different. In fact, some of the best places to stay are guest houses.

If you vary your accommodation from guest house to town and country house or farmhouse, you will discover one of the principles of Irish life: everything works on a personal basis. If you are on holiday to avoid people, a guest house is the last place you should book into. It is impossible not to be drawn into a friendly conversation, whether about fishing or politics. You will get a large, thoroughly uncontinental breakfast, and delicious evening meals with a choice within a set meal. Dinner is always punctual, at eight, after everyone has sat around by the fire over very large drinks. Lunch or a packed lunch can be arranged. All grades of guest house have hot and cold water, and heating in the bedrooms. Grade **A** guest houses have some rooms with private bathrooms, but their reputation is based on scrumptious food and comfortable surroundings. You can get full details of guest houses in the Northern Ireland Tourist Board and Bord Fáilte booklets entitled *Where to Stay in Northern Ireland* and *Be Our Guest*. As a general guide, a comfortable, even luxurious night's sleep will cost between £20 and £40, although the more basic guest houses cost no more than a farmhouse B&B. A delicious meal ranges between £10 and £20. Sometimes the owners provide high tea, sometimes the only meal they do is breakfast. Our selection of guest houses is included in the list of places to stay at the end of each county section.

Farmhouses, Town and Country Houses

Often these family homes make your stay, for you meet Irish people who are kind, generous and intelligent. This is also the most economical way to stay in Ireland if you don't want to stay in a tent or in a youth hostel. If you are not going to a place that is recommended, it is largely a matter of luck whether you hit an attractive or a mediocre set-up, but always watch out for the shamrock sign, the Bord Fáilte sign of approval. Wherever you go, you should get a comfortable bed (if you are tall, make sure it is long enough, as sometimes Irish beds can be on the small side), and an enormous breakfast: orange juice, cereal, two eggs, bacon, sausages, toast and marmalade, and a huge pot of tea or coffee. If you get tired of this fry-up, ask your hostess the night before for something different and she will be happy to oblige. Another thing—the coffee is invariably weak and tasteless; it's much safer to stick to tea.

Bed and breakfast per person ranges from £15 to £30 if you are sharing a bedroom (a single room is sometimes more expensive). You can get much cheaper weekly rates, with partial or full board. Very often you can eat your evening meal in the dining room of the B&B. Again, there will be masses to eat and piping hot—so much better than in most of the restaurants and cafés. There is flexibility over breakfast and other meals: they happen when it suits you, but you should give notice before 12 noon if you want to eat dinner.

Some houses serve dinner at between £9 and £15, and some 'high tea', which is less costly (between £6 and £8). 'High tea' is a very sensible meal which has evolved for the working man who begins to feel hungry at about 6pm. You get a plate of something hot, perhaps chicken and chips, followed by fresh soda bread, jam and cakes and a pot of tea. Sometimes you get a salad. This leaves you with plenty of time to go out and explore in the evenings—

whether to the pubs or the countryside! Some houses provide tea and biscuits as a nightcap for nibblers at around 10pm.

For people hitching or using public transport, the town houses are the easiest to get to and find, but my favourites are farmhouses, followed closely by country houses. The farms concentrate on dairy, sheep, crop farming or beef cattle and are often a mixture of everything. Tucked away in lovely countryside, they may be traditional or modern. The farmer's wife, helped by her children, makes life very comfortable and is always ready to have a chat, and advise you on the local beauty spots, good places to hear traditional music or where to go for a *ceili*. Some of the town and country houses are on fairly main roads, but they are generally not too noisy as there is so little traffic about. The type of house you might stay in ranges from the Georgian to the Alpine-style bungalow, from a semi-detached to a 1950s dolls' house. There are a bewildering number of architectural styles in the new houses beginning to radiate out from small villages.

It is wise to book maybe a night or two ahead during July and August, though it is rarely necessary. This means that you can dawdle in a place as much as you want.

Full details of Irish homes can be obtained from the Northern Ireland Tourist Board, and a booklet on farmhouses, town and country houses from any Bord Fáilte office, or write to Irish Farmhouse Holidays, Glynch House, Newbliss, Co. Monaghan or the Secretary, Town and Country Homes Association, Killadean, Bundoran Road, Ballyshannon, Co. Donegal.

Renting a House or Cottage

This is very easy. Ask the NITB for their self-catering bulletin or look in the back of the accommodation booklet and in newspapers. Every regional office of Bord Fáilte has a list of houses and apartments to let; there is also a short list of self-catering houses at the back of the *Guest Accommodation* booklet. Places to rent range from converted stable blocks, modern bungalows to stone-built cottages.

Youth Hostels

The Northern Ireland Youth Hostel Association (YHANI) is at 22 Donegall Rd, Belfast, ✆ (028) 9032 4733. The Irish YHA is called *An Oige* and has 44 hostels. These are distributed all over the Republic and there are a few in the Six Counties, often in wild and remote places, so that they are doubly attractive to the enterprising traveller. Members of the International Youth Hostel Association can use any of these and the hostels in Northern Ireland.

The youth hostels are sometimes the most superb houses, and they range from cottages to castles, old coastguard stations to old military barracks. You must provide your own sleeping sheet, and the hostel provides blankets or sheet bags. Most hostels have fully equipped self-catering kitchens, and some provide breakfast, packed lunches and an evening meal on request.

Charges vary according to age, month and location; during July and August it is slightly more expensive, and it is vital to book. This applies also to weekends. All YHANI and *An Oige* hostels may be booked from one hostel to another, or centrally by contacting the head office listed below. Most of the hostels are open all year round.

The average approximate cost of staying overnight ranges from £6.50 to £9. All enquiries, an essential handbook and an excellent map can be got from the *An Oige* Office, 61 Mountjoy Street, Dublin 1, ✆ (01) 830 4555, ✉ (01) 830 1600. Independent Holiday Hostels of Ireland (IHH) is a completely separate organization to YHA. It is a co-operative society of 112 hostels throughout the country, ranging from Georgian houses to restored mills. They are friendly, open to everyone (children are welcome in most hostels), and most have double and family rooms. All hostels will rent you sheets and provide duvets and blankets. The average price for a dormitory bed in high season is £7. Both YHA and independent hostels are listed in accommodation guides available at tourist offices.

Camping and Caravanning

The camping and caravan parks which meet the standards set by the Northern Ireland Tourist Board and Bord Fáilte are listed in a booklet available from the tourist offices.The sites are graded according to amenities and many of them are in beautiful areas. Laundry rooms, excellent showers and loos, shops, restaurants, indoor games rooms and TV make camping easy and also more civilized, especially if you have children. It is possible to rent tents and camping equipment.

For a complete list of sites, write to the NITB in Belfast and the main Dublin tourist office. It is also possible to rent caravans and motor homes. For full details check with the tourist offices. Overnight charges in the camping parks vary between £3 and £5 per person per night. If you are bringing your own caravan or camping equipment and have Calor gas appliances, the only ones on sale in Ireland which are compatible are those supplied by Gaz. Some caravan parks accept dogs if they are on a leash.

Farmers can be very tolerant of people turning up and asking if they can camp or park their caravan in a field. You must ask their permission first, and tell them how long you want to stay. Be polite, do not get in the way and you will find that they will give you drinking water, lots of chat, and even vegetables from their gardens.

Women Travellers

Irish men have an attitude towards women which is as infuriating as it is attractive. They are a grand old muddle of male chauvinism, with a dash of admiration and fear for their mothers, sisters and wives. Irish women have a sharpness and wit which makes them more than a match for 'your man' in an argument, but at the same time they work their hearts out.

If you are a lone female travelling through Ulster you will find an Ulsterman will always help you with your luggage, your flat tyre and stand you for a meal or a drink, without any question of you buying him a round. If one tries to chat you up in a bar, or at a dance, it is always a bit of 'crack', not to be taken seriously, and the game is abandoned at once if you get tired of it. They probably think that you ought to be travelling with somebody else, but it's only the women who will say so, suggesting, with a smile, that it must be a bit lonesome. If you walk into an obviously male preserve, such as a serious drinking pub, don't expect to feel welcome, because you won't be unless everybody is drunk and by that time you would need to scarper. A bit of advice, which does not apply just to women, was pithily put by an Irish politician: 'The great difference between England and Ireland is that in England you can say what you like, so long as you do the right thing. In Ireland you can do what you like, so long as you say the right thing.' If you are hitch-hiking on your own, or with another girl, you will get plenty of lifts, and offers to take you out dancing that night; your driver will never believe that you have to get on and be somewhere by a certain date, so the journey is passed in pleasant banter. You would be better off hitch-hiking with someone else if possible, although it is pretty safe on the whole.

History

I found in Munster, unfettered of any
Kings and queens, and poets a many—
Poets well skilled in music and measure,
Prosperous doings, mirth and pleasure.
I found in Connaught the just, redundance
Of riches, milk in lavish abundance;
Hospitality, vigour, fame,
In Cruachan's land of heroic name
I found in Ulster, from hill to glen,
Hardy warriors, resolute men;
Beauty that bloomed when youth was gone,
And strength transmitted from sire to son.
I found in Leinster the smooth and sleek,
From Dublin to Slewmargy's peak;
Flourishing pastures, valour, health,
Long-living worthies, commerce, wealth.

from 'Prince Alfrid's Itinerary'
(version by James Clarence Mangan)

If you happen to fall into conversation with an Irishman in any bar the subjects of religion and politics are bound to come up. With any luck you will have a cool glass of Guinness in front of you, for discussions on Ireland are inevitably rather emotional. The Irish are good talkers and have very long memories, so when you are in Ireland it's a good idea to have some idea of their history.

Many of Ireland's troubles have stemmed from her geographical situation—too far from Britain to be assimilated, too near to be allowed to be separate. Queen Elizabeth I poured troops into Ireland because she appreciated the strategic importance of Ireland to her enemies. Throughout the centuries Ireland has been offered help in her fight for independence, but it was never disinterested help; whoever paid for arms and fighting men in Ireland wanted to further some military, political, religious or ideological cause of their own. France in the late 18th century supplied arms to Ireland to distract England from other policies; and in Northern Ireland some of the guns were supplied by foreign powers to the IRA. Twenty-five years of membership of the European Union has paid huge dividends for Ireland. Not only has the economic disparity with the UK narrowed considerably, but Ireland has gained in self-confidence from being a leading player in a union where the centre of power is not London, but Brussels. The European Union is playing its own part too in resolving the troubles in the North of Ireland for the shared economics of membership is working its influence in undermining political and religious differences.

General History

Pre-Celtic Ireland

The hills and river valleys are scattered with ancient monuments dating from the Stone, the Bronze and the Iron Age. Most of them suggest some religious significance, though they have been swathed in romance and heroism by the Celtic story-tellers or *shanachies* in the cottages and castles. Unfortunately only a few survive today as 'memory men'.

The earliest record of man in Ireland is dated between 8,700 and 8,600 years ago, as deduced from fragments found at a camp in **Mount Sandel** near Coleraine. The people of this time lived a nomadic life, hunting and trapping; they could not move around very easily as the countryside was covered by forest, interrupted only by lakes and river channels. They used *curragh* boats, similar to the ones used today by fishermen in the west of Ireland, and built lake-dwellings or *crannógs*. No one is sure where these people came from but they had the island to themselves for 3,000 years. Then came **Neolithic** man, who perhaps is the Fir Bolg in Celtic mythology: at this stage everything is very vague. These people were farmers and gradually spread over the whole of Ireland, clearing the forest as best they could with their stone tools. They evidently practised burial rites, for they built chambered tombs of a very sophisticated quality, decorated with spirals and lozenge shapes. For example, the Great Burial Chamber at Newgrange in the Boyne Valley which dates from 2500 BC has a chamber large enough to contain thousands of cremated bodies. These people must have been very well organized, with the energy and wealth to spare for such an ambitious project—similar in its way to the pyramids, and a thousand years older.

Around 2000 BC yet another race appeared, who were skilled miners and metal-workers. They were called the **Beaker People**; or the Tuatha dé Danaan, as they are known in Irish legend. They opened up copper mines and started to trade with Brittany, the Baltic and the Iberian Peninsula. They had different beliefs about burial: their dead were buried singly in graves lined with stone slabs and covered with a capstone. Other peoples with different burial habits and funeral rituals also arrived at this time; it is not clear in what order they arrived, or to what extent they intermingled. They are named after objects associated with their culture—hence Bowl Food Vessel People, Urn People and Vase Food Vessel People. There are a thousand chambered graves, ring-shaped cairns, standing stones, rows and circles of stones left from these times, and the Boyne Valley culture; they hint at various rituals and, it has been suggested, at observations of the stars. They are often called 'fairy stones', and the chambered graves have been nicknamed 'Dermot and Grania's bed'.

The Celts

The first arrival of the Celts cannot be precisely dated; a few may have come as early as 900 BC, though the main waves of Celtic invaders occurred between 700 BC and 400 BC. These people had iron weapons and defeated the Beakers, whose legendary magical powers were no defence against the new metal. Known as the **Celts** or **Gaels**, the new invaders had spread from south Germany, across France, and as far south as Spain. Today everybody in Ireland has pride in the 'Celtic' past: epic tales sing the praises of men and women who were capable of heroic and superhuman deeds, and beautiful gold jewellery is preserved as proof of their achievements. The Celts brought to Ireland a highly organized social structure, and the La Tène style of decoration (its predominant motif is a spiral or whorl). Ireland was divided into different clans with three classes: the **free**, who were warriors and owned land and cattle; the **professionals**, such as the jurists, Druids, musicians, story-tellers and poets, who could move freely between the petty kingdoms; and, finally, the **slaves**. Every clan had a petty king, who in his turn was ruled over by the high king at Tara, County Meath.

The Gaels made use of many of the customs and mythology that had existed before their arrival, so their 'Celtic civilization' is unique. They were also very fortunate, for although they were probably displaced themselves by the expanding **Roman Empire**, once they got to Ireland they were isolated, and protected to some extent by England which acted as a buffer state. The Romans never extended their ambitions to conquering Ireland, so the Gaels were able to maintain their traditions, unlike Celts elsewhere in Europe. They spent most of their time raiding their neighbours for cattle and women, who were used as live currency. In their religion, the human head was all-important as a symbol of divinity and supernatural power—even when severed from the body it would still retain its powers. The warriors used to take the heads of their slain enemies and display them in front of their houses. The Gaels also believed firmly in an afterlife of the soul—to the extent that they would lend each other money to be repaid in the next world.

The Arrival of Christianity

Christianity was brought to Ireland in the 5th century AD by **St Patrick**, and quickly became accepted by the kings. One of them, **Cormac MacArt**, who ruled in Tara about a century and a half before St Patrick arrived, saw the light and told his court of Druids and nobles that the gods they worshipped were only craven wood. The Druids put a curse on him and soon afterwards he choked to death on a salmon bone; but before he died he ordered that he was not to be buried in the tomb of Brugh (Newgrange) but on the sunny east point by the River Rosnaree. When St Patrick lit a fire which signalled the end of Druid worship, legend has it that he was looking down from the Hill of Slane on to Rosnaree.

The Christians displayed great skill in reconciling their practices and beliefs with those of the pagans; a famous saying of St Columba was, 'Christ is my Druid'. The early Christians seem to have been ascetics, preferring to build their monasteries in the wild and inaccessible places. You can still see their hive-shaped dwellings on **Skellig Michael**, a windswept rocky island off the Kerry coast. The monasteries became universities renowned throughout Europe, which was submerged in the Dark Ages, and produced beautiful manuscripts like the famous *Book of Kells*.

The Viking Invasion

The tranquillity of Ireland, 'land of saints and scholars', was brutally interrupted by the arrival of the **Vikings** or **Norsemen**. They were able to penetrate the heart of the country through their skillful use of the rivers and lakes. They struck for the first time in 795, but this was only the start of a 300-year struggle.

Much treasure from the palaces and monasteries was plundered, for the buildings had no defences; so the monks built round towers in which to store their precious things at the first sign of trouble. Eventually the Norsemen began to settle down and they founded the first city-ports—Dublin, Wexford and Waterford—and started to trade with the Gaels.

Military alliances were made between them when it helped a particular king in the continuous struggle for the high kingship. After a short period of relative calm another wave of Norsemen invaded and the plundering began again; but **Brian Boru**, who had usurped the high kingship from the O'Connors, defeated the Vikings at Clontarf in 1014 and broke their power permanently. Unfortunately for the Gaelic people, Brian Boru was murdered by some Vikings in his tent just after the victory at Clontarf. Havoc and in-fighting became a familiar pattern, as the high kingship was fought over by the O'Briens, the O'Loughlins and the O'Connors. The Gaelic warriors wasted themselves and their people, for no one leader seemed strong enough to rule without opposition. The next invaders saw that their opportunity lay in the disunity of the Irish.

The Norman Invasion and Consolidation

In the mid 12th century the Pope gave his blessing to an expedition of **Anglo-Normans** sent by **Henry II** to Ireland. The Normans were actually invited over by the King of Leinster, **Dermot MacMurragh**, who had made a bitter enemy of **Tiernan O'Rourke** of Breffni by running off with his wife, Devorgilla. He also backed the wrong horse in the high kingship stakes, and the united efforts of the High King Rory O'Connor and O'Rourke brought about a huge reduction in MacMurragh's kingdom. So he approached Henry II, offering his oath of fealty in exchange for an invasion force of men with names like Fitzhenry, Carew, Fitzgerald, and Barry—names you still see in Irish villages. The Normans were adventurers and good warriors: in 1169 several Norman nobles decided to try their luck in Ireland, and they found it easy to grab huge tracts of land for themselves. The Gaels had faced so few attacks from outside their country that they were unprepared for battle. With inferior weapons, their main advantages were a knowledge of the bogs, mountains and forest, and their numbers. The Normans had a well-equipped cavalry, who rode protected by a screen of archers. Once they had launched a successful attack, they consolidated their position by building moats, castles, and walled towns. **Strongbow**, one of the most powerful of the Norman invaders, married MacMurragh's daughter and became his heir, but his successes and those of the other Norman barons worried Henry II. In 1171 Henry arrived in Ireland with 4,000 troops and two objectives: to secure the submission of the Irish leaders and to impose his authority on his own barons. He achieved both aims, but the Gaelic lords still went on fighting. In fact, the coming of the Normans began a military struggle which was to continue over four centuries.

The Bruce Invasion

In 1314 **Robert Bruce of Scotland** decisively defeated English forces at Bannockburn, and was in a position to try to fulfil his dream of a united Celtic kingdom, by putting his brother **Edward** on the throne in Ireland. At first his invasion was successful, but he left a trail of destruction behind him. The year 1316 was marked by famine and disease exacerbated by the war. His dream brought economic and social disaster to Ireland, and when Edward Bruce was defeated and killed at Dundalk few of his allies mourned his death. The Normans' control fluctuated within an area surrounding Dublin known as the Pale, and they became rather independent of their English overlord; in some cases, such as the de Burgos (Burkes), they became more Irish than the Irish. The Gaelic lords in the north and west continued to hold their territories. To do so they imported Scottish mercenary soldiers, called **gallowglasses**, who prolonged the life of the independent Gaelic kingdoms for more than two centuries after the defeat of Edward Bruce.

The Nine Years' War: Elizabethan Conquest and Settlement

Since the Norman invasion, Ireland had been ruined by continual fighting. By the late 16th century, **Queen Elizabeth I** was determined to bring the Irish more firmly under English control, especially the Ulster lords who had so far maintained almost total independence. Elizabeth took over the Irish policy of her father which had never been fully implemented; her government decided that all the Gaelic lords must surrender their lands to the Crown, whereupon they would be regranted immediately. At this time Ulster, today largely Protestant, was the most Gaelic and Catholic part of Ireland, and it was from here that the great **Hugh O'Neill** and **Red Hugh O'Donnell** launched a last-ditch struggle against Elizabeth. Initial successes bolstered the rebels' morale. Elizabeth, recognizing the gravity of the situation, sent over her talented favourite soldier, Essex.

Most of his troops died from disease and guerrilla attacks, and with no reinforcements he had little alternative but to make a truce with O'Neill. Disgrace and execution were his reward. In February 1600 Lord Mountjoy arrived in Ireland with 20,000 troops. Risings at Munster were crushed and with them the aspirations of Connacht and Leinster. The Gaelic chiefs seem to have been ruthless in their allegiances. They had hailed O'Neill as Prince of Ireland but now, antici-pating defeat, they deserted him. O'Neill's hopes were raised by the long-promised arrival of Spanish troops at Kinsale in 1601, but they only numbered 4,000. When they did do battle against Mountjoy, the Irish were left confused when the Spaniards failed to sally out as arranged.

The Flight of the Earls

O'Neill returned to Ulster on 23 March 1603 and made his submission to Mountjoy, only to learn in Dublin later that Queen Elizabeth had died the very next day. He is said to have wept with rage. Amongst all the nobles, only he might have been able to unite the Irish and beat Elizabeth. O'Neill had his titles and lands returned to him, but the Dublin government, greedy for his property, began to bait him. It took his land at the slightest excuse and forbade him to practise Catholicism; so, abandoning hope and his followers, he sailed to Europe. This 'Flight of the Earls' took place on the 14 September 1607, from the wild and beautiful shores of the Swilly. It symbolizes the end of Gaelic leadership and a new period of complete domination by the English. The Irish lords took themselves off to the courts of France and Spain or into the foreign armies. They had spent most of their energies warring among themselves and at the last moment deserted their country, and left the Irish peasants with no leadership at all.

The Confederation, Cromwell and the Stuarts

By the 1640s, Ireland was ready for rebellion again—there were plenty of grievances. **James I**, a staunch Protestant, dispossessed many Gaelic and old English families in Ireland because they would not give up Catholicism, and he began the **'plantation'** of the most vehemently Catholic province, Ulster, with Protestants. Previous plantations had not worked because of inclement weather, but James knew the Scots could skip about the bogs as well as the Irish. When **Charles Stuart** came to the throne, many Catholic families hoped that they might be given some religious freedom and retain their estates, but nothing was legally confirmed. In 1633 **Black Tom**, the Earl of Strafford, arrived with the intention of making Ireland a source of profit rather than a loss to the king. In his zeal he succeeded in alienating every element in Irish society. His enemies amongst the Puritans in Ireland and England put pressure on the king to recall him and he was eventually executed. English politics became dominated by the dissen-sion between the Roundheads and the Cavaliers and the hopeless Irish took note. Their maxim was 'England's difficulty is Ireland's opportunity'. Charles tried to deal with the growing unrest in Ireland by giving everybody what they wanted, but he no longer had enough power to see that his laws were carried out. The Gaelic Irish decided to take a chance and rebel; many of them came back from the Continental armies hoping to win back their old lands. In October 1641 a small Gaelic force took over the whole of Ulster and there were widespread uprisings in

Leinster. In Ulster, the Gaelic people had been burning for revenge and the new planted families suffered terribly. This cruel treatment has not been forgotten by Ulster Protestants.

The Dublin government was worse than useless at controlling the rebels. While the government waited for reinforcements from England, they managed to antagonize the old English, for they made the mistake of presuming that they would be disloyal to the Crown, and so viewed them with suspicion. The old English families decided to throw in their lot with the rebels since they were already considered traitors, but on one condition: a declaration of loyalty from the Gaelic leaders to the Catholic English crown which was now seriously threatened by the Puritans.

The Confederation of Kilkenny

By February 1642 most of Ireland was in rebel hands. The rebels established a provisional government at **Kilkenny**, and Charles began to negotiate with them, hoping to gain their support against the Puritans. Things were too good to last. The destructive factors that had ruined many Irish uprisings before and since, came into play: personal jealousy and religion. The old English were loyal to the king and wanted a swift end to the war; the Gaelic Irish were only interested in retrieving their long-lost lands and were ready to fight to the bitter end. This disunity was exacerbated by the rivalry between the Gaelic commander, **Owen Roe O'Neill** and the commander of the old English army, **Thomas Preston**. In October 1645 the Papal Nuncio arrived and the unity of the Confederates was further split: he and O'Neill took an intransigent stand over the position of the Catholic Church, which Charles I could not agree to.

The rebels won a magnificent victory over the Puritan General Munro at Benburb, but O'Neill did not follow it up. The confederates, torn by disunity and rivalry, let opportunities slip and they lost the initiative. Eventually they did decide to support the king and end their Kilkenny government, but by this time Charles I had been beheaded and his son had fled into exile. The Royalists were defeated at Rathmines in 1649 and the way was left clear for the Puritan leader, **Cromwell**, who landed in Dublin soon after. Cromwell came to Ireland determined to break the Royalists, break the Gaelic Irish, and to avenge the events of 1641 in Ulster. He started his campaign with the **Siege of Drogheda**, and there are the most gruesome accounts of his methods. When his troops burst into the town they put Royalists, women, children and priests to the sword; in all 3,552 dead were counted, whilst Cromwell only lost 64 men. Catholics curse Cromwell to this day. The same butchery marked the taking of Wexford. Not surprisingly, he managed to break the spirit of resistance by such methods and there were widespread defections from the Royalists' side. Owen Roe O'Neill might have been able to rally the Irish but he died suddenly. Cromwell's campaign only lasted seven months and he took all the towns except Galway and Waterford. These he left to his lieutenants.

By 1652 the whole country was subdued, and Cromwell encouraged all the fighting men to leave by granting them amnesty if they fled overseas. The alternative to exile was, for many families, something that turned out to be even worse: compulsory removal to Connacht and County Clare. Some had been neutral during all the years of fighting, but that was never taken into account. Cromwell was determined that anyone suspect should go to Hell or Connacht. The government had lots of land to play with after that. First of all they paid off 'the adventurers', men who had lent them money back in 1642. Next, the Roundhead soldiers, who had not been paid their salaries for years, got Irish land instead. Thus the Cromwellian Settlement parcelled out even more land to speculators, foreigners and rogues.

Stuart and Orange

After the **Restoration of the Monarchy** in 1660, the Catholics in Ireland hoped for toleration and rewards for their loyalty to the Stuart cause. They felt threatened by the fast-expanding Protestant community, but Charles II did not restore many Catholic estates because he had to keep in with the ex-Cromwellian supporters, although Catholics were given a limited amount of toleration. However, with the succession of Charles' brother **James**, who was a Catholic, things began to brighten up. In Ireland, the Catholic Earl of Tyrconnell became commander of the army in 1685 and, later, chief governor. By 1688 Roman Catholics were dominant in the army, the administration, the judiciary and the town corporations, and by the end of the year Protestant power in Ireland was seriously weakened. James frightened all those Protestants in England who had benefited from Catholic estates. They began to panic when he introduced sweeping acts of toleration for all religions. His attempts to re-establish the Catholic Church alienated the country to such an extent that the Protestant aristocracy eventually invited **William of Orange** over in November 1688 to relieve his father-in-law of his throne. James fled to France but soon left for Ireland, which was a natural base from which to launch his counter-attack. By the date of his arrival in March 1689, only Enniskillen and Londonderry were in Protestant hands.

The Siege of Londonderry and Battle of the Boyne

The subjugation of the city of Londonderry was James' first aim. In a famous incident celebrated in Orange songs, a group of apprentice boys shut the city gates to the Jacobite army, and so began the famous Siege of Londonderry. The townspeople proved unbreakable, though they were reduced to eating rats and mice and chewing old bits of leather. Many died of starvation during the 15-week siege, but just as they were about to give in, the foodship *Mountjoy* forced its way through a great boom laid across the River Foyle. When William himself arrived at Carrickfergus in June 1690, James decided to confront him at the Boyne. William of Orange had an army of about 36,000 comprised of English, Scots, Dutch, Danes, Germans and Huguenots, against James' army of about 25,000, made up of Irish and French. William triumphed, as the result of his numerical and strategic superiority. James deserted the battlefield and Ireland with haste.

In the **Battle of the Boyne** James seems to have completely lost his nerve. The Jacobite forces had to retreat west of the Shannon to Limerick, and William promptly laid siege to it. So weak were its walls that it is said they could be breached with roasted apples. The defence of Limerick was as heroic as that of Londonderry. Patrick Sarsfield slipped out with a few followers and intercepted William's siege train and destroyed it. William then gave up and left for England leaving Ginkel in charge. The next year the French King Louis XIV sent over supplies and men to fuel the Jacobite cause, as he hoped to divert William in Ireland for a little longer. The Jacobite leader St Ruth, who landed with them, proved a disaster for the Irish; Sarsfield would have been a better choice. Ginkel took Athlone and Aughrim in June and July of 1691, after two battles in which stories of courage on the Jacobite side have provided inspiration to patriot poets and musicians. The last hope of the Catholic Irish cause was now Limerick.

The Treaty of Limerick

Sarsfield skilfully gathered together what Jacobite troops were left. (St Ruth had been killed by a cannonball, and rather typically had appointed no second-in-command.) Ginkel tried to storm the town from both sides, but still Limerick held out and so he was forced to negotiate with Sarsfield. Honourable terms were made for the Jacobites, and Sarsfield signed the famous **Treaty of Limerick** in October 1691. The next day a French fleet arrived and anchored off the Shannon estuary, but Sarsfield stood by the Treaty; Catholics were to have the same rights as they had had under Charles II and any Catholic estates which had been registered in 1662 were to be handed back. Catholics were to be allowed free access to the bar, bench, army and parliament. Sarsfield was to be given a safe passage to the Continent with his troops. But the Treaty was never honoured, except for the last clause which got all the fighting men out of the country. This was one of the dirtiest tricks the English played; William of Orange in fact supported the treaty, but being unsure of his own position he complied with the treachery. Eleven thousand Irish Jacobites sailed away to join the French army, forming the Irish Brigade. Over the years many came to join them from Ireland, and were remembered in their native land as the **Wild Geese**.

The Orange/Stuart war still lives vividly in the imagination of the people today. The Siege of Londonderry has become a sign of Protestant determination: 'no surrender 1690' is scrawled, usually in bright red paint, on the walls and street corners of Loyalist areas in Northern Ireland. The Battle of the Boyne is remembered in a similar way.

The Penal Laws

The defeat of the Catholic cause was followed by more confiscation of land, and the **Penal Laws**. A bargain had been struck with the Protestant planters who were allowed to keep a complete monopoly of political power and most of the land in return for acting as a British garrison to keep the peace and prevent the Catholics from gaining any power. To do this they passed a series of degrading laws. Briefly they were as follows. No Catholic could purchase free-hold land. Any son of a Catholic, turning Protestant, could turn his parents off their estate. Families who stayed Catholic had their property equally parcelled out amongst all the children, so that any large estates soon became uneconomic holdings. All the Catholics were made to pay a tithe towards the upkeep of the Anglican Church. All priests were banished. No Catholic schools were allowed and spies were set amongst the peasants to report on 'hedge schools', a form of quite sophisticated schooling that had sprung up; priests on the run taught at these schools and celebrated Mass. A Catholic could not hold a commission in the army, enter a profession nor even own a horse worth more than £5. These anti-religious laws had the opposite effect to that intended: Catholicism took on a new lease of life in Ireland. In addition, **economic laws** were introduced that taxed heavily anything that Ireland produced—cloth, wool, glass and cattle—so that she could not compete with England. The trading regulations were disadvantageous to the non-conformist Ulster Protestants and many of them left. Then, gradually things began to relax; the Catholics had been well and truly squashed. The Protestants began to build themselves grand and beautiful houses; the draughty, damp tower houses could be left to decay. (Irish squires were famous for their hard drinking; the expression 'plastered' comes from the story of a guest who was so well wined and dined at a neighbour's housewarming party that he fell asleep against a newly plastered wall. He woke up next morning to find that his scalp and hair had hardened into the wall.)

As the 18th century progressed, however, there were signs of aggression amongst the peasantry; agrarian secret societies were formed with names like the **White Boys**, **Hearts of Oak**, and the **Molly Maguires**. They were very brutal and meted out rough justice to tenants and landlords alike. If any peasant paid rent to an unfair landlord, he was likely to be intimidated or have his farm burnt down. In Ulster, peasant movements were dominated by sectarian land disputes. The Catholics were called the **Defenders** and the Protestant groups the **Peep-O'Day Boys**. In the 1770s the Penal Laws were relaxed a little and Catholics were allowed to bid for land, and they incensed the Protestants by bidding higher. After a particularly bad fight between the two sides which the Protestants won, the **Orange Order** was founded in 1795. A typical oath of one of the early clubs was, 'To the glorious, pious and immortal memory of the great and good King William, not forgetting Oliver Cromwell, who assisted in redeeming us from popery, slavery, arbitrary power, brassmoney and wooden shoes'.

The **American War of Independence** broke out in 1775 and Ireland was left undefended. There were fears of an invasion by France or Spain and a general feeling that there ought to be some sort of defence force. The **Volunteers** were organized with officers from the Protestant landowning class; but as the fears of invasion receded they turned their considerable muscle to the cause of political reform, and Britain began to fear that they might follow the example of the American colonies. When America sought independence, Irish Protestants and Catholics alike watched with approval, particularly since many of the rebel Americans were of Ulster/Scots blood. The landowners had their own parliament in Dublin, but all important matters were dealt with by London. A group of influential landowners began to think that Ireland would be much better off with an independent Irish parliament. In 1783, the British Government, influenced by the eloquence of the great speaker **Henry Grattan**, acknowledged the right of Ireland to be bound only by laws made by the king and the Irish parliament. Trade, industry and agriculture began to flourish, and the worst of the Penal Laws were repealed or relaxed.

Grattan's Parliament

Grattan's Parliament was really an oligarchy of landowners, but they at least understood the problems of the economy and tried to bring a more liberal spirit into dealings with Catholics and dissenters. Grattan wanted complete Catholic emancipation, but for that the Irish had to wait. Yet Trinity College was made accessible to those of all religious persuasions, although Catholics were forbidden by their bishops to go there. The great Catholic Seminary at Maynooth was founded, and endowed with money and land from the Protestant aristocrats, who were worried that the priests educated at Douai might bring back with them some of those frightening ideas of liberty and equality floating around France. Dissenters were given equal rights with the Established Church at this time.

Dublin was now a handsome Georgian city, a centre for the arts, science and society. To pay for all this pleasure landowners began to sublet their estates to land-hungry tenants. In the early 1790s, fear and anger swept through Europe in the form of the French Revolution and the governments of Europe, whether Catholic or Protestant, drew nearer together in mutual fear. Many, who at first were delighted with the revolution in France, became disgusted with the brutality of its methods. The Irish government disbanded the Volunteers and got together a militia and part-time force of yeomanry. It was nervous of a French invasion and increasingly of a middle-class organization, the 'United Irishmen', who were sick of a government which only spoke for a tiny proportion of the population.

Wolfe Tone and United Irishmen

The aim of the United Irishmen was to throw open the Irish parliament to all Irishmen, irrespective of their rank or religion. Many United Irishmen were from Ulster non-conformist backgrounds. Initially the movement was to be non-violent, but when war broke out between England and France, all radical societies were forced to go underground. No liberal ideas could be tolerated during the war effort. **Wolfe Tone** was a Dublin lawyer and a prominent United Irishman; he crossed over to France to try and persuade the French Directory to help.

The Protestant Wind

Wolfe Tone succeeded brilliantly in arguing a case for French intervention and, on the night of 16 December 1796, the last great French invasion force to set sail for the British Isles slipped past the British squadron blockading the port of Brest, anchoring off Bantry Bay five days later. They waited one clear, calm day for the frigate carrying the Commander-in-Chief to arrive; then the wind changed and blew from the east, remembered in all the songs as a 'Protestant Wind'. The fleet endured the storm for three days, then the ships cut cable and headed back for France. Only Wolfe Tone and his ship, *The Indomitable*, remained and, as Tone put it, 'England had not such an escape since the Armada'.

Meanwhile, in the Irish countryside, increasingly brutal attempts were made by the militia and the yeomanry to stamp out sedition. In Ulster, where the United Irishmen were strong, efforts were made to set the United Irishmen against the Orangemen, many of whom had joined the yeomanry. This continual pressure forced the society to plan rebellion. However, government spies had infiltrated its ranks, and two months before the proposed date many of the leaders were arrested. By this time many Irish peasants had joined the United Irishmen, inspired by the heady doctrine of Tom Paine's *Rights of Man*. The increased power of the Irish parliament had not meant more freedom for them; on the contrary the heretics and alien landlords now seemed to have more power to persecute them in the forms of tithes and taxes. Yet the Gaelic-speaking peasants had little in common with the middle-class agitators, and their anger was even more explosive.

The 1798 Rebellion

In May 1798 the rebellion broke out. The United Irish leaders had planned a rebellion believing that they could count on an army of over 250,000. However, the absence of leadership and careful planning resulted in local uprisings with no central support; even those which achieved some success were quickly crushed. In Ulster there were two main risings, under **McCracken** and **Munro**. The risings both enjoyed brief success during which time the rebels treated any Loyalist prisoners well—a marked contrast to what had happened in other counties. But the sectarian battles between the Peep-O'Day Boys had already soured the trust of the Catholics, and many of them did not turn up to help the mixed bunch of United Irishmen. Poor Wolfe Tone and others who had started the society with such hopes for affectionate brotherhood saw their ideals drowned in a sea of blood. Nugent, the commander of the government forces in Ulster, decided to appeal to the rebels who had property to lose, especially those in the rich eastern counties, and he proclaimed a general amnesty if the Antrim rebels gave up their arms. The rebels of Down did not get off so humanely; when they had been routed and shot down they were left unburied in the streets for the pigs to eat. McCracken and Munro were executed.

The Races of Castlebar

Whilst the war between France and England became more embittered, Wolfe Tone succeeded in raising another invasion force. On 22 August 1798, **General Humbert** arrived in Killala Bay with 1,000 men and more arms for the rebels, although most of them had dispersed.

Humbert captured Ballina and routed 6,000 loyalist troops in a charge called the 'Races of Castlebar'. But there were not enough rebels and Humbert had to accept honourable terms of surrender in September. Only a few weeks later, another unsuccessful French expedition arrived with Tone on board and entered Lough Swilly. It was overcome by some British frigates and Wolfe Tone was captured. He appeared before a court martial wearing a French uniform and carrying a cockade. The only favour he asked was the right to be shot, which was refused, whereupon he cut his own throat with a penknife and lingered in agony for seven days. The rebellion of 1798 was one of the most tragic and violent events in Irish history, and it had the effect of making people try to bring about change in a non-violent way. In the space of three weeks, 30,000 people, peasants armed with pitchforks and pikes, women and children, were cut down and shot. The results of the rebellion were just as disastrous. The ideas of political and religious equality were discredited, because of the deaths and destruction of property. The British Government found that an independent parliament was an embarrassment to them, especially since the 'Protestant garrison' had not been able to put down the peasant rising without their help.

The Union

Pitt, the British prime minister, decided that union between Great Britain and Ireland was the only answer. First he had to bribe the Protestants to give up their power and many earldoms date from this time. Then the **Act of Union** was passed, with promises of Catholic emancipation for the majority. Pitt really did want to give them equality, for he saw that it was a necessary move if he wished to make Ireland relatively content. Unfortunately Pitt was pushed out of government, and **George III** lent his considerable influence to those opposed to Catholic emancipation. He claimed, with perfect truth, that the idea of it drove him mad. The Union did not solve any problems: the Catholics felt bitterly let down and the temporary Home Rule of Grattan's parliament was looked back to as an example. Irreconcilable nationalism was still alive and kicking. Union with England was disadvantageous to Ireland in the areas of industry and trade and many poorer Protestants were discontented—although from now on the Ulster non-conformists supported the Union, for many had been disillusioned by the vengeance shown towards Protestants by the Catholic peasantry. The terms of the 1801 Act were never thought of as final in Ireland, although the English failed to understand this.

The Liberator: Daniel O'Connell

Catholics still could not sit in parliament or hold senior judicial, military or civil service posts. Between the Union and 1828 efforts to address this imbalance came to nothing. Then the Catholics found a champion among themselves: a Catholic lawyer called **Daniel O'Connell** who believed that 'no political change is worth the shedding of a single drop of human blood'. O'Connell founded the **Catholic Association** which, amongst other things, represented the interests of the tenant farmers. Association membership was a penny a month and brought in a huge fighting fund. Most important of all, the Catholic priests supported him, and soon there were branches of the association everywhere. A turning point for Irish history and the fortunes of Daniel O'Connell came with the Clare election in 1828, when the association showed its strength. O'Connell had an overwhelming victory against the government candidate when all the 40-shilling freeholders voted for him. The whole country was aflame: they wanted Daniel at Westminster. Wellington, the Prime Minister of the day, was forced to give in, and the **Emancipation Bill** was passed in April 1829. But this was not a gesture of conciliation, for at the same time he raised the voting qualification from 40 shillings to a massive £10. Protestant fears had been raised by the power of such a mass movement, for tenant farmers had dared to vote in opposition to their landlords, even though voting was public. To English Catholics Daniel was also a 'Liberator'.

For 12 years O'Connell supported the Whig government and built up a well-disciplined Irish party whose co-operation was essential to any government majority. He was then able to press for some very necessary reforms, and when the viceroy and his secretary were sympathetic much was achieved. But with the return of the Conservatives in 1840, O'Connell decided it was time to launch another popular agitation campaign, this time for the repeal of the Union. His mass-meetings became 'monster meetings', each attended by well over 100,000 people. The government refused to listen on this issue; British public opinion was firmly against it and in Ulster there was a distinct lack of enthusiasm. Daniel O'Connell arranged to have one of his biggest meetings yet, at Clontarf, where Brian Boru had defeated the Vikings. The Government banned it and O'Connell, unwilling to risk violence, called it off. He himself was arrested for conspiracy and sentenced by just the sort of packed jury he had been trying to abolish. Luckily for him, the House of Lords was less frightened and more just; they set aside his sentence. But by then O'Connell's influence had begun to fade, and some Irish began to look to violence to achieve their aims.

The Young Irelanders

Within the Repeal Association was a group of young men who called themselves the **Young Irelanders**. They had founded *The Nation* newspaper to help O'Connell, but they soon began to move in a different direction. They believed that culturally and historically Ireland was independent of England and fed their enthusiasm on the painful memories of 1798, composing heroic poetry which they set to old ballad tunes. They were useless at practical politics and did not have the support of the clergy. In 1848 they responded to the spontaneous and romantic uprisings in Europe with one of their own. It was a dismal failure and alienated many people who had been in favour of the Repeal of the Union. The movement was not to become respectable again until 1870.

The Great Hunger

The diet of an ordinary Irishman was six pounds of potatoes and a pint of milk a day, and he lived in miserable conditions. The Cromwellian and Williamite plantations, together with the effect of the Penal Laws, left the Catholics with only 5 per cent of the land. Except in the North, where a thriving linen industry had grown up, the people had to make their living from farming. Absentee landlords became more of a problem after the Union, their agents greedier and their rent demands even higher. It was the farmer at the bottom of the pyramid who paid heavily for what he got. From 1845–49 the **potato blight** struck, with tragic results.

The population of Ireland, as in the rest of Europe, began to rise quickly in the late 18th century, perhaps because the potato could feed large families on small plots of land. The most deprived and populated area of Ireland was the west, where the potato was the only crop that would grow; it alone sustained the fragile equilibrium of large families on tiny holdings. The scene was set for agricultural and social catastrophe. As the potato rotted in the ground, people ate turnips, cabbage, wild vegetables and even grass, but these could not supply more than a few meals. Gradually, thousands of people began to die of starvation, typhus fever, relapsing fever and dysentery. Every day corn and cattle were leaving the country; nothing was done that might interfere with the principle of free trade and private enterprise. The government's attitude was rigid, though they did allow maize in, a crop in which nobody had any vested interest. Food distribution centres were set up and some relief work was paid for by the government. But this was not very sensible sort of work; mostly digging holes only to fill them in again. Something constructive like laying a network of railway lines might have interfered with private enterprise! Out of a population of eight and a half million, about one million died and another million emigrated.

Emigration

The Irish had been emigrating for years; first to escape persecution by fleeing to the Continent and then as seasonal labour for the English harvests. The Ulster Scots had set the first pattern of emigration to America. They had found that Ireland was not the promised land, after being lured over there by grants of land and low rents. Bad harvests, religious discrimination and high rents sent them off at the rate of 4,000 a year. Not many Catholics followed, for there were still restrictions on Catholic emigration. Many Irish went to Australia as convicts or free settlers. But the heaviest years of emigration were just after the famine, especially to the USA. The people travelled under appalling conditions in boats known as 'coffin ships' for the numbers that died in them. It took six to eight weeks to get to America in those overcrowded and disease-ridden conditions. By 1847 nearly a quarter of a million Irish were emigrating annually.

Priests followed their flocks out to America and Australia and founded churches wherever they were needed, so a distinct Irish Catholic Church grew up. Such an influx of starving, diseased Irish Catholics was quite another thing to the steady flow of a few thousand Ulster Scots, and initially a lot of people were prejudiced against them. Most of the emigrants left Ireland loathing the British in Ireland. Their children grew up with the same hatred, and sometimes became more anti-British than the Irish left in Ireland. This bitterness was soon transformed into political activity, aided by the Young Irelanders who had fled to America. Many of the emigrants had come from the west where the Gaelic language and culture existed undisturbed. The rest of Ireland, especially the east, was quite anglicized and became more so with the development of education and transport.

America and Irish Politics

In 1858, James Stephens founded a secret movement in Ireland called the Irish Republican Brotherhood (IRB). Shortly afterwards, he and John O'Mahony, a comrade from the uprising of 1848 who had fled to America, reorganized the Irish Catholics in America into a twin movement called the Fenian Brotherhood. The Fenians called themselves after the legendary Fianna Warriors and were dedicated to the principal of Republicanism. Because of the need for secrecy, the IRB was generally known at this time under the name of the Fenians, the American part of the organization, which was able to function openly. In Ireland, aided by money from America, the Fenians started up a newspaper, *The Irish People*, which was aimed at the urban worker. When the American Civil War was over many Irish American soldiers came over to help the Fenians in Ireland, but their military operations were always dismal failures. But Fenianism remained a potent force. The unfortunate execution of Allen, Larkin and O'Brien in 1867, who became known as the Manchester Martyrs, became further powerful propaganda for the Fenian Cause. John Devoy in America and Michael Davitt of the **Irish Land League** were imaginative enough to see that violence was not the only way to fight high rents. They made a loose alliance with Parnell, the leader of the Irish Party in the House of

Commons. John Devoy was head of the **Clan-na-Gael**, an organization which cloaked Fenianism. In America, through the Fenians, Parnell was able to collect money for the land agitators. John Devoy gave money and moral support to the revolutionaries in their fight for independence. The Clan created good propaganda for the Nationalists and, between the death of Parnell and the rise of **Sinn Féin** ('We, Ourselves'), did everything it could to drive a wedge between the USA and England, and to keep the States neutral during the First World War. It even acted as an intermediary between Germany and the IRB who were negotiating for guns.

The Irish Americans played such an important part in Irish politics that it is worth jumping forward in time for a moment to recount subsequent events. In 1918 **Eamon de Valera**, born in America, was elected by Sinn Féin as head of a provisional government. He came to America with high hopes during the War of Independence in Ireland. He wanted two things: political recognition from the government for the Dail Eireann—the Irish parliament set up in Dublin in 1919—and money. He failed in his first aim: he was rebuffed by President Wilson (himself of Ulster Scots blood). However, de Valera got plenty of money, 6 million dollars in the form of a loan, but he fell out with Devoy. He founded a rival organization called the **American Association for the Recognition of the Irish Republic** (AARIA). When Ireland split over the solution of partition and there was a civil war, the Republicans, who rejected the partition, were supported by the AARIA, whilst the Free Staters had Devoy and Clan-na-Gael behind them. The leading spirit of the AARIA was **Joseph McGarrity**, who later broke with De Valera when he began to act against the IRA. His group and their successors continued to give financial support to the IRA during the Troubles in Northern Ireland.

Tenants' Rights and the Land War

The Union Government was blamed by many in Ireland for the tragic extent of the famine, but the government was blind to the lessons it should have taught them. The famine had only intensified the land war and the 1829 Act simply enabled the impoverished landlords to sell their estates, which the peasants had no money to buy. So the speculators moved in, seized opportunities for further evictions and increased the rents. Tenant resistance smouldered, stimulated by the horrors of the famine.

Michael Davitt organized the resistance into the **National Land League**, with the support of Parnell, the leader of the Irish Party in the House of Commons. In the ensuing **Land War** (1879–82), a new word was added to the English language—'boycott'. The peasants decided not to help an evicting landlord with his crops and he had to import Orangemen from Ulster to gather in the harvest. The offending landlord was a Captain Boycott. The tenants wanted the same rights that tenants had in Ulster and fair rent, fixity of tenure and freedom to sell at the market value. They also wanted a more even distribution of the land; at that time 3 per cent of the population owned 95 per cent of the land.

Behind all the agitation at this time, and all the obstruction the Irish Party caused in parliament, was a desire for the repeal of the Union. But the politicians saw the problem as religion, over-population, famine, anything but nationalism. It did not enter English heads that the Irish might not want to be part of Britain—with the Union, in their eyes, Irishmen were on an equal footing with the rest of Great Britain, they were part of the Empire. The Union was also a security against foreign attack and must stay. Only one man said anything sensible on the subject and he was not listened to. **J. S. Mill** said that England was the worst qualified to govern the Irish, because English traditions were not applicable in Ireland. England was firmly *laissez-faire* in her economic policies, but Ireland needed economic interference from the government. This the English politicians had resolutely refused to do during and after the famine. Gladstone and other Liberals were aware of the discontent. They tried to take the sting out of Irish Nationalism by dealing with the problems individually, believing that then the nationalist grievance would disappear.

Killing Home Rule with Kindness

One of the first things to be dealt with was religion, for it could not be kept out of politics. The Protestant Ascendancy, by virtue of education, contacts, etc., still monopolized powerful positions, despite Catholic emancipation. This frustrated the middle classes and created an Irish Catholic national distinctiveness. There may have been no legal barriers any more, but there were unofficial ones. The Anglican Church of Ireland still remained the Established Church until 1869, and until then the Irish peasant had to pay tithes to it. The Catholic hierarchy wanted a state-supported Catholic education, but the government tried to have interdenominational schools and universities. This never satisfied the Catholic Church and consequently, much later on, it supported the illegal nationalist organizations. Unfortunately the government were unwilling to establish the Catholic Church in Ireland as they would have had problems with the Protestants in Ulster so, although the Catholic Church had consolidated its position, it was not conciliated.

The distress of the peasant farmers had, by this time, become identified with nationalism, so the government set out to solve the economic problems, thinking that this would shatter the nationalists. But they acted too late. Only in 1881 were the demands of the tenants met. Large amounts of money were made available to tenants to buy up their holdings, and, by 1916, 64 per cent of the population owned land. (Many of these new owners had the same surnames as those dispossessed back in the 17th century.) But Britain was remembered not for these Land Acts, generous as they were, but for the Coercion and Crime Acts which Balfour brought in to try to control the unrest and anarchy which existed in some parts of the country. The **Land Purchase Acts** took away the individual oppressor and left only the government against whom to focus discontent. The peasants had been given more independence and the landlords were virtually destroyed, so the Union became even more precarious. The Nationalists could not be bought off.

Home Rule for Ireland?

Parnell forced the government to listen, often holding a balance of power in the House of Commons, and for a while he managed to rally the whole Nationalist movement behind his aggressive leadership. The bait of universal suffrage was enough for the Fenians to try to overthrow the Union from within the system. The **Secret Ballot Act** in 1872 made this even more attractive than abortive rebellions. But the Home Rule League did not succeed, even though Gladstone and the Liberals, who were at that time in Opposition, had promised to support it. First of all, Parnell was a weakness as well as a strength. His aggressive tactics alienated many Englishmen and his Protestant origins upset some of the Catholic hierarchy, who thought he should have concentrated a little more on pushing for the Catholic university they wanted. Also, his affair with Kitty O'Shea and involvement in a divorce case shocked many Victorians and non-conformists in the Liberal Party. They demanded that he should be dropped from the leadership of the Irish Party and, when the Catholic hierarchy heard this, they also began to scold 'the named adulterer' and turned their congregations against him.

Another reason for the failure of the Home Rule Bill was that the predominantly Protestant and industrial North of Ireland had no wish to join the South. The North thought that it would be overtaxed to subsidize the relatively backward agrarian South, and the Protestants were frightened of being swamped by the Catholics. Their fear gave them a siege mentality; Parnell's divorce case was like a gift from heaven and gave them a reprieve. English opinion was still against Home Rule and it was only because the Irish Party had made a deal with the Liberals that there was any hope of their succeeding. With the fall of Parnell, the Irish Party split and lost most of its influence.

Parnell's fall in 1891 and the failure of the 1893 Home Rule Bill initiated a resurgence of revolutionary nationalism. The younger generation were shocked by the way in which the Catholic Church within Ireland condemned Parnell over the O'Shea case. And, as the moral authority of the Church was cast aside, so was one of the barriers to violence. Parnell's failure to work things through Parliament seemed to indicate that only violence would work. Young people began to join the Irish Republican Brotherhood (IRB), founded by James Stevens, and even the Church began to show more sympathy because at least nationalism was preferable to the atheistic socialism that was creeping into Dublin. Many of the priests had brothers and sisters in illegal organizations and it was inevitable that they would become emotionally involved.

Gaelic Cultural Renaissance

There was a new mood in Ireland at the end of the 19th century. The people were proud of being Irish and of their cultural achievements. Unfortunately only 14 per cent of the population spoke the Gaelic language (the famine and emigration that followed had seriously weakened its hold); English was taught in schools, knowledge of it led to better jobs and opportunities, and Irish music and poetry were neglected except by a few intellectuals. However, it was in the stories of Ireland's past, her legends and customs, that many diverse groups found a common ground. In 1884 the **Gaelic Athletic Association** started to revive the national game—hurling. In 1893 the **Gaelic League** was formed. Its president was **Douglas Hyde**, who campaigned successfully for the return of Gaelic lessons to schools and as a qualification for entry to the new universities. He never wanted the League to be a sectarian or political force, but it did provide a link between the conservative Catholic Church and the Fenians and Irish Nationalists. 'The Holy Island of St Patrick' developed an ideal: that of the Catholic, devout, temperate, clean-living Irishman. The Gaelic League and the Gaelic Athletic Association were used by the IRB as sounding boards or recruiting grounds for membership. The Liberals returned to power in 1906 and things began to look brighter for Home Rule. In 1910 John Redmond led the Irish Party and held the balance of power between the Liberals and the Conservatives. In 1914 Asquith's **Home Rule Bill** was passed, although it was suspended for the duration of the First World War. But six years later Ireland was in the middle of a war of independence and the initiative had passed from the British into the hands of the revolutionary nationalists. This happened because the British Government had left Home Rule too late; the time lag between when it was passed and when it actually might be implemented gave the Irish public time to criticize it and see its limitations. The nationalists began to despair of ever finding a parliamentary solution, for the British could now not force the North into Home Rule and were shutting their eyes to the gun-running which had been going on since the formation of the Ulster Volunteers. The Irish people were lukewarm about organizations like the IRB and its associated new Sinn Féin Party, founded by Arthur Griffith. In fact, military recruitment, relative prosperity, and the nominal achievement of Home Rule brought Ireland and the rest of

Britain closer together. The IRB's military council wanted to do something to stem the fragmentation of their movement. An event on Easter Monday in 1916 changed all that.

Easter Rebellion 1916

Plans for a national rising with German support were made. The support did not arrive; it was a confused situation yet the IRB leaders were determined it should go ahead and a rising commenced in Dublin. It happened very quickly. Suddenly the tricolour of a new Irish Republic was flying from the General Post Office in Dublin. Two thousand Irish nationalist volunteers, led by **Patrick Pearse** of the IRB, stood against the reinforcements sent from England and then surrendered about a week later. People were horrified at first by the waste of life, for many civilians got caught up in the gun battles; but then the British played into the hands of Patrick Pearse. All 14 leaders were executed after secret trials. Suddenly they were dead, and pity for them grew into open sympathy for what they had been trying to obtain. The Catholic Church was trapped in the emotional wave which advocated revolution. The party which gained from this swing was the Sinn Féin; it was pledged to non-violent nationalism and was the public front of the IRB. John Redmond, the leader of the Irish Party at Westminster, had urged everybody to forget their differences with England and fight the common enemy which was Germany, but the Irish Nationalists, who were negotiating with the Germans, saw things in a very different light. Many Irishmen did go and fight for Britain (some 200,000 men enlisted), but the feeling grew that Redmond was prepared to compromise over Home Rule and shelve it until it suited the British. Sinn Féin, under the influence of American-born Eamon de Valera, set out to mobilize popular support through propaganda and electioneering.

When in 1918 conscription was extended to Ireland even more people decided that **Sinn Féin** was the only party which could speak for them. It won all the Irish seats bar six. Redmond's party was finished. The only problem was that 44 of the Sinn Féin members were in English jails; those that were not met in Mansion House and set up their own Dail Eireann. Eamon de Valera made an audacious escape from Lincoln prison and was elected the first President of the Irish Republic in 1919. The Irish Volunteers became the **Irish Republican Army** and war was declared on Britain.

The North

Meanwhile in the North they had found a leader to defend the Union in Dublin-born **Edward Carson**. He was a leading barrister in London (he cross-examined Oscar Wilde in that notorious lawsuit), and was openly supported by the Conservatives in England. A solemn **Covenant of Resistance to Home Rule** was signed by hundreds of thousands of Northern Unionists. They would fight with any means possible not to come under an Irish parliament in Dublin. After the Easter rising of 1916, Carson was assured by Lloyd George that the six northeastern counties could be permanently excluded from the Home Rule Bill of 1914. When the **War of Independence** broke out in the South, the British offered them partition with their own parliament whilst remaining within Britain. Today their ties are with a liberal Britain, not the Catholic South.

The War of Independence

The British Government had been caught out by the Declaration of Independence by the Dail. The British were engaged in trying to negotiate a peace treaty at Versailles and the Americans had made it very clear that they sympathized with the Irish. Ammunition raids, bombing, burning and shooting began in Ireland, mainly against the Irish Constabulary. The British government waited until the Versailles Conference had come to an end and then started to fight back. The **Black and Tans** were sent over to reinforce the police; Lloyd George tried to play it down as a police situation. The Black and Tans got their name from the mixture of police and army uniform they wore. Their methods were notoriously brutal and it seemed that their reprisals were more vicious than the IRA incident that had provoked it. It became a war of retaliation.

Michael Collins was in charge of military affairs for the IRA and he set up an intelligence system which kept him well informed about British plans; he waged a vicious, well-thought-out campaign against the Black and Tans. By July 1921 a truce was declared because the British public wanted to try to reach a compromise. In October an Irish delegation, which included Griffith and Collins, went to London to negotiate with Lloyd George. They signed a treaty which approved the setting up of an Irish Free State with Dominion status, similar to Canada. The British were mainly concerned with the security aspect and they made two stipulations; that all Irish legislators should take an oath of allegiance to the Crown and that the British Navy could use certain Irish ports.

Civil War

The Republicans (or anti-treaty side) in the Dail were furious. They regarded it as a sell-out. They did not like the oath, or the acceptance of a divided Ireland. Michael Collins saw it as a chance for 'freedom to achieve freedom' and when it came to the debate on it in the Dail, the majority voted in favour of the treaty. De Valera was against the treaty and, as head of the Dail, he resigned; **Arthur Griffith** succeeded him. In June, when the country accepted the treaty, civil war began. The split in the Dail had produced a corresponding split in the IRA; part of it broke away and began violent raids into the North. The remainder of the IRA was reorganized by Michael Collins into the Free State Army. When he was assassinated, a man just as talented took over, **Kevin O'Higgins**. This period is remembered as the **War of Brothers**—men who had fought together against the Black and Tans now shot each other down. Finally, the Republicans were ready to sue for peace. De Valera, who had not actively taken part in the fighting but had supported the Republicans, now ordered a cease-fire. The bitterness and horror of the civil war has coloured attitudes to this very day. The differences between the two main parties, **Fine Gael** (pro-treaty) and **Fianna Fáil** (anti-treaty), are historical rather than political, although perhaps in foreign policy Fianna Fáil has taken a more anti-British line. Fine Gael held power for the first 10 years and successfully concentrated on building the 26-county state into something credible and strong. In 1926 de Valera broke with Sinn Féin because they still saw the Dail and the government in power as usurpers, as bad as the British, and refused to take up their seats. De Valera founded his own party, the Fianna Fáil. De Valera was a master pragmatist and succeeded in disappointing none of his supporters; the new state wanted a change and in 1932 he formed a government. He soon made it clear that Ireland was not going to keep the oath of allegiance or continue to pay the land annuities (the repayment of money lent to help tenants pay for their farms).

De Valera

In 1937 de Valera drew up a new **Constitution** which named the State Eire or Ireland. It declared Ireland a Republic in all but name and seemed a direct challenge to the Northern Ireland Government. Article 5 went like this: 'It is the right of the Parliament Government established by the Constitution to exercise jurisdiction over the whole of Ireland, its Islands and territorial seas'. Article 44.1.2. recognized 'the special position of the Holy Catholic, Apostolic Roman Church as the guardian of the Faith professed by the great majority of its citizens'. De Valera would not go so far as to 'establish' it, as the Church of Ireland had once been, and as the Catholic hierarchy wanted. (This article was removed from the Constitution in the 1970s.) Both parties had trouble with extremists in the 1930s; Fine Gael had to expel General O'Duffy of the Fascist Blue Shirt movement, and Fianna Fáil were embarrassed by their erstwhile allies in the IRA. De Valera dealt with the situation by setting up a military tribunal and declaring the IRA an illegal organization in 1936. The IRA did not die but went underground and continued to enjoy a curious relationship with the government and the public. When it got too noisy it was stamped on; but the IRA continued to be regarded nervously and with respect, for its ideals and its members' intransigence seemed to be in line with Ireland's dead patriots.

In 1939 Eire declared itself neutral during the Second World War which further isolated it from the rest of the British Isles. In 1949, Costello's Interparty Government inaugurated a Republic and broke Commonwealth ties. Relations between The North and The South remained cool until the tentative *rapprochement* in 1965 between Lemass (the Taoiseach of Eire) and O'Neill (the Prime Minister of Northern Ireland.) But relations cooled again rapidly as 'The Troubles' (1968–1970) began and two members of Taoiseach Lynch's Fianna Fáil ministry were implicated in gun-running for the IRA.

Northern Ireland

The North Today

It is very difficult to be impartial about the Troubles in Northern Ireland; the only certainty is that the vast majority of people in the North, on both sides of the argument, have paid a terrible price and now want it to stop so that they can get on with their lives. This was confirmed resoundingly on 22 May 1998, when 71.2 per cent of people in the North endorsed the Good Friday Agreement, which commits its signatories to 'partnership, equality and mutual respect as the basis of relationships within Northern Ireland'. At the time of writing, the cease-fire is holding; at times it has been shaky, but as the structures of the new government become reality, and the politicians of all the main parties are getting down to the business of running the state, the fragile peace is holding and gathering its own momentum. It is to the great credit of the Northern Irish people that they are united in their exasperation with the men of violence and are loudly demanding the establishment of a real and lasting peace.

The series of events that lead up to the present situation is discussed in more detail below. Before you read on, you may find it useful to look at the glossary of Northern Irish political parties and terms at the end of this chapter.

Discontent Amongst Ulster Catholics, 1921–69

The Ulster Protestants made up two-thirds of the population of Northern Ireland, and the Catholics the rest. Under the leadership of Edward Carson and James Craig, the Protestants had managed to wrest their bit of Ulster from the rest of Ireland, and preserve the Union with Britain. They utterly repudiated the idea of a Catholic Gaelic Republic of Ireland, and held themselves aloof from events in the Free State, later the Republic. No attempt was made to woo the Catholic Nationalists, perhaps because the Protestant leaders directed all their energies into preserving the Union. Unionists have a beleaguered mentality because they are constantly in a great state of anxiety about being turfed out of the Union with Britain and into the Republic of Ireland. They were anxious in the 1920s, and they are so now. The **Government of Ireland Act** in 1920 gave Westminster supreme authority over Northern Ireland. The **Ireland Act** of 1949 enshrined the constitutional guarantee which gave the Stormont Parliament the right to decide whether Northern Ireland would remain in the UK or not.

All Catholics were regarded as supporters of the **IRA**, an organization which was indeed a real menace to this shaky state. It was seen as imperative that Catholics should never be allowed into positions of power and influence. Sir Basil Brooke (1888–1973) was typical of the type of blinkered cabinet minister who ran the government for years. He, along with James Craig (1871–1940), first Prime Minister of Northern Ireland, encouraged Protestants to employ only Protestants, for he, like others, believed that the Catholics were 'out to destroy Ulster with all their power and might'. He became Prime Minister in 1943 and played an active role in linking the Orange Order, of which he was a leading member, with the government of the time. Protestant businesses tended to employ Protestants and Catholics employed Catholics. There were few mixed housing areas or mixed marriages. The Catholic priests fiercely defended their right to run Catholic schools—as they still do.

Government went on at a mainly local level through county and town councils. The Loyalists ensured that they always had a majority on the council through the use of gerrymandering. The local voting qualification also favoured Protestants, who were often wealthier, for the franchise was only granted to house-owners or tenants, and the number of votes allocated to each person could be as high as six, depending on the value of their property. Because the Protestant rulers controlled housing schemes and jobs, the working-class Protestants were given the lion's share of any housing or jobs that existed. Northern Ireland had a much lower standard of living than the rest of the UK, and any advantages were eagerly grasped by these workers, who displayed little feeling of worker solidarity with their fellow Catholics. They never could escape from their religious prejudices and preoccupations to unite against the capitalists, although the ruling class had feared their alliance during the 1922 riots over unemployment.

The Catholics themselves were ambiguous about the State; most of them in the 1920s were Republicans, and they never gave up hope that the Dublin Government might do something about it. Many believed that the Six Counties could not survive, and in the beginning, Nationalist Republican representatives refused to sit at Stormont. On the other hand, others had watched with horror the bloodshed and bitterness which resulted from the Civil War in the Irish Free State. After being educated, the bright ones emigrated rather than fight the system. The IRA attempted over the next 50 years to mount a campaign in the North, but they never got anywhere. The local Catholics did not back them, and the **B Specials** (the Protestant-dominated special police force) did their job well. 'The Specials' irritated and harassed law-abiding Catholics, which left them with a feeling of great injustice. For the time being the Protestant Unionists were able to dominate Catholic Nationalists in elections in a proportion of about four-to-one. This gave them a feeling of security, which was also bolstered by the gratitude of the British government for their loyalty and help during the Second World War, when the North of Ireland had been a vital bulwark for the rest of the UK.

The Civil Rights Movement—British Troops Move in

Yet things had to change, for as young and educated Catholics and Protestants grew up they began to agitate about the obvious injustices, and the **Civil Rights Association** was formed in

1967. Unfortunately, the marches which drew attention to their aims also attracted men of violence on both sides, and as the marches turned into riots, the Protestant Loyalists, including the **Royal Ulster Constabulary** (RUC) and B Specials, seemed to be in league with the Protestant mobs against the Catholics. At this point the discredited IRA failed to seize their opportunity to woo the Catholics, who were confused and frightened. The Catholics welcomed the British troops, who were brought in to keep the peace after the Loyalists and police beat up Civil Rights marchers at Burntollet, and later the inhabitants of the Bogside in Londonderry, in January 1969.

At that time **Terence O'Neill** had taken over from Lord Brookborough as Prime Minister at Stormont. Although of the same Unionist Ascendancy stock, he realized that something must be done to placate the Nationalists. The few liberal gestures that he made towards the Catholics and the Republic opened up a Pandora's box of fury and opposition amongst the Protestant Unionists, who found a leader in the **Reverend Ian Paisley**. The reforms O'Neill planned over housing and local government came too late, and he was swept away by the Protestant backlash when he called a General Election in April 1969. The brutality with which the police had broken up the Civil Rights marches had stirred support for the IRA, and the Summer Marching Season was marked by even more violence.

The IRA Exploit Events

The IRA organized itself to exploit the situation. It split into two after an internal struggle, and the murders and bombings which dominated events after this time are mainly the work of the Provisional IRA, commonly called the IRA. The British army lost the confidence of the Catholic community it had come to protect through heavy-handed enforcement of security measures. Besides, the IRA posed as the natural guardians of the Catholics, so there were cheers amongst the Catholic Nationalists when the IRA killed the first British soldier in October 1970. The IRA aimed to break down law and order; to them any method was legitimate, and any member of the army or police a legitimate target.

The Stormont government hastened to pass much needed reforms between 1969 and 1972. The RUC was overhauled, and the B Specials abolished. A new part-time security force was set up within the British Army and called the **Ulster Defence Regiment** (UDR). In 1971 a new Housing Executive was set up to allocate houses fairly, irrespective of religious beliefs. The IRA managed to conduct a destructive bombing campaign in the cities; innocent civilians were killed or injured and buildings destroyed. British soldiers responded to rioting in Derry in January 1972 by killing 13 people on what has become known as Bloody Sunday. A cycle of violence began to spiral, and society divided along sectarian lines even more than before.

UK Attempts to Solve the Problem

In 1972 the Stormont government and parliament were suspended by the British government, which had always retained full powers of sovereignty over it. Direct Rule from Westminster was imposed, and continued for 27 years. (The devolution of power to a new Stormont Assembly with both Unionist and Republican representation is under way with certain areas of government, for example, defence, reserved to Westminster.) The **Secretary of State for Northern Ireland** governed through ministers and civil servants; his role has changed under the new Assembly but he is still appointed by the Prime Minister of the United Kingdom and sits in the Cabinet. Members of Parliament from the constituencies of Northern Ireland were elected from various parties and sat in Westminster.

Internment was made legal in August 1971, and large numbers of terrorist suspects were imprisoned without trial. This hardened Catholic opinion against British justice, and the practice was gradually phased out after a couple of years. Subsequently, the Diplock system of Criminal Courts was introduced, which tried alleged terrorists by judges rather than juries. Various power-sharing initiatives between the largely Protestant Unionist parties and the Catholic and Nationalist SDLP did not get off the ground, so Direct Rule continued. The suspension of the Stormont Parliament removed the Constitutional guarantee of the 1949 Act but it was renewed in the 1973 Constitution Act, which established the principle that any change in the status of Northern Ireland would have to have majority consent.

The Sunningdale Agreement

In December 1973 the leaders of the Northern Irish parties, a new Executive, and Ministers from the United Kingdom and, for the first time, the Republic of Ireland met together at Sunningdale, and agreed to set up a **Council of Ireland** which would work for co-operation between Northern Ireland and the Republic. The Agreement provided for a new type of Executive in Northern Ireland, in which power was shared as far as possible between representatives of the two communities in a joint government. It was the dawn of new hope for the province, but the Unionist masses and the Republican terrorists did not want this new co-operation to work. Faced with a general strike called by the Ulster Workers' Council which paralysed the province, the government did not use the army to break the strike, but allowed intimidation by 'Loyalist' paramilitary organizations to win the day. The Unionist members of the Executive resigned, and Direct Rule had to be resumed. Many people believe that if the Sunningdale Agreement had been implemented, the whole of Ireland might be a stabler place today.

The Victims of the 'Troubles'

The province then suffered sectarian killings, bombings, and the powerful propaganda of the hunger strike campaign by IRA prisoners in the early 1980s. The economy was in the doldrums and the well-educated members of society, both Protestant and Catholic, left in droves. However since a cease-fire was established in 1994 things have improved, the economy has picked up and foreign investors are looking again at Northern Ireland. The spirit and bravery of the Ulster people remains unbroken; businesses continue to thrive and to compete in international markets. But the statistics in such a small population are grim: between 1969 and 2000, some 3,300 people have lost their lives and almost 4,000 have been injured and maimed, of whom around 2,300 have been civilians.

The Anglo-Irish Agreement

In 1985, after initial efforts by **Garrett Fitzgerald**, the leader of the Fine Gael Party in the Republic, and **Margaret Thatcher**, the British Prime Minister, the New Ireland Forum met in Dublin. It was agreed that Northern Ireland would remain in the United Kingdom as long as the majority so desired, and that the Dublin Government should have an institutionalized consultative status in relation to Northern Irish affairs.

The effect of the Agreement was largely positive; both governments made progress in the area of extradition and cross-border security, even after the revulsion over the IRA bomb attack in Enniskillen in 1987. The British Government grasped the nettle of injustice over the conviction of the 'Guildford Four' and the 'Birmingham Six', prisoners convicted of bombings on mainland Britain. The re-opening of these cases and the subsequent acquittal of the prisoners dissipated much bad feeling in the Republic of Ireland where there is great scepticism about British justice in relation to the Irish. One of the most important achievements of the Agreement was that the Irish Government formally accepted 'the principle of consent' by the people of Northern Ireland: any change in the Constitution Act of 1973 had to have majority consent. The Unionists were not mollified by this, for it was enshrined in the constitution of the Republic that the Irish Republic claim the whole island, and this claim had not been given up. The Agreement made the world realize that the 'Brits out' solution would mean forcibly transferring a million-strong Protestant population into a united Ireland that did not really want them, and the probability of bloody civil war.

The strong emotional link between the rest of the UK and the Northern Irish has changed since the beginning of the century. The Union was no longer regarded as a cause in itself; many English, Welsh and Scots knew little about the North, and questioned the lives lost and money spent maintaining the Union. The Nationalists had not rejected the IRA, who continued to work for the destruction of the six-county state through terror campaigns in Ulster. On mainland Britain and Europe, the IRA followed a campaign of bombing 'soft' British military targets, and assassinating British politicians, lawyers, and industrialists in order to turn British public opinion against the Union with Northern Ireland.

1990–1993

Inter-party talks began in Northern Ireland and, before they broke down, some progress was made in defining the three complicated relationships between the North and the UK, the North and the Republic, and the Republic and the UK. This meant there was a set of negotiating mechanisms for the peace process to be furthered. British policy continued to try and find the middle ground between opposing parties in the North, and it was hoped that the politics of the extremists would wither away.

The IRA carried out bombing attacks in the financial heart of London in 1992/93 and elsewhere. One such attack in a shopping centre in Warrington killed two children; there was worldwide condemnation of the atrocity, and a peace movement was launched in Dublin. The IRA could continue their campaign of violence indefinitely, but there were signs that key elements in the IRA wanted to try and change things through political action. In April 1993, **John Hume** of the SDLP started a dialogue with **Gerry Adams** of Sinn Féin. Both the British and the Irish Governments reacted furiously to this but popular nationalist support for the dialogue, in both the North and South, forced the governments to rethink their policy. Both Prime Ministers Major and Reynolds began a new policy of trying to draw the extremists into the political process and to aim at all-party talks for a lasting constitutional settlement which would bring peace. The North had just suffered the horror in October 1993 of the IRA bomb in a Belfast chippie which killed 10 people; and then the terrible revenge by extremist Loyalists who shot 14 people in a public house in Greysteel.

The Downing Street Declaration

On 15 December 1993, both the Irish and British Prime Ministers presented a **Joint Declaration** which addressed the competing claims of the Nationalists and the Unionists. The British Government declared in the document that Britain 'had no selfish strategic or economic interest in Northern Ireland' and recognized the right of the people of Ireland North and South to self-determination. Both Governments affirmed that the status of Northern Ireland could only be changed with the consent of 'a great number of its people'. In the event of an overall political settlement the Irish Government declared it would drop its claim to the six counties contained in articles 2 and 3 of the Irish Constitution. The Irish Government would establish a forum for peace and reconciliation at some later date. Both governments offered a place at the negotiating table to the extremists on both sides if they renounced violence.

Cease-fire

After a disappointing reaction to the Declaration and prevarication for several months, the IRA eventually announced 'a complete cessation of military operations' on 31 August 1994. In the following weeks the extremist unionist forces of the UFF, the UVF and the Red Hand of Ulster announced a cease-fire, conditional upon the IRA's continuing cease-fire. This brought great optimism for a real peace, and created an even stronger climate of belief amongst the people of the North that they must find politicians who were prepared to try new ways to settle their differences. Unfortunately, the main protagonists still disagreed over major issues such as the release of prisoners, the withdrawal of the British army, decommissioning of arms amongst terrorist groups, the future of community policing in Northern Ireland, and the role of the Irish Government in the future of the province.

The British and Irish Governments produced two important framework documents in 1995. These sought to provide a basis for discussion in a Northern Irish Forum with elected delegates from all the different parties. The documents proposed a new Assembly elected by proportional representation, a new relationship between North and South and between all the countries surrounding the Irish Sea. However, the discussions met stalemate over the **decommissioning of arms**. In February 1996, the IRA compromised the cease-fire with a bomb attack on Canary Wharf in London, in which two people were killed. The talks continued without Sinn Féin, little progress was made, and things looked very gloomy. In the UK, in May 1997 a new Labour Government with Prime Minister Tony Blair was not reliant on the Unionist vote in the House of Commons, and this gave him a freer hand all round. The Official Unionists, under the leadership of David Trimble, were breaking out of their reactionary 'Ulster Says No' mould.

In the British elections, Sinn Féin's **Gerry Adams** and **Martin McGuiness** won seats, although they did not take them up. In the Irish Republic, Fianna Fáil, under its leader, Bertie Ahern, was willing to talk to Sinn Féin about a new cease-fire, and Northern Ireland Secretary of State, **Mo Mowlam**, also promised to admit Sinn Féin to the talks if it called a new cease-fire. The American senator **George Mitchell**, who had accepted the delicate task of brokering all-party talks, suggested that the talks on the decommissioning of arms should take place at the same time, but separately, as the talks on the future of the province.

Sectarian tension became heightened through the late 1990s as progress towards peace continued. Orange Order marchers insisted, unhelpfully, on sticking to their traditional parade routes, some of which included Catholic neighbourhoods. In Drumcree, Portadown, this brought them into serious confrontation with Catholics, and the eruption of violent protest on both sides eventually led the head of the Orange Order Lodges to cancel or reroute some of the potentially violent 12 July marches. Horrible sectarian murders added to the tension but the restoration of the IRA's cease-fire in August 1997 improved matters considerably. In September 1997 the leaders of Sinn Féin joined the all-party talks. The Official Unionist Party dropped its demand that the decommissioning issue must be settled before any negotiations could begin so, in parallel, an independent commission on illegal arms decommissioning was set up.

At last, negotiations between all the concerned parties could begin; both the Irish and UK Prime Ministers made it clear that there was now a clear agenda and timescale, and that the talks must not get lost in prevarication.

On **Good Friday, 11 April 1998**, after many vicissitudes, the world was told that there had been a historic agreement. This Agreement mapped out radical new arrangements for a devolved Ulster Assembly, a Council of Ministers linking Northern Ireland and the Republic, and limited cross-border bodies which would work things out together. A new Council of the Islands would be set up which would link all the devolved assemblies in the UK, and in Dublin and London. The Irish Government promised to amend Articles 2 and 3 of its constitution which lay claim to the six counties. In return, the British Government stated that it would replace the Government of Ireland Act. The people of Ireland from both sides of the border voted their approval of the Agreement in a **Referendum** in May 1998. In the **Assembly** elections in June 1998 the UUP gained 28 seats, the SDLP gained 24 seats, Sinn Fein gained 18, DUP gained 20 and the other 18 seats were divided up between the smaller parties. There is the potential for the DUP, who oppose the Good Friday Agreement, to thwart proceedings, although so long as there are no defections to the anti-Agreement Unionist position, this should not happen. The SDLP make up the largest Nationalist Party, followed by Sinn Féin. **David Trimble** of the UUP was nominated as the First Minister.

Since the elections of June 1998, it has taken nearly 18 months rather than the 9 months originally envisaged for the Assembly to take up its powers. The principal issue has continued to be **decommissioning**. (Punishment beatings have numbered 168 between June 1998 and November 1999, suspicion of weapons purchase and other actions close to the breaking of the cease-fire have added to the strain.) The IRA has appointed a negotiator, as have other paramilitary organizations, to work with General John de Chastelaine on decommissioning, which must take place by May 2000. The Unionists are aware that over the next 25 years or so, the population will become more balanced as the Catholic population increases. The Nationalists too, are weary of the Troubles, and have seen their position improve over the years, and Sinn Féin are experiencing the dividends of joining the democratic process. Increasingly, there is a confidence that a new and brighter age for the people of Northern Ireland has begun.

The Republic Today

The Irish Republic has a titular Head of State, a **President**, who is elected for seven years by the vote of the people. The President is empowered on the recommendation of the Dail to appoint the Prime Minister (**Taoiseach**), sign laws and invoke the judgement of the Supreme Court on the legality of Bills. He is also supreme commander of the armed forces. The Irish parliament consists of the President and two Houses: the Dáil and the Senate. The Dail is made up of 166 members (TDs) elected by adult suffrage through proportional representation. The Senate is made up of 60 members: 11 are nominated by the Taoiseach; 49 are elected by the Dáil and county councils from panels representative of the universities, labour, industry, education and social services. The average length of an Irish government is three years.

In the 1970s and 1980s each Irish government has had to face unemployment, growing emigration and a huge national debt—in 1989 it was IR£24,827 million. In 1988, incomes measured by GDP per head were just 63% of those in the UK. As the new millennium begins, the Republic has overtaken the UK: in 1999 GDP growth was over 9 per cent a year, faster than anywhere in Europe. Government borrowing has fallen. Ireland has been a beneficiary of inward European investment in technology, food processing, pharmaceuticals and the marketing industries. This is partly because of its young, well-educated population and skilled work force. Emigration, so long a haemorrhage of the country's vitality, has almost halted, and a steady stream of former emigrants is now returning home to Ireland.

Developments within the EU may see a watering down of Irish neutrality, as they include a commitment by all members to a common security policy. The traditional lines of Irish parties are also changing from the pro- and anti-treaty (of 1921) stances. Former Irish President **Mary Robinson** (1990–97) left a legacy of flexibility and dynamism to politics here. Her enthusiasm and energy in helping all parts of Ireland, including the North, won her great popularity and a world profile.

Irish Political Parties

The origins of the two major parties, Fianna Fáil and Fine Gael, hark back to the violent differences between those anti the Free State Treaty, and those pro it in the 1920s. **Fianna Fáil** has established itself as the dominant ruling party; at the time of writing it is the largest party in the country. Its leader and Ireland's Taoiseach is Bertie Ahern.

Fine Gael is the second largest party in the country; it is close to other Christian Democrat parties in Europe and has strong European inclinations. The current leader is John Bruton. The **Labour Party** has found it difficult to gain popular support in the country as people have, up to now anyway, been very conservative and voted as their family do—either Fine Gael or Fianna Fáil. This is changing now as Labour has increased its powerbase in the last 15 years in Dublin and Cork and formed coalition governments either with Fianna Fáil or Fine Gael, although in the last election the Labour Party found its share of the vote decrease.

A Glossary of Political Parties and Terms

The following labels and identities crop up constantly in discussions on Northern Ireland:

Catholic: Approximately 610,000 people belong to the Roman Catholic Church in Northern Ireland.

Protestant: Term refers to Church of Ireland, Presbyterians and other non-Catholic denominations. The Church of Ireland numbers around 280,000 people, and Presbyterians some 340,000.

Unionist: Refers to one who supports the Union with Great Britain, and has no wish to share an Irish nationality with the Republic of Ireland. There are two main Unionist parties in Northern Ireland. The Official Unionists (UUP) were the original party and appear willing enough to negotiate a real settlement with Republicans. The Democratic Unionist Party (DUP), led by Ian Paisley, is more conservative and remains stridently Protestant.

Alliance: A label used for a party composed of moderate Unionists, both Protestant and Catholic, but it loses out to the more extreme parties.

Loyalist: Refers to a Protestant who is prepared to use violence to prevent a United Ireland, and maintain the Union with the UK

Nationalist: A label which refers to anyone who supports a united Ireland. In Northern Ireland, the Socialist Democratic and Labour Party (SDLP), formed in 1970, is committed to achieving a United Ireland through peaceful and democratic means. It is not linked, except through its aims, to Sinn Féin, the political wing of the IRA.

Taig: A term used by Loyalists to describe Catholics.

Fenian: A term for a Catholic that suggests that he or she is a Republican.

Republican: A supporter of a united Ireland. Often used as a synonym for an IRA supporter.

Republican Movement: This covers both Sinn Féin, and the IRA.

IRA: Is the label used to describe the Irish Republican Army, which did not disband after the Civil War in Ireland ended (1920–21). The IRA is outlawed in the Republic of Ireland and the United Kingdom. The objective of its members is to establish an Ireland free of British rule, with the six counties reunited with the rest of Ireland.

UVF and **UDA**: Both the Ulster Volunteer Force and the Ulster Defence Association are illegal Protestant terrorist organizations that recruit from the working class.

UFF: Ulster Freedom Fighters. An illegal Protestant paramilitary organization which engages in sectarian killings.

RUC: Royal Ulster Constabulary. Reorganized in the 1970s, this police force manages much of the security of Northern Ireland in co-operation with the British army. The Catholic Nationalists in Northern Ireland regard it with suspicion, because of its overwhelmingly Protestant Unionist membership. Catholics who join it are targeted for intimidation by the IRA. A radical review of the service is under way, including considerations for a change of name, uniform, means of recruitment and even the Loyalist oath currently taken by all officers.

The B Specials: Were a special, part-time reserve force within the RUC with particular powers to search out IRA members, operating from the 1920s until the 1970s.

UDR: Ulster Defence Regiment. A regiment of the British Army, many of its soldiers are part-time, and drawn from the Protestant population in Ulster. Over 200 UDR soldiers have been killed by the IRA, often when off-duty.

The Orange Order: A sectarian and largely working-class organization that originated as a secret Protestant working-class agrarian society known as the Peep-O'Day Boys. William of Orange (William III of England) became their hero, and the society changed its name to the Orange Order in 1795. Its members have a traditional fear of the Catholic majority in Ireland and are Unionist in politics. Orange Lodges are still active in Northern Ireland.

The Summer Marching Season: Is a reference to the Orange and Hibernian marches during July and August. Each side commemorates opposing events in the history of Ireland.

Gerrymandering: Refers to the policy of concentrating large numbers of Catholics with Republican views in unusually big electoral districts, whilst Protestant Unionists were in smaller districts. This meant that the Protestant Unionists were always certain to win a larger number of representatives, district by district. Gerrymandering gradually became the norm from the late 1920s until the electoral reforms at the beginning of the 1970s.

Civil Rights Movement: Began in the 1960s, inspired by American Civil Rights campaigner, Martin Luther King. The Civil Rights Association, founded in 1967, called for equal treatment in regard to jobs, houses and 'one-man-one-vote'.

Direct Rule: The Government of Great Britain had always retained full powers of sovereignty on all matters over the Northern Ireland government at Stormont. Thus, when the riots and bloodshed began to get out of control and the Stormont government seemed unable to implement reforms or control the police, in 1972 Direct Rule was imposed and remained for 27 years.

Religion

The reminders and symbols of a religious faith and deep love of God are everywhere to be seen in Ireland. The images which fill my mind are of a child in white, showing off her dress after her first Holy Communion, rags caught in brambles around a holy well, cars parked up a country lane, everybody piling out for Mass, umbrellas held high and skirts fluttering. The people of Ireland invoke and refer to the Virgin Mary and to Jesus often in their everyday talk. Roadside shrines to the Virgin are decorated with shells and fresh flowers, and many people still stop what they are doing to say the Angelus at noon and at sunset. Grey Neo-Gothic churches dominate country towns, whilst in smaller villages the chapel or church is a simpler building, planted around with dark yews and beeches above which the ceaseless cawing of rooks can be heard.

In Ireland everybody knows what you are—whether Catholic, Presbyterian, Church of Ireland, Baptist or Methodist; anything else is classed as 'heathen', and they feel sorry for you if you are nothing! The history of Ireland has had much to do with this feeling of religious identity, and, unfortunately, in the North this mix of politics and religion has produced individuals whose extreme Catholic or Presbyterian attitudes are reminiscent of 17th-century Europe. The bigotry that characterizes such attitudes has been a major factor in the political situation in the North today. Efforts are made by some clergy to organize ecumenical meetings, and these have brought greater understanding and tolerance. Ireland has not been immune from the general decline in church attendance everywhere in the Western world. The Catholic Church is still pre-eminent, but has been damaged by a series of scandals and a consequent loss of respect for the clergy. Increased materialism has also undermined the spiritual discipline and certainties of the past.

Pre-Christian Ireland

The Irish have been religious for five thousand years, and there are plenty of chambered cairns (mounds of stones over prehistoric graves) to prove it. The Celts who arrived in about 500 BC seemed to have been a very religious people, and they had a religious hierarchy organized by Druids. These people worshipped a large number of gods, and central to their beliefs and rituals was the cult of the human head. They believed that the head was the centre of man's powers and thoughts. Their stonemasons carved two-headed gods and the style in which they worked has a continuity which can be traced right up to the 19th century. There are heads in the Lough Erne district which are difficult to date. They could be pagan, Early-Christian or comparatively modern.

The origins of the earlier Tuatha dé Danaan are lost in legend: they may have been pre-Celtic gods or a race of invaders, themselves vanquished by the Celts. They are believed to have had magical powers and heroic qualities. Today they are remembered as the 'wee folk' who live in the raths and stone forts. Here they make fairy music which is so beautiful that it bewitches any human who hears it. The wee folk play all kinds of tricks on country people, from souring their milk to stealing their children, and so a multitude of charms have been devised to guard against these fairy pranks. I can remember being told about the fairies who used to dance in magic rings in the fields; the trouble was that if you tried to go up to them they would turn into yellow ragwort dancing in the wind.

Early-Christian Ireland

Christianity is believed to have come to Ireland from Rome in the 4th century, although St Patrick is credited with the major conversion of the Irish in the 5th century. The Irish seem to have taken to Christianity like ducks to water, although much of our knowledge of early Christianity comes through the medieval accounts of scholarly (but possibly biased) clerics. One explanation for the ease with which Christianity took over is that the Christians did not try to change things too fast, and incorporated some elements of the Druidic religion into their practices.

An example of the assimilation of the Druidic religion by the Christians is the continuing religious significance of the holy wells. Ash and rowan trees, both sacred to the Druids, are frequently found near the wells, and Christian pilgrims still leave offerings of rags on the trees as a sign to the Devil that he has no more power over them. Patterns (pilgrimages) and games used to be held at the wells, although they often shocked the priest, who would put the well out of bounds and declare that its healing powers had been destroyed. There are many other everyday signs of the way that the spiritual life of the Irish people harks back to pagan times. In cottages and farmhouses you might see a strange swastika sign made out of rushes. This is a St Brigid's cross, hung above the door or window to keep the evil spirits away. Fairy or sacred trees are still left standing in the field even though it is uneconomic to plough round them—bad luck invariably follows the person who cuts one down.

Monasteries in Early-Christian Ireland

By the end of the 6th century the Church was firmly monastic, with great monasteries such as Clonmacnoise in County Offaly and Clonfert in County Galway. These centres were responsible for big strides in agricultural development and were important for trade; they also became places where learning and artistry of all sorts was admired and emulated. The Ireland of 'Saints and Scholars' reached its peak in the 7th century.

The monks sought an ascetic and holy way of life, although this was pursued in a fierce and warlike manner. The ultimate self-sacrifice was self-imposed exile, and so they founded monasteries in France, Italy and Germany. The abbots, by the 8th century, had become all-powerful in Irish politics. Missionaries continued to leave Ireland and contribute to the revival of Christianity in Europe, and there was a blossoming of the arts with wonderful metalwork and painted manuscripts. By the 9th century, the monasteries were commissioning intricately carved stone high crosses, such as you can see at Ahenny in County Tipperary, Clones, County Monaghan, and Arboe and Donaghmore, County Tyrone.

Religious Discrimination

Religious discrimination is long-established in Ireland. Over the centuries Catholics and Protestants have suffered by not conforming to the established church, although Catholics have undoubtedly received the greatest share of discrimination and persecution. The Huguenots arrived when Louis XIV revoked the Edict of Nantes in 1686. They were Calvinists and intermarried easily with the other Protestant groups. (The Huguenots were very skilled and established the important linen industry, as well as weaving and lace-making.) The Presbyterians were the biggest group of dissenters, most of whom were Scots who settled in Ulster during the 17th century. They had been persecuted in Scotland because of their religious beliefs and now they found that Ireland was no better: they were as poor as the native Irish, and many found life so hard that they emigrated to America. Quakers, Palatines (German Protestants), Moravians, Baptists and Methodists also settled in Ireland, but their numbers have declined through emigration and intermarriage.

Religion in Ireland Today

The approximate membership of the main churches is as follows: Roman Catholic 3,242,000; Church of Ireland 220,570; Presbyterian 218,000. Other Christian denominations include Methodists, Baptists and Pentecostal. There is a very small number of Muslims and Jews. In the six counties of Northern Ireland about 40% are Catholics, 55% Protestant (Church of Ireland and Presbyterian) and others 5%. In the Republic the Catholic majority is obviously the controlling force in political and social life and the Protestant minority has bowed out gracefully. The Protestants used to represent almost 10% of the population but this figure has declined through mixed marriages and emigration.

In theory the modern state does not tolerate religious discrimination, and it is true that both Jews and Protestants have reached positions of importance and wealth in industry and banking. However, the Protestant classes had it so good during the hundreds of years of British Rule, it is not surprising that for a short time there was a legacy of antipathy towards anyone connected with the mainly Protestant Ascendancy.

The bishops' exhortations on divorce, contraception, abortion, AIDS, etc. are listened to with great earnestness by the politicians. The sanctity of the family is held to be of the greatest importance, although divorce has been introduced after a referendum in 1995 in the Republic, which resulted in a 50.3 per cent vote in favour and a 49.7 per cent vote against. Contraception is now readily available but women still go to England for abortions. Of course, in Northern Ireland, the laws of the land are quite secular, being laid down by the British government, but divorce is still quite unusual there, too, and the principal UK legislation on abortion, the 1967 Abortion Act, has not been extended to the province.

The parish priest is always a person of great importance in Irish society and he is usually very approachable. You might easily meet him in the village bar having a drink and a chat. Nearly every family has a close relative who is a priest or a nun, and Irish priests and nuns leave their native land in great numbers to serve overseas, taking their particular brand of conservative Catholicism with them.

Schooling is mostly in the hands of the Church (incidentally, Ireland has a very high standard of literacy and general education), and thankfully the days of the cane and the even crueller sarcasm of the priest-teachers described by so many Irish writers has disappeared. The people in the top positions in Ireland today mostly went to Christian Brother Schools (look in the Irish *Who's Who*). So did many county councillors and petty officials who organize Ireland's huge bureaucracy. The old-boy network is very strong for getting favours done, grants approved, and planning permission granted. In the six counties there are very few integrated schools; most Protestants go to state schools and nearly all Catholics to Church schools.

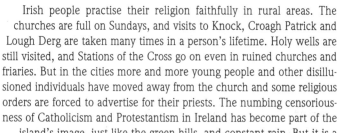

Irish people practise their religion faithfully in rural areas. The churches are full on Sundays, and visits to Knock, Croagh Patrick and Lough Derg are taken many times in a person's lifetime. Holy wells are still visited, and Stations of the Cross go on even in ruined churches and friaries. But in the cities more and more young people and other disillusioned individuals have moved away from the church and some religious orders are forced to advertise for their priests. The numbing censoriousness of Catholicism and Protestantism in Ireland has become part of the island's image, just like the green hills, and constant rain. But it is a theme which has been overplayed, and the reality is that people are really very tolerant of other religious communities within their society; this applies to Northern Ireland too. Great community involvement and care comes directly from the churches, and the social events are enjoyable and fun. The Irish are amongst the most generous when it comes to raising money for world disasters, and this charity work is usually channelled through the Church.

Death and weddings are always occasions for a bit of 'crack', and there is also a party whenever the priest blesses a new house. Irish couples spend more on their engagement rings and their weddings than their English counterparts; it's a really big occasion. The Irish wake has lost many of its pagan rituals—mourning with keening and games involving disguise, mock weddings, jokes and singing. Nowadays, the dead person is laid out in another room and people come in to pay their last respects, and then spend the rest of the evening drinking, eating and reminiscing.

Irish Saints

Every locality in Ireland has its particular saint. The stories that surround him or her belong to myth and legend, not usually to historical fact. One theory is that all these obscure, miraculous figures are in fact Celtic gods and goddesses who survived under the mantle of sainthood. Included below is a short account of lives of some of the most famous saints, about whom few facts are known.

Brendan (c. 486–575), Abbot and Navigator

This holy man is remembered for his scholastic foundations, and for the extraordinary journey he made in search of Hy-Brasil, believed to be an island of paradise, which he had seen as a mirage whilst looking out on the Atlantic from the Kerry Mountains. His journey is recounted in the *Navigato Brendan*, a treasure of every European library during the Middle Ages. The oldest copies are in Latin and date from the 11th century. The account describes a sea voyage which took Brendan and 12 other monks to the Orkneys, to Wales, to Iceland, and to a land where tropical fruits and flowers grew. The descriptions of his voyage have convinced some scholars that he sailed down the east coast of America to Florida. Tim Severin, a modern-day explorer, and 12 others recreated this epic voyage between May 1976 and June 1977. In their leather and wood boat, they proved that the Irish monks could have been the first Europeans to land in America. (It is possible to see the boat at the Lough Gur Centre in County Clare.) Christopher Columbus probably read the *Navigato*, and in Galway there is a strong tradition that he came to the west coast in 1492 to search out traditions about St Brendan.

The saint's main foundation was at Clonfert, which became a great scholastic centre. One of his monks built the first beehive-shaped cells on Skellig Michael, the rocky island off County Kerry. Other foundations were at Annaghdown in County Galway, and Inisglora in County Mayo. Brendan is buried in Clonfert Cathedral, and honoured in St Brendan's Cathedral in Loughrea, County Galway, where the beautiful mosaic floor in the sanctuary depicts his ship and voyage.

St Brigid (died c. 525), Abbess of Kildare

Brigid, also known as Briget, Bride and Brigit, is the most beloved saint in Ireland and is often called Mary of the Gael. Devotion to her spread to Scotland, England and the Continent. The traditions and stories that surround her describe her countless generous and warm-hearted acts to the poor, her ability to council the rulers of the day, and her great holiness. Her father was a pagan from Leinster and she was fostered by a Druid. (This custom of fosterage in Ireland existed right up to the 19th century.) She decided not to marry and founded a religious order with seven other girls. They were the first formal community of nuns and wore simple white dresses.

St Brigid has her feast day on 1 February, which is also the date of the pagan festival Imbolg, which marks the beginning of spring. She is the patron of poets, scholars, blacksmiths and healers, and is also inevitably linked with the pagan goddess Brigid, the goddess of fire and song. There is a tradition that St Brigid's Abbey in Kildare contained a sanctuary with a perpetual fire, tended only by virgins, whose high priestess was regarded as an incarnation and successor of the goddess. The two women are further linked by the fact that Kildare in Irish means 'church of oak', and St Brigid's church was built from a tree held sacred to the Druids. There is a theory that Brigid and her companions accepted the Christian faith, and then transformed the pagan sanctuary into a Christian shrine.

Kildare was a great monastic centre after Brigid's death, and produced the now lost masterpiece, the *Kildare Gospels*. Tradition says that the designs were so beautiful that an angel helped to create them. The St Brigid's nuns kept alight the perpetual fire until the suppression of the religious houses during the Reformation.

Brigid was buried in Kildare Church, but in 835 her remains were moved to Downpatrick in County Down, because of the raids by the Norsemen. She is supposed to share the grave there with St Patrick and St Colmcille, but there is no proof of this. In 1283 it is recorded that three Irish knights set out to the Holy Land with her head; they died en route to Lamiar in Portugal, and in the church there the precious relic of her head is enshrined in a chapel to St Brigid. The word 'bride' derives from St Brigid. It is supposed to originate from the Knights of Chivalry, whose patroness she was. They customarily called the girls they married their brides, after her, and hence the word came into general usage.

St Columban (died 615), Missionary Abbot

Columban, also known as Columbanus, is famous as the great missionary saint. He was born in Leinster and educated at Bangor in County Down under St Comgall, who was famed for his scholarship and piety. Columban set off for Europe with 12 other religious men to preach the gospel and convert the pagans in Gaul (France) and Germany. He founded a monastery at Annegray, which is between Austria and Burgundy, in AD 575, and his rule of austerity attracted many. Luxeuil, the largest monastery, and then Fontaines, were all established within a few miles of Annegray. When Columban was exiled by the local king, he and his followers founded Bobbio in the Apennines, between Piacenza and Genoa. Bobbio became a great centre of culture and orthodoxy from which monasticism spread. Its great glory was its library, the books from which are scattered all over Europe and are regarded as treasures. There are still many parishes in the region dedicated to St Columban.

St Colmcille (c. 521–97), Missionary Abbot

Along with St Patrick and St Brigid, Colmcille, also known as Columba and Columcille, is probably the most famous of the Irish saints. He spread the gospel to Iona and hence to Scotland. St Colmcille was a prince of Tyrconnell (County Donegal), and a great, great grandson of Niall of the Nine Hostages, who had been High King of Ireland. On his mother's side he was descended from the Leinster Kings. He was educated by St Finian of Movilla, in County Down, and also by Finnian of Clonard, and Mobhi of Glasnevin. He studied music and poetry at the Bardic School of Leinster, and the poems he wrote which have survived are delightful. A few are preserved in the Bodleian Library, Oxford. He chose to be a monk, and never to receive episcopal rank. He wrote of his devotion: 'The fire of God's love stays in my heart as a jewel set in gold in a silver vessel.'

In AD 545 he built his first church in Derry, the place he loved most. Then he founded Durrow and later Kells, which became very important in the 9th century when the Columban monks of Iona fled from the Vikings and made it their headquarters. In all, Colmcille founded 37 monastic churches in Ireland, and he produced the *Cathach*, a manuscript of the Psalms. At the age of 42 he set out with 12 companions to be an exile for Christ. They sailed to the island of Iona, off the west coast of Scotland, which was part of the Kingdom of Dalriada ruled over by the Irish King Aidan. He converted Brude, King of the Picts, founded two churches in Inverness, and helped to keep the peace between the Picts and the Irish colony. The tradition that he left Ireland because of a dispute over the copy he made of a psalter of St Finian is very dubious. The legend goes that the dispute caused a great battle, although the high king of the time, King Diarmuid, had tried to settle the dispute and had ruled against Colmcille, saying: 'to every cow its calf, to every book its copy'. The saint is supposed to have punished himself for the deaths he had caused by going into exile.

Colmcille was famous for his austerity, fasting and vigils. His bed was of stone and so was his pillow. From the various accounts of his life, Colmcille emerges as a charismatic personality who was a scholar, poet, and ruler. He died at Iona, and his relics were taken to Dunkeld (Scotland) in AD 849.

St Enda of Aran (died c. 535), Abbot

Famous as the patriarch of monasticism. He is described as a warrior who left the secular world in middle life. He had succeeded to the kingdom of Oriel, but decided to study for the priesthood. He was then granted the Aran Islands by his brother-in-law, Aengus, King of Cashel. He is said to have lived a life of astonishing severity, and never had a fire in winter, for he believed the 'hearts so glowing with the love of God' could not feel the cold. It is said that he taught 127 other saints, who are buried close to him on the islands.

St Kevin of Glendalough (died *c.* 618), Abbot

Many stories surround St Kevin, but we know he was one of the many Irish abbots who chose to remain a priest. He lived a solitary contemplative life in the Glendalough Valley where many people followed him, attracted by his rule of prayer and solitude. He played the harp, and the Rule for his monks was in verse. He is supposed to have prayed for so long that a blackbird had time to lay an egg and hatch it on his outstretched hand. His monastery flourished until the 11th century. In the 12th century St Lawrence O'Toole came to Glendalough and modelled his life on St Kevin, bringing fresh fame to his memory. The foundation was finally destroyed in the 16th century.

St Kieran (*c.* 512–545), Abbot

St Kieran, also known as Ciaran, is remembered for his great foundation of Clonmacnoise, where the ancient chariot road through Ireland crosses the Shannon River. Unlike many Irish abbots he was not of aristocratic blood, for his father was a chariot-maker from County Antrim, and his mother from Kerry. St Kieran attracted craftsmen to his order, and Clonmacnoise grew to be a great monastic school, where, unusually for Ireland, the position of abbot did not become hereditary. Kieran died within a short time of founding the school. Many kings are buried alongside him, for it was believed that he would bring their souls safely to heaven.

St Malachy (1094–1148), Archbishop of Armagh

Malachy is famous as the great reformer of the Irish Church. He persuaded the Pope, Eugenius III, to establish the Archbishops of Ireland separately from those of England. He also ensured that it was no longer possible for important ecclesiastical positions to be held by certain families as a hereditary right. For example, he was appointed Bishop of Armagh, although the See of Armagh was held in lay succession by one family. It was an achievement to separate the family from this post without splitting the Irish Church.

The saint was educated in Armagh and Lismore, County Waterford, and desired only to be an itinerant preacher. His great talents took him instead to be Bishop of Down and Connor, and in 1125 he became Abbot-Bishop of Armagh. He travelled to France, where he made a lasting friendship with Bernard of Clairvaux, the reforming Cistercian. The Pope appointed him papal legate in Ireland, and whilst abroad he made some famous prophesies; one was that there will be the peace of Christ over all Ireland when the palm and the shamrock meet. This is supposed to mean when St Patrick's Day (17 March) occurs on Palm Sunday.

St Patrick (*c.* 390–461), Bishop and Patron Saint of Ireland

St Patrick was born somewhere between the Severn and the Clyde on the west coast of Britain. As a youth he was captured by Irish slave traders, and taken to the Antrim coast to work as a farm labourer. Much controversy surrounds the details of Patrick's life. Popular tradition credits him with converting the whole of Ireland, but nearly all that can be truly known of him comes from his *Confessio* or autobiography, and other writings. Through these writings he is revealed as a simple, sincere and humble man who was full of care for his people; an unlearned man, once a fugitive, who had learnt to trust God completely. Tradition states that, after six years of slavery, voices told him he would soon return to his own land,

and he escaped. Later, other voices called to him from Ireland, entreating him 'to come and walk once more amongst us'.

It is believed that he spent some time in Gaul (France) and became a priest; perhaps he had some mission conferred on him by the Pope to go and continue the work of Palladius, another missionary bishop who worked amongst the Christian Irish. It is believed that some confusion has arisen over the achievements of Palladius and Patrick. Patrick, when he returned to Ireland, seems to have been most active in the north, whilst Palladius worked in the south. He made Armagh his primary see, and it has remained the centre of Christianity in Ireland. He organized the church on the lines of territorial sees, and encouraged the laity to become monks or nuns. He was very concerned with abolishing paganism, idolatry and sun-worship, and he preached to the highest and the lowest in the land. Tradition credits him with expelling the snakes from Ireland, and explaining the Trinity by pointing to a shamrock.

One of the most famous episodes handed down by popular belief is that of his confrontation with King Laoghaire at Tara, known as the seat of the high kings of Ireland, and the capital of Meath. It was supposedly on Easter Saturday in 432, which that year coincided with a great Druid festival at Tara. No new fire was allowed to be lit until the lighting of the sacred pagan fire by the Druids. St Patrick was camped on the Hill of Slane which looks onto Tara, and his campfire was burning brightly; the Druids warned King Laoghaire that if it was not put out, it would never be extinguished. When Patrick was brought before Laoghaire, his holiness melted the king's hostility and he was invited to stay. Although Laoghaire did not become a Christian, his brother Conal, a prince of the North, became his protector and ally.

Certain places in Ireland are traditionally closely associated with St Patrick, such as Croagh Patrick in County Mayo, where there is an annual pilgrimage to the top of the 2510-ft (765 m) mountain on the last Sunday of July; and Downpatrick and Saul in County Down. The cult of St Patrick spread from Ireland to many Irish monasteries in Europe, and in more modern times to North America and Australia, where large communities of Irish emigrants live. The annual procession on 17 March, on St Patrick's Day in New York has become a massive event, where everybody sports a shamrock and drinks green beer. However, quite a few Irish believe St Colmcille should be the patron saint of Ireland, not this mild and humble British missionary!

Oliver Plunket (1625–81), Archbishop of Armagh and Martyr

This gentle and holy man lived in frightening and turbulent times, when to be a practising Catholic in Ireland was to court trouble. He was born into a noble and wealthy family whose lands extended throughout the Pale. He was sent to study in Rome, and was a brilliant theology and law scholar. He became a priest in 1654 and in 1669 was appointed Archbishop of Armagh. Oliver was one of only two bishops in Ireland at that time, and the whole of the laity was in disorder and neglect. Apart from the hostility of the Protestants, the Catholics themselves were divided by internal squabbles. Oliver confirmed thousands of people, and held a provincial synod. He did much to maintain discipline amongst the clergy, to improve education by founding the Jesuit College in Drogheda, and to promulgate the decrees of the Council of Trent.

Oliver managed to remain on good terms with many of the Protestant gentry and clergy, but was eventually outlawed by the British government. The panic caused by the false allegations made by Titus Oates in England about a popish plot was used by Plunket's enemies, and he was arrested in 1678. He was absurdly charged with plotting to bring in twenty thousand French troops, and levying a charge on his clergy to support an army. No jury could be found to convict him in Ireland, so he was brought to England, where he was convicted of treason for setting up 'a false religion which was the most dishonourable and derogatory to God of all religions and that a greater crime could not be committed against God than for a man to endeavour to propagate that religion'. He was hanged, drawn and quartered at Tyburn in July 1681. His head is in the Oliver Plunket Church in Drogheda, County Louth, and his body lies at Downside Abbey, Somerset.

Topics

The Argory

The National Trust in Northern Ireland

The six counties of Northern Ireland are very fortunate in having the National Trust to protect and serve some of Ulster's most beautiful and environmentally important areas. Close to Belfast it has fulfilled one of the ideals of Octavia Hill, who was a national founding member of the Trust, to ensure 'open-air sitting rooms for urban populations'. So it is possible to wander in the **Minnowburn Beeches**, a popular beauty spot beside the Lagan river, or amongst the hazel and beech woods of **Killynether** beneath Scrabo, or to walk the promontory of **Ballymacormick** on Belfast Lough. Further into Co. Down, large areas are protected by the Trust's wildlife scheme, which covers all the foreshore of **Strangford Lough**, one of the most attractive landscapes in Ulster. Birdwatchers are encouraged to use the hides set up to watch flocks of wild fowl and nesting birds.

Heading towards the Mourne Mountains, the Trust has managed to combine amenity and conservation in a sensitive way at **Murlough**. Sand dunes and heathland rich in flora and fauna provide a wonderful stretch of views and walks bordering the lagoon of Dundrum Bay to the north and the Irish Sea to the south. Footpaths make the wild beauty of the Mournes and Slieve Donard accessible to walkers.

There are many National Trust areas of great beauty in the six counties. They are too numerous to list here but some obvious ones are the **Crom Estate** in Co. Fermanagh, and **Downhill** in Co. Londonderry with its exciting windy walks to the Mussenden Temple and Black Glen. The most impressive landscape in the six counties must be the coastline and **Glens of Antrim**. People have written reams about its beauty, geology, culture and legends, and it is still unspoilt today, especially when compared to the Co. Down coastline. This landscape is the glory of the north, and includes one of the natural wonders of the world, the **Giant's Causeway**, where the shrinkage of cooling molten lava caused columnar structures to form. Access is managed by the National Trust and no tourist paraphernalia spoils the view. It also owns and protects part of the headlands and beaches of this magnificent coast; you can follow paths that take you past the ruins of **Dunseverick Castle**, overlooking Rathlin Island, and on to the drama of **Fair Head.**

The National Trust in Northern Ireland was set up in 1936, and has gradually acquired properties which range in their areas of interest from architecture, botany, geology, horticulture and ornithology to industrial archaeology. **Patterson's Spade Mill**, south of Templepatrick, is the last water-driven spade mill in Ireland. It is a really fascinating place and the methods, skill and equipment of the mill, along with the buzz of activity, will keep you here much longer than you'd planned. The spades you see being made can be bought at the small shop, and regional variations in the shape and use of the spade are still followed.

The linen industry was an immense influence in the lives of many Ulster folk, and **Wellbrook Beetling Mill,** in a pretty glen near Cookstown, is well worth visiting. You can see how the linen was finished off, giving it its special sheen or texture.

Most people appreciate the National Trust through visiting the grand stately homes and their gardens which are under its protection. These are always preserved in style, and their decoration and furnishing usually restored in a sympathetic way. Humbler dwellings are also represented, for instance a Victorian bar in Belfast, and a traditional farmhouse, **Hezlett House**, near Coleraine. Examples of the 'big house' vary from a gentleman farmer's estate,

Ardress, Co. Armagh, to the stately grandeur of **Castle Coole**, Enniskillen, designed by James Wyatt. Some of the most fascinating aspects of these properties are the work areas, so different from the leisured world upstairs. Each estate was a self-sufficient entity with its own dairy, laundry, livestock, flour and saw mills, stables, and fruit and vegetable gardens. The National Trust is also responsible for maintaining some great gardens, two of which are world-famous for their plants and their design, **Mount Stewart** and **Rowallane**, both in Co. Down, see pp.177 and 178. For details of the National Trust properties in Northern Ireland, write to The National Trust, Rowallane, Saintfield, Co. Down BT24 7LH. You can become a member, which entitles you to free entry to its properties; family membership is also available. The National Trust also organizes lectures on art history, furniture, plants and wildlife. Most of the country house properties have restaurants or tearooms where you can get a decent bite to eat, and their shops usually stock an interesting range of books.

The Republic has no equivalent of the National Trust, although it has a few conservation bodies, amongst them *An Taisce*, which acts as an environmental watchdog. In the counties of Donegal, Monaghan and Cavan, the fate of the 'big house' is mostly one of dereliction and decay. An exception is **Glenveagh Castle** in Co. Donegal. It was gifted to the nation by Henry McIlhenny along with a vast acreage of mountainous wilderness, bog, lough and gardens. The castle is an attractive Gothic building, furnished in high Victorian style by McIlhenny. Nearby is **St Columb's**, a more humble house, originally a rectory. It contains a very individual collection of beautiful objects, pictures, porcelain, and furniture. Its outbuildings have been converted into an art gallery with a wonderful collection of 20th-century paintings. The place has been given to the nation by the artist Derek Hill, and, like Glenveagh, is run by the Office of Public Works. You can also take a tour around **Castle Leslie** in Co. Monaghan, a fine 19th-century mansion with impressive grounds and plenty of atmosphere.

The Gardens of Ulster

Ulster suffers more from the disadvantages of wind and cold than the rest of Ireland, yet it boasts three of the greatest gardens in the country, and a host of charming landscaped parks, country-house walled gardens, and some magnificent arboreta. It is true that the northern climate is tempered by the benign influence of the Gulf Stream, but, as with all great gardens, it is an individual with vision, talent and usually money who creates a great garden. Climate and soil is less important.

The gardens of **Mount Stewart** on the Ards Peninsula in Co. Down are a perfect example of vision and planning. The fine trees and the manmade lake were laid out by previous generations but genius came with Edith, the seventh Marchioness of Londonderry, in the 1920s. She managed to combine the beautiful, the stately, the whimsical and the bizarre in a series of formal gardens around the house which marry well with the 19th-century landscaping. In one area is a sunken garden filled with vivid colours—blues and purples—based on a plan Gertrude Jekyll sent to her. Lady Londonderry not only loved tender and unusual plants, but often used very ordinary plants in unusual ways, for example, hedging with cotinus. Her whimsical streak is revealed by the garden shaped into a shamrock by yew hedges with a topiary harp and, in the middle, a Red Hand of Ulster fashioned out of red begonias. Other pleasures are the Spanish and Italian gardens with their vast urns, loggias, pillars and terraces, and huge eucalyptus and Irish yews beyond. The bizarre is provided by the Dodo Terrace, adorned with concrete remembrances of Lady Londonderry's powerful friends who were known by the names of exotic or mythological animals. She was not only a great gardener but also a suffragette, founder of the Women's League and a famous London Society hostess who presided over the Ark Club, an elite group of men who included Winston Churchill and Harold Macmillan. Mount Stewart contains eighteen different gardens in all, including a wonderful rhododendron wood. Everything thrives in this sheltered position beside Strangford Lough in the lime-free soil.

Rowallane, near Saintfield in Co. Down, is another superb garden. It is the creation of two men, the Reverend John Moore and his nephew, Hugh Armytage Moore. The grounds are planted with many rare and special shrubs and flowers, some of which originated as chance seedlings at Rowallane; others have come from the legendary Slieve Donard nursery, now sadly defunct. The rock garden is made around natural outcrops of rock and the dwarf plants seem to thrive on the thin, peaty soil. The walled garden is well laid out with mature and colourful plants and there are beautiful rhododendron walks. The stonework around the garden is very atmospheric: some monumental pillars are made of natural balls of rock, others are pillars crowned with jagged stone.

The last of the trilogy of great Ulster gardens is **Glenveagh** in Co. Donegal. The magnificent backdrop of the mountains and lough, which give a wild and romantic prospect, makes the exploration of the garden an even more enjoyable pastime. Glenveagh Gardens were begun in the 1860s by Mrs Cornelia Adair, the wife of a notorious landlord who evicted all his tenants when he bought Glenveagh as a sporting estate. Perhaps the huge *Rhododendron fabconeri* dates from this time. An American, Henry P. McIlhenny, eventually bought the estate in 1937 and began to restore and develop the gardens in the 1950s. The ordered serenity of the walled garden with its mixed rows of vegetables, herbs and flowers, and the elegant Gothic orangery at the castle end, are very attractive. The gardens lead one into another; there is an Italian statuary garden, a flag-stoned terrace filled with enormous urns of scented azaleas, and the woodland walks; exotic plantings crowd the paths, which lead to great vistas. The gardens at Glenveagh are cared for by the Department of Public Works and are part of a large National Park. Be sure to bring some midge repellent with you because Glenveagh midges are particularly savage!

The National Trust in the six counties own other interesting and appealing gardens. In Co. Londonderry, it has **Downhill Castle,** or Palace, as it is known. The palace itself was built for the famous Earl Bishop Frederick Hervey in the 1780s. He chose the site for its grandeur, and the landscape and walk to the Mussenden Temple on the edge of a sea-cliff is very invigorating. But the gardens here are the creation of Miss Jan Eccles, who came as a warden in 1962. She has made a water meadow bright with the colours of candelabra primulas and irises, and a flower garden of roses, phlox and tree peonies. The walk through the Black Glen is planted with beautiful and unusual trees, and in springtime there are bluebells and wild garlic under-foot. The Bishop's Palace is now a picturesque shell. It was reputedly a most uncomfortable place to live, so perhaps it is best it should remain a romantic ruin amid a field of sheep.

Seaforde, which has a fine nursery garden, and **Castlewellan Arboretum and garden** are two other Co. Down gardens worth stopping for. They are both open all year. Throughout Ulster, small private gardens can also be visited by appointment. Close to Bushmills in Co. Antrim is a fine walled and informal garden at **Ballylough House**, and at **Benvarden**, near Devrock, is another charming walled garden with box hedges. Many of these smaller gardens are beside attractive old houses with lovely views. **Drumadravey House**, Irvinestown, Co.

Fermanagh; **Drenagh**, at Limavady, Co. Londonderry; **Greenfort** at Portsalon, Co. Donegal, and **Keady Rectory**, Co. Armagh, are just a few of the many you can visit. Be sure to make an appointment in advance; they are only open at the owners' convenience.

Finally, **Ardnamona**, overlooking Lough Eske in Co. Donegal, has a spectacular collection of rhododendrons and conifers collected in the late 19th century. The gardens had been left to go wild over many years, yet the rhododendrons obviously loved the moist soft climate and flourished. Many have seeded themselves, and their cinnamon-barked progeny flourish. It is possible to make an appointment to view the garden (go in May or June if you can) or, better still, book into the 1790s house, which is run as a comfortable country house B&B with memorable cooking.

Historic Houses

If you want to try to understand the Anglo-Irish, the best thing to do is look round one of their houses. The expression 'Anglo-Irish' has political, social and religious connotations. It is used to describe the waves of English settlers and their descendants who became so powerful in the land after the success of the campaigns of Elizabeth I of England. An optimistic view is held by some that Anglo-Irish is a tag that should only be applied to literature, and indeed it does seem ridiculous that, after three hundred years of living in a place, these landowning families are not counted as truly Irish. On the one hand, it is a fact that the sons of the Ascendency were educated in England, and served the British Empire as soldiers or civil servants, and that they beheld themselves as different from the native Irish; whilst on the other, many of these people felt a great and patriotic love for Ireland, led revolts and uprisings against British rule and, starting with the Normans, became, in the very apt, anonymous and undated Latin saying, 'more Irish than the Irish'.

Ireland's big houses were built by families who would be most offended if you called them English, although as far as the Gaelic Irish are concerned, that is what they are! 'The Big House' is another very Irish expression, applied to a landowner's house regardless of its size or grandeur. In fact, if you look through Burke's *Guide to Irish Country Houses* and the rather depressing, but fascinating, *Vanishing Houses of Ireland* (published by the Irish Architectural Archive and the Irish Georgian Society) you will get a very good idea of the variety and huge number of houses that belonged to the gentry.

The English monarchs always financed their Irish wars by paying their soldiers with grants of land in Ireland, and as the country was so unruly, the settlers lived in fortified or semi-fortified houses during the 17th century. There are only a very few examples of Tudor domestic architecture. The victory of William of Orange over James II was complete when the Jacobites surrendered at the Treaty of Limerick in 1696. Within a few years the Penal Laws were introduced, which severely restricted the freedom of both Catholics and non-conformists. The majority of big houses were built in the hundred years following the 1690s when the Protestant landowners settled down to enjoy their gains. The civil and domestic architecture that survives from these times is both elegant and splendid, and is to be found in every county.

The 'big house' usually consists of a square, grey stone block, sometimes with wings, set amongst gardens and parkland with stables at the back, and a walled garden. Sometimes it is called a castle, although the only attribute of a castle it may have is a deep fosse. A lingering insecurity must often have remained, for many are almost as tall as they are wide, with up to four storeys, rather like a Georgian version of the 16th-century tower house.

The buildings are completely different in atmosphere here from their counterparts in England. They have not undergone Victorian 'improvements' or gradually assumed an air of comfortable mellowness over the centuries. It was an act of bravado on the part of the Anglo-Irish to build them at all, for they had always to be on the alert against the disaffected natives, who readily formed aggressive agrarian groups such as the Whiteboys. They never had enough money to add on layer after layer in the newest architectural fashion; their houses remained as Palladian splendours or Gothick fantasies built during the Georgian age, when the fortified house could at last be exchanged for something a good deal more comfortable. The big houses that remain are full of beautiful furniture, pictures, *objets d'art* and the paraphernalia of generations who appreciated beauty, good horses, hard drinking and eating, and were generous and slapdash by nature. It is against this background of grey stately houses looking onto sylvan scenes and cosseted by sweeping trees that one should read Maria Edgeworth, supplying some details yourself on the Penal Laws, the famine, the foreignness of the landlords and their loyalties. The literature on the 'Big House' is huge, and if you read Thackeray, Trollope, Charles Lever, Somerville and Ross, and more Maria Edgeworth on the subject, you will not only be entertained but well informed. The big house, the courthouse, the jail and the military barracks were all symbols of oppression and not surprisingly many of them got burnt out in the 1920s; but these houses echo with the voices of talented and liberal people: the wit of Sheridan and Wilde, the conversations of Mrs Delany, the gleeful humour of Somerville and Ross, whisper through the rooms as you wander around.

In England there is a whole network of organizations and legislation to protect the historic house. The National Trust has several properties in Northern Ireland whose restored glory seems to be in mocking contrast to their counterparts in the Republic. Castle Coole in Co. Fermanagh and Springhill in Co. Londonderry are favourites, the latter because it still has the atmosphere of a gracious house, whose owners were never exceptionally rich, just thrifty in a typically Northern way. All these properties have entrance fees which vary from £2 to £4. The National Trust is described more fully on p.76.

In the Republic of Ireland there is no real equivalent of the National Trust, no Historic Building and Monuments Commission, no National Heritage fund. Although *An Taisce*, the National Trust for Ireland, does its best, it does not have the funds to buy property. This means there are no grants for repairs to buildings, and no effective legislation to protect them from dereliction or neglect. Even now the 'big house' is persistently regarded by the powers that be as tainted with the memories of colonialism and an oppressive age. They are labelled as 'not Irish', although the craftsmen who built and carved the wonderful details of cornicing, stucco-work and dovetailing, elegant staircases and splendid decoration were as Irish as could be. There are many desolate shells to glimpse on your travels, though it is still possible to go around quite a selection of well cared-for properties.

The Heritage Council has helped to change official attitudes, but it is the Irish Georgian Society which so far has done most to secure the future of the 'big house'. Founded in 1958 to work for the preservation of Ireland's architectural heritage, the society has carried out numerous rescue and restoration works on historic houses. Financed almost entirely by members and donations, one of its great achievements was the restoration work done on Castletown House in Co. Kildare, Ireland's largest and finest Palladian country house. It was bought by the Hon. Desmond Guinness in 1967, the founder and then president of the Irish

Georgian Society, and they had their headquarters at Castletown until 1979. From 1979 the house was owned and maintained by the Castletown Foundation, a charitable trust who continued with the restoration work and kept the house open to the public. In January 1994 Castletown became the property of the State and is now the responsibility of the Office of Public Works. The Irish Georgian Society is now based at 74 Merrion Square, Dublin 2, © (01) 676 7053. The growth of tourism has been of great help in the survival of these great houses, and state-funded organizations have started to look after some of them.

If these gracious buildings and their gardens and parkland interest you, book into the country-house hotels such as Rathmullen House in Co. Donegal, Galgorm Manor, Co. Antrim or Hilton Park, Co. Monaghan. For more details of country-house lodgings, *see* **Practical A–Z**, 'Where to Stay', pp.34–5, and entries at the end of each county chapter.

'Hidden Ireland' is the collective name for a number of privately owned historic houses throughout Ireland offering accommodation and often dinner, © (01) 668 1423, *www.indigo. ie/hiddenireland/*. They do not cover the six counties, so if you want to stay in an interesting old house in the North contact the Tourist Office or the National Trust. John Colclough runs specialized tours of public and private houses and castles in Ireland. You can contact him at Irish Country House Tours, 71 Waterloo Road, Dublin 4, © (01) 668 6463. Also worth buying is 'Friendly Homes of Ireland', another collection of B&Bs which includes some private historic homes. Booklet available from John Colclough (*see* above) and from tourist offices (£1).

Later Architectural Forms

Palladian: The term used to describe a pseudo-classical architectural style taken from the 16th-century Italian architect, Palladio. Sir Edward Lovett Pearce introduced the Palladian style to Ireland, which consisted of symmetrical pavilions flanking the central block of the house, and it was continued by his pupil, Richard Cassels, also known as Castle. The most perfect Palladian house in the British Isles is Bellamont House in County Cavan, designed by Pearce, which has fortunately been restored recently, but is not open to the public.

Neoclassical: A style of building similar to that of Palladio, but more directly inspired by the civilization of Ancient Rome. It became popular in the 1750s until the Gothic Revival.

Gothick: An amusing and romantic style popular in the late 18th century, spelt with a 'k' to distinguish it from the serious, and later, Gothic Revival. Gothick Castles were built by Francis Johnston and the English Paine brothers, who came over to Ireland with John Nash during the 1780s. Towers and battlements were added to more severe classical houses. Castleward in Co. Down is a house that is classical on one side and Gothick on the other.

Gothic Revival: From the 1830s onwards many houses and churches were built in a style harking back to the Tudor and perpendicular forms; the popularity of these gradually gave way to the more severe style of the Early-English and Decorated Gothic. The English church architect Augustus Pugin (1812–52) equated Gothic with Christian and Classicism with pagan. He designed a number of churches and cathedrals in Ireland. J. J. McCarthy (1817–82), an Irish architect, was very strongly influenced by Pugin; you can see McCarthy's work at St Patrick's (Roman Catholic) Cathedral, Armagh.

Hibernio-Romanesque: A style which was popular in church architecture from the 1850s onwards. It fitted in with growing national feelings to lay claim to an 'Irish style' which existed before the Anglo-Norman invasion.

Irish Rococo Plasterwork: The great period of rococo plasterwork in Ireland began with the Swiss Italian brothers Paul and Philip Francini, who came to Ireland in 1739. They were great stuccodores, and modelled plaster figures, trophies, fruit and flowers in magnificent combinations. The Irish craftsmen quickly learned the technique, and between 1740 and 1760 many beautiful ceilings were created. These craftsmen tended to leave out figures, and concentrate instead on birds, flowers, and musical instruments. The ceilings are graceful, yet full of life, with a swirling gaiety that make Adam ceilings, which later became the fashion, seem rather stilted. Ardress House in Co. Armagh has a wonderful ceiling dating from the late 18th century. It was created by Michael Stapleton, whose style is reminiscent of the Francini Brothers.

Selected Architects

W. J. Barrie (1826–67). Designed the Ulster Hall in Belfast and palatial houses for the rich linen merchants of Belfast—e.g. Danesfort in Malone Road, currently the HQ of the Electricity Board, which is a medley of French, Italian and English chateau style.

Richard Cassels, also known as Castle (*c.* 1690–1751). Cassels is responsible for some of the most beautiful country houses in Ireland. He was of Huguenot origin (his family came from Germany to England), and part of the circle surrounding Lord Burlington, the wealthy and scholarly aristocrat who did so much to bring neoclassicism to Britain. Cassels came to Ireland in the 1720s. He was also involved in designing the Newry Canal, begun in 1730, which linked the coalfield of Coalisland in County Tyrone to Newry, a distance of 18 miles (28.8km). It was the first major canal in the British Isles. It is thought that Florence Court in Co. Fermanagh is his work, with the Palladian pavilions added later to the designs of Davis Ducart.

Francis Johnston (1760–1829). An architect in Armagh, and responsible for many of the fine buildings there, such as the Observatory. He moved to Dublin in 1793. He also designed a number of 'Gothick' castles.

Sir Charles Lanyon (1813–89). He was born in Belfast, and built the Custom House there in 1857. He also designed Queens University buildings, Sinclair Seamen's Church and the Scrabo Tower. Lanyon was adept at creating country houses in the Italian style: imposing and florid buildings adapted from Italian palaces and villas of the High Renaissance Period.

John Nash (1752–1835). English architect who designed grand country houses, amongst which are Killymoon Castle and Caledon in Co. Tyrone. His elegant neoclassical style can be seen in the terraces of Regent's Park, London, and in the Royal Pavilion, Brighton.

Sir Edward Lovett Pearce (1699–1733). He was born in Co. Meath, and served as a soldier. He visited Venice in his early twenties, where he made drawings of the buildings there and in other Italian cities. He was the leader of the Irish Palladians, and he designed the interior of the largest and most splendid of all Irish country houses, Castletown in Co. Kildare. He also designed Bellamont Forest in Co. Cavan. Richard Cassels was one of his pupils. Pearce became an MP and, in 1730, Surveyor-General.

Alfred Brumwell Thomas (1866–1948). He was primarily a London architect but he designed the imposing Belfast City Hall which was completed in 1906. His other principal works were the town halls of Stockport, Woolwich and Clacton.

There are many little islands lying off the magnificent coastline of Ulster, some of which you can only visit if you have a boat or can persuade a local boatman to take you. The islands described below can be reached by organized ferry or boat trips in the summer, so you can easily include them in your itinerary. For details of these services and contact telephone numbers, *see* under the individual counties.

Tory Island

One of the most wonderful trips can be made to Tory Island, off the coast of West Donegal. It is a journey of dreamlike landscape, whether you leave from Bunbeg, Magheraroarty or Downings. The rocky headlands of the mainland shore, blurred with olive and ochre, and the pure colour of the water are continually changing in the light of these North Atlantic skies. With luck you will get a day with some sun: you will never forget such intensity of colour. The crossing to Tory is often rough, so pray for a light wind. The length of the journey varies depending where you sail from: Magheraroarty to Tory is the shortest crossing, about 40 minutes; from Downings it takes 1½ hours and from Bunbeg about 75 mins, but the scenery is so lovely the time passes quickly. You may hear Ulster Gaelic spoken either by the locals or a boatload of Gaelic students from Belfast; it is seldom heard outside the classroom. Then there is the excitement of landing at the little fishing harbour in West Town with your first sight of the ancient Tau cross, so elementary with its T shape, before walking on into the simple white-washed village.

Tory in Gaelic means Place of Towers. The island is three miles long and about one mile wide and is very barren, with only a few fuchsia bushes to stand up to the wind. The islanders have a long history of independence from the mainland, and, according to ancient records, Tory was ruled by Balor, the God of Darkness, whose people lived by raiding the mainland. The two villages on the island are brightly painted and in West Town there is a small hotel, a bar where you might happen on a *ceilidh* (frequent in the summer), and a café.

Walking on the island is an exhilarating experience; the road passes through boggy land, wild flowers and streams, accompanied all the while by glorious birdsong. A glimpse into the houses of East Town shows a simple way of life with a few chickens and the odd beast grazing. The road then leads on to the shore and more fishing boats. Most visitors climb up the stony high ground edged with dramatic sea-cliffs to Balor's Fort, a magnificent outcrop of rock scattered with nesting seabirds and spray from the shifting ocean. There are no fences to detract from the freedom of standing on the edge of such a landscape, but it is not a place for small children.

The West side of the island is equally beautiful, without the cliffs but with dangerous rocks where many boats have been wrecked. You can walk the island in a day but this would give you no time to explore the little church in West Town, the ruined round tower or the Gallery. This is part museum and part selling gallery, where you can buy the naïve painting of the islanders. A school of painting grew up here in the 1980s after Derek Hill, the painter who lives near Churchill in Donegal, encouraged James Dixon to try out his paints. Many of the momentous events in the islanders' memory are celebrated in the subject matter of the paintings. The wreck of the gunboat *Wasp* in 1884, when most of the crew perished, recurs repeatedly. The *Wasp* had been sent to make the islanders pay their taxes. This naïve school of painting has given the island an international reputation, and it is a welcome way for some islanders to make a little money. Farming is virtually non-existent, and fishing is in decline. The islanders, who number about 130, have to work abroad, and there are always financial pressures to move to the mainland. Tourism is another source of income.

Rathlin

Another exciting trip can be made to Rathlin Island, or Raghery as it is called locally. It is eight miles off the coast of Antrim and there are many regular sailings from Ballycastle during the summer. The island is shaped like an upside-down L and is about eight miles long and two miles wide. It is farmed in a way that you do not often see nowadays: small grazing fields, or fields allowed to ripen into hay, and very little tillage. Simple farm houses, surrounded by fields of sheep and cattle, give way to boggy ground strewn with rocks and little loughs glinting with dragonflies. The cliffs on the western side of the island are very dramatic, and thousands of seabirds breed on these and the black volcanic rockstacks. One of the best places to view the birds is from the area around the West lighthouse, which is a nature reserve. It is fascinating to watch the activities of the puffins, razorbills, fulmars and guillemots, whose cries can be heard above the swell of the sea. Waders love the reedy edges of the loughs and marshy boglands, as do the curlews and snipe. The birdwardens can arrange to show you the birds of prey: kestrel, buzzard and peregrine falcon, among others. Walking around the island (or hiring a bicycle) is a pleasure; there are very few cars, only the odd tractor crawls along the roads. You might hear a cuckoo or a corncrake, which have disappeared in the more intensely cultivated places.

Many people come to Rathlin to dive in the waters around the island and see some of the many wrecks driven onto the rocks by the relentless wind. Many have also been sent to their deep resting place by the treacherous currents and whirlpools—the Slough-na-moreore over-falls to the south brought an end to 50 currachs in AD 440; and to the northeast, in the 17th century, another tragic story involved the loss of four sons in a notorious tide race known afterwards as the MacDonnells Races. The stories of shipwreck, rescue and salvage would fill a huge book, and a few experienced islanders will lead divers to the most accessible wrecks.

The history of Rathlin has many tragic incidents, including a number of massacres in the 16th and 17th century when they were caught up in the struggles between Scotland, Ireland and England. In the 19th century the famine reduced the population dramatically, although Rathlin folk have always been able to fish, and today continue to make a small amount of money from potting for lobster and crab. Salvage has been an important part of their livelihood too, and the tradition is still strong. The last big vessel to go down off Rathlin was the *Erlo Hills* in 1981, a motor trawler of 178 tonnes. In 1987, Richard Branson's transatlantic hot air balloon *Virgin Flyer* ditched in the sea three miles north of Rathlin. For their help in the recovery of the balloon, the Rathlin islanders received a donation of £25,000 from Branson to help fund community projects.

The Manor house used to belong to the Gage family. It has been restored and is now being developed as a centre for island activities as well as a place to stay and eat. The Richard Branson Activity Centre is mainly a hostel for groups of divers and walkers, and there is a pleasant guest house. Rathlin has changed a great deal in the last ten years with a wind-powered electricity system and a new piped water supply. The roads have been improved and Church Bay developed for islanders and visitors alike, yet it remains an unspoilt and beautiful place, with very friendly people and plenty to do.

The Copeland Islands

These three small islands, Lighthouse Island, Great Copeland and Mew, lie in the mouth of the Belfast Lough, just off the harbour town of Donaghadee. They are low, green isles full of charm, and make a splendid day's outing. A regular boat goes from Donaghadee in the summer months; take a picnic as there are no shops, only a few holiday cottages. Lighthouse Island (lighthouse no longer working) is a bird observatory run by the National Trust. It is possible to apply for a permit to stay at the self-catering accommodation in the converted lighthouse. It is worth staying overnight to see the fascinating sight of the manx shearwaters who breed in the rabbit burrows venturing out to feed—they don't dare come out during the day because of the predatory gulls. Seabird populations are monitored here, and you might see the ringing of birds—the variety is enormous. Great Copeland is given over to grazing sheep, and Mew, the smallest island, has a powerful lighthouse, sadly soon to lose its human operator. If you come here in spring it is wonderful to see the wild narcissi which have spread throughout the islands and there are plenty of little rocky bays and springy groves to picnic on.

Linen

The role of linen in the province of Ulster has been enormously important. This wonderful cloth was produced on a huge commercial scale in the 19th and early 20th centuries when embroidered and patterned linen was considered a necessity in every well-off home, and was exported all over the world. Very little flax is grown in Ulster today, and linen manufacture has shrunk to a small, high-quality business. The impact of linen on a largely rural society, and its huge employment of women as the industrial mills developed, is very much a part of the complex history and identity of Ulster.

Everyday memories of the industry are alive, and the ruined mills can be seen in many places in the Lagan Valley. The bleaching greens and the retting dams may have disappeared, but the beshawled mill girls with their swollen red and blue feet, bare in all weathers, rushing to work in the early hours of the morning, still haunt the streets of Belfast. Driven by a harsh timetable of long hours with scarcely a moment's rest, youngsters started 'officially' at the age of twelve. Their toil helped to keep the family alive. Originally weaving was done largely on a hand loom in rural cottages, but, as the machinery grew more sophisticated and factories were established, people were drawn into the linen centres such as Lisburn and Belfast. The work was cruel, although it was one of the reasons the Ulster people survived the famine times a little better than in other parts of Ireland. So many people were involved in the making of linen, whether it was the farmer and his labourers who grew and harvested the flax, the women who hand-embroidered the finished linen at home, or the workers in the scutch mills, the weaving mills, the beetling mills and the bleachworks. Belfast grew into a bustling city with a complex of factory chimneys on each side of the river Lagan. The mills were huge, box-like buildings, usually of red brick, with smokestacks and steep glass roofs to give light to the machine rooms. These linen mills went into a decline with the introduction of man-made materials, yet mill girls were still going to work with bare feet in the 1950s.

Linen is made from the strong fibres (the phloem tubes) in the stem of the flax plant. Flax had been grown in Ireland since early Christian times, but it was in the more settled times, following the victory of William III over James II at the Battle of the Boyne in 1690, that its manufacture into linen was actively encouraged by the government. In Ulster, the credit for the establishment of the linen industry has traditionally been given to Louis Crommelin, a French Huguenot skilled in the manufacture of linen, who came to Ireland under the patronage of another Huguenot, Ruigny, the Earl of Galway. He was employed as Overseer of the Royal Linen Manufacture and he established a factory in Lisburn, Co. Down with French artisans brought over from Holland. The linen industry was gradually strengthened by the encouragement given to Protestant traders to settle in the area, and the generous copyhold leases granted to them by landlords eager to cultivate the industry.

The process of harvesting the flax for linen was as follows. After the flax with its blue flowers had been in bloom for three or four weeks, the crop was pulled out by its roots, deseeded of its immature seeds with a special comb, and put into retting dams until it had decayed; this made it easier to detach the phloem tubes. The dams were small and about 3½ feet deep to allow the water to become warm enough to rot, or ret, easily. The labourers who had the unpleasant task of lifting the rotten sheaves of flax from the dams smelt for weeks afterwards, and their wages were supplemented with extra whiskey to encourage them! The flax was then dried in stooks and later in large ricks, sometimes taking a long time depending on the weather. Eventually, it was taken to the scutch mill where the unwanted parts of the plant were knocked off by being bruised between teethed wooden rollers and hit with a blunt wooden blade. The working conditions were awful as it was so dusty, and if the workers lost concentration they could be horribly mangled in the machinery. After the scutching came the hackling, when the linen fibres were pulled through a special comb; they now looked like coarse brown beige hair, and could be spun into thread, and then woven into cloth.

Lisburn became an important centre for linen-making during the 18th century and beyond. The importance of the industry in Ulster is recognized in the excellent museum there, the Irish Linen Centre, ☎ (028) 9266 3377. It has a marvellous exhibition on the process of linen-making, a very good linen shop and a relaxing café—three very good reasons for making a special trip to go there. You might even be curious enough to look at the burial place of Louis Crommelin, the Protestant refugee, in the venerable graveyard of Lisburn Cathedral. It is also possible to tour modern-day linen factories in what is known as the Linen Homelands in the Lagan Valley; the Belfast and local tourist offices keep details of the tours. The factories today produce high-quality linen used for high fashion, or else make linen fibres which can be blended with other types of fibre. Most of the linen is actually imported from Belgium. Linen table napkins, clothes and sheets can still be bought. Try the Lamont Factory Shop, Stranmillis, Embankment, Belfast, ☎ (028) 9066 8285. Another interesting trip can be made to the Ulster Folk and Transport Museum in Cultra, Holywood, Co. Down, which has many exhibits and special demonstrations on the making of linen.

Music

Traditional Irish music is played everywhere in Ireland, in the cities and the country. Government sponsorship helped to revive it, especially through *Radio an Gaeltachta* (Irish-language radio) in the west. Now there is great enthusiasm for it amongst everyone: a nine-year-old will sing a lover's lament about seduction and desertion, without batting an eyelid, to a grandfather whose generation scarcely remembered the Gaelic songs at all. The 1845–49 famine silenced the music and dancing for a while, but today Ireland has one of the most vigorous music traditions in Europe.

Serious traditional music is not in this sweet, folksy style. Listening to it can induce a state of exultant melancholy, or infectious merriment; whatever way, it goes straight to your heart. The lyrics deal with the ups and downs of love; failed rebellions, especially that of 1798; soldiering, dead heroes; religion and homesick love for the beauty of the countryside.

The bard in pre-Christian society was held in honour and a great deal of awe, for his learning and the mischievous satire in his poetry and music. After the Cromwellian and Williamite wars, he lost his status altogether; music and poetry were kept alive by the country people who cheered themselves up during the dark winter evenings with stories and music. The harp is, sadly, scarcely used nowadays, except when it is dragged out for the benefit of tourists at medieval banquets. The main traditional instruments used are the *uillean* pipes, which are more sophisticated than the Scottish bagpipes, the fiddle (violin) and the tin whistle. The beat and rhythm is provided by a handheld drum made from stretched goat hide called the *bodhran*. The accordion, the flute, guitar and the piano are used by some groups as well. These instruments are played singly or together.

The airs, laments, slip jigs, reels and songs all vary enormously from region to region, and you might easily hear a Monaghan man or a Donegal fiddler discussing with heated emotion the interpretation of a certain piece. Pieces are constantly improvised on, and seldom written down; inevitably some of the traditional content gets changed from generation to generation. A form of singing that had almost died out by the 1940s is the *Sean-Nós*, fully adorned, sung in Gaelic and unaccompanied by instruments. Now the *Sean-Nós* section in music festivals is overflowing with entrants.

You will have no difficulty in hearing traditional ballads or folk music in the local bars or hotels; players usually advertise in the local newspaper or by sticking up a notice in the window. The group of players seem only too happy to let you join in, and as the atmosphere gets smokier the music really takes off. In 1951 Comhaltas Ceoltoírí Eireann was set up for the promotion of traditional music, song and dance. It now has two hundred branches all over the country, and their members have regular sessions (*seisiún*) which are open to all. Ask at the local tourist office or write to *Comhaltas Ceoltoírí Eireann*, 32 Belgrave Square, Monkstown, Co. Dublin, ✆ (01) 280 0295. Seisiúns are informal sessions of music, ceilidhs and traditional cabaret and are a popular feature of the traditional music scene.

For information on local musical happenings contact ✆ (066) 32323 or ✆ (066) 32134—there is bound to be a *fleadh* going on somewhere near you. The All-Ireland Fleadh is held at the end of August in a different town every year, and smaller festivals are held all over the country. At these you can hear music of an incredible standard brimming over into the streets from every hall, bar, hotel and private house. It takes a great deal of stamina and a lot of jars to see the whole thing through. Do not expect a formal concert-hall environment, as music and 'crack' thrive best in small, intimate gatherings, and are often unplanned sessions in the local bar.

The six counties do not have an organized body such as CCE, although traditional music is played in many bars and festivals. Look in the newspapers, and try *Artslink*, a monthly guide to what's on. You can also ask in the local tourist offices.

If you get a chance to watch the Orangemen marching with their flute bands (practising ground for the celebrated James Galway when he was a youngster), you will see how important music is to every Irishman. Boys beat the great Lambeg drums till their knuckles bleed, while the skilful throwing of the batons makes a great performance—well worth seeing, in spite of its sectarian associations.

Today Ireland is producing some good musicians of a completely different type from the folk groups. The local bands that play in the bars play jazz, blues, and a rhythmical and melodious combination of pop and traditional instruments. Look in the local newspaper of any big town or ask in a record shop; they will know what gigs are on and probably be able to sell you a ticket as well. Some of the top names on the rock and pop scene come from Ireland, for instance Van Morrison, U2, The Corrs, Ash and Boyzone.

Tracing Your Ancestors

If you have any Irish blood in you at all, you will have a passion for genealogy; the Irish seem to like looking backwards. When they had nothing left—no land, no Brehon laws, no religious freedom, they managed to hold on to their pride and their genealogy. Waving these before the eyes of French and Spanish rulers ensured that they got posts at court or commissions in the army. There is no such thing as class envy in Ireland: the next man is as good as you, and everybody is descended from some prince or hero from the Irish past. It is the descendants of the Cromwellian parvenus who had to bolster up their images with portraits and fine furniture. Now the planter families have the Irish obsession with their ancestors too.

The best way to go about finding where your Ulster ancestors came from is to write to the Public Record Office in Belfast. First find out as much as possible from family papers and the records of the Church and State in your own country; your local historical or genealogical society might be able to help. Find out the full name of your emigrant ancestor, the background of his or her family, whether rich, poor, merchant or farmer, Catholic or Protestant. Start your enquiries as far in advance of your visit as you can. The search is becoming easier as church and civil records are being computerized by Irish Genealogy Ltd (IGL). For more information about the IGL write to: IGL Northern Manager, 2 Mellon Road, Castletown, Omagh BT78 5QY, ☎ (028) 8224 2241.

In America, immigrant records have been published by Baltimore Genealogical Publishing Company in seven volumes, and list the arrival of people into New York between 1846 and 1851. In Canada, the Department of Irish Studies, St Mary's University, Halifax is very helpful. In Australia, the Civil Records are very good: try the National Library, Canberra, the Mitchell Library, Sydney, and the Society of Australian Genealogists, Richmond Villa, 120 Kent Street, Sydney. The following addresses are important sources of information in Ulster (please enclose a S.A.E. with your enquiry):

Public Record Office (PRONI), 66 Balmoral Avenue, Belfast BT9 6NY, ✆ (028) 9066 1621. Main source of manuscript information for genealogical research in Ulster. Open Mon–Fri, 9.15–4.45.

General Register Office, Oxford House, 49 Chichester Street, Belfast BT1 4HL, ✆ (028) 9025 2000. Records of all births and deaths since 1864 and copies of all marriage registrations since 1922 in Northern Ireland are held here. Central records prior to 1922 are held in Dublin but the Registrar-General in Belfast will arrange for searches to be made, for a small fee, of any births, marriages or deaths in Northern Ireland before 1922.

Donegal Ancestry, Makemie Centre, Back Lane, Ramelton, Co. Donegal, ✆ (074) 51266.

Ulster Historical Foundation, 12 College Square East, Belfast BT1 6DD, ✆ (028) 9033 2288. Records relating to Belfast, Co. Antrim and Co. Down.

Heritage World, The Old School, Pomeroy Road, Donaghmore, BT70 3HG, ✆ (028) 8776 7039. Records relating to Co. Tyrone and Co. Fermanagh.

Armagh Ancestry, 42 English Street, Armagh BT61 7BA, ✆ (028) 3752 1802. Records relating to Co. Armagh.

Heritage Centre, 4–22 Butcher Street, Londonderry, BT48 6HL, ✆ (028) 7137 3177.

Association of Ulster Genealogists and Record Agents. Members' list and details of services from AUGRA, 18 Harberton Park, Belfast BT9 6TS.

If your ancestors were Presbyterian, **the Presbyterian Historical Society,** Church House, Fisherwick Place, Belfast, may be able to help. **The Ulster Historical Foundation**, which is attached to the Northern Ireland Public Record Office, will undertake searches.

Potatoes and the Famine

Potatoes were the main food of the peasant in the 19th century. The whole family would sit around a *rishawn* (basket) made of willows placed on the three-legged iron pot in which they had been boiled. The summer months were known as the hungry months, as the old crop of potatoes was finished. The last Sunday in July, or the first Sunday in August, was the ancient feast of *Lughnasa* (Lammas), a celebration of the start of the new harvest. Sometimes a delicious mixture of new potatoes, milk, chopped onion, spices and melted butter would be eaten from the first digging of the new potatoes. This is known as a Calcannon. The potato crop enabled large families to live on tiny, subdivided holdings on the poorest land. The spuds were grown in lazy beds, the farmers using spades to build up ridges of soil on these stony hillside farms. Today they are no longer cultivated; many were abandoned in the famine times.

The potato blight, a fungal disease which struck between 1845 and 1849, had fatal consequences for the peasants living on this subsistence economy, especially in the west. Huge suffering, death and disease followed, with the departure of millions of folk for Britain, Australia, Canada and America.

The effects of the famine and emigration were enormous, and still affect Ireland today. The population of Irish-speaking small farmers declined dramatically by 1847; nearly a quarter of a million emigrated every year. The landscape was emptied of people, villages were deserted, and the more prosperous farmers increased their land holdings. Very often all but the eldest son in a family emigrated; he was left to carry on with the farm, and he did not marry until very late in life, usually when his parents were dead. The wandering labourer who had an important place in society gradually died out as a class after the famine. These wandering labourers went to hiring fairs all over the provinces to be taken on by comfortable farmers, as the better off were called. Many were poets and storytellers and helped to keep the myths and tales of an ancient oral tradition alive. The spade was the essential tool that each labourer carried with him. Every region in Ireland had its own variation of spade made by the blacksmith to suit local conditions. You can see them being made at Patterson's Spade Mill at Templepatrick, Co. Antrim. It is the only mill of its kind left in Ireland (*see* p.153).

The Bowl Game (pronounced to rhyme with Owl)

This is traditionally played in Co. Armagh, along country lanes, and is known as 'road bowls' or 'bullets'. The ball is made of very heavy iron (28oz/795g), and the object of the game is to cover the greatest distance with the fewest number of bowls. The best players are strong and skilful, and the ball is a dangerous missile. It is illegal to play on public roads, but this did not stop it happening in the past; small children were stationed along the roads to warn competitors of oncoming traffic and the police. Today, the game has been saved from extinction and accommodated into the tourist calendar.

Museums and Heritage Centres

Ulster has a superb collection of museums, interpretative centres, historic farms, houses, folk and ecology parks. The variety is enormous and the few mentioned below are only meant as pointers, as each county has its own centres of interest. The many facets of social, cultural, industrial and natural history are identified and explained in these places.

The **Ulster Folk and Transport Museum**, close to Belfast, is the best of its type in Ireland, and provides hours of interest. The railway collection is superb, and includes the largest locomotive in Ireland. The well-kept grounds are laid out with traditional buildings in which the crafts, farming methods and textile history of Ulster is explained with examples of the beautiful embroidery, lace and patchwork produced by the cottagers.

The importance of linen is the main theme of the very attractive and well laid out **Lisburn Museum**. The permanent exhibition 'From Flax to Fabric' uses sound, life-like models, and artefacts from the past. They show the processes involved in linen manufacture, tracing the story of flax as it was harvested, spun and woven in small cottages during the last part of the 18th century, and its subsequent concentration and manufacture in huge factories at the turn of the 19th century. The enormous social and historical effects of the success of the linen industry are also covered. A resident weaver is busy with his hand loom recreating the beautiful damask of the past which is available in the museum shop; it is even possible to book in for a linen tour, visiting local factories where very different technology produces the same quality of linen as in the past.

The Knight Ride in Carrickfergus is a thrilling expedition for children, and involves a monorail ride through the history of the town since AD 531. The **US Rangers Centre** and **Andrew Jackson Centre** close by will be of interest to North Americans. The Scottish Irish Presbyterians were a familiar and honoured part of the American melting pot. They settled the frontier, founded the kirk, built the schools, and contributed quite a few presidents. The **Ulster American Folk Park** near Omagh explores this link, as do many other smaller heritage centres in Ulster. The Northern Ireland Tourist Board (NITB) produces an Ulster American Heritage Trail guide which details many connections with the two main migrations from Ulster to America; the first, mainly Presbyterian migration in the 18th century, and then the later, mainly Catholic migration in the 19th century. The NITB also produces a guide detailing the centres where the Allied Forces were based in Northern Ireland during the Second World War.

Stretching back into the myths and legends of Ulster as a place of importance is **Navan Fort** (*Emain Macha*) near Armagh, the capital of the Kings of Ulster from 600 BC. It is a pleasant walk to the grassy hill fort, and the Visitor Centre, close by, uses the latest technology to bring those far off times to life. The **Planetarium** in Armagh is of great interest, with its insight into the workings of the universe and hands-on computers in the Hall of Astronomy.

The Visitor Centre at **Glenveagh National Park**, Co. Donegal is also excellent, mixing history and natural history in a stimulating way. **The Tower** in Derry is an award-winning museum which details the intricate and fascinating history of the city and county. The scene is set by the giant cannon in the entrance.

Other worthwhile sojourns can be spent in **Enniskillen Castle Museum**, **Monaghan County Museum**, and the **Armagh County Museum** with its pleasant old-fashioned glass cases. The **Ulster Museum** in Belfast has a splendid collection of Irish antiquities, a notable art section, costume, fine silver and glass, and an area devoted to natural history. Finally, a small private museum, the **Carrothers Family Heritage Museum** near Lisbellow in Co. Fermanagh presents a very intimate history of a family whose lives were touched by the momentous events of the First World War, and the natural life of the world around them. The collection includes newspapers, letters from the front, birds' eggs and fossils.

The Fairy People

The Fairy People, or *Daoine Sidhe*, are a rich part of Irish folklore. According to peasant belief, they are fallen angels who are not good enough to be saved and not bad enough to languish in Hell. Perhaps they are the gods of the Earth, as it is written in the *Book of Armagh*; or the pagan gods of Ireland, the *Tuatha de Danaan*, who may also have been a race of invaders whose origins are lost in the mists of time. Antiquarians have different theories but, whatever they surmise, these fairy people persist in the popular imagination; they and their characteristics have been kept alive in tradition and myth.

The Fairy People are quickly offended, and must always be referred to as the 'Gentry' or the 'Good People'. They are also easily pleased, and will keep misfortune from your door if you leave them a bowl of milk on the window-sill overnight. Their evil seems to be without malice, and their chief occupations are feasting, fighting, making love and playing or listening to beautiful music. The only hardworking person amongst them is the leprechaun, who is kept busy making the shoes they wear out with their dancing. It is said that many of the beautiful tunes of Ireland are theirs, remembered by mortal eavesdroppers. The story is that Carolan, the last of the great Irish bards, slept on a rath which, like the many prehistoric standing stones in Ireland, had become a fairy place in folk tradition, and forever after the fairy music ran in his head and made him the great musician he was. Some of the individual fairy types are not very pleasant, and here are brief descriptions of a few.

The banshee, from *bean sidhe*, is a woman fairy or attendant spirit who follows the old families, and wails before a death. The keen, the funeral cry of the peasantry, is said to be an imitation of her cry. An omen which sometimes accompanies the old woman is an immense black coach, carrying a coffin and drawn by headless riders.

The leprechaun, or fairy shoemaker, is solitary, old and bad-tempered; the practical joker amongst the 'Good People'. He is very rich because of his trade, and buries his pots of gold at the end of rainbows. He also takes many treasure crocks, buried in times of war, for his own. Many believe he is the dé Danaan god Lugh, the god of arts and crafts, who degenerated in popular lore into the leprechaun.

The leanhaun shee, or fairy mistress, longs for the love of mortal men. If they refuse, she must be their slave; if they consent, they are hers, and can only escape by finding another to take their place. The fairy lives on their life, and they waste away, but death is no escape. She has become identified in political song and verse with the Gaelic Muse, for she gives inspiration to those whom she persecutes.

The Pook seems to be an animal spirit. Some authorities have linked it with a he-goat, from *púca* or *poc*, the Gaelic for goat. Others maintain it is a forefather of Shakespeare's Puck in *A Midsummer Night's Dream*. It lives in solitary mountain places and old ruins, and is of a nightmarish aspect. It is a November spirit, and often assumes the form of a stallion. The horse comes out of the water and is easy to tame if you can only keep him from the sight of water. If you cannot, he will plunge in with his rider and tear him to pieces at the bottom.

Writing and the Visual Arts

Patrick Kavanagh, the poet from County Monaghan who could phrase things so aptly, defined parochialism and provincialism as opposites: 'The provincial has no mind of his own: he does not trust what his eyes see until he has heard what the metropolis...has to say on any subject... The parochial mentality, on the other hand, is never in any doubt about the social and artistic validity of his parish. All great civilisations are based on parochialism—Greek, Israelite, English.'

All the best in Ulster painting and writing is based on this parochialism or, as Seamus Heaney calls it, 'the sense of place'. The best poets writing in Ulster today have a wonderful 'sense of place' in their depiction of its countryside and its people with all their prejudices and weaknesses as well as their strengths. Sam Hanna Bell, who writes with such love and understanding about the people of Co. Down and the historical forces that have shaped Ulster, conveys this sense of place in his novels. Other novelists to enjoy are Colin Bateman, Shan Bullock, who wrote so evocatively of Co. Fermanagh; and the writings of Patrick Kavanagh, Bernard McLaverty, William Carleton and Anne Crone, whose novel *Bridie Steen* may haunt you for ever. Amongst contemporary poets try Seamus Heaney, John Hewitt, Paul Muldoon and Maeve McCuckian. These are just some suggestions for you to explore the literature more deeply and to gain a sense of the richness of Ulster through the imagination and sheer ability which characterizes the Irish writer.

The visual arts in Ulster are also very rewarding. The Ulster Museum has some fine paintings, and if in Armagh you should try to visit the museum there which has a good collection. Works by Ulster artists are memorable, especially those of Colin Middleton and John Luke. In Co. Donegal there is an excellent small collection of art at the Glebe Gallery, Churchill; it is not an exhibition of Ulster Art, but it has some of the best work of Derek Hill, who bequeathed his collection to the Irish nation and who has been painting in Donegal for the last 40 years. The leading contemporary artists in Ulster are Basil Blackshaw, T. P. Flanagan and Tom Carr; they all paint wonderfully rich landscapes whose colours evoke their deep feelings for their countryside. James MacIntyre paints evocative pictures of a rural way of life: ricks of hay being made, a woman feeding her hens—an Ulster which is still there but which now has to be searched out. Other names to look out for in galleries are Neil Shawcross, Jack Packenham, Malcolm Bennett, Rita Duffy, Catherine Harper and Barbara Freeman. Make sure you pick up a copy of *Artslink*, an excellent calendar of what is happening in the arts month by month.

The Water Gate, Enniskillen

County Fermanagh

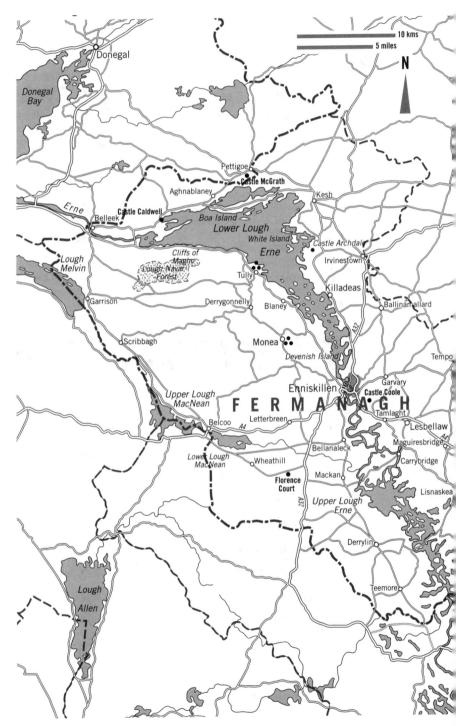

County Fermanagh

Omagh

Clabby

npo

Brookeborough

Eshnadeelada

snaskea

Derrynawilt

Donagh

Newtownbutler

Crom Estate

This is the lakeland of Ireland, bounded with limestone mountains in the south-west and scattered with drumlins which speckle the lakes with islands. A third of the county is under water: the lake system of the Erne with its mass of lakelets in the upper lough, and the great boomerang of Lower Lough Erne. Then there are the two Lough MacNeans in their mountain fastness, which together with the county's share of Lough Melvin have until recently discouraged incoming populations, so it is a place of long-lasting traditions and folk-lore. Even today, few strangers settle in this area, although the lakes attract summer visitors.

The countryside in which these beautiful lakes are scattered is mostly composed of little rushy farms where sheep and cattle graze. The higher ground is covered in hazel scrub, whilst in the limestone upland to the western edge of the country the soil is so poor that natural species have survived undisturbed by the tractor or fertilizers of the farmer. There are some lovely ash woods at Hanging Rock and Marble Arch. Here too are the famous Marble Arch Caves on Cuilcagh Mountain, which you can explore with a guide. The county also has two exquisite Georgian mansions under the care of the National Trust—Castle Coole and Florence Court. The coarse fishing is legendary, and every year in May fishermen have great fun at the Ulster Fishing Festival, which spreads events all over the myriad lakes. You can explore the lakes by chartering a cabin cruiser and there are plenty of opportunities for water-skiing. The waterways of the upper and lower Erne are now connected to the great waterway of the Shannon by the Ballyconnell and Ballinamore canal, which passes through some very unspoilt scenery.

Sports and Activities

Cruising: The area comprises over 300 square miles (800 sq km) of island-studded lakes and rivers, with over 70 free jetty-moorings and only one lock. Many companies rent out cruisers by the day or week. Prices range from £380 a week for a four-berth cruiser in the low season and £900 for an eight-berth in the high season. They welcome complete novices and give free lessons on how to handle boats. You can get a complete list from the tourist office in Wellington Road, Enniskillen, © (028) 6632 3110. Try the Carrybridge Boat Company, Lisbellaw, © (028) 6638 7034, or Manor House Marine, Killadeas, © (028) 6862 8100.

Erincurrach Cruising, at Blaney, Enniskillen, operates a one-way boat rental between the Erne and the Shannon, © (028) 6864 1737.

Boat Tours: *The Kestrel* leaves from the Round O Quay in Enniskillen for cruises round the islands every day from July to September, and includes a stop at Devenish Island. It is possible to hire the Kestrel for private groups from £100. You could also try *Inishcruiser*, Killadeas, © (028) 6862 8550, which is equipped with a bar and facilities for up to 60 people. Boats over 10hp must be registered with the Portora Locks Warden. The Share Centre, Lisnaskea, organizes tours of Upper Lough Erne on a powered Viking Longship, Easter–Sept, © (028) 6772 2122. Ferry to White Island from Castle Archdale (off the B82) every day except Monday, June–Sept 10am–7pm, Sunday 2–7pm. Ferry to Devenish Island from Troy point, 3 miles north of Enniskillen (junction of A32/B82), April–Sept, Tues–Sat 10–7, Sunday 2–7.

Water-skiing and canoeing: Through the cruiser-hire companies listed above, or The Water Sport Centre, Drumrush Lodge, Kesh, © (028) 6863 1578, or Lakeland Canoe Centre, Enniskillen, © (028) 6863 24250.

History

The history of this county is similar to that of the rest of Ulster. The Maguires were the chief Gaelic family here before the plantation. In the 17th century, Scottish undertakers arrived to provide a population loyal to the English crown. Many grand houses were built by the big landowners in the 18th century (two of these are mentioned above).

Fermanagh has a vast and largely unrecorded ancient history, which you will get glimpses of through the beautiful carvings and stone statues still to be seen in graveyards and the Enniskillen Museum.

Those of you of a reflective turn of mind will be fascinated by the pagan idols; their impassive stone heads are to be found on the islands and secret peninsulas of Lough Erne. Usually they are mixed up with the gravestones of the newer religion, Christianity. The two seem to mingle quite happily. There are many remains of Christian hermitages, and on Devenish Island on Lough Erne is a superb collection of ecclesiastical ruins dating from the 6th century. The headlands of the loughs are wooded and often enough their interest is enhanced by the ruins of Plantation castles from the 17th century. This county and the town of Enniskillen has unfortunately suffered greatly since the 'Troubles' started in 1969: many lone Protestant farmers have

Birdwatching: The waterways are the home of kingfishers and great crested grebes. The Erne basin is an important breeding ground for redshank, snipe, lapwing and curlew. Contact Eddie McGovern, Fermanagh District Council TIC, Wellington Road, Enniskillen, ✆ (028) 6632 3110.

Fishing: The Fermanagh lakelands are renowned for their coarse fishing. Brown trout and salmon fishing are also excellent in the rivers and loughs. Lough Melvin is notable for three unusual species of trout: the gillaroo, the sonaghan and the ferox. The Lakeland Visitor Centre in Enniskillen stocks permits, licences and a useful booklet on local waters, ✆ (028) 6632 3110. Lough Melvin Holiday Centre, Garrison, ✆ (028) 6865 8142, specializes in angling holidays.

Bicycle Holidays: Kingfisher Cycle Trail tour, ✆ (028) 6632 0121, ✉ (028) 6632 5511: 30–40 mile rides.

Golf: Enniskillen Golf Club in Castle Coole Estate, ✆ (028) 6632 5250. Castle Hume Golf Club, Enniskillen, ✆ (028) 6632 7077.

Horse Riding: Drumhoney Stables, Lisnarick, ✆ (028) 6632 1892. Letterview Riding Centre, Leggs, Belleek, ✆ (028) 6865 8163.

Riding Holidays: Necarne Castle, Irvinestown, ✆ (028) 6862 1919, ✉ (028) 6862 8382. Weekend or weekly riding breaks in this internationally recognized equestrian park.

Pot-holing: Marble Arch Caves, Florencecourt, ✆ (028) 6634 8855.

Belleek Visitor Centre: 20-minute guided tour of the pottery, ✆ (028) 6665 8501, ✉ (028) 6665 8625.

been murdered by the IRA, and British soldiers ambushed on the narrow country roads which follow the curves of the lakesides. The most notable tragedy was an IRA bomb blast which killed 11 people at the Enniskillen cenotaph on Remembrance Sunday in 1987.

Fermanagh has never been a rich county. Its population has always lived by farming, fishing and, nowadays, tourism. The local people welcome tourists.

Getting There and Around

By air: From Belfast International Airport.

By rail: There is no train service.

By bus: Six Ulsterbus express buses run daily from Belfast to Enniskillen; two from Dublin. Good local bus links from Enniskillen to country areas. Enniskillen bus station, ✆ (028) 6632 2633.

By car: Car hire from Lochside Garage, Tempo Road, Enniskillen, ✆ (028) 6632 4366.

By bike: Bicycle hire from Cycle Ops, Mantlin Road, Kesh, ✆ (028) 6863 1850; Lakeland Canoe Centre, Castle Island, ✆ (028) 6863 2456.

Enniskillen, Lakeland Visitor Centre, Wellington Road, ✆ (028) 6632 3110.

There are lots of tiny festivals and sporting events in villages thoughout the summer. Ask at the tourist office. The following are amongst the most interesting:

May: Coarse fishing festival.

June: Fermanagh County Fleadh.

August: Fishing Festival on Lough Melvin, based at Garrison. West Ulster Hound Show and Drag Hunt, Lisbellaw.

October: Antique and Fine Art Fair, Enniskillen.

Enniskillen and Around

Enniskillen is built on a bridge of land between Upper and Lower Lough Erne, and at first sight the medieval conglomeration of town and castle makes you think this is a very ancient town, although modern shops, supermarkets and offices soon spoil the illusion. Before the plantation, the Maguires held sway over this lakeland area and used it as the centre for their watery dominions. Enniskillen's name comes from Cathleen, one of the women warriors of the Fomorian invaders. Her husband Balor was head of a pirate gang quartered on the rock island of Tory, off the Donegal coast. He later resurfaced as the Celtic god of darkness, whose one eye could strike you dead (*see* **Old Gods and Heroes**, p.245). Enniskillen is famous for its home regiments (the Air of the Inniskillings became the tune of 'The Star Spangled Banner'), so you might say that there is a certain fighting tradition down here. Visit the **County Museum** (*open all year, Tues–Fri, 10–5; Sat–Mon, 10–1; adm;* ✆ *(028) 6632 5000*), which is housed in Maguire's Keep, a 15th-century building. Attached to it is the **Water Gate**, a fairytale building with towers and fluttering standards. The museum is one of the best and friendliest of local museums. It displays some of the strange head sculptures found in the locality, and explains the history of Fermanagh from the Middle Stone Age to the end of the Early-Christian period. There is also an audio-visual display on the Maguires of Fermanagh. British regiment

Band stand, Enniskillen

enthusiasts will be interested in the soldiering relics of the Royal Inniskilling Fusiliers which can be seen in the same building.

You should take a walk through the centre of Enniskillen, which is rather a jumble. The winding main street takes on about six names during its course; and you might be impressed enough by the local souvenir brooches made from fishing flies to buy one of these unusual ornaments. This is a handy place to buy the delicate cream-coloured Belleek china, as the town which produces it sometimes runs low on stocks. In the old **Buttermarket** you can buy a variety of hand-crafted goods. There are plenty of fishing tackle and bait shops, and some good bakeries for sandwich material. The **Church of Ireland cathedral** dates from the mid-17th century, but was extensively remodelled in the 19th century. In the chancel and choir hang the colours of the Royal Inniskilling Fusiliers together with the pennons of the Inniskilling Dragoons, which were raised in the town.

Close by is St Michael's Catholic Church, which was built in 1875 to plans by John O'Neill, although the spire (designed by the original architect) dates from 1992. Inside are some fine paintings depicting scenes from the life of Christ. Four are by the Scottish artist Charles Russell (1852–1910), whilst the Holy Family scene is by Michael Joseph Healy (1873–1941).

For a good view of the town and surrounding area, you could climb the 108 steps to the top of the **Cole Monument** (*open May–Sept, daily 2–6; adm*). It was built between 1845 and 1857 in Forthill Park at the eastern end of town (Sir Galbraith Lowry Cole was a distinguished general and politician).

Just outside Enniskillen to the northwest is the **Portora Royal School**, founded in 1608. As a public school it had amongst its more famous pupils Oscar Wilde. About 1¼ miles (2.4km) southeast of the town on the main Belfast to Enniskillen road (A4) is **Castle Coole** (*open daily April & Sept on weekends and bank holidays 1–6; May–Aug Fri–Wed 1–6; open daily at Easter; adm; ✆ (028) 6632 2690*), an assured and beautiful neoclassical house which has recently been carefully restored by the National Trust. This entailed replacing the Portland stone blocks of the façade. It was built between 1790 and 1797 with an agreeably simple symmetry, and the main block with colonnaded wings was designed by James Wyatt. Inside, 18th-century furniture is still in the rooms for which it was made. English plasterer Joseph Ross, who had worked for Adam at Syon and Harewood, made the long journey to supervise the creation of the ceilings. The building accounts of the house survive, and, since the cost of the construction exceeded the estimates, restraint may have been exercised in the decoration, keeping it elegant but simple. In the surrounding parkland there is a lake which has a very long-established colony of greylag geese. The saying is that if they leave Castle Coole, so will the Lowry-Corrys, Earls of Belmore, whose seat it is.

The Islands in Lower Lough Erne

Lower Lough Erne stretches in a broad arc with a pattern of 97 islands, with Belleek at one end and Enniskillen at the other. Ripe for exploration, Lough Erne's scattered islets hold many treasures. You should not miss **Devenish**. Here St Molaise founded a monastic community in the 6th century, which was probably a more than usually perilous venture in that remote water kingdom, where paganism persisted long after Christian practices had taken hold in more accessible parts. However, there is a legend which credits these parts with a visitation by a character from the Old Testament, for the prophet Jeremiah is said to have his grave in the waters of Lough Erne. His daughter was married to the son of a high king of Ireland, and she brought as her dowry the Stone of Destiny, the coronation stone of Scone, the same stone that Fergus, who also cropped up in County Antrim (*see* p.142) took to Scotland. This story is almost as good as the variation of the Old Testament flood story recounted by the 9th-century cleric annalists, in which Beith, Noah's grandson, landed in Ireland with a whole ark of beautiful women—which is said to account for the comeliness of all Irish women today! Devenish island has a complete round tower, with an elaborately decorated cornice. Another ruin on the island incorporating some outstanding decoration is the 12th-century Augustinian **Abbey of St Mary**. Here St Molaise rested from his labours, listening spellbound to bird song which, it was said, was the Holy Spirit communicating. The reverie lasted a hundred years, and when he looked around after that interval this abbey had been built. You will find it a few miles outside Enniskillen off the main road to Omagh (A32). For transport to the island *see* 'Sports and Activities', p.96.

Another island with more tangible supernatural associations is **White Island**, in Castle Archdale Bay, north of Enniskillen, famous for its eerie statues. All eight of them are lined up in a row against the wall of a 12th-century church. Like many of the sculptures found in Fermanagh and nearby districts, there is a pagan quality about these objects. There are conflicting theories about just what the figures represent. Possibly they are of Christian origin employing archaic pre-Christian styles, dating between the 7th and 10th centuries. It is sometimes possible to hire a boat from **Castle Archdale** to **Inismacsaint**, a tiny island which has an ancient cross, possibly dating from a 6th-century monastery of which nothing remains, although there is a romantic ruin of a medieval church.

Boa Island, joined to the mainland by a bridge at each end, is the largest of the islands. Its name comes from *Badhbha*, war goddess of the Ulster Celts, and traditionally it remained the centre of the Druidic cult long after Christianity had arrived in Ireland. In the old cemetery, **Caldragh**, at the west end of the island, there is a strange 'Janus' figure with a face on each side. Such figures (several have been found in the Fermanagh area and in Cavan) are thought to have had ritual significance; a hollow in the figure's head may have held sacrificial blood. To find it, follow the A47 past the village of Kesh for about 5 miles (8km). Look for an insignificant signpost to Caldragh on the main road, then climb over a gate and through a field to this half-forgotten graveyard, full of bluebells in the spring.

The Northern Shore of Lough Erne

Killadeas is a fishing village looking on to Lough Erne. In the graveyard of the chapel there are some ancient, sculptured stones. One called the Bishop's Stone depicts a man with a crozier and bell. It is certainly pre-Norman. There is also a carved stone figure in the churchyard which dates from the 9th century. The country round the lough is full of the dips and hollows of the glacial-drift drumlins. Because of flooding problems in former years, you will notice few waterside town settlements although there are plenty of rushes, a source of thatching material. Just beyond the lough is **Castle Archdale Country Park** (*open from early morning till dusk*) on the B82. It is an old demesne now opened up for walking in the beautiful forest along nature trails, and for camping, boating and fishing. There is a marina, café, shop and an exhibition centre (*open Tues–Sun, June–Sept*). The old castle is a pretty ruin. The ferry to White Island goes from here. From the jetty you overlook **White Island**

and **Davy's Island**; it is a good place for setting off by boat to some of the nature reserve islands. Perhaps the loveliest aspect of this part of the shore is the flowers that decorate the water's edge.

Kesh is a busy little fishing village on the A35 where you can hire cruise boats. It is possible to learn the old skills of spinning and weaving at Ardress, near Kesh. There is a boat-building industry here specializing in traditional broad-beamed eel boats, as this is a centre for eels (though subsidiary to Lough Neagh). From Kesh you can make your way to the pretty little island of **Lustybeg**, which has holiday chalets for hire. Another 'Janus' figure was discovered here, and is now in the Enniskillen Museum. Following the curve of the shoreline west you reach **Pettigo**, which is just in County Donegal, with newer houses straggling on and over the border into Fermanagh. Pettigo is an angling village which has grown up by the River Termon about a mile from where it flows into Lough Erne. It was on the pilgrims' route to Lough Derg, which lies in Donegal about 4 miles (6km) away, so it is busy in summer. The ruins of the 17th-century **Castle Magrath**, with its keep and circular towers at the corners, are on the outskirts of the village, next to the rectory. The B136 joins up with the A47 here and leads you to **Castle Caldwell**, which is situated on a wooded peninsula jutting out into the lough—a romantic situation for a romantic and enterprising family. One of the Caldwells had a barge on which music used to be played for his pleasure. Unfortunately, a fiddler over-balanced on one of these occasions and was drowned. You can see his fiddle-shaped monument with its warning:

> *On firm land only exercise your skill*
> *There you may play and safely drink your fill.*

In the 19th century the Caldwells promoted the original porcelain industry at nearby Belleek, using clay found on their estate. This clay has a high feldspar content, which gives this delicate china its texture and robustness. Now their castle lies in ruins. Visitors can wander in their gardens above the shore, admiring the view that in 1776 made Arthur Young, the agriculturalist, exclaim that there was 'shelter, prospect, wood and water here in perfection'. You can use the special wildfowl hides to watch the plentiful ducks, geese and other birds; these grounds also have the largest breeding colony of black scooters in the British Isles.

Further up the River Erne, at **Belleek** you reach another border village. For anglers there's a joky saying that you can hook a salmon in the Republic and land it in Northern Ireland. But it's more famous for its distinctive lustreware, which is produced as attractive ornaments rather than anything utilitarian. The 19th-century **pottery** is very attractive; it has a small museum, guided tours and a video presentation. Also in Belleek is an exhibition centre detailing the history of Lough Erne through exhibits and video (*open March–Oct, daily 10–6; adm;* © *(028) 6865 8866*).

The Southern Shore of Lough Erne

On your way along the southern shore, on the A46, the road hugs the waterline, for limestone cliffs loom overhead, rising to the height of 2,984ft (909m) at Magho. You may be tempted to venture above the lough and see how the countryside looks from the mountainous and wooded roads around Lough Navar. To visit the forest, go inland via Derrygonnelly on the B81, which is off the A46. From the **Lough Navar Forest** viewpoint you can see the splendid sight of the lough spread out in front of you, with the hills of Donegal in the distance, and the ranges of Tyrone, Sligo and Leitrim in a grand panorama. The forest entrance, opposite Correl Glen, is about 5 miles (8km) west of Derrygonnelly. It takes you on a 7-mile (11km) scenic road which is full of nature trails and little lakes, and has a camp site. The Ulster Way footpath runs through the forest up to a height of 1,000ft, and runs down to Belcoo, between Upper and Lower Lough MacNean. This mountainous area is full of caves.

The plateau on the southern shore is covered with forest lands, and behind them are the Cuilcagh Mountains rising to the south. If you stick to the loughside you will pass the plantation-era **Tully Castle** (*open April–Sept, 10–7; rest of year 2–7; adm*) and, further inland towards the south, a better-preserved castle at **Monea** (*free access always*). Both show the Scottish style brought to this country by Scottish settlers. Monea was built in 1618 by Malcolm Hamilton, a rector of Devenish Island. The castle front shows two circular towers which are square on the top storey, and the crow-stepped gables add to its Scottish air.

Up into the Western Mountains

For spectacular sights, nature has more on her side than architecture, so head towards the mountains in the west. You can take winding, confusing roads cross-country from Monea, but for a simpler route take Enniskillen as a starting point and follow the A4.

At **Belcoo** you reach a village lost in the mountains, situated on a narrow strip of land separating the two Lough MacNeans. In this place patterns (pilgrimages) to the St Patrick's Well are held on Bilberry Sunday, the last Sunday in July—the date of the Celtic *Lughnasa* or festival of fertility, a tradition which surely indicates the chain of pagan and Christian practices which have lingered on here longer than anywhere else and which gave the playwright Brian Friel the name for his highly successful play *Dancing at Lughnasa.*

If you go back by **Lower Lough MacNean** you will see the **Hanging Rock** from the minor road which goes to Blacklion across the border. Limestone has endowed this place with characteristic caverns. They stretch in a sort of underground labyrinth through the Cuilcagh Mountains, and some remain to be explored. Do not go pot-holing by yourself; apart from anything else, streams run into the caverns. You can see this for yourself from the scenic Marlbank loop road (unnumbered but signposted off the A4 Enniskillen–Sligo road), which takes you round from Florence Court to Lower Lough MacNean where the Sruh Croppa stream disappears into a crevice called the Cat's Hole. (***Marble Arch Show Caves** are open daily March–Sept from 10am, weather permitting; last tour 4.30pm; adm exp. Call ahead before setting out, © (028) 6634 8855.*). A 1¼-hour tour includes an underground boat trip. Take a jumper and flat shoes.

The wooded demesne of **Florence Court** (*open April–Sept, Sat–Sun 1–6; May–Aug, daily except Tues 1–6; grounds open all year, 10–7; adm; © (028) 6634 8249*) is situated under the steep mountain of Benaughlin. This means 'Peak of the Horse' in Gaelic, and the white limestone showing through the scree at the foot of the eastern cliff did indeed once portray the outline of a horse, though it is getting more and more difficult to distinguish. Florence Court, home of the Coles, earls of Enniskillen, is about 8 miles (13km) southwest of the town they helped to fortify in Plantation times, on the A4 and A32 Swanlibar road. Built in the mid-18th century for Lord Mountflorence, sadly the house has suffered fire damage, but there is still some fine rococo plasterwork. It is beautifully situated in woodland with views across to the Cuilcagh Mountains. In the gardens is the original Florence Court yew, from whose seedlings grew *Taxus baccata fastigiata*, now found all over the world.

Upper Lough Erne

Upper Lough Erne and the maze of waters from the Erne river system provide quite a challenge for the explorer, so arm yourself with a good map. This area bridges the less water-strewn area of east Fermanagh whose pretty towns you may pass through. Some bear names of founder planter families. **Brookeborough** is on the A4, near the home of the Brooke family, who were prominent in Northern Irish affairs. Basil, the first Viscount Brookeborough (1888–1973), was Prime Minister of Northern Ireland—remembered, perhaps unfairly, for his *laager* mentality towards Roman Catholics. The town of **Maguiresbridge** is named after the reigning chieftains, who were deposed by the planters.

This area is rich in folk tradition; you might meet someone with the secret of a cure, both for animal and human ailments. If you are interested in the distinctive sculptures you may have seen at the Enniskillen Museum or elsewhere, go and search out **Tamlaght Bay** near Lisbellaw on the A4, where at **Derrybrusk Old Church** you can see some more strange carved heads on a wall. At nearby **Aghalurcher Churchyard**, near Lisnaskea off the A34, you can see gravestones carved with what seems to be a rather macabre funerary motif, typically found in Fermanagh: the skull and crossbones. **The Crom Estate** (*open Easter–end Sept, daily 2–6; car park fee*) on the shores of Upper Lough Erne is a huge acreage of woodland, parkland and wetland. It is under the protection of the National Trust and is an important nature conservation area. You approach it on a minor road off the A34 in Newtownbutler. **Lisnaskea**, also on the A34, is rather an interesting market town with a restored market cross whose ancient shaft has fine carving. In the middle of the town is a ruined 17th-century castle built by Sir James Balfour, which was burnt down in the 19th century. On the main street is a folk-life display at the library (*open Mon, Tues and Fri, 9.15–5; Wed, 9.15–7.30; Sat, 9.15–12.30; adm free*). A cruise boat leaves the jetty here for 1½-hour tours of Upper Lough Erne (*see* p.96).

The upper reaches of Lough Erne are scattered with 58 little 'islands'. Meandering streams cut through the marshy wetlands, creating these prettily named islands which are really tiny districts or townlands, not islands at all, for most of them are easy to walk and drive around. Some of them are inhabited, though on an increasingly part-time basis. You need to hire a boat to explore them properly. One sad story illustrates the difficulties associated with island living even in these easier days: a postman living on Inishturk Island was frozen to death when his boat was trapped in ice during the hard winter of 1961. **Cleenish Island** can be reached from Bellanaleck on the A509 by a bridge. There are some remarkable carved headstones in the graveyard. Even more interesting is the collection of carved slabs on **Inishkeen**, accessible by causeway from Killyhevlin, which is just off the Dublin Road (A4) on the outskirts of Enniskillen. **Belle Isle** is a townland (it is hardly discernible as an island any more, being linked to the mainland by roads), which claims to be the spot where the *Annals of Ulster* were compiled in the 15th century by Cathal MacManus, Dean of Lough Erne. **Galloon Island** is large, with another ancient graveyard where you may, if you persevere, discern the curious carvings on the 9th- or 10th-century cross shafts which depict a man hanging upside down.

Some think this might be Judas Iscariot, or else St Peter. There is a marina at **Bellanaleck** and **Carrybridge**, near Lisbellaw, where it is possible to hire cruisers and rowing boats with which to explore this secret wetland area, where cattle enjoy grazing the distinctive grasses and there is plenty of coarse fishing. If you wish to walk about here, be sure to wear long wellington boots. A mile west of **Lisbellaw**, on Carrybridge Road, Tamlaght, is a small private **museum** (✆ *(028) 6638 7278; adm*) with exhibits collected by the **Carrothers** family. Birds' eggs, fossils, newspapers and letters conjure up a lost world.

Shopping

Crafts: Belleek china, fishing-fly brooches and Irish lace in giftshops in Enniskillen main street. Also at the Belleek Visitor Centre in Belleek itself. Ardess Craft Centre, Kesh, sells a range of local pottery, woven rugs and other crafts. Enniskillen Craft and Design Centre, The Buttermarket, Down Street, ✆ (028) 6632 4499.

Crystal: Main Street, Belleek. Glasses, vases and lamps of handcut lead crystal.

Pottery: Ann McNulty Pottery, Enniskillen Enterprise Centre, Down Street, Enniskillen.

Antiques: Forge Antiques, Circular Rd, Lisbellaw.

Where to Stay

Enniskillen

Killyhevlin Hotel, Dublin Road, ✆ (028) 6632 3481, 🖷 (028) 6632 4726 (*expensive*). Comfortable modern hotel overlooking its own little lake. The bar is a great chatting place for fishermen. Lord and Lady Anthony Hamilton, **Killyreagh**, Tamlaght, ✆ (028) 6638 7221 (*moderate*). Comfortable 19th-century country house. Fishing, riding and tennis arranged. **Dromard House**, Dromard, Tamlaght, ✆ (028) 6638 7250 (*moderate*). Comfortable rooms in converted stable loft. **Riverside Farm**, Mrs Fawcett, Gortadrehid, Culkey, ✆ (028) 6632 2725 (*inexpensive*). The River Sillies at the bottom of the farm holds the record for coarse fishing. Comfortable and friendly. **Corrigans Shore**, Clonatrig, Bellanaleck, ✆ (028) 6634 8572 (*inexpensive*).

North Fermanagh

Tempo Manor, Tempo, ✆ (028) 8954 1450, 🖷 (028) 8954 1202 (*expensive*). Victorian Manor house overlooking gardens and lakes. Mr A. Stuart, **Jamestown House**, Magheracross, near Ballinamallard, ✆ (028) 6638 8209, 🖷 (028) 6638 8322 (*moderate*). A gem of a Georgian house. Superb cooking and lots to do all around—water-skiing, fishing, riding.

Lakeview House, Drum Crow, Blaney, ✆ (028) 6864 1263 (*moderate*). Grade A farmhouse with lough view. **The Cedars**, Castle Archdale, Irvinestown, ✆/🖷 (028) 6772 1493 (*moderate*). Grade A guest house. Mrs Pendry, **Ardess House**, Kesh, ✆ (028) 6863 1267 (*inexpensive*). Wholefood cooking. Courses run at the craft centre in the grounds. **Castle Archdale Youth Hostel**, Irvinestown, ✆/🖷 (028)

6862 8118 (*inexpensive*). Family rooms and group accommodation in a historic listed building.

South Fermanagh

Lanesborough Arms, High Street, Newtownbulter, ✆ (028) 6773 4488, 🖷 (028) 6773 8049 (*moderate*). Refurbished 18th-century town house. **Tullyhona House**, Marble Arch Road, Florence Court, ✆ (028) 6634 8452 (*inexpensive*). Nice old house, set in its own grounds beside Upper Lough Erne. Fine home-cooking.

self-catering

The following are for rent by the week:

Lusty Beg Island Chalets, Boa Island, ✆ (028) 6863 2032. Sleep 6; from £620 high season. **Rose Cottage**, a National Trust cottage on Florence Court Demesne, ✆ (028) 6634 8249. £185 low season. **Crom Cottages**, Crom Estate (National Trust) near Lisnaskea, ✆ (028) 6773 81118 or NT Central Reservations, ✆ (01225) 791199. Seven converted cottages available. **Belle Isle Estate Cottages**, Lisbellaw. Traditional cottages—garden cottage, coach house and bridge house—on lovely estate at the northern end of Upper Lough Erne. Sleep 4/6; from £200 per week low season. Contact Rural Cottage Holidays (*see* below) or Mr C Plunket, ✆ (028) 6638 7231, 🖷 (028) 6638 7261. **Innish Beg Cottages**, Innish Beg, Blaney, Derrygonnelly, ✆/🖷 (028) 6864 1525. Five cottages with views over Lower Lough Erne. Rowing boat for hire and private shoreline. £220/£450 per week high season. **Shannon-Erne Luxury Cottages**, Teemore. Six traditional-style cottages on the banks of the canal. Sleep 4. From £225 per week; through Rural Cottage Holidays, Central Booking Office, ✆ (028) 9024 1100, 🖷 (028) 9024 1198.

Eating Out

Enniskillen

Franco's Pizzeria, Queen Elizabeth Road, ✆ (028) 6632 4424 (*moderate*). Food includes pasta, pizza and fish. **Blakes of the Hollow**, 6 Church Street, ✆ (028) 6632 2143 (*inexpensive*). Pub offering good lunches. Live traditional music some nights. **Melvin House and Bar**, 1 Townhall Street, ✆ (028) 6632 2040 (*inexpensive*). Good lunches. **Crow's Nest**, 12 High Street, ✆ (028) 6632 5252 (*inexpensive*). Serves oysters, cottage pie, ham.

North Fermanagh

The Cedars, Castle Archdale, Drumall, Lisnarick, ✆ (028) 6862 1493 (*moderate*). Excellent steaks. **Hollander**, 5 Main Street, Irvinestown, ✆ (028) 6862 1231 (*moderate*). **Fiddlestone Bar**, Belleek; sandwiches. **Florence Court House**, ✆ (028) 6634 8249 (*inexpensive*). Lunch only: quiche, stews, wheaten bread.

South Fermanagh

The Sheelin, Bellanaleck, ✆ (028) 6634 8232 (*moderate*). Excellent for lunch or dinner. A traditional cottage with climbing roses round the door. Delicious and original menu. **Le Bistro**, Ernside Centre. ✆ (028) 6632 6954 (*moderate*). **Wild Duck Inn**, Lisbellaw, ✆ (028) 6638 7258 (*inexpensive*). Pub grub.

Entertainment and Nightlife

Theatre: Ardhowen Theatre, Enniskillen, ✆ (028) 6632 5400.

Traditional music: Blakes of the Hollow, Church Street, Enniskillen.

Caledon court house

County Tyrone

County Tyrone

10 kms
5 miles

N

Sperrin Mountains

lenelly Valley   Sperrin
Cranagh

Owenkillew   Glenhull

Beaghmore
Stone Circles

Dunnamore

Creggan

Drum Manor
Forest Park   Cookstown

Carrickmore   A29

Pomeroy   Ardboe

The Rock   Lough

milecross   Stewartstown   Neagh

Donaghmore   Coalisland

Dungannon

Ballyreagh   A4

Ballygawley   Greystone   Blackwater   M1

Lurgan

Carnteel   Moy   Craigavon

Blackwater   A28   Portadown

Benburb

Caledon   Armagh

This is the heart of Ulster, the land called after *Eoghan* (Owen), one of the sons of High King Niall of the Nine Hostages, who lived in the 4th century AD and was the progenitor of the O'Neill dynasty. The least populated of the six counties, Tyrone is celebrated in many a poignant song by emigrant sons (some of whom found fame and fortune in America). The Sperrin mountains cover a large part of the north, the highest at 2,240ft (683m) being Sawel, which is on the border with County Londonderry. In these lonely hills locals have panned for gold for hundreds of years, and recently excitement has been generated by the discovery of large deposits of this precious metal. Lough Neagh forms Tyrone's eastern border for a few miles in the east, but the county's main attractions are its chattering burns, flora and fauna, and peaceful glens. It is a land of hillside, moorland and good fishing.

Only in the southeastern area is it well-wooded, and there is a much quoted tag about 'Tyrone among the bushes, where the Finn and Mourne run'. The land in this region is more fertile and well-planted with trees; the farmers here keep cattle as well as sheep. Many of the farmhouses are still of white-washed stone with gaily painted doorways. The linen industry is important at Moygashel, and there are many small businesses in the main towns, such as milling.

The plantation families have their traditions and big houses in the southeast too. Some of the loveliest, such as Caledon, are still occupied by their original families, whilst the most unusual, Killymoon Castle, was saved from ruin by a farmer who bought it for £100 in the 1920s. Neither of these houses is open to the public, but it is possible to stay in the grounds of another large Georgian mansion at Baronscourt, the home of the Duke of Abercorn. Here there is a golf course and coarse fishing, and water sports on Lough Catherine. There is fishing on the Rivers Mourne, Owenkillew, Camowen and Glenelly for brown trout and salmon. There is much to attract the walker and naturalist too, in the forests and moorland of the Sperrin Mountains.

Tyrone is an undiscovered county without the romance of Donegal or the repu-tation of the Antrim Coast, but it inspires pride and praise from its native dwellers. Tyrone people are well known for their music and their talent with language, both the spoken and written word; notice how many writers and poets come from this part of the world, the most notable being William Carleton, John Montague, Brian Friel and Flann O'Brien.

History

This region is rich in folklore and ancient ways. Its history lives on in the language: some of the local expressions recall the Gaelic, although it is no longer spoken, and a few turns of phrase will take you back to the days of Elizabeth I. For example, a 'boon' is a company of people in the house, to 'join' is to begin, to 'convoy' is to accompany, and 'diet' is the word for food.

County Tyrone's past is similar to that all over Ulster, and it can be well illustrated by concen-trating on the ownership of the lands and estate of Caledon, a small village close to the border with County Monaghan. This was O'Neill territory, and the natives fought vigorously against

the English forces from the mid-17th century on, but by the 18th century the region was planted with Scottish undertakers. The story of Captain William Hamilton is typical of that of many of the new landlords; a Cromwellian soldier and one of the Hamiltons from Haddington in East Lothian, William was granted the Caledon estate of Sir Phelim O'Neill after the Battle of Benburb in 1646. By 1775 the Hamilton line, which had intermarried with the Osserys—Earls of Ossery and Cork—had become very extravagant. As a result of the family's debts, the property was sold to a Derry merchant's son, James Alexander, who had acquired a vast fortune in the service of the East India Company. The most distinguished member of this family (which still owns the estate) was Viscount Alexander of Tunis.

The tenants and small farmers in this area are for the most part descended from Scottish Presbyterians, but in the hilly Sperrins there are still a good many Catholics—descendants of the ousted O'Neills and their septs.

Getting There and Around

By air: Belfast International Airport and Dublin Airport are about 70 and 86 miles (112 and 137km) from Omagh respectively.

By rail: There is no railway line running through County Tyrone. The nearest station is Portadown, ✆ (028) 3835 1422.

By bus: Ulsterbus maintains a good service to all parts of the county. Omagh bus station, ✆ (028) 8224 2711. Strabane bus station, ✆ (028) 7138 2393.

By car: Cars for hire from Johnston King Motors, 82 Derry Road, Omagh, ✆ (028) 8224 2788.

By bike: Conway Cycles, 1 Market Place, Omagh, ✆ (028) 8224 6195.

Sports and Activities

Fishing: For brown trout, sea trout and salmon on the River Blackwater, near Omagh, and on the Mourne River System which includes the Strule, Owenkillew and Glenelly. Licences from Foyle Fisheries Commission, Derry, or local fishing tackle shops. For the Ballinderry River, you need a Fisheries Conservancy Board game rod licence and permission (from tackle shops or tourist offices). Permits are available from tackle shops in Caledon, Cookstown, Omagh, Moy and Aughnacloy. Try the Strule, Oweneagh, Camowen and Owenkillew rivers for brown and sea trout.

Maps of fishing area and permits from Tyrone Angling Supplies, Bridge Street, Omagh. The Department of Agriculture, ✆ (028) 9052 3434, offers pike and perch fishing in Creeve Lough and White Lough, and brown trout fishing in Brantry Lough. Also pike fishing in lakes on Baronscourt Estate, ✆ (028) 8166 1683. Book well in advance.

Walking: In the valleys of the Glenelly, Owenreagh, Owenkillew and Camowen Rivers; in the 12 Sperrin forests, in particular Drum Manor, near Cookstown, and Gortin Glen Forest Park with its nature trails and wild deer. Other forest parks with nature trails: Favour Royal, Gollagh Woods, and Fardross Forest where you can see red squirrels. Riverside walks by Wellbrook Beetling Mill, near Cookstown.

The Ulster Way signposted walking trail goes through the Sperrins. For details and a map, write to the Sports Council, House of Sport, Upper Malone Road, Belfast, ✆ (028) 9038 1222. Walking Holidays in the Sperrins, contact ✆ (028) 7930 0050, ✉ (028) 7930 0009, *activities@Sperrins.iol.ie*. Walking Festival in the Sperrins in June. Call ✆ (028) 7188 73735 for more details.

Tourist Information

Cookstown, 48 Molesworth Street, ✆ (028) 8676 6727; open April–Oct.

Cranagh, Sperrin Heritage Centre, 274 Glenelly Road, ✆ (028) 8164 8142; open June–Sept.

Dungannon, Ballygawley Road, (028) 8776 7259; open all year.

Strabane, Abercorn Square, ✆ (028) 7188 3735; open April–Sept.

Omagh, 1 Market Street, ✆ (028) 8224 7831; open all year.

Festivals

May: Omagh *Feis* with Irish dancing and music.

Last week of July: Bilberry Sunday *Feis* with traditional music and dancing at Altadaven, 2 miles (3.2km) south of Favour Royal.

July: Clogher Valley Agricultural Show, Augher.

August–September: Sheepdog trials in Gortin.

Rough shooting: Over the Sperrin Mountains. Applications to Seskinore Game Farm, ✆ (028) 8284 1243. Also contact Ian Whiteside at Sperrin Sports, 112 Seskinore Rd, ✆ (028) 8284 0149, or Baronscourt Estate ✆ (028) 8166 1683. Book well in advance.

Clay Pigeon Shooting: Baronscourt Estate, ✆ (028) 8166 1683. Also Altglushan, Cappagh, ✆ (028) 8775 8201.

Pony-trekking: At Moy Riding School, 131 Derrycaw Road, Moy, ✆ (028) 8775 3925.

Golf: At Killymoon Golf Club, Cookstown, an 18-hole parkland course, ✆ (028) 8676 3762. Newtownstewart Golf Club, ✆ (028) 8166 1466. Omagh Golf Club, an 18-hole parkland course, ✆ (028) 8224 3160.

Open farm: Altmore Open Farm, 3 miles south of Pomeroy, ✆ (028) 8735 8977. 175-acre sheep farm in the Sperrins with rare breeds and poultry. Open daily.

Working Mill: Silverbrook Mill, 18th-century corn mill and 19th-century flax mill, Brook Road, Dunnamanagh; at time of writing was ready to install a permanent tenant and run tours. Call ✆ (028) 7188 3735 for details. Benburb Valley Heritage Centre. Guided tours of 19th-century linen mill on the banks of the Ulster Canal. Ten miles south of Dungannon. *Open East–Sept, Tues–Sat 10–5, Sun 2–5,* ✆ (028) 3754 9752.

Traditional Music Evenings of craic, traditional music, dance, stories and poetry at Teach Ceoil and the Fernagh Ceili house. Enquire at the Omagh tourist office, ✆ (028) 2824 7831 or Commhaltas Ceoltoiri Eireann in Omagh, ✆ (028) 8224 2777, ✉ (028) 8225 2162.

Strabane and Environs

Strabane (*An Srath Ban*: the white holm) is a border town and almost the twin of Lifford, across the Foyle in Donegal. The Finn joins the Foyle here as well. Strabane and its environs enjoy a notoriety in EU figures, for this area is an unemployment blackspot. It is, however, a bustling town with friendly people. It is also the birthplace of John Dunlap, printer of the American Declaration of Independence. You should try to visit Grays (*open 24 Mar–end Sept, daily except Thurs and Sun, 12–6; adm*), the 18th-century printing shop in Main Street where he worked, which is owned by the National Trust. There is a collection of 19th-century hand-printing machines in working order. Another Strabane-born notable is that curious wit Brian O'Nolan, alias Flann O'Brien. He wrote *The Poor Mouth* and other stories, and his column in *The Irish Times* between 1937 and 1966 became a byword for a debunking type of humour. There is not much else of particular interest in the town, except the fishing tackle shops near the bridge and a factory that produces a phenomenal quantity of ladies' tights.

The Tyrone Hills

East of Strabane you pass into the **Tyrone Hills**, which consist mainly of the Sperrin mountain range, extending into County Londonderry. This is perfect walking country, full of glens and mountain passes to beyond Plumbridge. At Gortin, a tiny hill village with a broad street, the B45 heads south to Omagh through Gortin Gap, a pretty mountain pass.

Plumbridge is a small crossroads village at the western end of the beautiful Glenelly Valley. A few miles on, following the B47, is the **Sperrin Heritage Centre** (*open daily April–Oct; adm;* © *(028) 8164 8142*), situated between the villages of Cranagh and Sperrin. Here there is a comprehensive and interesting display of Sperrin wildlife, showing all the animals and birds you might be lucky enough to see whilst walking in the glens around here. One very special bird you might spot is the hen harrier. Look out for the cloudberry, an alpine species which grows low to the ground on a single patch west of Dart Mountain. The Heritage Centre also has a craft shop and tea room, and plenty of historical and cultural information. One of the great saints of Ireland, St Brigid, is strongly associated with this area; there are not many houses which do not have a St Brigid cross hanging above the door to

Blacksmith at the Ulster-American Folk Park

ward off evil. These crosses look rather like swastikas, and are made of rushes. Most of the people living up in these moorlands are sheep-farmers, and regularly during the spring and the autumn there are sheep fairs and sheepdog trials in Gortin. The Glenelly and Owenkillew Rivers are very good for trout fishing. You need a Foyle Fisheries Commission rod licence, which is available from tackle shops in nearby towns. If you follow the B47 from the Centre onwards to Draperstown (a scenic route), you pass Goles Forest, planted with conifers. Alternatively, the B48 from Gortin to Omagh passes through the wild and beautiful **Gortin Glen Forest Park**, where there are nature trails amongst the conifer trees. The Ulster Way also passes through it. The country lanes around about are bright with gorse and primroses in spring, and the lambs make a very pretty sight. Another visitor centre, the **Ulster History Park** (*open daily April–Sept, rest of year Mon–Fri only; adm;* © *(028) 8164 8188*), traces human settlement and society from 8000 BC to the 17th century. You find this on the B48, at Cullion, 7 miles north of Omagh.

A couple of miles southeast of Strabane on the pretty, unnumbered Plumbridge road, at **Dergalt**, is the Wilson homestead (*call* © *(028) 7188 3735 for opening hours; adm*), maintained by the National Trust. This comparatively humble dwelling is where President Woodrow

Wilson's grandfather (among many other children) was reared before he set off for the States to become a newspaper editor. The house provides a preview of what is available on a grander scale at the American Folk Park (*see* below). **Newtownstewart**, on the A5 10 miles (16km) south of Strabane, is a 17th-century plantation town. It is attractively laid out on a large main street. Nearby on the B84 lies Baronscourt Estate, which has a fine mansion house and gardens which you can tour (*by appointment only, © (028) 8166 1683*). There are cottages for rent, coarse and game fishing, pony-trekking, golf and water-skiing on Lough Catherine.

Ulster American Folk Park

Open Easter–Sept, Mon–Sat 11–6.30, Sun 11.30–7; rest of year, Mon–Fri 10.30–5; adm; © (028) 8162 43292.

The Folk Park is between Newtownstewart and Omagh, sandwiched between the A5 and the Plumbridge road. It was developed with funds made available by the Mellon family of Pittsburg, in order to illustrate the life the emigrants left in Ireland, and those they encountered in their new land, by reconstructing the buildings they inhabited. The Irish village has a meeting house, the central focus of the Ulster Presbyterians' worship; a forge, a school house and county shop. The New World buildings include log cabins, a clapboard farmhouse and various barns complete with implements. While you are here, look out for the Ulster tartan, for near here a piece of tartan material was discovered in a bog, with the result that the so-called 'Ulster tartan' is full of tanned browns. The ancestral home of the Mellons, and the boyhood home of Archbishop John Hughes of New York, are very spartan and simple, and established showpieces. There is a fair bit of outdoor walking, so take along some good strong shoes and a raincoat.

East of Omagh, at Creggan, you will find a **visitor centre** (*open daily April–Sept, 11–6.30; Oct–March, 11–4.30; adm*) with bog trails, archaeological exhibits and a restaurant.

Omagh

Omagh, capital of Tyrone, is separated from the other large town of the county, **Cookstown**, by the Black Bog, which accounts for the turfcraft souvenirs you may find as a welcome alternative to the more usual Irish linen hankies or crochet also displayed for your attention.

Tragically, since 15 August 1998, the world has known Omagh as the site of the most devastating single act of violence in the history of the Troubles; 29 people were killed by a bomb that day in the city centre, and the effect on the entire community will be felt for many years to come. There is now a small memorial garden at the site, on the corner of Market Street beside Strule Bridge, where the flowers and poems left by devastated family and friends tell any visitor all they need to know about the terrible price paid by innocent people in Northern Ireland.

Some people tell you that there is something French about this town, with its twin-spired church and a reputation for liveliness. Brian Friel, the playwright, is a native. Any of his plays are worth making a special effort to see; he gives a profound and lyrical insight into Irish culture. Omagh is a good spot for fishing, which can be found on the Camowen and Owenreagh Rivers. Those wanting to hear musical talent should time their visit to coincide with the West Tyrone *Feis* in May, also known as the Omagh *Feis*, which has plenty of Irish music and dancing.

Omagh is near other forest areas: **Seskinore Forest**, near Fintona, and **Dromore Forest**, further west. Should you wish to strike across the moor country you can go by Mountfield on the A505 from Omagh, which will take you by the Black Bog, a nature reserve; any other little roads you encounter may take you past some of the many antiquities which testify to Bronze or earlier Stone Age inhabitants of this area.

At **Pomeroy**, on the B4 15 miles (24km) east of Omagh, high in the mountains and equidistant from Cookstown and Dungannon, there are the remains of seven stone circles. More famous are the **Beaghmore Stone Circles**, outside Cookstown and near Dunnamore; these intricate alignments (on a northeast axis) represent the remarkable architecture of the late Stone Age or early Bronze Age. Their formation has been likened to a clock pointing for the last six thousand years towards the midsummer sunrise. They certainly look very impressive in the wild landscape that surrounds them. To get there, take a minor road off the A505 through Dunnamore, and travel on a few miles going north. Near to Cookstown at Corkhill is **Wellbrook Beetling Mill** (*open Easter and July–Aug, daily except Tues, 2–6; April–June and Sept, weekends and bank holidays, 2–6; adm; © (028) 8675 1735*), a hammer mill powered by water for beetling. (This alarming-sounding process is the final stage of linen manufacture.) The mill is situated about 4 miles (7km) west of Cookstown, half a mile off the A505 Cookstown–Omagh road, in a lovely glen with wooded walks along the Ballinderry River and the mill race.

Cookstown is situated in the middle of Northern Ireland, near the fertile heartland which traces its course beside the Bann in Londonderry and continues down by Lough Neagh. There are two Nash buldings in its environs. On the outskirts southeast of the town is **Killymoon Castle**, a battlemented towered construction which contrasts with the simple Church of Ireland parish church known as St Laurane's at the southeast end of the main street. The conspicuous Puginesque Catholic church, sited on a hill in the middle of town, provides a good landmark.

Arriving at Cookstown, you will be impressed by the long, wide main street; if you are of a cynical turn of mind you may think it a good street for leading a charge against insurgents. Cookstown has a good Nationalist tradition, exemplified by the energetic Miss Bernadette Devlin, now McAliskey, who was active in the Civil Rights Movement and Nationalist Party in the 1970s. There is also a strong Scottish Protestant tradition with the ancestors of those who settled here in the 17th century.

Places to visit nearby include the loughside **Ardboe High Cross**, about 10 miles (16km) east on the shore of Lough Neagh. The cross is a 10th-century monument with 22 remarkable sculptured scriptural panels covered with scenes from the Old and New Testaments. These scenes are easily recognizable, unlike those on many of the other high crosses you may see, which are usually so weathered that you need to concentrate to read the theme. South of Cookstown, in **Tullaghogue Rath** (pronounced '*Tullyhog*'), the O'Neills, the great chieftains of Tyrone, were inaugurated. In 1595 Hugh O'Neill gave in to the British, and seven years later the Lord Deputy Mountjoy had the throne smashed to prevent any future ceremonies. At the foot of Tullaghogue hill, in what is now Loughry Agricultural College, is the mansion where Jonathan Swift stayed while writing *Gulliver's Travels*; the portraits of his two loves,

Stella and Vanessa, still hang in the house. It is sometimes possible to visit it; ask at the door. **Drum Manor Forest Park** close by, to the east of Cookstown on the A505, has a butterfly garden and a forest trail for the disabled (*open all year daily 10am–dusk; adm; parking fee;* ℗ *(028) 8776 2774*).

Dungannon, a city on a hill, looks like your average planter town, with a planned main street and a Royal School founded in the time of James I of England. It was, in fact, the centre for the great O'Neills until the 'Flight of the Earls' deprived the Gaels of their native leaders (*see* **History**, p.42). It is now a quietly prosperous town with a long-established textile industry specializing in Moygashel fabrics, and Tyrone crystal-glass. At the beginning of the 17th century, in order to promote good Protestant education, James I of England and Ireland (James VI of Scotland) provided Royal Schools as well as charters for land. You may notice the **Royal School, Dungannon** which is on Northland Row in the centre of the town. The present building dates from 1786 and outside it is a statue of one of its most famous 'old boys', Major General John Nicholson, whose exploits in India inspired such respect that there was even a sect called 'Nikkul Seyn'. Another Indian connection is the **police station** in the town centre, which looks like a castle with projecting apertures for missile-throwing. Apparently it was built according to plans for a fort in the Khyber Pass because some clerk in Dublin got into a muddle. This is the usual explanation for many of these exotic-looking stations which are scattered about Ireland.

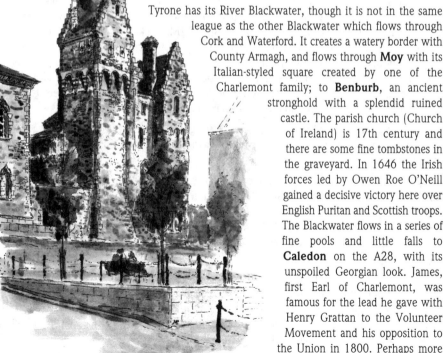

Former RIC station, Dungannon

Tyrone has its River Blackwater, though it is not in the same league as the other Blackwater which flows through Cork and Waterford. It creates a watery border with County Armagh, and flows through **Moy** with its Italian-styled square created by one of the Charlemont family; to **Benburb**, an ancient stronghold with a splendid ruined castle. The parish church (Church of Ireland) is 17th century and there are some fine tombstones in the graveyard. In 1646 the Irish forces led by Owen Roe O'Neill gained a decisive victory here over English Puritan and Scottish troops. The Blackwater flows in a series of fine pools and little falls to **Caledon** on the A28, with its unspoiled Georgian look. James, first Earl of Charlemont, was famous for the lead he gave with Henry Grattan to the Volunteer Movement and his opposition to the Union in 1800. Perhaps more intriguing to the traveller is the **Clogher Valley**, which is border country with the Republic and so enjoys that anomalous status of being either frontier outpost or lost territory. A narrow gauge railway used to run through the valley connecting the two sides. This place evidently has a long history of habitation, for many ancient earthworks have survived. The countryside is very pleasant and fertile, and extends for 25 miles (40km). There are some interesting villages and the River Fury runs through the valley. In the townland of Gort, between Ballygawley and Augher, is the ancient graveyard of Errigal Keerogue with a fine early high cross and a superb view over the woodland and rich agricultural countryside.

Just north of **Augher**, off the B83, is the **Knockmany Forest**, a government-run forestry plantation on Knockmany Hill. At the top, look for the **Knockmany Chambered Cairn** said to be the burial place of Queen Aine, Queen of Oriel, a 6th-century kingdom whose centre was Clogher. The cairn is a passage grave dating from Neolithic times. This type of monument consists of a stone-built passage leading to a terminal chamber, often cruciform in shape, and covered by a mound or cairn of stones. The remarkable thing about this grave is its incised decoration, in patterns of concentric circles, zig-zags and other designs, which are similar in style to the great earthworks in the Boyne Valley, County Meath. This country, besides being a fisherman's haunt, is well forested. The 19th-century landlords who once owned vast tracts of land have disappeared, but their old estates, such as Favour Royal and Fardross, gave their names to public parkland and forests where it is possible to camp and have picnics. At Favour Royal, you can walk from the river to St Patrick's well and chair at Altadaven, a secret, mossy place.

If you are interested in the way things used to be on these large estates, it is worth seeking out the work of Miss Shaw, a governess whose photographs from the turn of the century are incorporated in an anthology called *Faces of the Past* by B. M. Walker. Another documentor of earlier ways was the prolific William Carleton (1794–1869), 'the Irish Dickens', who was born at Springtown just outside Augher, and who made no bones about the hardships of peasant life, paying tribute to some of the great spirits who existed unsung in rural isolation. His most famous work is *Traits and Stories of the Irish Peasantry*. If you are interested in Carleton's work, ask to see the archive material in the Library in Fivemiletown.

Augher and Clogher are within striking distance. **Augher** lies between the Blackwater River and Augher Lake. You can see the 19th-century **Castle of Spur Royal** just to the west of the village as you pass by on the A4.

Clogher village is on a site of prehistoric importance, as well as being of great ecclesiastical significance. It was the original seat in the 5th century of the diocese of Clogher, one of the oldest bishoprics in Ireland. In the porch of **St MacCartan's Cathedral** there is a curious stone called 'the *Clogh-oir*' or Gold Stone. There are two 9th-century high crosses in the graveyard, and you can climb the tower and get a stunning view of the Clogher Valley. Ask at the rectory for access.

Behind this centre of ancient Christianity is the even older hill-fort of **Ramore**. Archaeologists have investigated it for evidence about the Iron Age, and perhaps the mysterious '*Clogh-oir*' comes from an idol of those times. It was certainly the site of the palace of the kings of Oriel; the tradition of the dynasty survives but not the dates, other than that they were pre-5th century. The hill-fort itself is now just a grassy mound, and always accessible.

Benburb has a picturesque ruin of a castle on a cliff overhanging the Blackwater River; this early 17th-century castle replaced an earlier O'Neill stronghold. The demesne surrounding the castle is freely accessible and the Servite Priory in the grounds has a popular open day on the third Sunday in June. The Benburb Heritage Centre (*open April–Sept, Tues–Sat 10–5, Sun 2–7; adm*) operates from the 19th-century linen mill; it also has a hostel and a café, ✆ (028) 3754 9752.

Shopping

Glass: Tyrone Crystal, Oaks Road, Dungannon, ✆ (028) 8772 5335. The glassworks give you a guided tour, and you can buy imperfect glassware very cheaply.

Antiques: Viewback Antique Auctions, 8 Castle Place, Omagh.

Where to Stay

East Tyrone

Tulldowey House, 51 Tulldowey Road, Dungannon, ✆ (028) 3754 8230, @ (028) 3754 8881 (*moderate*). Old house, en suite bedrooms, very refurbished. Mrs N. Brown, **Grange Lodge**, 7 Grange Road, near Dungannon, ✆ (028) 8778 4212, @ (028) 8772 3891 (*moderate*). Comfortable Georgian house by the Blackwater River. **Braeside House**, 23 Drumcovis Road, Coagh, Cookstown, ✆ (028) 8673 7301 (*moderate*). Four rooms, one en suite in old house.

Mr & Mrs McNeice, **Charlemont House**, 4 The Square, Moy, Dungannon, ✆ (028) 8778 4755 (*inexpensive*). Georgian townhouse with period furnishings and lots of atmosphere with a view of the Blackwater River at the back. Nice garden.

West Tyrone

Captain R. M. Lowry, Blessingbourne, near Fivemiletown, ✆ (028) 8952 1221 (*expensive*). You can imagine you are staying in the time of leisurely house parties when you stay in this attractive Victorian mansion set in wooded grounds. You are made to feel part of the family. The rooms are very comfortable, and the cooking first-rate. **Corick House**, 20 Corick Road, Clogher, ✆ (028) 8254 8216, @ (028) 8254 9531 (*expensive*). 17th-century house, full of history, in lovely grounds.

The **Valley Hotel**, 60 Main Street, Fivemiletown, ✆ (028) 8952 1505 (*moderate*). Comfortable, cheery, grade B accommodation. The **Royal Arms**, 51 High Street, Omagh, ✆ (028) 8224 3262, @ (028) 8224 4860 (*moderate*). Traditional hotel in the town centre. **Deer Park House**, 14 Baronscourt Road, Newtownstewart, ✆ (028) 8166 1083 (*moderate*).

self-catering

An Creagán, Creggan, Omagh, ✆ (028) 8076 1112, @ (028) 8076 1116. Eight traditional-style cottages; sleep 6, from £300 per week high season. **Mote Cottage**, Omagh. Traditional white-washed cottages with flowers around the door; sleep 2, from £180 per week high season. **Baronscourt Cottages**, Golf Course Road, Newtownstewart, ✆ (028) 8165 8602. Nine cottages by a private lake. **Capt. R. M. Lowry**, Blessingbourne, ✆ (028) 8952 1221. Two apartments.

East Tyrone

Tullylagan Country House, near Cookstown, ✆ (028) 8676 5100 (*moderate*). **Mellon Country Inn**, 134 Beltany Road, Newtownstewart, ✆ (028) 8166 1224 (*moderate*). Good steak. **Tommy's Bar** (*inexpensive*) in Moy is a very authentic pub. **Cookstown Courtyard**, 56 William Street, Cookstown, ✆ (028) 8676 5070 (*inexpensive*). Set lunch, home-made pies and puddings. **Suitor Gallery**, Ballygawley. Good home-baking in tea-room.

West Tyrone

Rosamund's Coffee Shop, Station House, Augher, ✆ (028) 8554 8601 (*inexpensive*). Home-made stew during the day. The **Caledon Arms**, 44 Main St, Caledon, ✆ (028) 3756 8161 (*inexpensive*). **Number 15**, Church Street, Dungannon, ✆ (028) 8775 048 (*inexpensive*). Café in bookshop. **Nature Trail**, 20 Bridge St and 39 Castle St, Omagh. Whole foods, herbal remedies and vegetarian dishes.

County Londonderry

Cottage near Bellarena

County Londonderry

This is a rich and varied region. The traditions of war and tumult vie with the gifts of learning and song in the people who inhabit this friendly land. The countryside ranges from stormy sea coast and wild mountain ranges to sheltered valleys, well-wooded from years of far-sighted planting. The coastline from Magilligan to Downhill is scattered with golden strands. Historic Derry is a spire-dreaming city which arouses fierce passions in the hearts of its inhabitants.

The city and the whole county have suffered because of the 'Troubles', which started in the 1960s. The fighting in the streets, the bombing and the upset to normal life have taken their toll on the lives of the inhabitants. Yet some good things have happened: new housing schemes have been implemented, sports centres built and, where shops and stores were destroyed, new buildings have gone up. Derry City has been rejuvenated in recent years through its craft village, heritage centre, and award-winning Tower Museum. The people of the province are determined to survive, and not give in to the men of violence. None the less, people live in tribal areas; those who have tried to live in a mixed estate have been intimidated into moving out.

The economy of County Londonderry is subsidized heavily by the British government, and there is a lot of unemployment in places like the Bogside. Several international companies have set up factories and there are traditional linen and shirt-makers, though these are now struggling in the face of competition from Third World countries.

History

The O'Neills were the overlords here before the county was planted with settlers who came over with the London City Companies. These London City Companies became owners of huge tracts of land, through grants from James I in the early 1600s. It was at this point that the county and its main

123

Sports and Activities

Walking and other activity sports: Roe Valley Country Park, centre for walking, fishing, canoeing, rock-climbing, orienteering. Also countryside museum and visitor centre. Call ✆ (028) 7172 2074 for details. Ness Woods, Derry (off A6 to Belfast) Nature trails, waterfall.

Outdoor activity specialists: Swiss Lodge, 4 Chapel Road, Waterside, Derry. Freephone ✆ (0800) 7317153. McNamara Walking Tours of the City of Derry, ✆ (028) 7126 5536. Stephen McPhilemy walking tours, 70 Marlborough St, ✆/✉ (028) 7128 9051.

Coarse fishing: River Bann.

Deep-sea fishing: Between Lough Foyle and Portrush. Boat hire from: Robert Cardwell, 119 Bushmills Road, Coleraine, ✆ (028) 7082 2359; Joe Mullan, Portrush, ✆ (028) 7082 2209.

Game fishing: For brown trout and salmon on the Agivey, Clady, Roe, Bann and Faughan Rivers. Game-rod licence from Foyle Fisheries Commission, 8 Victoria Road, ✆ (028) 7134 2100, ✉ (028) 7134 2720. Glenowen Co-operative, ✆ (028) 7137 1544. Provides guides, licences, package fishing trips.

Swimming and leisure centres: In Templemore, Lisnagelvin, St Columb's Park and Brooke Park—all in Derry.

town became Londonderry. Previously, it had been known as Derry-Colmcille after the oak grove in which it once stood, and after St Colmcille who had established a religious settlement here in AD 546. A subtle point is made, to those 'in the know', whether reference is made to Londonderry or Derry. The former perhaps indicates Loyalist politics; but the county and its city are generally known as Derry, so we have named Derry City accordingly in this text. Derry was granted to the Irish Society of London 'for the promotion of religion, order and industry'. The city had been ruined in the fighting between the English forces and those of O'Neill and O'Doherty, the chief Irish septs (clans) of the region. It was rebuilt with strong walls which protected it from would-be conquerers during three major sieges in the 17th century, earning it the title 'Maiden City'.

Getting There and Around

Derry is a terminal for railway and bus services, and is a useful halfway house for those moving east or west.

By air: to Belfast Airport, ✆ (01849) 422888. The City of Derry Airport has flights to Manchester, Glasgow, Jersey and London Stansted, ✆ (028) 7181 0784.

By car: Avis Car Hire, City of Derry Airport, ✆ (028) 7181 1708. Desmond Motors, City of Derry Airport, ✆ (028) 7181 2220.

By sea: to Larne and Belfast ferryports.

By rail: mainline services from Belfast to Derry link several coastal towns along the way, ✆ (028) 7134 2228.

Golf: Benone Golf Course, Downhill, ✆ (028) 7775 0555. Castlerock Golf Club, 65 Circular Road, Castlerock, ✆ (028) 7084 8314. City of Derry Golf Club, 49 Victoria Road, ✆ (028) 7131 1610. Radisson Roe Park Resort, Limavady, ✆ (028) 7772 2222.

Pony-trekking: Hilltop Farm, Castlerock, ✆ (028) 7084 8629.

Gliding: The Ulster Gliding Club, Bellarena, ✆ (028) 7166 3080.

Museum visits: (other than those mentioned in detail in text) **The Amelia Earhart Centre**, Ballyarnet, Derry (*open Mon–Thurs 9–5, Fri 9–1; adm free; ✆ (028) 7135 4040*); **The Heritage Library**, 14 Bishop Street, Derry (*open Mon–Fri 9–5 ✆ (028) 7126 9792*); **Garvagh Museum and Heritage Centre**, Main Street, Garvagh. Stone Age artefacts, farming implements (*open June–Aug, Thurs and Sat 2–5; ✆ (028) 2955 8216*).

Plantation of Ulster Visitor Centre, High Street, Draperstown, (*open daily Easter–Sept 11–5, Oct–Easter Mon–Sat 11–5, Sunday 10–5; adm; ✆ (028) 7962 7800*); **Railway Museum**, on Foyle Road, close to Craigavon Bridge, Derry: you can take a trip on a 1934 diesel railcar on the 1½-mile track beside the Foyle, (*open Tues–Sat, 10–4.30; museum free, charge for ride; ✆ (028) 7126 5234*).

By bus: Ulsterbus connects Derry with Belfast, and there is a good local bus network, ✆ (028) 7126 2261. Lough Swilly Bus Company, ✆ (028) 7126 2017.

By coach: Airporter provide an express bus service to Belfast City and International airports, ✆ (028) 7126 9996.

Tourist Information

Derry: 44 Foyle Street, ✆ (028) 7126 7284, ✉ (028) 7137 7992; open all year.

Derry: Bord Fáilte Information Centre, 44 Foyle Street, ✆/✉ (028) 7136 9501; open all year.

Limavady: 7 Connell Street, ✆ (028) 7772 2226, ✉ (028) 7772 2010; open all year.

Festivals

February/March: Derry *Feis*, Easter week.

March: Celtic Spring Film Festival, Derry.

May: Jazz & Blues Festival.

July/August: Maiden City Festival, incorporating the Apprentice Boys Marches in Derry, Castledawson and many other towns. Contact the Apprentice Boys Memorial Hall, ✆ (028) 7126 3571, or look in the local newspapers—*The Derry Journal* or *The Sentinel*.

October: Two Cathedrals Classical Music Festival.

October/November: Banks of the Foyle Halloween Carnival.

November: Foyle Film Festival; Northwest Arts Festival, mainly located in Derry.

The A2 takes you along the Foyle Plain and by-passes Eglinton (the site of Derry City Airport) and travels through **Ballykelly**. This town was settled by people brought in by the Fishmonger's Company of London in 1618. There are two handsome churches here, the Tamlaghtfinlagan Parish Church, which is 18th-century Gothic with a graceful spire and fine tombstones; and the neoclassical Presbyterian Church. It is close to a British army base and in 1970 hit the headlines when off-duty soldiers were blown up in a pub here. The next town along the coast, still following the A2, is **Limavady**, beautifully situated in the Roe Valley with fine mountain scenery to the north and southeast. Before the Fishermongers Company arrived, Limavady was an important centre of the territory of the O'Cahans, a *sept* under the lordship of the O'Neills, although no trace remains of their castle now. The town is associated with the famous 'Londonderry Air', noted down by Miss Jane Ross in 1851 from a passing fiddler called Denis O'Hempsey (*see* below). William Connolly, speaker of the Irish House of Commons before the Act of Union in 1800, and builder of the beautiful Castletown House near Dublin, was the son of a Limavady blacksmith.

Precious gold representations of a masted boat, collars and a necklace fashioned in the Celtic La Tène style were found at Broighter near the coastal marshes surrounding the estuary of the River Roe. They are now in the care of the National Museum, Dublin. Further up the coast, underneath the forest-covered Binevenagh Mountain, is the triangle of **Magilligan Point**. A Martello Tower, built during the Napoleonic wars, guards the entrance to Lough Foyle. The strand is well known for its shells, the herbs that grow among the dunes, the birds, and for the plagues of rabbits commemorated in a special Magilligan grace. The names of local villages such as Bellarena and the Umbra recall the foundering of the Armada; folklore would have you believe that some of the darker-hued Magilliganites are of Spanish descent. This part of the world also has connections with the Irish music tradition. At the end of the 18th century, interest in the Gaelic cultural achievement began amongst a group of scholarly men; foremost amongst them was Edward Bunting who did so much to preserve Irish airs and ancient music. He helped to organize a great assembly of Irish harpers in Belfast in 1792. One of the oldest harpers, a blind man called Denis Hempsey, or O'Hempsey (c. 1695–1807), lived near Magilligan. He provided Bunting with many old tunes and airs and had played before Prince Charles Edward Stuart at Holyrood Palace in 1745. It is rather symbolic that so many of the last Irish harpers were blind—as if they suffered physically the fate which had befallen their culture. Men like O'Hempsey or Carolan continued to play the old Irish airs and to wander through Ireland, yet they had no status in the English framework of society. The Gaelic lords who had given them a home and patronage had fled, and the Gaelic society in which they had played no longer existed. It is only fair to say, however, that the anglicized Earl of Bristol and Bishop of Derry presented O'Hempsey with a house near Magilligan. Benone Strand is an extension of Magilligan, a glorious seven-mile sandy arc.

Downhill to Coleraine

From Limavady you can cut inland through the Roe Valley to Dungiven on the B68 and pass through the Country Park which has many fine picnic spots and walks by the River Roe. However, if you want to take advantage of the superb coastline you should go on from

Magilligan following the A2 to Downhill, and on up to the pretty resort of **Castlerock**, which has a superb sandy beach stretching for miles. A really worthwhile expedition can be made to the **Palace of Downhill** and **Mussenden Temple** (*open daily, 10–14 April 12–6; June and Sept, Sat and Sun 12–6; July–Aug and Easter, daily 2–6; glen and grounds always open; adm free; ✆ (028) 7038 48728*), a ruined castle just off the A2 at Downhill village, built by the famous Earl-Bishop, Frederick Augustus Hervey (1730–1803), one of the most interesting and enlightened Church of Ireland bishops. The palace and the surrounding coastline is in the care of the National Trust. At the entrance the caretaker has planted a marvellous garden of primulas and cottage flowers, and the palace itself is sited on a windswept hill with wonderful views of the Inishowen hills and the Antrim headlands. The Earl-Bishop who built it was extravagant and well-travelled; he built up a great art collection with the episcopal revenues from his Derry bishopric (which in the 18th century was the second-richest in Ireland), and a second princely residence at Ballyscullion near Bellaghy, which is totally ruined. Downhill was built in the late 18th century. The landscaped estate which still remains includes the Mussenden Temple perched on a cliff overlooking the sea, the ruins of the castle, family memorials, gardens, a fish pond, woodland and cliff walks.

The bishop was a great advocate of toleration, contributing generously both to Catholic and Presbyterian churches. One of his amusements was party-giving. If you go down to the Mussenden Temple, the story of the great race he organized between the Anglican and the Presbyterian ministers before a dinner party is recounted. There was suspicion that he was more of a Classicist than a Christian: his temple, on a cliff edge, is modelled on the Roman temple of Vesta, and suggesting a certain independent interpretation of religion. The ruins of the palace lie within the boundaries of a farm, but the temple and the little valley beside it provide splendid picnic spots.

Eastwards along the coast is **Portstewart**, a seasoned little resort town which is overlooked by the castle-style convent (*not open to the public*). Inland from Portstewart is **Coleraine** (*Cuil Raithin*: fern recess), which is supposed to have been founded by St Patrick. Most of what you see was developed by the Irish Society of London. Whiskey from Coleraine is now made by Bushmills Distillery (*for information about tours of Old Bushmills Distillery, call ✆ (028) 2073 1521*); it is still held in high repute and indeed is supplied to the House of Commons.

The Coleraine campus of the University of Ulster is a centre for talks and tours during the summer, and there is a good **theatre** here called the Riverside. The campus has a rare collection of Irish-bred daffodils and narcissi which are in full bloom mid to late April. (*Free access always.*) The River Bann runs through the town and was the scene of early habitation. At **Mount Sandel**, on Coleraine's outskirts, Mesolithic flints have been found which indicate the presence of the earliest settlements in Ireland. There is much archaeological evidence to suggest that they date from 7000 BC. Later the mound of Mount Sandel became a royal seat of local Celtic kings, and finally, a Norman fort. If you are in the British Museum in London you will see some of those Bannside antiquities, the most spectacular of which is a huge hoard of Roman coins, evidently seized by Irish pirates, and now returned to England.

On the A2, northwest of Coleraine is **Hezlett House** (*open April–June and Sept, Sat and Sun only; July–Aug, daily except Tues; adm; ✆ (028) 7084 8567*), a thatched 17th-century cottage, which was once a rectory. It has a cruck or truss roof, and is owned by the National Trust.

Bellaghy to Moneymore

You can follow the River Bann through its valley by taking the A54. The valley is farmed by the industrious descendants of Scots and English, who were tenants of the London Companies and arrived in the region in the early 17th century. The countryside is very pretty in a cultivated way. Before the Bann reaches Lough Neagh it broadens out into Lough Beg, and in the marshy area around the lake is Church Island, so called because of its ruined church and holy well. A spire has been constructed among the ruins—one result of Earl-Bishop Hervey's building ventures. He wanted to be able to see the spire from his palace at Ballyscullion. The local people still leave offerings at the holy well on the island. The birdlife around the lake is superb; many water-fowl, snipe and swans can be seen. Seamus Heaney, the poet, comes from this area and the strength of his feelings for this land is apparent in his poetry.

You can find out more about this internationally loved poet at the **Bellaghy Bawn** (*open April–Sept, Mon–Sat 10–6, Sun 2–6, rest of year closes at 5; adm*), a fortified farmhouse, built for the London Vintner's Company around 1618. Inside this fine *bawn* are a series of rooms through which you are taken on a tour and local history is explored since prehistoric times. There is an audio-visual presentation by Seamus Heaney, who explains how local places and experiences have influenced his poetry.

Sheep market, Draperstown

Besides a café, there is a library with manuscripts and original works by Seamus Heaney, as well as works by other Northern poets and artists. **Moneymore**, further south, is a sister town to **Draperstown**, because it was developed by the same London Company of Drapers. One mile (1.6km) outside Moneymore on the B18 is the most attractive of residences, **Springhill** (*open July–Aug, daily except Thurs; June & Sept, Sat & Sun only; adm; © (028) 8674 8210*), built in the late 17th century as a fortified manor house by the Lennox-Conynghams, a settler family, with its outbuildings in Dutch style. It is a proper country gentleman's house with soft shadowed interiors, a lovely library and portraits, including one with a following gaze. The artist's trick was to paint the eyes so that they seem to be watching you wherever you stand. There is a small costume museum, and implements are on show in the outbuildings. The grounds are beautiful; the yew thicket is said to be a vestige of the ancient forest of Glenconkeyne, and there is a herb garden—essential for any household in the 17th and 18th centuries.

Maghera to Londonderry

Here you are on the edges of the Sperrin mountains, which this county shares with Tyrone. If you love walking, the Sperrins Sky Way, a twenty-mile route, starts at Barony Bridge,

Moydamlaght Forest, near Draperstown, and runs along the Sperrin Ridge, finishing at Eden, east of Plumbridge.

Maghera, the mountain heartland of the county, is a small and busy town at the foot of the Glenshane Pass. It is said to be the meeting place of the mountain and plains people, rather like Dungiven on the other side of the mountain. At the southeast end of the town there is an ancient church of St Lurach (*always accessible*) with a square-headed doorway, dating perhaps from the 18th century. The massive lintels are decorated with a carved, interlaced pattern, and a sculpture of the crucifixion.

The steep, straight road through the **Glenshane Pass** will take you on to **Dungiven** or you can explore the charming countryside around **Draperstown** and on to **Feeny** travelling on the B40. Draperstown has a visitor centre and craft shop. You will pass by **Banagher Forest Glen**, which is a nature reserve. Close by, to the west, is Sawel, at 2,240ft (683m) the highest mountain in the Sperrin range. North of the forest, off the B74 from Feeny, is **Banagher Church**, founded by a St Muriedach O'Heney. The church itself is probably 12th century, with a square-headed doorway and massive lintels. In the graveyard is a stone-roofed tomb or oratory with the figure of O'Heney in relief—he who bequeathed to his descendants the power to be lucky with the sand from his tomb. The church is always accessible to the public. On the eastern side of **Dungiven** (on the A6) is a fine ruin of an **Augustinian priory**; only the chancel with a Norman arch remains. The elaborate altar tomb erected in the late 14th century is very striking. It is carved with a figure in Irish dress grasping a sword, and commemorates an O'Cahan, whose family were the lords of this territory before the plantation.

Derry City

Derry or Londonderry (*Doire*: oak grove) is a symbolic city situated on the River Foyle. Before the 1960s it was probably best known for its association with the pretty 'Londonderry Air' (better known as 'Danny Boy'), but has until recently been one of Northern Ireland's troublespots. The strife is not unprecedented, for it has survived three sieges.

History

The land on which the settlement of Derry grew up was granted to St Colmcille (St Columba), by Aimire, Prince of the O'Neills, in AD 546. St Columba built a monastery on the oak-crowned hill. He eventually left the monastery, and founded many other religious settlements, the most important of which was Iona, the isle off the west coast of Scotland. From here Christianity spread over Scotland. St Columba wrote, homesick for this place:

> *Derry, mine own small oak grove,*
> *Little cell, my home, my love.*
> *Oh. Thou Lord of lasting life,*
> *Woe to him who brings it strife.*

St Columba never outgrew his love for the city. He would have sympathized with the emigrant families who left Derry for America during the 18th and 19th centuries, among them the forebears of such famous figures as Davy Crockett and President James K. Polk.

Derry suffered at the hands of the Norsemen, and then an expedition burned the abbey in 1195. By the end of the 16th century, the English built a fort in Derry, in order to attack the

O'Neill of the time, and later a small town was built from the ecclesiastical ruins. This was completely destroyed in 1608 by Cahir O'Doherty and his supporters. It was after this that the city and the county were granted by James I to the London Livery companies, who rebuilt the walls and planned the streets, which still remain. Derry acquired its prefix 'London' because of the position occupied by the London Livery companies in the building and development of the city. Derry is the most complete walled city in Ireland: with early 17th-century walls about a mile (1.6km) in circumference, pierced by seven gates, six bastions and many cannon.

Derry was first besieged during the rebellion of 1641, then during the Cromwellian wars of 1649, and finally there was the historic siege of 1689. This last siege still plays a very important part in the mind of the Ulster Unionist, for it sums up the courage and righteousness of the Protestant settlers who resisted with the cry, 'No surrender.' The city was being assailed by James II, who had lost his throne in England and was trying to repair his fortunes in Ireland with the help of Louis XIV of France. Thirteen apprentice boys rushed to the gates of the city and shut them in the faces of his approaching army. This secured Londonderry for William III, who had been invited to take over from James II by the English parliament. The siege that followed resulted in many deaths, for the city had no stores of food. Citizens ate rats, dogs, and the starch for laundering linen. A boom was placed across the River Foyle to prevent food supplies reaching the city, but this was eventually broken after 105 days, and the city was relieved by the forces of the Lord Deputy Mountjoy, commanded by Captain Browning, at Ship Quay on 28 July. Every year, the anniversary of the shutting of the gates is celebrated on the Saturday nearest 18 December, and the Raising of the Siege on 12 August. There are marches around the city, with bands and drummers.

City Centre/City Walls

Derry is a place well worth visiting, and on most of the approaches to its centre you will see its image across the water, a fine city within its walls, built around the curve of the Foyle. Some ugly buildings have been allowed to mar its elegant profile, but not as yet too many, although the docks are no longer crowded with folk sailing to a brand new world, as they were in their thousands in the 19th century.

The city is now a modern industrial centre, noted for its manufacturing of clothing, but its skyline is still relatively untouched, and a walk around the historic walls gives you a good view of the docks and the wide River Foyle. Big ships still harbour here, although in the days of the British Empire they carried exotic cargo such as silk from Bombay. The old city is bounded by its walls. To the northwest of them is the Republican and historical **Bogside**, with its much-repainted and photographed 'Free Derry' monument and colourful murals. A guided walking tour of the walled city is an excellent way to begin exploring; these depart from the tourist office on Foyle Street several times a day.

Derry has many attractions to offer the visitor: interesting museums, charming old streets and the Craft Village, off Shipquay Street. Great efforts have been made to improve the cultural life of the city, and its own spontaneous creativity in theatre, poetry, and the arts has brought a welcome energy. One of the greatest changes has been the development of three huge, ugly retail complexes—Quayside, Foyleside and the Richmond Centre—which are a fair indicator of a new-found commercial confidence in a stable future for the city. Another major development is the relocation of the Verbal Arts Centre to a building beside the city walls. The Verbal Arts Centre is a valuable resource for it encourages and supports all forms of written and

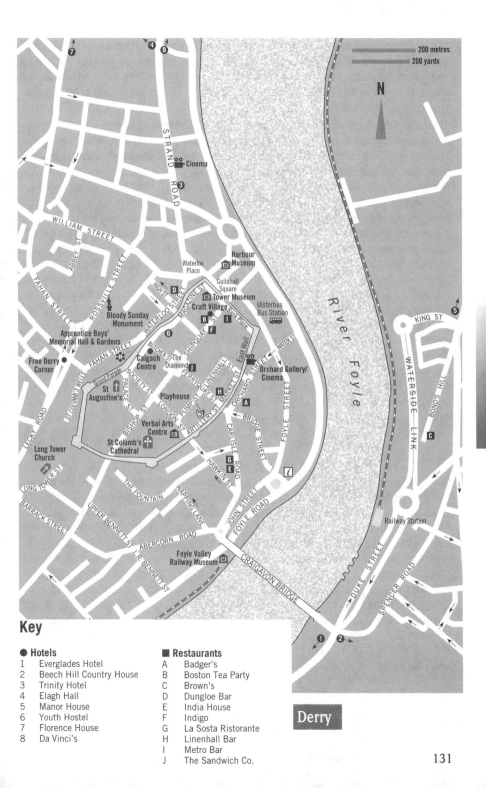

Key

● Hotels
1 Everglades Hotel
2 Beech Hill Country House
3 Trinity Hotel
4 Elagh Hall
5 Manor House
6 Youth Hostel
7 Florence House
8 Da Vinci's

■ Restaurants
A Badger's
B Boston Tea Party
C Brown's
D Dungloe Bar
E India House
F Indigo
G La Sosta Ristorante
H Linenhall Bar
I Metro Bar
J The Sandwich Co.

Derry

131

spoken creative expression. Literary festivals, readings and traditional story-telling, poetry and writing workshops will all take place in this adaptable building furnished with the best of Irish craftsmanship and art. The 18th-century idea of a coffee house where you meet and discuss ideas is being followed in the style of the coffee house here. (The centre is likely to re-open at its new home in late 2000.)

The walls of Derry have been restored, making for a very interesting walk around the old part of the City. They are entered by seven gates, and all along the circuit are views towards the Foyle, or into the Bogside and beyond to the hills. Information plaques mark every structure of note along the walls, and there is some unofficial graffitti too. If you start at Shipquay Gate opposite the Guildhall, you will see some of the cannon used in the siege of 1689. Walking on in a westward direction you come to Ferryquay Gate where the gates were slammed and locked by the determined apprentice boys in the face of James II's troops. Moving on, you soon come to the long low plantation Church of Ireland Cathedral, **St Columbs**, (*chapter house museum open April–Oct, Mon–Sat 9–5; Nov–March, 10–4; adm*), which lies between Fountain Street and Bishop Street, and is an example of planters' Gothic. The building was founded by the Corporation of London in 1633, and restored in 1886. The Cathedral was the first specifically Protestant Cathedral to be built in the British Isles after the Reformation. The roof rests on stone corbels carved into heads representing past bishops of Derry. The philosopher George Berkeley (1685–1753) was Dean here between 1724 and 1733, and the well-known cleric, the Earl of Bristol, was Bishop between 1768 and 1803. He was extremely rich and cultured, favoured Catholic Emancipation and opposed the tithe system. The bishop's throne incorporates the chair which was used at the consecration of the cathedral in 1633. The cathedral bells ring out through the city on every important religious, civic or national occasion; the peal is made up of twelve bells, eight of them dating from the 17th century. It has a number of exhibits illustrating the spirit of the 17th-century siege; and the stained glass windows depict incidents from it. The small museum inside is well worth visiting for its relics of the siege and mementos of Cecil Frances Alexander, composer of such famous hymns as *Once in Royal David's City* and *There is a Green Hill Far Away.*

Bishop's Gate, nearby, has fine stone carvings. It actually dates from 1789 when the original was replaced with this triumphal arch. The terraced housing area behind the walls here is the Fountain, a dwindling Protestant preserve, the only one this side of the city. Now as you turn the corner, you can see the Double Bastion with its cannons which still point out over the Bogside where the Jacobite army was camped. There is a wonderful view from here, and you can clearly see the large wall murals of the Bogside. (The area immediately below the walls is a well-used football patch for the youngsters from the Bogside.) You will come to **St Augustines Church**; set amongst mature trees, somewhere here is the site of St Columcille's (St Columba's) monastery; which as the plaque proudly says, means 1,400 years of continuous Christian settlement. On the corner opposite is the Apprentice Boys' Hall; along the walls here are sycamore trees, planted to commemorate the apprentice boys. Overlooking the Bogside is the base of a monument to the Reverend George Walker, who rallied the dispirited Derry people to continue their defiance. The original statue was destroyed by an IRA bomb in 1973, and when a replacement was commissioned the IRA vowed they would blow that one up as well (it now resides safely behind a high fence, a few metres along the street past the Apprentice Boys Hall). The rest of the wall brings you back down Magazine Street with its attractive 18th-century houses to Shipquay Gate again; notice the fine Presbyterian Church in

Upper Magazine Street with its classical lines. This area has been much rebuilt, as hardly a single building was left undamaged through the ceaseless IRA bombing campaign of the 1970s.

The **Craft Village**, a representation of Derry between the 16th and 19th centuries, is worth a look, not least for a coffee break in one of the cafés—or a browse amongst the craft shops. **The Courthouse** (1813) in Bishop Street is a good example of Greek Revival architecture; as the city's main symbol of British justice, it received a great deal of IRA attention, and the scars of numerous car-bombs are still evident.

To visit the **Bloody Sunday Memorial,** pass through the Butcher's Gate. It is down to the right, close by the road. This commemorates 30 January 1972 when a civil rights march ended in 13 deaths after the Parachute Regiment opened fire on the marchers—government inquiries into the incident are even now continuing (*see* **History,** p.58). Close by, just outside the city walls, is the interesting 18th-century **Church of St Columba**, also called Long Tower Church. It is built on the site of a 12th-century monastery called Templemore. Saint Columba is further commemorated in a boys' school of that name further down the street. **St Eugene's Roman Catholic Cathedral**, off Infirmary Road and Great James Street, has a fine east window and high altar. It was built in Gothic style in 1873. **The Orchard Gallery** in Orchard Street (*✆ (028) 7126 9675*), will give you a taste of modern Irish art. **The Calgach Centre** in Butcher Street (*✆ (028) 7126 9792*) preserves genealogical data from 1663, but its main attraction is a multi-media exhibition on the history of the Celts in this area, based on the mythical idea of a 'fifth Irish province', the shared heritage and state-of-mind that connects those of Irish descent, no matter where they live (*open Mon–Fri 10–6, also Sat June–Sept 10–4; two showings daily of the Fifth Province; adm; ✆ (028) 7137 3177*).

Southeast across the Craigavon Bridge is the **Waterside**, which remains largely Protestant. The **Tower Museum** (*open daily July–Aug; rest of year, Tues–Sat, 10–5; adm; ✆ (028) 7137 2411*) in O'Doherty Tower, Union Hall Place, preserves the treasures of the Corporation of London, including a two-handed sword said to belong to Sir Caher O'Doherty, who raided Derry in 1608. This is an outstanding museum, the winner of several awards, and it does help you to grasp both the complex history of ancient Derry and the effects of the Troubles. Artefacts from the Spanish Armada ships wrecked off the coast in 1588 are also on display. It is well worth devoting a couple of hours to the displays, but leave time to go to the less fashionable but fascinating **Harbour Museum**, in Harbour Square (*open Mon–Fri, 10–1 and 2–5; free; ✆ (028) 7137 7331*). Ship models in glass cases, a replica of a 30ft curragh in which St Columcille (Columba) would have

The Guildhall, Londonderry

133

sailed to Iona, and Derry's maritime history are set out. It is possible to tour the **Guildhall**, which has impressive stained-glass windows depicting the city's history.

Within the walls, you will notice some attractive Georgian houses, some with medieval foundations. At the top of the hill on the Diamond, the central square of the old town, excavations were undertaken to try to uncover an early settlement, possibly the Columban foundation. However, they only revealed domestic material from the early 17th-century settler population. The old workhouse is now the **Workhouse Museum** in Glendermott Road (*open July–Aug, Mon–Sat 10–4.30; Sept–June, Tues–Sat 10–4.30; adm; ✆ (028) 7131 8328*), with exhibits on the famine; upstairs is the original workhouse dormitory in the same condition as it was for the poor souls who were sent there. In another room is the Atlantic Memorial Exhibition, which draws on the importance of the Foyle and Derry during the Second World War; the British Royal Navy, the Canadian and the US Navy had bases here. Other museums of interest are the Foyle Valley Railway Centre, the Amelia Earhart exhibition and the Harbour Museum.

Shopping

Paintings: The McGilliway Gallery, 6 Shipquay Street. Irish paintings, mainly landscape.

Bookshops: Bookworm, Bishop Street. Terrific section on books of Irish interest. Foyle Books, Craft Village. Second-hand books.

Food: Life Tree, Spencer Road, Derry.

Antiques: Forge Antiques, 24 Long Commons, Castlerock. The Whatnot, 22 Bishop Street, Derry. The Smithy, 782 Coleraine Road, Portstewart.

Crafts: The Donegal Shop, 8 Shipquay Street, Derry. Tower Museum Shop, Craft Village, Derry. Patricia Gavin, Endymion, creates elegant clothes in tweed and other textiles. Call ✆ (028) 7131 1060 for appointment.

Pottery: Tom Agnew, Brook Road, Dunamanagh, produces useful objects for everyday living in wonderful muted shades of stoneware.

Where to Stay

Derry

Everglades Hotel, Prehen Road, ✆ (028) 7134 6722, ✉ 7134 9200 (*expensive*). Overlooking the River Foyle. Bland and comfortable. **Beechhill Country House Hotel**, 32 Ardmore Road, ✆ (028) 7134 9279, ✉ 7134 5366 (*expensive*). Lovely grounds and well-known for good cuisine. **The Trinity Hotel**, 22–24 Strand Road, ✆ (028) 7127 1271, ✉ 7127 1277 (*expensive*). Modern city-centre hotel. **Da Vinci's**, 15 Culmore Rd, ✆ (028) 7126 4507 (*moderate*). 60-room hotel complex (opening April 2000), 10-min walk from the city.

Mrs Elizabeth Buchanan, **Elagh Hall**, Buncrana Road, ✆ (028) 7126 3116 (*inexpensive*). 18th-century farmhouse, 2 miles (3.2km) from the city centre, overlooking the hills of Donegal. Mrs Davidson, **Manor House**, 15 Main Street, Eglinton, (near Derry City Airport), ✆ (028) 7181 0222 (*inexpensive*). Attractive manor house. **Oakgrove Manor Hostel**, 4 Magazine Street, Derry, ✆ (028) 7137 2273, ✉ 7137 2409 (*inexpensive*). This YHANI hostel is the only accommodation inside the city walls, but there's little else to recommend it. **Florence House**, 16 Northland Rd, ✆/✉ (028) 7126 8093 (*inexpensive*). Small, comfortable B&B located near the walled city.

Elsewhere in County Londonderry

Ardtara Country House, 8 Gorteade Road, Upperlands, near Maghera, ✆ (028) 7964 4490, ✉ 7964 5080 (*expensive*). Fine 19th-century house, comfortable and welcoming. **Brown Trout Inn**, 209 Agivey Road, Aghadowey, ✆ (028) 7086 8209 (*expensive*). Pretty grounds, near the river, with good food.

Mrs Josephine King, **Camus House**, 27 Curragh Road, Coleraine, ✆ (028) 7034 2982 (*moderate*). Listed 17th-century house overlooking the River Bann. Mrs Welch, **Streeve Hill**, 25 Dowland Rd, Drenagh, Limavady, ✆ (028) 7776 6563, ✉ 7776 8285, *hidden.ireland@indigo.ie*, (*moderate*). Lovely early 18th-century house, with delicious food, and walks in parkland and moon garden.

Mrs Hegarty, **Greenhill House**, Aghadowey, Coleraine, ✆ (028) 7086 8241, ✉ 7786 8365 (*inexpensive*). Pretty Georgian farmhouse, good home-cooking. Mrs Craig, **Ballycarton Farm**, 239 Seacoast Road, Bellarena, ✆ (028) 7775 0216 (*inexpensive*). Modern farmhouse in very scenic area close to Magilligan Nature Reserve. Mrs Henry, **Carneety House**, 120 Mussenden Road, Castlerock, ✆ (028) 7084 8640 (*inexpensive*). Old farmhouse on the A2. Mrs Kane, **Ballyhenry House**, 172 Seacoast Road, Limavady, ✆ (028) 7772 2657 (*inexpensive*). Farmhouse with good home-cooking and comfortable rooms.

The Flax Mill Hostel, Mill Lane, Gortnaghey Road, Dungiven, ✆ (028) 7774 2655 (*inexpensive*). Converted stone mill, 16 beds, traditional music in pub close by. **Drumcovitt House**, 704 Feeny Road, Feeny, ✆/✉ (028) 7778 1224, *drumcovitt.feeny@btinternet* (*inexpensive*). Lovely 18th-century house in scenic countryside. Also self-catering cottage. **The Old Rectory**, 4 Duncrun Road, Bellarena, ✆ (028) 7775 0477 (*inexpensive*). Pretty house beneath Binevenagh Mountain. **Downhill Hostel**, 12 Mussenden Rd, Downhill (028) 7084 9077. One of the most comfortable and sociable hostels in Ireland, located right on a glorious stretch of beach, east of Portstewart.

self-catering

Lough Beg Coach Houses, Ballyscullion Park, Bellaghy, ✆ (028) 7938 6235, ✉ 7938 6416. Six well-appointed cottages on large estate, bordering Lough Beg, sleep 6. Full Irish breakfast and dinner can be ordered. Close to game and coarse fishing. Games room, horse-riding and lovely walks. **Drumcovitt Barn**, Feeny (*see* above). **Barnmill Cottages**, Limavady, ✆ (028) 7776 2105, ✉ 7776 3321. Attractive apartments close to beaches and game fishing on River Roe.

Eating Out

Derry

Beech Hill Country House, 32 Ardmore Road, ✆ (028) 7134 9279 (*expensive*). Delicious imaginative food such as home-made tagliatelle with chicken, and sumptuous puddings.

India House, 51 Carlisle Road, ☎ (028) 7126 0532 (*moderate*). Spicy, well-cooked and reasonably priced menu. **Browns**, Bar and Brasserie, 1 Bonds Hill, ☎ (028) 7134 5180 (*moderate*). Diverse menu based on good quality lamb, fish and veg. **Badger's**, 16 Orchard Street, ☎ (028) 7136 0736 (*moderate*). Grills, salads; lively bar and restaurant. **La Sosta Ristorante**, 45a Carlisle Road, Derry, ☎ (028) 7137 4817 (*moderate*).

The **Boston Tea Party**, Craft Village (*inexpensive*). Good snacks during the day. **Dungloe Bar**, 41 Waterloo Street (*inexpensive*). Pub grub and traditional music. **Indigo**, 27 Shipquay Street (*inexpensive*). Relaxed café-bar with tasty Asian-influenced menu and vegetarian options. **Linenhall Bar**, 3 Market Street, (*inexpensive*). **Metro Bar**, 3 Bank Place (*inexpensive*). Soup, stews. **The Sandwich Company**, The Diamond (*inexpensive*). Excellent rolls, salads.

Elsewhere in County Londonderry

Ardtara House, 8 Gorteade Road, Upperlands, Near Maghera, ☎ (028) 7964 4490 (*expensive*). Creative menu using the freshest ingredients. **Radisson Roe Park Hotel**, Limavady, ☎ (028) 7962 2212 (*expensive*). Sophisticated menu in golf-resort hotel.

Ballymaclary House, 573 Seacoast Road, Benone, ☎ (028) 7775 0283 (*moderate*). **Salmon Leap**, 53 Castleroe Road, Coleraine, ☎ (028) 7035 2992 (*moderate*). Good buffet lunch. **Trompets**, 25 Church Street, Magherafelt, ☎ (028) 7963 2257 (*moderate*). Delicious nouvelle cuisine-style food, but plenty of it. Cheaper set lunch menu.

Morelli's, The Promenade, Portstewart, ☎ (028) 7083 2150 (*inexpensive*). Ice-cream and pasta. **Brown Trout Inn**, 209 Agivey Rd, Mullaghmore, Aghadowey, ☎ (028) 7086 8209 (*inexpensive*). Well-established, with good pub food.

Lucille's Sandwich Bar, 17 Catherine Street, Limavady (*inexpensive*). Sandwiches, hot snacks. **Ditty's Home Bakery**, 44 Main Street, Castledawson (*inexpensive*). Pies, excellent bread, lasagne, also in Magherafelt. **Mary's Bar**, 10 Market Street, Magherafelt (*inexpensive*). Good pub food.

Entertainment and Nightlife

arts

Orchard Street Cinema, Derry ☎ (028) 7126 2880. Mostly art-house films. Strand Road Cinema, Strand Road, Derry. Seven-screen cinema for new release movies. The Playhouse, 5–7 Artillery Street, Derry, ☎ (028) 7126 8027. Non-sectarian community arts centre with theatre performances and drama workshops. The Verbal Arts Centre (to re-locate in 2000), ☎ (028) 7126 6946.

Outside Derry: Riverside Theatre, Cromore Road, Coleraine, ☎ (028) 7035 1388.

pubs and nightclubs

Linenhall Bar, 3 Market Street. Grand Central, 27 Strand Road. The Metro, Shipquay Street. Henry J Cocktail bar, corner of Magazine/Castle Street describes itself as a chapel of cocktails and monastery of music. The Townsman Bar, 33 Shipquay Street. Badgers, Orchard Street. Squires Night Club, 33 Shipquay Street.

The Frosses

County Antrim

The Antrim coast has a well-deserved reputation for being one of the loveliest and most spectacular in Europe. The coast road (A2) passes through exquisite little fishing villages and areas of protected beauty. The famous Giant's Causeway—one of the wonders of the natural world—the wild beauty of Fair and Torr Heads, and the ruined Dunluce Castle, all contrive to make a trip here more than worthwhile. A little way inland are the Nine Glens of Antrim, which have been celebrated in poetry and song the world over because of their scenic beauty.

Especially beautiful is Glenariff, with its waterfalls, the 'Mare's Tail' being the most spectacular. The glen is an excellent example of a post glaciation U-Valley; it is virtually geometric. The valley of the River Bann extends along the Londonderry border to Lough Neagh, the largest inland sheet of water in Britain: 150sq miles (388sq km) in all.

The weather on the east coast is variable, as it is in all parts of Ireland, although it is more inclined to be sunny and dry with a brisk breeze off the sea. The traveller who can brave the cold Atlantic water will enjoy the breakers which roll into Whitepark Bay, and the fine sandy beaches around Portrush. The cyclist will find the roads quite strenuous, with hills and hairpin bends, but will be well rewarded with the views; whilst the walker can follow the Ulster Way, a marked trail which explores the Antrim Coast and Glens. A splendid adventure is to take the boat out to Rathlin Island and spend the day watching the huge sea bird population on the cliffs there, and revelling in the island's unspoilt beauty.

County Antrim shares Belfast, the capital city of Northern Ireland, with County Down; Belfast is dealt with in a separate chapter (*see* pp.157–70).

History

Antrim lies very close to Scotland, with only a narrow strip of water in between, so it is not surprising that there are strong links between the two. Even the accent of the peoples are similar. Before the Celts invaded, the Scotti people moved easily between Scotland and Ireland, crossing the Moyle or North Sea Channel here. (This is the shortest ferry link to the mainland, and the same shifting of populations goes on today.) The word Scots is derived from the 4th-century Irish verb 'to raid', and the Romans called Ireland 'Scotia' because it was from here that all the raiders came. It was not until the 12th century that its meaning was transferred to the country now called Scotland.

Up until the 6th century the ancient Kingdom of Dalriada extended from the Antrim coast, including the islands of Rathlin and Iona, to the west of Scotland. By the late 14th century the clan MacDonnell held the balance of power and their territory straddled both sides of the Atlantic up until the Elizabethan era. The time of the Dalriadic kings and the Scotti people is shrouded in half-myth and legend, but it has given rise to some interesting theories on who are the true natives of this land; some of which have been used as cultural propoganda. The Scottish Presbyterians, whose forebears were settled here in the Jacobite plantations, have claimed that they were coming back to their original home, and that the Catholic Celts who were driven into the mountains were in fact the interlopers who had come up from the south.

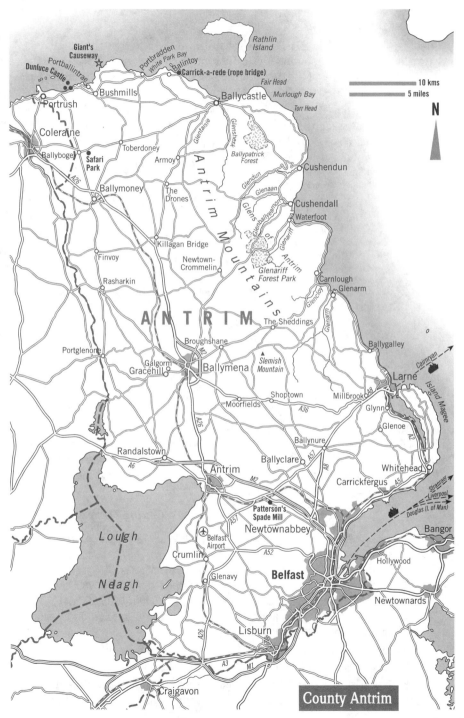

Giant's
Causeway
Portballintrae
Dunluce Castle
Portrush
Bushmills
Portbradden
White Park Bay
Balintoy
Carrick-a-rede (rope bridge)
Ballycastle
Rathlin
Island
Fair Head
Murlough Bay
Torr Head

Coleraine
Ballyboge
Safari
Park
Toberdoney
Armoy

Glenshesk

Glentaisie

Ballypatrick
Forest

Cushendun

Ballymoney
The
Drones
Killagan Bridge
Newtown-
Crommelin

Glendun
Glenaan
Glens of Antrim
Glenballyeamon
Cushendall
Waterfoot

Finvoy

Rasharkin

Glenariff
Forest Park

Glenariff

Carnlough
Glenarm

Portglenone

Broughshane

Glencloy

The Sheddings

Ballygalley

Galgorm
Gracehill
Ballymena

Slemish
Mountain

Glenarm

Cairnryan

Larne

Island Magee

Moorfields
Shoptown
Millbrook

Glynn

Glenoe

Randalstown

Antrim

Ballynure

Ballyclare

Whitehead

Carrickfergus

Stranraer
Liverpool
Douglas (I. of Man)

Lough

Patterson's
Spade Mill

Belfast
Airport

Crumlin

Newtownabbey

Bangor

Neagh

Glenavy

Belfast

Hollywood

Newtownards

Lisburn

Craigavon

County Antrim

10 kms
5 miles

N

139

Sports and Activities

Angling: The Bann, Main, Braid, Clough and Glenwhirry rivers have an abundance of brown trout, and salmon. Lough Neagh has its own variety of trout called dollaghan. The Inver, Glynn, Bush, Carey, Margy, Dun and Roe are all excellent for sea trout, salmon and brown trout. Call local tourist offices for details.

Sea and shore-fishing: Is very good all along the Antrim Coast. Boats can be hired; for a full list of operators and their addresses, refer to the Northern Ireland Tourist Board *Information Bulletin 9*, or try the Ulster Cruising School, Carrickfergus Marina, Carrickfergus, ✆ (028) 9336 8818. Best contacts for local sea fishing knowledge are: Joe Mullan, Tackle Shop, 74 Main Street, Portrush, ✆ (028) 7082 2209; Frank O'Neill, Red Bay Boats, Cushendall, ✆ (028) 2177 1331.

Cruising: On Lough Neagh and the River Bann. Contact the Ulster Cruising School, Carrickfergus, ✆ (028) 9336 8818.

Scuba-diving: Off Rathlin Island. Contact Tom Cecil, The Harbour, Rathlin, ✆ (028) 2076 3915.

Pony-trekking: Through the Ballypatrick forest at Watertop Farm, 188 Cushendall Road, Ballyvoy, Ballycastle, ✆ (028) 2076 2576. Also at Mourneview Stables, 33 Paisley's Road, Carrickfergus, ✆ (028) 9336 4734.

Whatever the theories of the past may be, today the Jacobite plantations continue to have an effect, in that there are pockets of staunch Presbyterians loyal to Britain who would man a Unionist army given half a chance. These Unionists live mainly in the rich plains, whilst there is a Catholic Nationalist fringe along the coast and in the glens; the two do not mix easily.

Stepping back into the mists and fantasy of legend, there are stories of Fionn MacCumhail (Finn MacCool) and of Oísín, his son; stories of the sons of *Uísneach* who died for Deidre's beauty; and of the Children of Lir, condemned to spend their lives as swans on the waters of the Moyle. The place-names of prehistoric remains, glens, mountains and caves abound with allusions to these myths (*see* **Old Gods and Heroes**, pp.243–8).

Getting There and Around

By air: Belfast International Airport is about 25 miles (40km) from Larne.

By sea: Stranraer or Cairnryan in Scotland are about 2½ hours by ferry from Larne; P&O Ferries, ✆ (0990) 980980. The Seacat, between Stranraer and Belfast, takes 1½ hours, ✆ (0990) 523523. P&O Jetliner, ✆ (0990) 980777, goes from Cairnryan to Larne in 1 hour. Ballycastle to Campelltown Ferry, ✆ (0990) 523523.

By rail: There are frequent train services from Belfast to Larne, which connect with ferries, and with buses travelling to the villages in the glens.

By bus: Ulsterbus operates the 'Antrim Coaster' which runs in summer between Belfast and Portstewart, stopping at most towns around the Antrim coast. Ulsterbus and

Golf: The best of many courses are: Ballycastle, a lovely seaside 18-hole course, ✆ (028) 2076 2536; Cairndhu Golf Course, outside Larne, an 18-hole parkland course, ✆ (028) 2858 3324; Royal Portrush Golf Course, three links courses by the sea, ✆ (028) 7082 2311.

Train trips: The Railway Preservation Society of Ireland runs the Portrush Flyer between Belfast and Portrush on several Saturdays each summer. The journey takes two hours and costs about £15 one way; call ✆ (028) 9335 3567 for details and dates, as these change every year.

Tennis: The Ballycastle Tennis Club, ✆ (028) 2076 3022.

Open farms: Leslie Hill Heritage Farm Park, Ballymoney, ✆ (028) 2766 6803; Watertop Farm, Ballycastle, ✆ (028) 2076 2576; Loughside Open Dairy Farm, Ballycarry, ✆ (028) 9335 3312.

Bird and wild animal sanctuary: T.A.C.T. Talnotry Cottage, 2 Crumlin Road, Crumlin, ✆ (028) 9442 2900. Home-made scones in an ornamental garden; the owners look after injured birds and small mammals. Call to arrange time for visit.

Bicycle Hire: Ardclinis Activity Centre, 11 High St, Cushendall, ✆ (028) 2177 1340. Check with Portrush tourist office for cycle shops offering rental in summer season, ✆ (028) 7082 3333.

the Old Bushmills Distillery operate an open-topped bus between 27 June and 28 August from Coleraine along the Giant's Causeway, via Portstewart, Portrush, Portballintrae, Bushmills, and back. Call ✆ (028) 7034 3334 for information.

By car: Avis, Rent-a-Car, Ferry Terminal, Larne Harbour, ✆ (028) 2827 0381. Hertz Rent-a-Car, Ferry Terminal, Larne Harbour, ✆ (028) 2827 8111.

By bike: The Raleigh Rent-a-Bike network operates in Ballymena, at RF Linton and Sons, 31 Springwell Street, ✆ (028) 2565 2516. The Skerries Pantry, 6 Bath Street, Portrush, ✆ (028) 7082 4334. Cushendall Activity Centre, 42 Layde Road, ✆ (028) 2177 1344.

getting to Rathlin Island

By boat: Daily crossings from Easter to September. From September to Easter, a limited service is arranged by the tourist office, 7 Mary Street, Ballycastle, ✆ (028) 2076 2024. The boat leaves Ballycastle at about 10.30am every day and returns in the afternoon. A return ticket costs £7.80. Four sailings per day during summer.

Tourist Information

Ballymena, Council Offices, 80 Galgorm Rd, ✆ (028) 2566 0300; open all year.
Giant's Causeway, Visitor Centre, ✆ (028) 2073 1855; open all year.
Portrush Dunluce Centre, Sandhill Rd, ✆ (028) 7082 3333; open April–Sept.
Antrim, 16 High St, ✆ (028) 9446 5156; open all year.

Ballycastle, 7 Mary Street ✆ (028) 2076 2024; open all year.

Belfast, 59 North Street, ✆ (028) 9024 6609; open all year.

Carrickfergus, Antrim Street, ✆ (028) 9336 6455; open all year.

Cushendall, 25 Mill Street, ✆ (028) 2177 1180; open Mar–Dec.

Larne, Narrow Gauge Road, ✆ (028) 2826 0088; open all year.

Festivals

Late May: Northern Lights, Ballycastle. Music festival and street entertainment.

June: *Feis na ngleann*—Gaelic music, crafts and sports in the Glens of Antrim.

Late June: The Northern Ireland Game Fair and Festival of the Countryside. Shane's Castle, Antrim.

Mid July: The Lughnasa Medieval Fair and Craft Market, Carrickfergus Castle. **14 July**: Ulster Harp Derby, Down Royal, Maze, Lisburn.

Last weekend of August: Ould Lammas Fair, Ballycastle.

The Antrim Coast

From Belfast to Larne

If you start off from Belfast for the Antrim coast, take the A2 loughside road passing the industrial districts and comfortable suburbs of Whiteabbey and Greenisland to the oldest town in Northern Ireland, **Carrickfergus**.

The town takes its name from one of the Dalriadic kings, Fergus, who foundered off this point on one of his journeys between Antrim and Scotland. The kings of Scotland were descended from his line and, therefore, the kings and queens of England. He is said to have brought his coronation stone from Ireland to Scone. Certainly the rock of redsandstone embedded with pebbles, now in Westminster Abbey, is like rock found along the Antrim coast. The town is lovely, very well kept and pedestrianized in parts with some good craft shops.

Carrickfergus Castle (*open April–Sept, Mon–Sat, 10–6, Sun, 2–6; Oct–Mar, Mon–Sat, 10–4, Sun, 2–4; adm*) is the most prominent sight in the town: a massive, rectangular, unbuttressed four-storey tower built by John de Courcy in the years after 1180. (John de Courcy and his kinsmen were very successful Normans who conquered much of Counties Down and Antrim.) In 1210, King John of England slept here during his tour of Ireland. The de Courcys renewed their oaths of allegiance to him at this time, but in reality were very much a law unto themselves. The castle has been a museum since 1928, and houses an impressive array of weapons and armour on display, plus the history of such Irish regiments as the Inniskilling Dragoons. The video presentation and costumed guides give a lively insight into the 800 years of the castle's history. Beside this splendid fortification lies the grand marina, where there are pleasure boats for hire. Carrickfergus has an old **parish church** founded by St Nicholas in 1185, and rebuilt in 1614. The famous Ulster poet Louis MacNeice (1907–63), who was associated with the group which included C. Day Lewis, Auden and Spender, wrote of the skewed alignment of the aisle:

> *The church in the form of a cross but denoting*
> *The list of Christ on the cross in the angle of the nave.*

His father was the rector here for a while. There's also a monument to Sir Arthur Chichester here, one of the loveliest pieces of 17th-century craftmanship in Ulster. The **Knight Ride** in Antrim Street is a heritage exhibition and ride through history in the best Disney traditions. You can buy a joint ticket for this and the castle (*open April–Sept, Mon–Sat, 10–6; Sun, 12–6; ✆ (028) 9336 6455*). Also worth visiting here is the **US Rangers'** and **Andrew Jackson Centre** (*open April–Sept, Mon–Fri 10–1 and 2–6, Sat and Sun 2–6; April, May & Oct, Mon–Fri 10–4, Sat and Sun 2–4; adm; ✆ (028) 9336 6455*). The exhibitions are devoted to the 1st Battalion US Rangers, raised in Carrickfergus in 1942. Antrim's **Gasworks Museum** (*June–Aug, Sun only 2–5; adm*) is the only complete Victorian coal-fired gasworks in Ireland.

On your way north out of Carrickfergus you pass **Kilroot**. Here in the ruined Church of Ireland church, Dean Swift (1667–1745), best remembered for his savage and ironic book *Gulliver's Travels,* began his clerical life. At Whitehead, less than a mile up the coast, there are excursions on vintage trains every Sunday in June, July and August. You can go up the coast as far as Portrush on the Portrush Flyer from York Street. The train is formed from preserved coaches and is hauled by a powerful mainline locomotive. The road to Larne takes you along by the lough, which is almost landlocked by Island Magee, a small peninsula with popular beaches such as Brown's Bay and Mill Bay. There is a ferry from Larne to Ballylumford on Island Magee and it is fun to walk along the Gobbins, basalt cliffs on the east side of the peninsula.

Before you get to Larne you will pass one of the glens that break through the Antrim plateau—**Glenoe**, with four waterfalls. It is now under National Trust care. The little village of **Glynn** is actually on the shore of Larne Lough, and was the setting for a film called *The Luck of the Irish.*

Although there are some hideous buildings and unecological views produced by the industrial sites round **Larne**, it is an important port and the gateway to the Antrim coast proper, so you cannot very well avoid it. There are railway services at regular intervals to and from York Street Station in Belfast. These connect with the sailing times of the boats between Larne, and Stranraer and Cairnryan. It's the shortest sea crossing from Ireland to Scotland, taking only 70 minutes once you are in open sea. **The Railway Bar** on the Main Street is good for a jar, if you have time to spare before a crossing.

On **Curran Point**, a promontory south of the harbour, you can see **Olderfleet Castle**, a corruption of the Viking name *Ulfrechsfiord.* The castle is 13th-century and ruined, with free access. If you have time to kill waiting for a ferry, a brisk 15-minute walk will take you past the Cairnyan ferry dock to Chaine Memorial Road, where a replica of a medieval round tower, 95ft (29m) tall, looks out to sea. Around here, so many Middle Stone Age artefacts have been found that the term 'Larnian' is often used to describe the Mesolithic culture of Ireland. You may not be surprised to learn that the discovery of so many early sites in the Black North (i.e. in 'Protestant' areas like Larne or Mount Sandel, near Coleraine), has given rise to an interesting theory of history: that there were anthropological differences between the two warring factions of the northeast—the aboriginal Protestants (heirs of the Dalriadic kingdom who came back from Scotland to claim their land), and the Celtic Catholic invaders. A rather incredible figure from Larne's more recent past was the romantic novelist Amanda McKittrick Ros, who was wife of the stationmaster here. *Delina Delaney* and *Poems of Puncture* were among her better known works; the young Aldous Huxley and his mates, while at Oxford, formed a reading circle to admire their awfulness. She died in 1939, convinced that she would still be remembered in a thousand years. It seems she did not realize that people responded to her writings with derision, or at best kindly laughter. In *Delina Delaney* we are told that the blood of Madame de Maine 'boiled to overflowing as she thickly smutted her handkerchief with its carmine stain'. Next she feels her every nerve in her body 'dance to the quivering tune of her bloody pores'.

From Ballygally to Ballycastle

Beyond Larne, still on the A2 coast road, some 60 miles (96km) of wonderful maritime scenery stretches ahead of you. This area is like a pictorial textbook, with examples of nearly every rock formation and epoch. For the average visitor, this means views of lovely mountains, looming white cliffs, glens, trout streams and beaches. For the geologist, it is fascinating: there are Archean schists over 300 million years old which formed the first crust over the once-molten earth, lava fields, glacial deposits, raised beaches and flint beds. The red sandstone which colours the beaches was formed from the sands of a desert which existed 110 to 150 million years ago in the Triassic epoch. This was succeeded by a sea which formed Lias clays, which in turn were changed into chalk by a later invasion of the sea. This happened between 120 to 170 million years ago, and we have the white headlands of **Fair Head** to remind us. After the Ice Age, the Glens of Antrim were formed by the movement of the inexorable glaciers which gorged out the valleys. It is best to imagine the glens as being part of a giant hand with ten fingers, and the spaces in between forming a series of short steep valleys running out towards the sea from the eastern edge of the Antrim plateau. The glens drain in a northeasterly direction and look straight across the sea of Moyle to Scotland. They were isolated from the rest of County Antrim by the difficult terrain of the Antrim plateau with its bogs and high ground near Glenarm. Today on the Garron plateau it is still possible to lose oneself, and to see wild ponies and goats grazing.

The A2 coast road links each of the nine glens. From south to north, they are Glenarm, Glencloy, Glenariff, Glenballyeamon, Glenaan, Glencorp, Glendun, Glenshesk and Glentaisie. The glens are rich in legend and history; most of the favourite characters of Irish legends make an appearance somewhere. The Children of Lir, who were changed into white swans by their wicked stepmother, were sentenced to spend three hundred years swimming on the bleak sea of Moyle—an ancient name for this stretch of the North Channel, which lies along the northeastern shores of the glens. Thomas Moore (1779–1852) tells their sad story in the 'Song of Fionnuala':

> Silent, oh Moyle be the roar of thy waters,
> Break not ye breezes your chain of repose,
> While mournfully weeping Lir's lonely daughter
> Tells to the nightstar her sad tale of woes!

Deidre and the sons of Uisneach landed near Ballycastle after they had been in exile, and were lured from there to their death at Emain Macha, near Armagh. Fionn MacCumhail (Finn MacCool) mistakenly killed his faithful hound Bran in Glenshesk, and his son Oísín (Ossian) is buried in the glens. His grave is marked by a stone circle in **Glenaan**. Other relics of the past are the megalithic monuments built by agricultural people about 5,000 years back, and the raths dotted all over the area. These were lonely farmsteads 1,500 years ago.

The glens have had a turbulent history. Originally Richard de Burgh, Earl of Ulster, conquered them, and they were sold to the Bissetts in the early 13th century. Five generations later the last of the Bissetts, Margery, the daughter of Eoin Bissett and Sabia O'Neill, became the sole heir to the glens. At this time John More MacDonnell of Kintyre, Lord of the Isles, was looking for a wife and he came to woo her. They were married in 1399, and from then on the glens have been in possession of the MacDonnells, who became known as the MacDonnells of Antrim. They still live at Glenarm Castle, and were created Earls of Antrim in the 17th century. The MacDonnells did not keep the glens easily; they spent a lot of time fighting other claimants to their territory, particularly the McQuillans, the O'Neills and Sir Arthur Chichester. In 1559 Sorley Boy MacDonnell tricked the McQuillans by spreading rushes over the bog holes which lay between the hostile camps above Glendun; and when the McQuillans and their allies the O'Neills led a cavalry charge, their horses sank into the swamps and riders became easy prey to the arrows and axes of the MacDonnells. Even today there is a saying, 'A rush bush never deceived anyone but a McQuillan'.

The remoteness of the glens has caused the people of these parts to have a great sense of regional unity and an affinity with their neighbours on the Scottish coast. They also retained the Irish language until the last quarter of the 19th century. When the Gaelic League set out to revive the Irish language early last century, they held a great *feis* (festival) in 1904 at which people competed in Irish dancing, singing and instrumental music, story-telling, crafts and hunting. A *feis* has been held every year since in one of the nine glens in late June.

From Larne you follow the A2 beneath cliffs and through the Black Cave Tunnel to **Ballygally**. Here there is a very Scottish-style castle, now a hotel. It is well worth a look inside to see the interior of a Scottish Bawn House. You can also have a drink in the bar in the dungeon. A couple of miles inland you can get a panorama of the Scottish coast, with the 'beehive' outline of Ailsa Craig from the Sallagh Braes. **Glenarm**, 'glen of the army', is one of the oldest of the glen villages, dating from the 13th century. The castle here belongs to the

MacDonnells, who are descended from Sorley Boy MacDonnell, Queen Elizabeth's great enemy. It is not open to the public, but if you go into Glenarm Forest you can look back at this turreted castle, which reminds many of the Tower of London. Those who are looking for folk music may well find it in the village itself.

This part of the coast is full of chalk and limestone. Glenarm exports it from the little harbour, and there used to be quarries at **Carnlough**, which is the town at the foot of Glencloy (glen of the hedges) although it is not particularly interesting. This area has long been inhabited and farmed, with dry-stone walls enclosing the land. Although Carnlough attracts local holiday-makers because of its sandy beach, solitude can be found on **Garron Moor**, and in the other little glens. On your way round the Garron Point to Red Bay you will notice a change in the geology from limestone to the Triassic sandstone exposed on the shore. All along the A2 coast road you will find breathtaking sea views. The road was built from 1834 to ease the hardships of the glens' people—as a work of famine relief—but it also gave them a route out, resulting in a much diminished population.

Glenariff (Ploughman's glen), is the largest and most popular of the glens with its waterfalls: *Ess na Larach* (Tears of the Mountain) and *Ess na Crub* (Fall of the Hoof). With names like these you can understand how easy it was for poets to praise these valleys. Moira O'Neill, one of the 'landscape rhymers', wrote the *Songs of the Glens of Antrim*, which encapsulate the simple lifestyle and pleasures of the 19th-century glensfolk.

Waterfoot is at the foot of the Glenariff River, by the lovely Red Bay, so called because of the reddish sand washed by the streams from the sandstone. There are caves in the cliffs above, which were once inhabited. The village is often the venue for the Glens of Antrim *Feis*. In the glen you will see steep climbing mountains and a green narrowing valley floor which gives some aptness to Thackeray's description, 'Switzerland in miniature'. This is perfect ground for nature rambles, with lovely wild flowers and the moorland of **Glenariff Forest Park**. This magnificent national nature reserve has a camp site and visitor centre in the glen. There is a beautiful walk beside the waterfalls and cascades of the glen. You can spend an hour or a whole day's hike here, and it is best to bring walking boots.

Along the east flank of the valley you can see the remains of a narrow-gauge railway which a century ago transported iron. On the west side, at the Alpinesque cliffs of Lurigethan, you can look for the mound of **Dunclana Mourna**, home of Fionn MacCumhail and his son, the poet Oísín. According to legend, the warrior Fionn was the leader of a mighty band called the *Fianna*; he was renowned for his wisdom gained through eating the Salmon of Knowledge; for his shining beauty (Fionn means fair); and for his bravery. His deeds were recounted in the legends and epics of Scotland, as well as Ireland. Fionn is the giant of the Giant's Causeway at the northern point of the county. He took up a sod of land to throw at another giant, leaving a hole which became Lough Neagh in the southeastern corner of the county, and forming the Isle of Man.

Continuing on the coast road, we get to **Cushendall**, called the capital of the glens. It lies at the foot of the **Glenballyeamon** (Edwardstown Glen), a somewhat lonesome glen, and the two glens **Glenaan** (Glen of the Colt's Foot or Rush Lights) and **Glencorp** (Glen of the Slaughter). Cushendall is delightfully situated on the River Dall, and there is an excellent golf course and camping facilities and a good bar called Pat's. An interesting building is **Turnley's Tower** at 1 Millstreet, right at the crossroads of the town. Built in 1820 as a 'Place of confine-

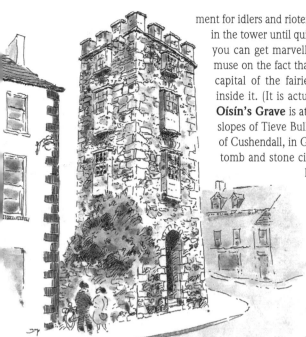
The Curfew Tower, Cushendall

ment for idlers and rioters', its garrison of one man lived in the tower until quite recently. On **Tieveragh Hill** you can get marvellous views over the coast, and muse on the fact that you might be standing on the capital of the fairies—they are supposed to live inside it. (It is actually a rounded volcanic plug.) **Oísín's Grave** is at the end of a path on the lower slopes of Tieve Bulliagh about 2 miles (3km) west of Cushendall, in Glenaan. It is in fact a megalithic tomb and stone circle but, as usual in Ireland, it has a lovely story associated with it. This Celtic Orpheus was entranced by a vision of the golden-haired Niamh, and followed her to her father's kingdom of Tír na Óg. He returned to find his companions dead and St Patrick preaching. He died unconverted, for the priests' music was not sweet to him after that of his father, Fionn. Further up the road is **Beagh's Forest**, which stands in splendid open country from where you can look back at the mountains Trostan and Slievenanee, where St Patrick is said to have spent many lonely hours in his youth watching sheep. A mile out of the village, on the way to Cushendun and by the sea, are the ruins of **Layde Church** which contains many MacDonnells' monuments and was in use up to 1790.

Cushendun village and its beach are in the care of the National Trust. Clough Williams-Ellis, who designed the pretty cottages here, also designed the seaside village of Portmeirion in Wales. There are marvellous walks around the village and surrounding area, and a camp site. The River Dun is famous for salmon and sea trout, but you have to ask the local Cushendun fishing club for permission to fish. Within the hidden glen of **Glendun** (Brown Glen) and its wood, Draigagh, there is a massive rock carved with a crucifixion scene, supposedly brought over from Iona. The poet John Masefield, whose wife came from here, was perhaps thinking of this glen when he wrote 'In the Curlew Calling Time of Irish Dusk', for it is full of wildlife and flowers. Continue along the A2 northwards to **Ballypatrick Forest**, where there is a scenic drive, a camp site, picnic area and walks. Opposite the entrance to Ballypatrick Forest is **Watertop Open Farm**, where you can see the animals at close quarters and hire a pony for trekking.

You have not finished with the glens yet, but you have some wonderful views from the headlands coming up. Go by **Torr Head**, traversing a twisty road from Cushendun through Culraney Townland, which remained an enclave of Scots Gaelic speakers until about 70 years ago. Here you can look to the Mull of Kintyre, only about 15 miles (24km) away. You can understand why this part of Ireland felt nearer to Scotland than any other kingdom.

Between here and Fair Head is **Murlough Bay** where the kings of Dalriada had their summer residence. There are no remains, but the tree-fringed beach is charming. It is in the care of the National Trust, and the best way to reach it is from Drumadoon. At **Fair Head**, reached from Ballyvoy, you can look down from the highest cliffs in the northeast, but still more impressive is the heather-covered top with its three lakes.

Ballycastle is a particularly attractive resort town. Although it's fairly lively, with lawn tennis courts in the old harbour, golf and other amusements nearby, this is the landscape for the two saddest stories of Ireland. According to legend, the Children of Lir, condemned to imprisonment as swans by their wicked stepmother, haunted these waters. At the east end of the Ballycastle sands is a rock called *Carrig-Usnach*, where the ill-fated Deidre landed with her lover and his two brothers, the sons of Uisneach, at the treacherous invitation of King Conor who, desiring her beauty, had lured them back from Scotland.

Ballycastle is divided into the market end and the harbour end. The diamond-shaped market place is the site of the Ould Lammas Fair held at the end of August. Visitors from the nearby Scottish islands travel over for this ancient, famous fair. It was given a charter in 1606 and is, therefore, the oldest of Ireland's big traditional fairs, although keep away if you don't like swarming crowds. There are large cattle and sheep sales; about five hundred stalls selling hardware, food and crafts; and fun at night, with dancing in the street. There is a rhyme that goes:

> *Did you treat your Mary-Ann*
> *To dulse and yellowman*
> *At the Ould Lammas Fair in Ballycastle?*

Ballycastle Museum (*open June–Sept, 12–6, other times by appointment;* ✆ *(0128) 2076 2024*) in Castle Street is worth a visit. Ballycastle was a stronghold of the MacDonnells. At the ruined **Bonamargy Friary**, east of the town, the great coffins of some of these redoubtable chiefs lie in the vault. Also associated with the town was the Boyd family who developed the coal mines; the entrances to these may be seen if you go across the golf course to the foot of Fair Head. **The Corrymeela Community House** is also along here. (*Corrymeela* means 'Hill of Harmony'.) This place is an interdenominational conference centre, and groups of Catholic and Protestant children come and holiday together here. The town is also famous for its tennis tournament on the grass courts which overlook the sea. These are available for hire. There is a fine beach, friendly pubs, and plenty of old-fashioned shops where you can find seaside essentials like film, shrimping nets, buckets and spades. There is a forest drive around the beehive-shaped **Knocklayd Hill** and good fishing in the River Margy.

County Antrim is very well endowed with home bakeries, and the potato bread, known as 'Fadge,' is quite a speciality around Ballycastle. Also sold here is the dulse and yellowman of the Fair rhyme: dulse being dried seaweed, salt and chewy; and yellowman being one of the most delicious confections you can imagine—a bit like the inside of a Crunchie bar. Ballycastle is a splendid touring centre, and the other glens which make the quorum of Nine Antrim Glens can be visited from here.

Glenshesk (the Sedgy Glen) is well wooded, lying east of Knocklayd Hill. **Breen Wood**, at the head of the Glen, is a nature reserve with very old oaks which probably witnessed the fights between the O'Neills and MacDonnells for mastery of the area. On the other side of the Hill of Knocklayd lies the last glen, **Glentaisie**, called after Taisia, a princess of Rathlin.

She seems to have been something of a warrior, winning a great battle on this broad glen which now carries the main road (A44) from Ballycastle to Armoy.

Another short expedition that can be made from the town is to **Kinbane Head**, a couple of miles to the northwest and stronghold of Colla MacDonnell, Sorley Boy's brother. Now it stands as a picturesque ruin on its narrow white promontory, reached from the B15 going to the Giant's Causeway. A better known tourist attraction is the swinging **Carrick-a-rede** rope bridge, north of Ballycastle, and about a mile on from Kinbane Head. The bridge is a narrow, bouncy bridge of planks with wire handrails, and it still gives a thrill to cross it. The views are tremendous, and a small salmon fishery still operates on the ocean side. (The bridge is dismantled between September and April.)

One of the prettiest towns on the coast is **Ballintoy**: if you catch it on a good day it looks like a Mediterranean fishing village with its white church and buildings. You can walk west from here to **Whitepark Bay**, a great curve of beach with sand dunes which is a National Trust property. On the edge of the cliffs is **Dunseverick Castle**, of which only one massive wall remains. In under the cliffs is the little hamlet of **Portbraddan** with a tiny church dedicated to St Gobhan (patron saint of builders), said to be the smallest church in Ireland. You will get a good close-up view of traditional salmon netting at this hamlet of four houses. The nets are set out to catch the salmon swimming along the coast to find the river where they were spawned. You should take your time here; beachcombers can find fossils, flower enthusiasts can examine the dunes, and there is even evidence of a Stone Age settlement at the east end.

Rathlin Island

Fair Head gives you a good view of **Rathlin Island**, called Raghery by the local people. The story goes that Fionn MacCumhail's mother was on her way to get some whiskey for him in Scotland, and she took a stepping stone to throw in on her way across the Moyle. This was Rathlin. This L-shaped island lies about 8 miles (13km) from Ballycastle, and 14 miles (22km) from the Mull of Kintyre, rising with white cliffs from the sea. It is populated by families who retained their Scots Gaelic longer than any other community; and it has a fascinating history, mostly of battles over the island's strategic position. Pirates and smugglers throughout the centuries have used it as a refuge and a hiding place for contraband. It was a good hideout for Robert the Bruce: he had to take refuge in one of the caves underneath the east lighthouse, and here he saw the determined spider that inspired the saying, 'If at first you don't succeed, try and try again.' This was in 1306 when, with renewed resolve, he fought for and gained the Scottish throne at Bannockburn. In Early-Christian times, the island's remote position provided a tranquil home for monks, until the Vikings came to plunder in the 9th century. There are traces of a monastic settlement and a stone sweat house at Knockans, between Brockley and the harbour; and a prehistoric mound-fort known as Doonmore, near the Stone Age settlement at Brockley. East of the harbour is a Celtic standing stone.

In more modern times Rathlin was used in an experiment to establish a wireless link with Ballycastle by Marconi, the discoverer of the wireless. In 1898 his assistant successfully managed it. The island is inhabited by about a hundred people who farm and fish. There is a guesthouse and restaurant. If you decide to pitch a tent, do ask at the appropriate farmhouse first.

As you approach Rathlin in the boat, you will see the beautiful white cliffs of the island and the endless wheeling of the sea birds which rest all over it. The most dramatic place to watch them is from the west lighthouse where the volcanic rock stacks are covered with puffins, fulmars, kittiwakes, razorbills, shearwaters and guillemots. Buzzards, waders, wild geese, ravens and peregrine falcons can be seen at different times of the year. There are no cars for hire on Rathlin which is a blessing, and the roads are silent except for the odd tractor and car belonging to one of the families who live there. The island is small enough to walk around in a (long) day or even better you can hire a bicycle. The verges of the roads are starred with wild orchids and there are hardly any bushes, let alone trees, to block the magnificent views of mountainy bog and little lakes. You might hear a corncrake calling, which is rare enough nowadays. You should be able to arrange to go lobster-fishing with one of the locals; the best place to ask is in the pub on the quay. There is good sport to be had catching eels around the wreck of the cruiser *Drake*, which was torpedoed in the First World War. There is good shore fishing, and deep-sea angling boats may be hired at Ballycastle, Ballintoy, and Portballintrae. Scuba-diving trips are organized by a local man (*see* 'Sports and Activities', p.140). The journey to Rathlin takes just 45-minutes, but if the weather turns bad you may not be able to return to the mainland the same day (*see* 'Getting Around').

The Giant's Causeway and Environs

The **Giant's Causeway** is a UNESCO world heritage site (the only one in Ireland), and this accolade only confirms what tourists have known for centuries: that the mix of black basalt columns, white chalk, sea, moorland and sandy beaches makes for a spectacular coastline. About 60 million years ago there was great volcanic activity, and basalt lavas poured out to cover the existing chalk limestone landscape. It actually baked the chalk into a hard rock— very unlike the soft chalk of southern England. These lava flows and eruptions were separated by several million years, allowing tropical vegetation and soils to accumulate. The cooling of the basalt lavas was very variable. When exposed to the air or water, they cooled rapidly and formed skins like that on the top of custard. If they cooled slowly at depth, they shrank to form remarkably even polygonal columns like the Giant's Causeway. Here the Ice Ages have eroded the cliffs and graceful arches have been formed by the action of the sea and weather.

The Giant's Causeway

There is a 5-mile (8km) circular walk past the strange formations. The National Trust, which manages the Causeway, has made great efforts to make the site accessible to the thousands who visit each year, retaining the beauty and natural habitat of the area. No souvenir shops and ice-cream vans mar the scenery as they do in other parts of this beautiful coastline. The Trust now owns 104 acres (42ha) of the North Antrim cliff path between the causeway itself and the ruins of Dunseverick Castle beside Whitepark Bay. You will find the Giant's Causeway on the B146, a looproad off the A2 between Ballycastle and Bushmills. Car parking is provided, and a shuttle bus covers the one kilometre from there to the Causeway itself; otherwise access is by foot only. The **Visitors' Centre** (*open July–Aug, daily, 10–7; earlier closing time during the rest of the year; car park adm; © (028) 2073 1852 for more details*) at the entrance includes a tea room and shop, as well as comprehensive interpretative displays, and information on the geology and history of the area. Next to the Centre is the **Causeway School Museum** (*open July and August, 11–4.30*), which takes you back to a small country school *circa* 1920.

You can walk a couple of miles north along another coastal path to **Portballintrae**, a picturesque fishing village, past a huge strand with strong Atlantic rollers (be careful of the undertow), called Runkerry. Here, a Spanish galleon, the *Girona*, was sunk off the Giant's Causeway. It contained the most valuable cargo yet found. You can see the recovered treasures in the Ulster Museum, Belfast.

Bushmills, which lies on the A2 inland from Portballintrae, is famous for its whiskey distillery which claims to be the oldest in the world. Whiskey (coming from the word *usquebaugh*, *uisce beatha* or sweet water) is one word that the English have taken from the Irish. Before whiskey became a genteel drink, 'the best Coleraine' was admitted to be a connoisseur's drink. Peter the Great in 1697 on his study tour of Europe was amongst many to appreciate the Northern Irish liquor. Bushmills distillery can be visited (*a tour of the distillery takes about one hour; open daily April–Oct, rest of year Mon–Fri only, © (028) 2073 1521; adm*).

If you like adventure stories of the old-fashioned historical variety, read one of George Birmingham's novels—say, *Northern Iron*. He lived between 1806 and 1872; his books are amusing and give a great insight into 'Victorian Ireland'. He used to live round here, and incorporates scenes from Irish life on this part of the coast and elsewhere in the North in his work. Many of Charles Lever's (1806–72) novels are set round here too. His books are more thrilling, and they helped to create the tradition of the rollicking devil-may-care young Irishman.

From the quiet little town of Bushmills you can move via the A2 on to Northern Ireland's biggest seaside resort, **Portrush**. Before you reach this uninspiring mecca of amusements and fish and chips, visit **Dunluce Castle**, sometimes translated as Mermaid's Fort (*open April–Sept, Mon–Sat, 10–7, Sun, 2–7; Oct–Mar, Mon–Sat, 10–4, Sun, 2–4; adm; © (028) 2073 1938*), whose bold ruins keep watch over the magnificent coastline. You can see it from the A2, 3 miles (5km) before you reach Portrush. Its long, romantic history is set out in a leaflet available at the entrance. Its kitchen actually fell into the seas while it was inhabited. Anyone approaching it along the shore (you can scramble from the White Rocks, a range of chalk cliffs accessible from the main road) may see the rare meadow cranesbill flower called the Flower of Dunluce. Portrush is on a promontory jutting out into the Atlantic. It has a small harbour which is popular with yachtsmen sailing in the west, and from here you can take boat cruises to see the Causeway Coast and the Skerries, a group of rocky islands where the great auk (now extinct) used to nest. Crowded in summer, it's not the most appealing place along the coast to stay—except perhaps for golfers, trying out the renowned Royal Portrush course—though its Victorian/Edwardian main buildings have their own contribution to make to the unique flavour of a Northern coastal resort. Just west is the more personable resort of **Portstewart**, which also boasts excellent golf courses, as well as a huge stretch of sandy beach. An adventurous option in good weather is to hire a bike and cover a loop from Portrush to the Causeway, down to Bushmills (for a well-earned whiskey) and back; it is possible to cover all of this in a single energetic but rewarding day.

Mid-Antrim

As you set off through mid-Antrim via **Ballymena** you will be passing through the richest farmland in the North. The farmers here are among the most modern and hardworking in Ireland. If you are here during the summer you will see the Loyalist flag, with a white background and red hand on a red cross, fluttering from many a household. This area has also benefited from the linen industry, which was greatly boosted in the late 17th century by the Huguenot weavers, who sought refuge here from the religious intolerance of Louis XIV of France. Louis Crommelin is credited with having started the linen industry, and northeast of Ballymena on the B64 is the little village of **Newtown-Crommelin** which is called after him. It is now a lonely sheep-rearing settlement, though in the past bauxite was mined on the moors around it. Ballymena itself is a very prosperous town; the rumour is that all the farmers roundabout have bank accounts in the tax haven of the Isle of Man. (A riddle asks—'Why are pound notes green?'—because Ballymena men pick them before they are ripe.)

Another spot worth stopping at is the little Moravian settlement of **Gracehill** just outside Ballymena, where you can see some of the communal buildings dating from the 18th century around the green. These Moravians came from Eastern Europe. Their Protestant sect, also known as the United Brethren, was founded in Saxony, before they came to Ireland in 1746. The village is linked to **Galgorm** by a bridge over the River Main. You can get a glimpse of the 17th-century Galgorm Castle, which is surrounded by a lawn and stately trees. The little village itself is delightful, with thatched cottages along one main street which runs by the river to the castle.

Off the A26 to Coleraine, just on the outskirts of **Ballymoney**, is **Leslie Hill Historic Park and Farm** (*open April–May and Sept, Sun and public holidays, 2–6; June, Sat and Sun, 2–6; July and Aug, Mon–Sat, 11–6, Sun, 2–6; adm; © (028) 2766 6803*). The 18th-century farm buildings include the Bellbarn (a threshing barn), a dovecote, a typical cattle byre and the payhouse. You can also see the old stables which now house newborn piglets. The famous traveller and agriculturist Arthur Young visited Leslie Hill in 1776, and much admired the lovely grounds, pretty lake and island. The estate has been lived in by the Leslie family for 350 years, and the big house is a classic Georgian stone-cut building dating from 1760 (*only open to groups and advanced booking is advised*). A few miles to the north in the tiny village of Benvarden Dervock, **Benvarden House and Garden** (*open June–Aug, Tues–Sun 2–6; adm; © (028) 2074 1331*) is worth a visit with its attractive 18th-century garden and pleasure grounds.

When you make your way down to Antrim Town and Lough Neagh you will see the distinctive shape of **Slemish Mountain**, east of Ballymena, where St Patrick spent his youth after capture by Irish pirates. To get to it, take the B94 from Broughshane; turn left after a mile, right after 3 miles (5km) (signposted), right after half a mile, and follow the road between dry-stone walls to Slemish car park. From the top, which is a steep climb of about 700ft (213m), you get a wonderful view. This lonely, extinct volcano has been a place of pilgrimage on St Patrick's Day, 17 March, for centuries. At **Broughshane**, a mile beyond the village on the A42, is **Carncairn Daffodils Centre** (*adm free*) where you can buy bulbs which have frequently won prizes in the Chelsea Flower Show. At **Dreen**, near Cullybrackey, is the ancestral home of US President Chester Arthur (1881–5). It is a thatched cottage which has been restored and furnished (*open to the public from April to September in the afternoons; adm*).

Two miles south of Temple Patrick on the A6 is **Patterson's Spade Mill** (*open April, May and Sept, Sat and Sun, 2–6; June to Aug, daily except Tues, 2–6 ; adm; © (028) 9443 3619*). It is the only water-driven spade mill left in Ireland, and you can see a traditional forge where nine regional types of spades are produced, although in its heyday the Mill used to produce around 300 different types. It has been restored by the National Trust and there is a fascinating guided tour; the busy, glowing workshop is full of exciting bangs and clangs showing the way things used to be done. Best of all you can go away with your own sturdy spade.

Antrim Town stands a little way back from Lough Neagh. The town has an old nucleus with a 9th-century round tower in almost perfect condition on Steeple Road (north of the centre), but it is being encircled by new housing and shopping centres. The ruined **Antrim Castle and Gardens** (*open Mon–Fri 9.30–9.30, Sat 10–5, Sun 2–5; © (028) 9442 8000*), c. 1662, are worth a visit. The former stable block is now an arts centre, but of the castle itself only a tower remains, the rest destroyed by fire in 1922. The gardens have been carefully restored and include geometrical borders in the 17th-century Anglo-Dutch style and a wooded walk.

Shane's Castle, outside Randelstown, is a ruin on a private estate, which is now open to the public. It is on the site of the ancient stronghold of Edenduffcarrick. The castle was for many centuries associated with the O'Neills of Clandeboye; the sculptured head in the south wall of the tower, about 30ft from the ground, is known as the Black Head of the O'Neills. The tradition is that, if anything should happen to the head, the O'Neill family will come to an end.

Lough Neagh, the largest stretch of inland water in the British Isles, is surrounded by flat marshy land, so you do not get a good view of it from the road. It is famous for the eels, which spawn in the Sargasso Sea, swim across the Atlantic, and struggle up the Bann in springtime, all 20 million of them (though now, as many as possible are captured at Coleraine and brought to Lough Neagh in tankers). The eels take about 12 years to mature, and the main fishery is at **Toomebridge**, a very large co-operative managed by local fishermen and farmers. **New Ferry**, at the top of Lough Beg, is a haven for coarse fishermen as well as water skiers.

Lisburn in the Lagan Valley in the southern tip of County Antrim has a **Planters Gothic Cathedral**. Louis Crommelin lived here and there is an excellent **museum and Irish Linen Centre** which includes a re-creation of a linen-weaving workshop; the workshop produces specialist linen which you can buy (*open all year; © (028) 9266 3377*).

Shopping

Bread: Good bakeries all over the county; especially good soda and potato breads.

    Whiskey: The Old Bushmills Distillery, Bushmills, © (028) 2073 1521. Tours and free sampling.

Delicacies: dulse (seaweed) and yellowman (confectionery) in Ballycastle grocery shops. Also wonderful sausages and black pudding at Wysner Meats, 18 Ann Street, Ballycastle, ✆ (028) 2076 2372.

Crafts: Giant's Causeway and Cushendun National Trust Shops, open April to September. Irish Linen Centre, Lisburn. Forge Pottery, Antrim. Orchard Crafts, Castlecroft, Main Street, Ballymoney.

Markets: For vegetables and clothes at Ballymena on Saturdays, the market car park beside the leisure centre on the Larne Road link.

Fresh eels: Lough Neagh Fishermans' Co-operative Society, Toomebridge, ✆ (028) 7965 0618.

Where to Stay

North Antrim

Bushmills Inn, Main Street, Bushmills, ✆ (028) 2073 2339, 🖷 2073 2048 (*expensive*). Comfortable, good service, excellent food. Sir William and Lady Moore, **Moore Lodge**, Kilrea, Ballymoney, ✆ (028) 2954 1043 (*expensive*). Very up-market, with excellent fishing on the River Bann. **Causeway Hotel**, 40 Causeway Road, Giant's Causeway, ✆ (028) 2073 1226, 🖷 2073 2552 (*expensive*). Delightful family-run hotel.

Maddybenny Farmhouse, 18 Maddybenny Park, Portrush, ✆/🖷 (028) 7082 3394. Comfortable, easy-going atmosphere, with the best breakfast in Northern Ireland. Horse riding available. The **Londonderry Arms Hotel**, 20 Harbour Road, Carnlough, ✆ (028) 2888 5255, 🖷 2888 5263 (*moderate*). This was originally built as a coaching inn by the Marchioness of Londonderry, whose mother was the Countess of Antrim. It later came into possession of her grandson, Sir Winston Churchill, who sold it in 1926. It has a delightful old-world atmosphere. **Drumnagreagh Hotel**, 408 Coast Road, Glenarm, ✆/🖷 (028) 2884 1651 (*moderate*). Small hotel with stunning views.

Dunaird House, 15 Buckna Road, Broughshane, ✆ (028) 2568 62117 (*inexpensive*). Welcoming, modernized farmhouse. Mr and Mrs McCurdy, **Rathlin Guesthouse**, The Quay, Rathlin Island, ✆ (028) 2076 3917 (*inexpensive*). This is a very friendly guest house from where you can explore the beautiful island. **Harbour House**, 36 Kerr Street, Portrush, ✆ (028) 7082 2130 (*inexpensive*). Restored 18th-century house. **Colliers Hall**, 50 Cushendall Road, Ballycastle, ✆ (028) 2076 2531 (*inexpensive*). Guest house one mile outside Ballycastle.

Island Farm, 13 Islandranny Road, Bushmills, ✆ (028) 2073 1488 (*inexpensive*). Friendly B&B on castle farm. **The Villa**, 185 Torr Road, Cushendun, ✆ (028) 2176 1252 (*inexpensive*). Victorian villa, set off the road in own gardens, comfortable and close to the beach. **Margaret's House**, 10 Altmore Street, Glenarm, ✆ (028) 2884 1307 (*inexpensive*). Welcoming old house, close to the hills and beach. **Glenkeen Guesthouse**, 59 Coleraine Rd, Portrush, ✆ (028) 7082 2279 (*inexpensive*). Good value B&B just out of the centre of town, all rooms en-suite.

South Antrim

Galgorm Manor, Ballymena, ✆ (028) 2588 1001, 🖷 2588 0080 (*luxury*). A spectacular 17th-century castle with lovely lawns transformed into a plush hotel. **Adair Arms Hotel**, Ballymoney Road, Ballymena, ✆ (028) 2565 3674, 🖷 2564 0436 (*moderate*). Attractive old 23-room hotel. **Dunadry Hotel and Country Club**, 2 Islandreagh Drive, Dunadry, ✆ (028) 9443 2474, 🖷 9443 3389 (*expensive*). Comfortable, modern hotel near Belfast International airport.

Manor Guest House, 23 Olderfleet Road, Larne, ✆ (028) 2827 3305, 🖷 2826 0505 (*inexpensive*). Grade A guest house on the seafront. **Craig Park**, 24 Carnbore Road, Bushmills, (028) 2073 2496, 🖷 2073 2479 (*inexpensive*). Comfortable country house near Giant's Causeway. **Keef Halla Guest House**, 20 Tully Road, Nutts Corner, Crumlin, ✆/🖷 (028) 9082 5491 (*inexpensive*). Grade A, comfortable and modern, 5 minutes from Belfast International airport.

self-catering

Ballinlea Mill, 34 Kilmahamoque Road, Ballycastle, ✆/🖷 (028) 2076 2287. Restored mill-house, sleeps 8. From £300 per week low season. **Briarfield**, 65 Dickeystown Road, Glenarm, ✆ (028) 2884 1296. Cottage, sleeps 4; from £150 per week low season.

All the following cottages can be booked through Rural Cottage Holidays Ltd., NITB, ✆ (028) 9024 1100, 🖷 9024 1198. They are all attractive traditional dwellings, restored and furnished to a high standard. Cost varies with the season, but a cottage sleeping 6 is £410 per week at the top rate:

Slemish Cottage, Broughshane. 100-year-old farmhouse with lovely views, sleeps 6. **Manns Cottage**, Broughshane. Equally attractive, sleeps 10. **Bellair Cottage**, Glenarm. In the glens above Glenarm, whitewashed farmhouse, sleeps 6. **Strand House**, Cushendun. In pretty National Trust village, sleeps 7. **John O'Rocks**, Cushendun. Just a few steps from a sandy beach, sleeps 6. **O'Harabrook**, Old Dairy, Ballymoney. Three apartments in stone-built outhouses on large farm; each apartment sleeps 6.

hostels

Whitepark Bay Youth Hostel, 150 Whitepark Road, Whitepark Bay, ✆ (028) 2073 1745, excellent facilities, with views onto the beach; some family rooms. **Ballycastle Backpackers Hostel**, 4 North Street, Ballycastle, ✆ (028) 2076 3612. Seafront houses. **Moneyvart Youth Hostel**, 24 Layde Road, Cushendall, ✆ (028) 2177 1344, 🖷 2177 2042. North of village, in the glens, some family rooms. **Sheep Island View Hostel**, 42a Main St, Ballintoy, ✆ (028) 2076 9391. Handy position for seeing the Causeway coast; comfortable new hostel with ocean views, bikes for rent.

Eating Out

North Antrim

The **Ramore Restaurant**, The Harbour, Portrush, ✆ (028) 7082 4313 (*expensive*). You can promise yourself a superb meal here: the chef has won many awards. Good value food during the day in the wine bar downstairs.

Bushmills Inn, Main Street, Bushmills, ✆ (028) 2073 2339 (*moderate*). Delicious cold salmon and salads in a bistro-style restaurant. **Hillcrest Country House Restaurant**, 306 Whitepark Road, Giant's Causeway, ✆ (028) 2073 1577 (*moderate*); *à la carte* and high tea. Also a B&B. **Magherabuoy House Hotel**, Portrush, ✆ (028) 7082 3507 (*moderate*). Hearty meals. **Marine Hotel**, Ballycastle, ✆ (028) 2076 2222 (*moderate*). Simple but good cooking in large hotel. **Old Bank House**, Church Street, Ballymoney, ✆ (028) 2766 2724 (*moderate*). Good steak and ale pies.

Harbour Bar, Portrush. Great atmosphere. **National Trust Tearooms**, Cushendun (*inexpensive*). Light meals during the day, 12–6. *Summer only*. Also **Giant's Causeway** (*inexpensive*). *Open Mar–Oct, daytime only*. **Brown Jug**, 23 Main Street, Ballymoney (*inexpensive*). Salads, quiche. *Daytime only*. **Rathlin Guesthouse**, The Quay, Rathlin Island, ✆ (028) 2076 3917 (*inexpensive*). Snacks, sandwiches, high tea.

McCuaig's Bar, The Quay, Rathlin (*inexpensive*). Pub grub. **Market Square**, Lisburn (*inexpensive*). Salads, snacks. **Leslie Hill Open Farm**, Ballymoney (*inexpensive*). Scones, cakes, teas. **Sweeney's Wine Bar**, Seaport Avenue, Portballintrae, ✆ (028) 2073 2405 (*inexpensive*). Grilled meats, vegetarian meals.

Mid and South Antrim

Dunadry Inn, 2 Islandreagh Drive, Dunadry, ✆ (028) 9443 2474 (*expensive*). The wine bar here is open during the day. It is conveniently close to the airport, and unexpectedly good. **Galgorm Manor**, Ballymena, ✆ (028) 2588 1001 (*expensive*). Opulent dining. **Ginger Tree**, 29 Ballyrobert Road, Newtownabbey, ✆ (028) 9084 8176 (*expensive*). Delicious Japanese food.

The Londonderry Arms, Carnlough, ✆ (028) 2888 5255 (*moderate*). Very good fish, and wonderful views of the sea and glens. **Manley**, State Cinema Arcade, 70a Ballymoney Road, Ballymena, ✆ (028) 2564 8967 (*moderate*). Cantonese and Peking cooking. **Water Margin**, 8 Cullybackey Road, Ballymena, ✆ (028) 2564 8368 (*moderate*). Cantonese cooking. **Dobbins Inn**, 6 High Street, Carrickfergus, ✆ (028) 9335 1905 (*moderate*). Rich *à la carte* food and bar meals. **Jourdans**, 50 Main Street, Kells, ✆ (028) 9389 1258 (*moderate*). Pub grub and more sophisticated meals.

Entertainment and Traditional Music

The Harbour Bar, Portrush. **The Central Bar**, Ballycastle. **McCarrolls Bar**, Ballycastle. **The House of McDonnell**, Ballycastle. **McCollam's Bar**, Cushendall.

The shipyards from Victoria Park

Belfast

Belfast is probably known to most people through the exposure brought by the Troubles. Press and television news reports have recorded the bombings, the military involvement and the sectarian murders, giving the impression of a war-torn city, constantly in a state of unrest and dangerous to visit. This is simply not the case. The visitor will be surprised at how 'normal' the streets are—full of people shopping at Marks & Spencer and the various chain stores which now proliferate in all British cities. Military patrols and armoured police vehicles are a rare sight, where once they were an everyday part of life in the city. The people too share a cautious optimism about the peace process, and while old sectarian divisions die hard, there is almost unanimous support for a permanent political resolution to the violence. The Belfast people are friendly and sympathetic to the tourist, answering any queries with the good humour and interest which is a characteristic of the Irish. There are many opportunities to see good theatre, art shows, classical and pop concerts, whilst a strong intellectual and historical sense makes for interesting conversations and well-stocked bookshops. The well-educated young are still leaving for opportunities abroad, but many are coming back with a wealth of experience. Belfast is losing its parochial image aand becoming more European-minded, and the bars and cafés more sophisticated. The new Waterfront Hall and Hilton seem to be new symbols for Belfast, just as the Europa Hotel and the Opera House became symbols of surviving the bomb and bullet during the worst of the troubles in the 1970s. A highly ambitious project underway in 2000 is the Odyssey Centre, which is to incorporate a sports stadium, science centre and IMAX cinema.

Belfast (in Gaelic *Beal Feirst* : the mouth of the sandy ford) is the administrative centre of the six counties that make up Northern Ireland. It has one of the most beautiful natural settings of any city: ringed by hills which are visible from most parts of the town, and hugging the shores of the lough. It has been a city officially only since 1888. In the 19th century it grew from an insignificant town by a river ford into a prosperous commercial centre and port, with great linen mills and the famous shipyards of Harland & Wolf. The Titanic, built here and so tragically sunk by an iceberg, was considered an outstanding engineering feat.

Architecturally, Belfast is made up of some grand Victorian public buildings and the red-brick streets which characterize many British towns. The prosperous 'big houses' which make up the smart Malone Road area, and line the lough on either side, were built by the wealthy middle class who had benefited from the linen industry. The workers in the factories and shipyards divided themselves between the Catholic Falls Road area and the Protestant Shankill Road. Unemployment became worse as the linen and ship-building industries declined, nurturing the conditions in which the terrorist armies could thrive. The division of these working class areas from the city centre was made explicit by the Westlink motorway, which runs north-south and creates a boundary line through the west side of the city.

By air: Belfast International Airport, ✆ (028) 9442 2888, is 19 miles (30km) from the city. The airport coach leaves every ½ hour from the Great Victoria Street Bus Station (just behind the Opera House entrance on Glengall Street). Belfast City Airport, ✆ (028) 9045 7745, is 4 miles (7km) from the city centre. It is served by local UK airlines only—no international flights. Take a train to Sydenham Halt from Central Station or Great Victoria Street station, or bus no.21 or taxi from City Hall, Donegall Square.

By boat: Larne to Cairnryan Ferry and Jet Liner, ✆ (0990) 980777. The Larne ferry service always links in with a train to Belfast. The station is just beside the ferry terminal building. Belfast–Liverpool car ferries, ✆ (0990) 779090. Hoverspeed Sea Cat, Belfast–Stranraer, 4 crossings per day; journey takes 1½ hours, ✆ (0990) 523523. Belfast–Isle of Man Steam Packet, ✆ (0990) 523523.

By rail: From Belfast Central Station, East Bridge Street, trains go to all destinations except Larne Harbour. Larne Harbour is served by York Gate Station. All rail transport enquiries, ✆ (028) 9089 9411. Please note there are no left luggage facilities in any Northern Ireland railway station.

By bus: Ulsterbus operates within the city suburb and throughout the province. Their coaches also go to the Irish Republic, and mainland UK. The main Belfast bus stations are: Europa Centre, Great Victoria Street (entrance in Glengall Street), for destinations in Counties Armagh, Tyrone, Londonderry, Fermanagh and West Down, and the Republic of Ireland. For all destinations in County Antrim and East Down go to the Laganside Bus Centre (east of Albert Clock Tower). Enquiries and timetables for all Ulsterbus destinations, ✆ (028) 9033 3000, open daily 7.30–8.30. No left luggage facilities.

City buses are red and cover most routes within Belfast. City bus enquiries, ✆ (028) 9024 6485. City stopper buses nos.523–538 provide an additional service on the Falls Road and Lisburn Road.

Parking: The centre of Belfast is taboo for parking. It is very clear where not to park: there are large notices on the pavements and double yellow lines. Excellent car parks and pay-and-display areas ring the centre of the city. The tourist office has a list and map of all car parks in the Belfast area.

By bike: McConvey Cycles, 467 Ormeau Road, ✆ (028) 9049 1163.

City bus tours: All tours leave Castle Place. For details call ✆ (028) 9045 8484.

Walking tours: Tours of the old town or pub tours, call ✆ (028) 9024 6609. Belfast City Centre and Laganside walk or Belfast Town and Gown walk, call ✆ (028) 9049 1469.

Northern Ireland Tourist Information Centre, 59 North Street, ✆ (028) 9024 6609, ✉ 9031 2424. Open Mon–Sat, 9–5.15. Extended opening hours in summer.

Bord Fáilte, 53 Castle Street, ✆ (028) 9032 7888, ✉ 9024 0201. Open March–Sept, Mon–Fri 9–5, Sat 9–12.30.

useful addresses

Emergency Services, ✆ 999.

Royal Victoria Hospital, Grosvenor Road, ✆ (028) 9024 0503.

AA, 108/110, Great Victoria Street, ✆ (0990) 500600. (24-hour rescue service, ✆ 0800 887766.) **RAC**, 14 Wellington Place, ✆ (0990) 722722. (24-hour rescue service, ✆ 0800 828282.)

Lost Property: Musgrave Police Station, Ann Street, ✆ (028) 9065 0222, ext. 26049.

Youth Hostel Association, 22 Donegall Road, ✆ (028) 9032 4733, ✉ 9043 9699.

USIT/Belfast Student Travel, ✆ (028) 9032 4073.

Festivals

November: Belfast Festival at Queens. Festival Box Office, College Gardens, 8 Malone Rd, ✆ (028) 9066 5577/9066 6321. The arts scene really hots up for three weeks. Classical, jazz, pop and folk music events are on in church halls and every available space. So too are films, plays and art exhibitions. The most successful fringe shows from Edinburgh come to the city, and the festival proper attracts internationally known stars. Events take place mainly around the university area.

Early May: Belfast Civic Festival Concert, Lord Mayor's Show.

August: *Féile an Phobail*: music, drama, Irish language events, carnival, parade.

Late August/Sept: Folk Festival: local and international performers, *céili.*

Key

● Hotels

1   Europa Hotel
2   Dukes
3   Wellington Park Hotel
4   Ash Rowan Town House
5   Lisdara Town House
6   Camera Guest House
7   Queens University Common Room
8   Eglantine Guest House
9   Liserin Guest House
10 Windermere Guest House
11 Belfast International Youth Hostel
12 Queens Elms
13 The Ark
14 The George

■ Restaurants

A   Roscoff's
B   Deanes
C   Sun Kee
D   Manor House
E   Ashoka
F   Chez Dalbert
G   Antica Roma
H   Belfast Castle
I   The Other Place
J   Scarletts
K   Villa Italia
L   Cafe Bongo
M   Speranza
N   La Salsa
O   Maggie May's

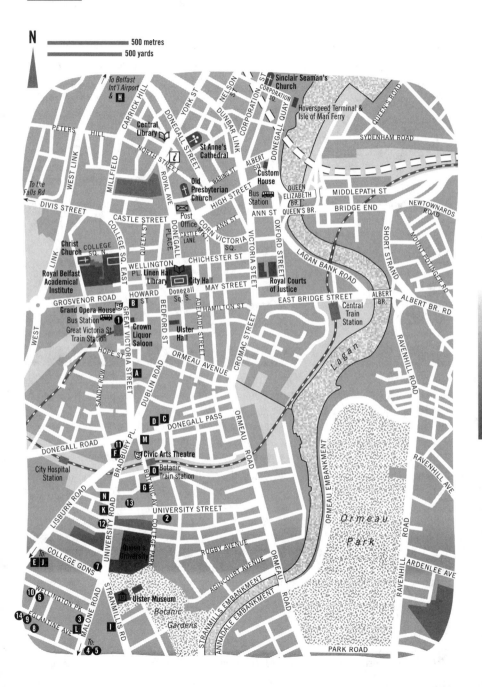

Belfast

N

500 metres
500 yards

To Belfast
Int'l Airport
& H

Sinclair Seaman's
Church

Hoverspeed Terminal &
Isle of Man Ferry

Central
Library

St Anne's
Cathedral

PETERS
HILL

WEST LINK
LINK

CARRICK HILL

YORK ST

DONEGALL STREET

NORTH STREET

ROYAL AVE

DONEGALL LINK

NELSON ST

DUNBAR LINK

WARING ST

CORPORATION ST

CORPORATION
SQ.

DONEGALL QUAY

QUEEN'S ROAD

SYDENHAM ROAD

To the
Falls Rd

DIVIS STREET

CASTLE STREET

MILLFIELD

Old
Presbyterian
Church

HIGH STREET

ALBERT
SQ.

Custom
House

Bus
Station

ANN ST

QUEEN
ELIZABETH
BR.
QUEEN'S BR.

MIDDLEPATH ST

BRIDGE END

NEWTOWNARDS
ROAD

Post
Office

Christ
Church

COLLEGE
SQ. N.

COLLEGE SQ. EAST

QUEEN ST

DONEGALL
PLACE

CASTLE
LANE

CORN MARKET

CASTLE STREET

CORN
VICTORIA
SQ.

CHICHESTER ST

ANN ST

VICTORIA STREET

OXFORD STREET

Royal Courts
of Justice

LAGAN BANK ROAD

SHORT STRAND

MOUNT POTTINGER RD

ALBERT BR. RD

Royal Belfast
Academical
Institute

GROSVENOR ROAD

WELLINGTON
PL.

Linen Hall
Library

City Hall

Donegall
Sq. S.

MAY STREET

HAMILTON ST

EAST BRIDGE STREET

ALBERT
BR.

Central
Train
Station

RAVENHILL ROAD

Grand Opera House

Bus Station

Great Victoria St
Train Station

HOWARD
ST

B

GREAT VICTORIA STREET

BEDFORD ST

ADELAIDE STREET

CROMAC STREET

Lagan

WEST

HOPE ST

SANDY ROW

Crown
Liquor
Saloon

Ulster
Hall

DUBLIN ROAD

ORMEAU AVENUE

A

D C

DONEGALL PASS

ORMEAU ROAD

ORMEAU EMBANKMENT

Ormeau
Park

RAVENHILL AVE

DONEGALL ROAD

M

F 11

Civic Arts Theatre

BRADBURY PL.

City Hospital
Station

Botanic
Train station

G

O

N

K

13

UNIVERSITY STREET

2

RUGBY AVENUE

AGINCOURT AVENUE

ORMEAU EMBANKMENT

ANNADALE EMBANKMENT

ARDENLEE AVE

LISBURN ROAD

12

UNIVERSITY ROAD

COLLEGE PARK

BOTANIC AVENUE

To:
E J

COLLEGE GDNS

Queen's
University

1

STRANMILLS RD

RAVENHILL ROAD

10 6

WELLINGTON PK

14 9 8

EGLANTINE AVE

3

L

I

MALONE ROAD

Ulster Museum

Botanic
Gardens

STRANMILLS EMBANKMENT

To:
4 5

PARK ROAD

161

Sports and Activities

Golf: 18-hole course at Carrickfergus Golf Club, 7 miles (12km) northeast of Belfast on the A2, ✆ (028) 9363 3713. Blackwood Golf Centre, Crawfordsburn Road, Clandeboye, ✆ (028) 9185 2706. Balmoral Golf Club, Lisburn Road, ✆ (028) 9038 1514 (18-hole).

Leisure centres: Maysfield Leisure Centre, East Bridge Street, ✆ (028) 9024 1633, is central and has a pool, gym, squash and sauna. Contact Belfast City Council, Leisure Services Dept, ✆ (028) 9032 0202, for a list of other leisure centres.

Organized tours: Citybus run 3½ hours tours which take in all the main sights of Belfast including Stormont and Belfast Castle. Also a Living History Tour which takes in the areas of Belfast associated with the Troubles. It lasts 2½ hours; ✆ (028) 9045 8484. Guided walking tours which include a tour of pubs, historic Belfast, the University area and Laganside walk are all available. Details from the tourist office, ✆ (028) 9024 6609.

Lagan Valley Walk: A towpath winds for 10 miles along the banks of the river. It starts from close by the Belfast Boat Club at Stranmillis, and ends upstream at Moore's Bridge, Lisburn, ✆ (028) 9049 1922.

Lagan Weir and Lookout Centre: Donegall Quay. Platform views of the busy waterway. Industrial and folk history of the Lagan River and Belfast. *Open April–Sept, Mon–Fri 11–5, Sat 12–5, Sun 2–5; Oct–March, closed Mon, Tues–Sun shorter winter hours; adm; ✆ (028) 9031 5444.*

Central Belfast

The city centre is pedestrianized for security reasons, but you will see nothing else out of the ordinary, unless you are extraordinarily unlucky. The centre of Belfast has been spoiled by awful shopping arcades and the usual range of British high street shops, which on the up-side means that shopping is convenient and there are now a few decent cafés. There also a few specialist interior decoration, furniture, and Irish design shops worth looking out for (*see* below under 'Shopping'). The city centre is quite compact and is easy to walk around.

Because Belfast is a 19th-century town it lacks the graciousness of Dublin; its city fathers were plutocrats, rather than aristocrats. Two of the most attractive buildings are on Great Victoria Street: the **Grand Opera House** and the **Crown Liquor Saloon,** the latter a gas-lit High-Victorian pub decorated with richly coloured tiles. It has been preserved by the National Trust, but has not been gentrified and its old clientele still drink there. The Opera House was also designed in High-Victorian style (by Robert Matcham, the famous theatre architect) with rich, intricate decorative detail, including carved elephants. It was restored in the 1970s by the architect Robert McKinstry, and painted on the ceiling is a fine fresco by Cherith McKinstry. Even if you don't have an evening to spare, both buildings are worth a quick look around, and the Crown is generally good around lunchtime for a quiet pint with lunch.

Although many of the splendours of Belfast date from its period of mercantile importance, there was a great quickening of spirit here in the 18th century. United Irishman Henry Joy McCracken, whose family first published *The Belfast Newsletter* in 1737 (the longest-running newspaper in the world), was a son of the city. Other 18th-century personalities include William Drennan, who coined the phrase 'the Emerald Isle' and founded the **Royal Academical Institution**, a distinguished building between College Square East and Durham Street designed by Sir John Soane, the eminent London architect, classical scholar and collector. It was built between 1808 and 1810 in a style that is classical in proportion. The institution is now a school, but it is possible to look around it. The prospect is a little spoiled by the great College of Technology, built on the corner of the lawn. The **City Hall** (*guided tours available; adm free; ✆ (028) 9027 0456*) in Donegall Square, built between 1896 and 1906 in Portland stone, is a grand composition with a central dome and corner towers borrowed from Wren's St Paul's Cathederal. Unfortunately the 18th-century Donegall Square has been replaced with a medley of different styles since the 19th century. The **Linen Hall Library** (*open Mon–Fri 9.30–5.30 (Thurs 9.30–8.30), Sat 9.30–4; ✆ (028) 9032 1707*) is one of the last survivors in the British Isles of the subscription library movement, so important to civilized Europe in the late 18th/early 19th century. Still a rich storehouse of books of Irish interest, it also has a comfortable room where you can sample periodicals, magazines and the day's flurry of newspapers. The librarians are polite and helpful, and the prints which line the walls echo the feeling of an earlier age.

Just along the way is the Robinson Cleaver Building, overlooking Donegall Place. This flamboyantly Victorian department store now houses a mixture of boutiques. The **Customs House** and **Courts of Justice** in Custom House Square and the **Ulster Hall** in Bedford Street with its impressive organ are all rather grey self-important buildings in heavy Victorian style. In Corporation Square is **Sinclair Seamen's Church** designed by Charles Lanyon and built in 1853. The pulpit incorporates the bows, bowsprit and figurehead of a ship, the organ displays starboard and port lights, and the font is a binnacle.

Southeast of here, following the Lagan, is the newly built and prestigious Waterfront Hall, a large concert hall and conference centre. **St Anne's Cathedral** in Donegall Street was built in

The Grand Opera House

1899 in Romanesque style, of the Basilican type. It is very imposing inside with some fine stained-glass windows and mosaics. In the nave is the tomb of Lord Carson, the Northern Unionist leader, who died in 1935.

About 10 minutes' walk away from Donegall Square, going south down Great Victoria Street, is the leafy university area. This neighbourhood best reflects the character of the city, and is by far the most pleasant part of town in which to stay. Lisburn Road, in particular, has seen dozens of new cafés and art galleries spring up in the wake of the cease-fire, and the student population ensures the area's vitality.

You pass the imposing Tudor-style red-brick Queen's University building to go into the **Botanic Gardens** (*gardens open from 8 to sunset; Palm House Mon–Fri 10–5, weekends 2–4*). The gardens are small but beautifully laid out with formal flower beds. The restored Victorian Palm House is a splendid combination of graceful design and clever construction. Richard Turner, a Dubliner, whose iron-works produced it, was also responsible for its design. It is made of sections which comprise the earliest surviving cast-iron and curvilinear glass architecture in the world. Inside the Palm House are tender and exotic plants.

Set inside the Botanical Gardens is the **Ulster Museum** (*open Mon–Fri 10–5, Sat 1–5, Sun 2–5; adm free except for special exhibitions* ; ✆ *(028) 9038 3000*). It has a variety of well-displayed and informative collections ranging from giant elk antlers to patchwork, jewellery and Irish antiquities. Of special interest is the outstanding modern art collection with a good representation of Irish artists including Sir James Lavery, whose wife was the Irish colleen on the old Irish pound notes. The Ulster Museum also has a unique collection of treasure from the wreck of the Spanish Armada vessel, the *Girona*. In 1588 Philip II of Spain ordered the greatest invasion fleet ever assembled to put an end to the growing power of England. Of the 130 ships that set sail, 26 were lost on, or just off, the coast of Ireland. In 1968 a fabulous hoard of gold and silver coins, heavy gold chains, a beautiful gold salamander pendant set with rubies, rings, ornamented crosses and a filigree brooch were all recovered off the coast of Antrim. As recently as 1999 a set of delicate gold, jewelled cameos was made complete by the addition of the twelfth cameo. The temporary exhibitions are invariably excellent, and there is a programme of lectures, art films and talks, and children's weekend activities. It also has a café over-

looking the gardens. The streets leading off the University are attractive and tree-lined with some good restaurants and cafés, small art galleries and design shops—all a far cry from the wastelands of the 'other' Belfast beyond the Westlink Motorway.

If you want to see the **Republican enclaves** in west Belfast, which are brightened by gaudy wall paintings and political slogans, take a black taxi. These run like miniature buses and serve areas such as the **Falls**, where public buses do not venture. Unemployment and poverty are obvious in the streets here, and tourists stick out like sore thumbs. These neighbourhoods are economically and socially depressed, and visitors should exercise caution, as they might in parts of London or New York. The communities are closed to strangers and it would not be wise to go drinking in the pubs or illegal clubs, nor to walk about these parts at night. The Unionist working-class area in west Belfast lies beside the Falls, in the notorious Shankhill Road, which has political murals of its own. The so-called 'peace line', a high barrier, divides the two communities. Sandy Row, a short distance from Great Victoria Street and Shaftesbury Square, is another working-class Unionist area. It seems less threatening to walk around, and there are plenty of little bakeries and small shops which gives it a bustling air. The bulk of the enclaves where the kerbstones are painted red, white and blue are over the river to the east, along Newtownards Road.

The Suburbs of Belfast

Parliament House, Stormont, can be seen from the Newtownards Road (A20) about 2 miles (4km) east from the city centre. It is a very imposing Portland stone building in English Palladian style, with a floor space covering 5 acres (2ha) and standing in a park of 300 acres (121ha). Next door is **Stormont Castle**, built in Scottish baronial style, which houses government departments.

There are many fine parks around Belfast. In south Belfast, in the upper Malone Road (B103) area, is **Barnett's Park**. Within the attractive parkland is an early 19th-century house with an art gallery, a permanent exhibition on Belfast parks and a restaurant (*open all year, Mon–Sat 10–4.30; adm free*). Nearby is **Dixon Park** (*open daily till dusk; adm free; © (028) 9032 0202*), where rose-fanciers will get a chance to view the Belfast International Rose Trials, the finals of which take place in the third week of July. The park borders the River Lagan, and in summer about 100,000 roses are in bloom. Continuing up the Malone Road, those of you interested in Neolithic sites should visit the Giant's Ring, near Ballylesson, about a mile south of Shaw's Bridge. The Giant's Ring is a circular grassy embanked enclosure over 600ft (187m) in diameter with a chambered grave in the centre. The dolmen in the centre is called Druid's Dolmen. The original purpose of the site is disputed but it was probably ritualistic; its date is unknown. The giant it is named after is possibly Fionn MacCumhail, a favourite to tag onto such places (*see* **Old Gods and Heroes**, p.247). In the olden days, farmers used to stage horse-races in this huge circle. It is always accessible and free. Shaw's Bridge, just mentioned, is very picturesque and spans the River Lagan. It was originally built *c*. 1650, and is to be found off the B23. You can walk for 10 miles (16km) along the tow path of the River Lagan, past the public parks. Start at the Belfast Boat Club, Loughview Road, Stranmillis, and end at Moore's Bridge, Hillsborough Road Lisburn.

On the northern side of the city, on the Antrim road (A6), the baronial-style Belfast Castle appears unexpectedly from the wooded slopes of Cave Hill. It was built by the third Marquess of Donegall in 1870. His family, the Chichesters, were granted the forfeited lands of Belfast and the surrounding area in 1603; the Gaelic lords of the area, the O'Neills, lost everything and fled to the Continent. The planted grounds of the castle are open to the public, and always accessible. There is a pleasant restaurant open for full meals or snacks in the Castle itself and a Heritage Centre with exhibits on flora and fauna of Cave Hill (*call ☎ (028) 9077 6925 for more details*). An easy climb to the summit of Cave Hill (1,182ft/368m) gives stunning views over the city and Belfast Lough. There are five caves and the earthwork of MacArts Fort, named after a local Gaelic chieftain of the Iron Age. It was here that the United Irishmen, Wolfe Tone and his followers, took their oaths of fidelity in 1798 (*see* **History**, p.47). **Belfast Zoo** (*open April–Sept daily 10–5, Oct–March, Sat–Thurs 10–3.30, Fri 10–2.30; adm; ☎ (028) 9077 6277; city bus routes nos.8, 9, 10, 45–51*), located on the slopes below Cave Hill, is beautifully planted with flowers, shrubs and trees. The zoo has won awards for its emphasis on large enclosures, its breeding programme, and mainly small animal collection. It is great fun to view the penguins and sealions from underwater, and a rare opportunity to see a spectacled bear and red panda.

There are several interesting places within easy reach of Belfast which are worth a visit. Northeast of the city, follow the A2 past the huge cranes (among the world's largest) of the ship-yards and the aircraft works at Sydenham until you arrive at the wooded suburb of **Cultra**, about 6 miles (9km) from the city centre. Here, in a parkland of nearly 200 acres (80ha), is the **Ulster Folk and Transport Museum** (*open daily July–Aug 10.30–6, Sun 12–6; April–June and Sept, Mon–Fri 9.30–5, rest of the year 9.30–4; adm; ☎ (028) 9042 8428; train from Central Belfast stops at Cultra Station in the grounds of the museum*). The museum provides a unique opportunity for visitors to explore the past of the province. It is the best museum of its type in Ireland, and gives a wonderful insight into what life in the countryside was like all over Ireland until 60 years ago. It is an open-air museum with representative buildings of rural Ulster: a linen scutch mill, a blacksmith's forge, a spade mill and farm houses of different regional styles. These are all furnished appropriately. Real fires burn in the grates and visitors are able to immerse themselves in the atmosphere of Ulster's agricultural communities. An instructive collection of carriages and railway engines will be found across the Belfast–Bangor road on the opposite side of the museum, housed in a great building by the architect Ian Campbell. At **Helen's Bay**, a couple of miles (3.2km) north of Cultra, two lovely beaches joined by a path flank **Crawfordsburn Country Park**, with a stream flowing through the woods to the sea. The wooded demesne of Clandeboye Estate has protected this area from the work of the housing developer. In the distance can be seen the delightful **Helen's Tower**, erected in Victorian times by the first Marquess of Dufferin and Ava to the memory of his mother. The 19th-century English poet Alfred Lord Tennyson's lines are inscribed in the tower:

> *Helen's Tower, here I stand*
> *Dominant over sea and land.*
> *Son's love built me and I hold*
> *Mother's love in letter'd gold...*

It was erected at a time of destitution caused by the famine of 1845, and gave employment to many. It has become a symbol of Ulster; another Helen's Tower was raised in northern France near Albert to commemorate the appalling losses suffered by the men of Ulster in the First World War. **The Somme Heritage Centre** (☎ (028) 9182 3202) on the A21 Newtownards–

Bangor road carries on the theme. Clandeboye Estate is opened from time to time for charitable purposes, but it is not possible to see inside the tower.

Shopping

The centre of Belfast is full of shopping arcades and pedestrian malls, and all the British high street stores are represented. Shuttle buses can take you to and from the large car parks on the outskirts of the centre. A large number of city buses stop at the City Hall, which is very central. The more unusual shops are situated in Bedford Street, Dublin Road, and Donegall Pass, where you will find interior design outlets, antiques and bric-a-brac. Expensive women's clothes shops are to be found amongst the cafés and food stores on the Lisburn Road.

Clothes: Paul Costelloe, Bradbury Place, stocks Irish designers. House of de Courcy, Lisburn Road; international designer clothes for women.

Interior Design: Tom Caldwell, Bradbury Place; original *objets d'art* as well as wallpapers and fabrics. The Natural Interior, Dublin Road.

Crafts: Craftworks, Bedford Road; Irish design of every sort.

Antiques: Alexander the Grate, Donegall Pass. Blue Cat, Bedford Street.

Bookshops: The University Bookshop, University Terrace (opposite Queens College). Dillons, Fountain Street. Waterstone's, Royal Avenue. Bookfinders, University Road.

Sports Equipment: Surf mountain, Brunswick Street. Graham Tiso, Cornmarket. S.S. More, Chichester Street.

Irish Linen: Irish Linen Stores, Fountain Centre, College Street. Lamont Factory Shop, Stranmillis Embankment.

Irish Shirts: Smyth and Gibson, Bedford Road. Top quality shirts made in Derry. Other desirable accessories too.

Where to Stay

luxury

Europa Hotel, Great Victoria Street, BT2, ✆/✉ (028) 9032 7000. Very central, modern hotel which has been bombed so many times everybody has lost count; it has recently been completely redecorated. The **Culloden Hotel**, 142 Bangor Road, Holywood, BT18, ✆/✉ (028) 9042 5223, ✉ 9042 6777. In the suburbs on the northeast of Belfast Lough, it is very plush with lovely grounds and luxurious old-style furnishings. One of the nicest hotels in Belfast. **Dukes Hotel**, 65 University Street, BT7, ✆/✉ (028) 9023 6666. Quiet and central, close to good restaurants. **Clandeboye Lodge Hotel**, Estate Road, Clandeboye, Bangor, BT19, ✆/✉ (028) 9185 2500. Luxurious hotel adjoining Blackwood Golf Course. The **Wellington Park Hotel**, 21 Malone Road, BT9, ✆ (028) 9038 1111, ✉ 9066 5410. Modern and comfortable, close to the Botanic Gardens, with secure car parking.

moderate

Ash Rowan Town-House, 12 Windsor Avenue, BT9, ✆ (028) 9066 1758. 10 minutes from the city centre; cosy and attractive. Breakfasts only. **Lisdara Town**

House, 23 Derryvolgie Avenue, Malone Road, BT9, ☎ (028) 9068 1549. Comfortable 1870s town house in quiet residential avenue, within easy reach of the city centre. **Camera Guest House**, 44 Wellington Park, BT9, ☎/☎ (028) 9066 0026. Victorian terraced house.

inexpensive

All of the following offer good value B&B in the quiet and leafy streets of the university district; often busy in summer, so try to book ahead.

Eglantine Guest House, 21 Eglantine Avenue, BT9, ☎ (028) 9066 7585. **Liserin Guest House**, 17 Eglantine Avenue, BT9, ☎ (028) 9066 0769. **Windermere Guest House**, 60 Wellington Park, BT9, ☎ (028) 9066 2693. **The George**, 9 Eglantine Ave, BT9, (028) 9068 3212. **Queen's University Common Room**, College Gardens, University Road, BT9, ☎ (028) 9066 5938, ☎ 9068 1209. **YWCA Hostel**, 70 Fitzwilliam Street, cnr Lisburn Road, BT9, ☎ (028) 9024 0439; good and central.

self-catering

Belfast International Youth Hostel, 22 Donegall Road, BT12, ☎ (028) 9032 4733, ☎ 9043 9699. Very clean, modern purpose-built hostel. 'Backpacker' coffee shop has cooked breakfasts and meals. **Queen's Elms**, Queen's University, 78 Malone Road, BT9, ☎ (028) 9038 1608, ☎ 9066 6680. Rooms are mainly singles with access to cooking facilities. **The Ark**, 18 University Street, BT7, ☎ (028) 9032 9626. Terraced house, close to city centre.

Eating Out
expensive

Roscoff's, Lesley House, Shaftesbury Square, ☎ (028) 9033 1532. Michelin star. Venison with salsify and wild mushroom is typical of the imaginative menu. Dinner is an expensive affair, but there are reasonable set lunches. Book ahead. *Closed Sun.* **Deanes**, 38 Howard Street, ☎ (028) 9056 0000. Successful, well-run restaurant with brasserie in basement.

moderate

Sun Kee, 38 Donegall Pass, ☎ (028) 9031 2016. Best Chinese restaurant in Belfast. **Ashoka**, 363 Lisburn Road, ☎ (028) 9066 0362. Reliable Indian. **Chez Delbart**, 10 Bradbury Place, ☎ (028) 9023 8020. Crêpes. **Deanes Brasserie**, (in basement), 38 Howard Street, ☎ (028) 9056 0000. Excellent food, cheaper than restaurant above. **Antica Roma**, 67 Botanic Avenue, ☎ (028) 9031 1121. Lively décor. Imaginative pasta and sauces. **Belfast Castle**, Antrim Road, ☎ (028) 9077 6925. Lovely city views.

inexpensive

The Other Place, Stranmillis Road. Good hamburger and chips, Ulster fry. **Scarletts**, 423 Lisburn Road. Snack menu and bistro. **Villa Italia**, 39 University Road, ☎ (028) 9032 8356. Lively and popular. *Evenings only.* **Café Bongo**, 42 Malone Road, ☎ (028) 9066 3667. Thai green chicken curry, exotic ambience, good music. *Evenings only.* **Speranza**, 16 Shaftesbury Square, ☎ (028) 9023 0213. Pizzas, pasta. **La Salsa**, 23 University Rd, (028) 9024 4588. Lively and informal, frozen margaritas and surprisingly good Mexican food. *Evenings only.* **Maggie May's**, 45 Botanic Avenue. Big servings, good value vegetarian meals.

Cafés

Belfast has some good cafés, where you can eat sophisticated salads, exotic, well-prepared food, or simple, inexpensive meals. Like the restaurants, however, few have effective non-smoking areas, and most are yet to master the art of a good cappuccino.

Bookfinders Café, 47 University Road. In bookshop; vegetarian meals. **Bonnie's Museum Café**, 11a Stranmillis Road. Pies, filled baguettes, soups. **Café Poirot**, 51 Fountain Street. Salads, sandwiches, cakes. **Cargoes**, 613 Lisburn Road. Mediterranean salads, café in delicatessen. **Roscoff Café**, 21 Fountain Street. Great for breakfasts and snacks. Part of the growing empire of excellent Roscoff eateries. **Roscoff Café**, 19 Arthur Street. This has an express takeaway area and a more relaxed area for snacks and lunch. **Equinox**, 32 Howard Street. Café in sophisticated interior design and gift shop. Excellent salads, coffee, milkshakes. **Smyth & Gibson**, Bedford Street. Famous Derry shirtmakers with a coffee outlet downstairs that does try for decent latte and cappuccino, and it's non-smoking.

Pubs, Bars and Nightlife

The atmosphere in the bars mentioned below is friendly and unthreatening. Traditional, folk and popular music is played in some places whilst hearty local specialities such as champ and stew are served in others.

In Pottinger's Entry, **The Morning Star** is an attractive old pub which serves excellent meals. **Bittles** in Upper Church Lane is another good lunchtime stop, whilst **The Duke of York** in 3 Commercial Court has live music in the evenings. **White's Tavern**, 41 Winecellar Entry, also has live music on Thursday. The most architecturally distinguished bar in Belfast is the **Crown Liquor Saloon** in Great Victoria Street (*see* p.162). A fine Victorian extravagance, which has been faithfully restored and is maintained by the National Trust. Irish stew and oysters at lunchtime. **Lavery's Gin Palace**, 12 Bradbury Place, is an old favourite for a wide range of age-groups during the day. Pub grub. **Morrison's Spirit Grocers** in Bedford Street is a cleverly decorated theme bar.

live and traditional music

Fibber Magee's, Blackstaff Square, decorated as a grocer's shop with traditional music. **The Rotterdam**, Pilot Street. Folk and traditional music. **Kelly's Cellars**, 30 Bank St. Traditional and blues. **Liverpool Bar**, Donegall Quay. **Front Page**, 106 Donegall Street. Food and live music.

nightclubs

The Limelight, Ormeau Avenue, promotes young bands—U2 and Oasis started here; very young crowd. **Robinson's Bar**, attached to Fibber Magee's, has some truly awful duos and bands but also the occasional gem, plus there's a nightclub upstairs. **The M Club**, Bradbury Place.

The best sources of information for music events are the *Belfast Telegraph* or *That's Entertainment*, a free listings magazine available from tourist offices and hotels.

The Grand Opera House, Great Victoria Street, ✆ (028) 9024 1919. **Belfast Waterfront Hall**, Lanyon Place, ✆ (028) 9033 4400. Concert and conference centre which accommodates up to 2,235 people in the main hall. Major stars from the classical music world perform here, as well as pop stars. **Lyric Theatre**, 55 Ridgeway Street, off Stranmillis Road, ✆ (028) 9039 1081. Serious Irish, European and American drama. **The Old Museum Arts Centre**, College Square North, ✆ (028) 9023 5053. Avant-garde dance, theatre, comedy.

St Anne's Cathedral, Donegall Street, ✆ (028) 9032 8332. The cathedral is a venue for occasional lunchtime recitals, and there are wonderful sung services on Sunday. **The Ulster Hall**, Bedford Street, ✆ (028) 9032 3900. Another venue for concerts, comedy shows and has a wonderful organ; there are a series of subscription concerts here and lunchtime recitals in the summer. Classical music concerts in the **Whitla Hall**, Queen's University, ✆ (028) 9027 3075, during the Arts Festival and throughout the year.

Listings for what is on can be found in the *Belfast Telegraph* and *Artslink*, a monthly programme, a free copy of which can be found at tourist offices or galleries.

film

The more avant-garde and art house films are shown at the **Queen's University Film Theatre**, ✆ (028) 9024 4857, in a narrow lane off Botanic Avenue. The big new-release cinema complex is **Virgin**, at the north end of Dublin Road.

art galleries

The Troubles seem to have generated a creative urge amongst Ulster artists which is both exploratory and introspective. Ulster artists such as Tom Carr, T. P. Flanagan, Brian Ferran, Basil Blackshaw and Brian Ballard have produced excellent works. They paint various subjects, often Ulster scenery, also nudes, and interpretations of ancient and modern Irish myths. *Entry to all the private, commercial galleries is free.*

The **Ormeau Baths Gallery**, ✆ (028) 9032 1402, is worth visiting and for the shows which are usually by Irish and Ulster artists. *Open Tues–Sat 9–5.* Other galleries are the **Bell Gallery**, 13 Adelaide Park, ✆ (028) 9066 2998; **Crescent Arts Centre**, 2–4 University Road, ✆ (028) 9024 2338, which also includes the **Fenderesky Gallery**, open Tues–Sat; **The Higgins Gallery**, Malone House, Barnett Demesne, Upper Malone Road, ✆ (028) 9068 1246; **Eakin Gallery**, 237 Lisburn Road, ✆ (028) 9066 8522; **Blue Yellow Gallery**, Boucher Crescent, (028) 9066 0791.

The **Old Museum Arts Centre**, College Square North, ✆ (028) 9023 5053; **The Townhouse Gallery**, 125 Great Victoria Street (prints, etchings), ✆ (028) 9031 1798; **Emer Gallery**, Great Victoria Street, ✆ (028) 9023 1377; **Tom Caldwell Gallery**, Bradbury Place, ✆ (028) 9032 3226; and, of course, the **Ulster Museum**, Botanic Gardens (off Stranmillis Road), ✆ (028) 9038 3001.

poetry readings

Ulster has also produced poets of international renown; Seamus Heaney started writing here when he was at Queen's University in the 1960s, as did Paul Muldoon at a later date. During the Belfast Arts Festival in November you could be lucky and hear them and other talented poets reading their work.

The Temple of the Winds

County Down

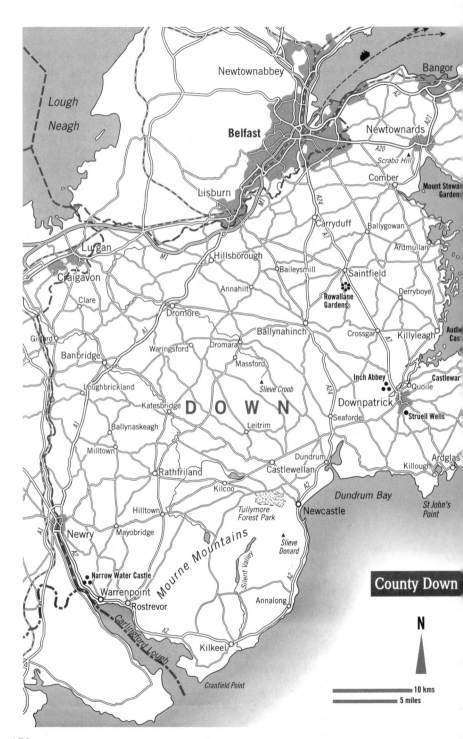

Lough
Neagh

Newtownabbey

Bangor

Belfast

Newtownards

A20

Scrabo Hill

Comber

Mount Stewart
Garden

Lisburn

Carryduff

Ballygowan

Lurgan

Hillsborough

Ardmullan

Craigavon

Baileysmill

Saintfield

Derryboye

Clare

Annahilt

Rowallane
Gardens

Dromore

Gilford

Ballynahinch

Crossgar

Killyleagh

Audle
Cas

Banbridge

Waringsford

Dromara

Massford

Inch Abbey

Castlewar

Loughbrickland

Slieve Croob

A24

Quoile

Downpatrick

Katesbridge

D O W N

Leitrim

Seaforde

Struell Wells

Ballynaskeagh

Milltown

Dundrum

Ardglas

Rathfriland

Castlewellan

Killough

Kilcoo

Dundrum Bay

St John's
Point

Hilltown

Tullymore
Forest Park

Newcastle

Newry

Mayobridge

Slieve
Donard

Narrow Water Castle

Mourne Mountains

Silent Valley

Warrenpoint

Rostrevor

Annalong

Carlingford Lough

A2

Kilkeel

Cranfield Point

County Down

N

10 kms

5 miles

172

Sea-bordered and close to mainland Britain, this county has excited the envy and lust of waves of invaders. Its farmlands are amongst the richest in Ireland, it has an attractive coastline, the famous Mourne Mountains, and a wealth of interesting historical buildings. For sailing enthusiasts there is the beautiful and sheltered water of Strangford Lough; for anglers, exciting sea-fishing off Ardglass and Portavogie. And there are plenty of opportunities for hill-walking, golfing, bird-watching and swimming. The climate has a reputation for being sunnier than other parts of Ulster. The people are mostly farmers and fish-erfolk, although, this close to the city of Belfast, there are quite a few dormitory towns, light industries and ugly big roads.

The county is rich in monuments from pre-history: there are cairns, standing stones, and dolmens dating from 3000 BC scattered around the Strangford Lough and Lecale district, and evidence of man in the form of middens and flint tools dating from 6000 BC.

History

St Patrick is associated strongly with this county. After spending his boyhood as a slave in County Antrim, he spent 21 years in France preparing himself for his mission to bring Christianity to Ireland. In AD 432 he was on his way back to County Antrim, but was forced by bad weather conditions to land at the Slaney River between Strangford and the River Quoile. He founded an abbey nearby, at Saul near Downpatrick, where he died on 17 March AD 461. He is buried in the vicinity of Down Cathedral in Downpatrick. From St Patrick's work, and that of his missionaries in the following century, Christianity flourished and Ireland became a centre of great learning. In fact, during the Dark Ages in Europe, when the Roman Empire was in ruins, the monasteries of Ireland kept the light of Christianity alive. The monastery founded by St Comgall in Bangor in the middle of the 6th century boasted three thousand students, but this famous place, like so many others in Ireland, was destroyed by the Norsemen (Vikings) in AD 824.

In the 17th and 18th centuries, County Down was planted with Scottish and English settlers, and the native Irish retreated into the hilly country around the Mourne mountains. County Down remains, like Antrim, a cornerstone of Loyalist Ulster, flying the Ulster flag with its red hand against a white background.

Sports and Activities

Sea-angling: In Strangford Lough for tope, skate, haddock, conger eel. Fishing trips arranged from Portaferry. For local knowledge of Carlingford Lough, contact Peter Wright, 152 Portaferry Road, Newtownards, ✆ (028) 9181 2081. Quinton Nelson, ✆ (028) 9188 3403.

Shore-angling: Off Ardglass and Portavogie. Contact Peter Wright, 152 Portaferry Road, Newtownards, ✆ (028) 9181 2081. For the Ardglass area, contact Captain R. Fitzsimons, Harbour-Master, ✆ (028) 4484 1291.

Game fishing: For brown trout and salmon on the River Bann near Hilltown, Spelga Dam, and Shimna River in Tullymore Forest Park.

Coarse fishing: In the River Quoile basin. Contact the local tourist office.

Sailing: In Strangford Lough. There is a sailing school on Sketrick Island in Strangford Lough where there are residential or day-long courses on all aspects of sailing. Contact Bangor and Strangford Sailing School, 13 Gray's Hill, Bangor, ✆ (028) 9145 5967 or ✆ (028) 9754 1592. Sailing boat charter from Terry Anderson, Down Yachts, 37 Bayview Road, Killinchy, ✆ (028) 9754 2210.

Pleasure cruises: Weather permitting, cruise boats leave from Bangor and Donaghadee in summer at 10.30, 2.30 and 7.30pm for short cruises. Information is posted at piers or call ✆ (028) 9127 0069. Trips to Copeland Islands, ✆ (01247) 883403.

Sub-aqua and scuba diving: Peter Wright, 152 Portaferry Road, Newtownards, ✆ (028) 9181 2081.

Bathing: Tyrella Strand, Dundrum Bay, Millisle.

Getting There and Around

By air: To Belfast International Airport.

By boat: To Larne Ferry port from Stranraer and Cairnryan in Scotland. Many crossings daily between Stranraer and Belfast.

By rail: Northern Irish Railways run a suburban service to Holywood and Bangor.

By bus: Ulsterbus runs an excellent network of services to all parts of County Down, ✆ (028) 9033 3000.

By bike: The Raleigh Rent-a-Bike network operates throughout County Down. Your local dealer is Ross Cycles, 44 Clarkhill Road, Newcastle ✆ (028) 4377 8029.

Tourist Information

Bangor, ✆ (028) 9127 0069.
Newry, ✆ (028) 3026 68877.
Warrenpoint, ✆ (028) 4175 2256.
Kilkeel, ✆ (028) 4176 2525.

Newcastle, ✆ (028) 4372 2222.
Downpatrick, ✆ (028) 4461 2233.
Portaferry, ✆ (028) 4272 9882.

Golf: At Ardglass, ✆ (028) 4484 1219; Bangor, ✆ (028) 9127 0922; Downpatrick, ✆ (028) 4461 5947; Donaghadee, ✆ (028) 9188 3624; The Royal County Down (links) Course at Newcastle, ✆ (028) 4372 3314; Scrabo Golf Club, ✆ (028) 9181 2355.

Pony-trekking: Mount Pleasant Trekking Centre, Castlewellan, ✆ (028) 4377 8651 and Mourne Riding School, 98 Castlewellan Road, Newcastle, ✆ (028) 4372 4351.

Walking: In the Mourne Mountains. The Ulster Way goes through Comber and along the shores of Strangford Lough, around the coast through Ardglass and Newcastle into the Mournes. Contact the Field Officer, Sports Council for Northern Ireland, House of Sport, Upper Malone Road, Belfast, ✆ (028) 9038 1222, for more details.

The tourist office in Newcastle gives out details of walks in the Mournes. Lovely walks on National Trust property in the Murlough Nature Reserve, near Newcastle, in the arboreteum of Castlewellan, at Castleward, Rowallane and Tullymore Park, Newcastle.

Bird-watching: At the Castle Espie hide, and at Salt and Green Islands, Mount Stewart Gas House and Island Reagh—all on Strangford Lough. Call The Wildfowl Wetlands Trust, Saintfield, ✆ (028) 9187 4146, or Strangford Wildlife Centre, ✆ (028) 4488 1411, for more details.

Open farms: Ark Open Farm, 296 Bangor Road, Newtownards. Rare breeds including Irish Moiled Cattle, ✆ (028) 9181 2672. Slievenalargy Open Farm, Largy Road, Kilco, near Castlewellan, ✆ (028) 4484 2268. Rare breeds of cattle, sheep, pigs and ponies.

Festivals

17 March: St Patrick's Day celebrations at Downpatrick, Newry and Cultra.

June: Castleward Opera. Contact Castleward, Strangford, ✆ (028) 4488 1204.

End of June: Portaferry to Galway—Hooker Regatta.

Early/mid-July: Booley Fair, Hilltown. Demonstrations of vanishing skills such as weaving, stone-carving, shoeing horses and other smithy work. Traditional music and dancing, street stalls and sheep fair.

July: Scarva hosts a sham fight in a traditional pageant which has gone on for over 200 years. It is a symbolic enactment of the Battle of the Boyne between two horsemen in period costume—William of Orange and James II.

July: Orange marches all over County Down.

July: Ulster Harp Derby at the Down Royal Race Course.

July: Kingdom of Mourne Festival in Kilkeel, Cranfield and Annalong.

August: Fiddlers Green Festival, Rostrevor. Five-day festival.

August: Ulster Pipe Band Championship.

October: Newry and Mourne Arts festival.

The **Ards Peninsula**, which runs along the length of the east shore of Strangford Lough, takes its name from rocky coast (*ard*: rock). This finger of land curving round the Down mainland contains some of the most charming villages and towns created by the Scottish and English settlers. In between these towns are earlier sites: raths, holy wells and monastic ruins. You are never more than 3 or 4 miles (5 or 6km) from the sea. Prepare yourself for an exhilarating climate, for this is the sunniest, driest and breeziest bit of Ulster.

Start from **Bangor**, a seaside resort popular with the Edwardians, as you will see from the architecture. It was a famous centre of learning in the 6th and 7th centuries, and from here Sts Columbanus and Gall set off to found Luxeuil Monastery in Burgundy, and St Gall Monastery in Switzerland. St Comgall, who founded this monastery in the middle of the 6th century, trained men like Columbanus and Gall to spread the word of Christ. The plundering Norsemen in the 9th century ravaged the town. All that remains from these times is the tower of the **Abbey Church** (*open to the public*) opposite Bangor railway station. The church has a pretty painted ceiling and ancient settler gravestones. A very interesting interlude can be spent in the Victorian castle (*open all year during normal working hours; © (028) 9127 1200*), used as the town hall, which has a permanent display on Bangor as an ancient place of learning. Apart from the Edwardian seafront, which has a great many B&Bs and small hotels, and a fine marina for visiting yachtsmen, there is not much to attract one to Bangor. The beach has an over-used look and the shops are tacky, though there is a lively market in the square on Wednesdays.

Donaghadee, a pretty seaside town with an attractive 19th-century harbour and a good number of pubs, used to be linked with Portpatrick in Scotland by a regular sailing boat. It has the feeling of an old port where generations of men and women have waited for the wind and the tide to change. The poet John Keats stayed at Grace Neill's Bar on the High Street, as did Peter the Great of Russia. (Gracie's is still one of the most attractive pubs in the town.) You can go out stream fishing at night in the summer with a white feather as a lure. Or at weekends go out to the **Copeland Islands**—long, low islands covered with spring turf and rabbit's trails, enchanting in spring and summer. It is possible to reach them and also to go out stream-fishing on a regular boat.

Following the coast road through **Millisle** down to **Ballyhalbert** you will pass some golden strands. There are pebbly beaches further on at **Cloughy Bay**. Notice the Scottish influence: snug, unpretentious houses and carefully worked fields. Many of the road names—taken from the townlands, early units of land-holding—are intriguing: Ballydrain, Ringboy, Balloo, Bright, and Scollogs Town. The National Trust maintains much of the little village of **Kearney**, which has pretty white washed cottages and coastal walks.

The most picturesque town on the Ards is **Portaferry**, situated where the tip of the Ards forms a narrow strait with the mainland of Down. On the waterfront you look across to Strangford village. The street here is wide, and the brightly painted old houses are attractive to look at. In Castle Street is the **Aquarium Exploris** (*open April–Sept, Mon–Fri 10–5, Sat 11–6, Sun 1–6; rest of the year, 10–5, Sun 1–5; adm; © (028) 4272 8062*), where in spacious tanks you can see many of the sea animals that inhabit Strangford Lough; there is also plenty of interesting background information on the geology and plant life of the lough. On summer evenings you might be lucky and hear some open-air music. A ferry runs between Portaferry and Strangford every half-hour, and the journey of five minutes is well worth it for the view up Strangford Lough. If you are an artist, you may be so won over by the charms of this part of the peninsula that you will want to enrol in one of the painting courses held here in the summer.

The Strangford Shore

On the A20, which hugs the Strangford Shore, you can enjoy the beauty of this nearly land-locked water. Scattered with small islands, this area is of special interest to naturalists. The National Trust has a wildlife scheme operating which covers the entire foreshore of the lough, totalling about 5,400 acres (2,000ha). Vast flocks of wildfowl gather here, as do seals and other marine animals. There are birdwatching facilities at Castle Espie, Mount Stewart Gashouse, and Island Reagh (*see* 'Sports and Activities', p.175). Strangford was named by the Viking invaders (*strang* means strong) after the strong tides at the mouth of the lough. Here, in Norman times, the wealthy knights encouraged the monks to settle amongst the lovely scenery. At **Greyabbey** (*An Mhainistir Liath*: the grey monastery), you can visit one of the most complete Cistercian abbeys in Ireland (*open April–Sept, Tues–Sat 10–7, Sun 2–7; Oct–March, Tues–Sat 10–4, Sun 2–4; adm;* © *(028) 9054 3033*). Built in the 12th century by the wife of John de Courcy, Affreca, it represented the new monastic orders that were introduced to repress Irish traditions. The Pope was determined to stop the independence shown by the Irish abbot-prince who combined temporal and spiritual power and often ignored pronouncements from Rome. A physick garden has been developed, planted as it may have been in medieval times, a vital part of the monks armoury against illnesses (*open same times as monastery; adm*). The pretty 18th-century house, Rosemount, is not open to the public. Kircubbin, a fishing village much used by yachts and leisure boats, has the interesting ruined church of Innishargie and associations with the 1798 rising.

Approximately 15 miles (24km) east of Belfast on the A20 to Newtownards, following the lough, the demesne wall of **Mount Stewart**, the home of the Londonderry family, appears. The 18th-century house and grounds are now in the care of the National Trust. (*open April–Sept, Mon–Sat 10.30–6, Sun 12–5.30; Oct–March, Sat 10.30–6 and Sun 12–5.30; adm for house, garden and temple;* © *(028) 4278 8387*). Edith, Lady Londonderry, 7th Marchioness (1879–1959) and one of the foremost political hostesses of her generation, created the wonderful gardens some 70 years ago for her children. There are some lovely topiary animals, colourful parterres and wonderful trees. If you ever come across her children's story *The Magic Inkpot*, you will recognize some of the place names from round here. Also in the grounds is the **Temple of the Winds**, inspired by the building in Athens and built in 1780 for picnicking in style. In the Mount Stewart school house you can buy patchworks and handmade cottage furniture. The tearoom in the house itself is painted beautifully with the animals from the Ark. Edith, Lady Londonderry, nicknamed all the famous men and women of the day who were her friends after animals in Noah's Ark; it is fun to guess who is who.

To complete the tour of the Ards, a quick visit to **Newtownards** will be rewarding, particularly for medievalists. The town square is also impressive and worth a visit. On the outskirts of the town on the road to Millisle is **Movilla Abbey**, built between the 13th and 15th centuries. There was an earlier establishment here founded in the 6th century by St Finian, a contemporary of the great Irish saint, Columba, also known as Colmcille. Unfortunately the two men did not get on. The story goes that it was St Finian's psalter that St Columba copied so stealthily, and they had a battle over it which caused many deaths. Columba was an O'Donnell prince as well as a cleric, and he was so dismayed at the bloodshed he had caused that he exiled himself and founded the famous church at Iona, an island off the coast of Scotland. From here Christianity spread to most of Scotland. The psalter he had copied became the warrior *Book of the O'Donnells* and was borne before them into battle; it is now in the National Museum, Dublin. It is always possible to see the Abbey.

Newtownards has a 17th-century market cross and a fine town hall. You won't fail to notice the prominent **tower** on Scrabo Hill, a memorial to one of the Londonderry Stewarts and a good lookout point. The tower (*open Easter and June–Sept daily exc Friday 11–6.30; free access to park*) stands on a granite outcrop and has 122 steps to the top. All around are woodland walks and the remains of old quarries where wildlife thrives. You

Dodo Terrace, Mount Stewart

might see a peregrine falcon. There is a small visitor centre with an audio visual show. Close to the pretty little village of Saintfield is another wonderful garden in National Trust care. This is **Rowallane** (*open April–Oct, Mon–Fri 11–6, Sat–Sun 2–6; Nov–Mar, Mon–Fri 11–5; adm; ✆ (028) 9751 0131*), famous throughout the horticultural and botanical world for its shrubs and trees. The best time to see it is early spring when the azaleas and rhododendrons are a riot of colour. There are also some interesting pillars and other structures in the garden made from Mourne stone, large round boulders of deep grey.

Mid-Down

Mid-Down is drumlin country until you reach Slieve Croob, around Ballinahinch. Harris, a local historian who described Down in the 18th century, had a rather droll phrase for the countryside contours: they are like 'eggs set in salt'. Cap this with C. S. Lewis' recipe for his native county: 'earth-covered potatoes'. (Lewis, the Belfast-born novelist and critic, who died in 1963, was most famous for his children's stories, *The Chronicles of Narnia*.)

To explore mid-Down you might start from **Comber**, a pleasant town with a prominent statue of Robert Gillespie, one of Ulster's military heroes in the Indian campaigns. Near here, off the A22 to Killyleagh, you can visit **Nendrum** (*open April–Sept, 10–7; always accessible; adm free*). This is one of the most romantic of the monastic sites, founded by a pupil of St Patrick on Mahee Island, and reached by a causeway through Island Reagh. It consists of a hill-top crowned with three circular stone walls, a church, a round tower stump, a sundial and cross slabs. It is always accessible and has a small museum. If you have time it is worth taking a little detour at Balloo to **Ardmullan**. Whiterock yacht club is always a hive of activity and it looks out onto the islands of Strangford Lough—including Braddock Island where there is a bungalow designed by T. W. Henry, brother of the better-known painter Paul Henry. The little village of **Killyleagh** has a lovely-looking castle, still lived in by its original family, who came from Ayrshire in the mid-17th century. It is the oldest inhabited castle in Ireland, and is not open to the public. Pop concerts are sometimes held in the castle grounds. On the A22 a couple of miles out of Killyleagh is **Delamont** (*open daily April–Sept, 9–dusk, Oct–March 9–5; © (028) 4482 8333*). It is a country park with fine views of Strangford Lough and the Mournes. Among its attractions is a heronry which you can view from a hide, lovely walks and a restored walled garden. You can also go pony-trekking. Going west on the B7 you come to the **Ulster Wildlife Centre** at **Crossgar** (*open Mon–Fri 10–4; Sun afternoon by arrangement; © (028) 4483 0282*). Here you can learn about wetland raised bog and meadowland flora and fauna. The Victorian conservatory is planted to attract butterflies and there are also guided walks, a tea-room and shop.

If you continue down the west side of Strangford, you cross the River Quoile and arrive at **Downpatrick**, an attractive Georgian town built on an old hill-fort which reputedly belonged to one of the Red Branch Knights (*see* **Old Gods and Heroes**, p.248). It is sited at the natural meeting-point of several river valleys, and so has been occupied for a long time, both suffering and benefiting from the waves of settlers and invaders—missionaries, monks, Norsemen, Normans and Scots (the army of Edward Bruce). **St Patrick's gravestone**, a large bit of granite, may be seen in the Church of Ireland Cathedral graveyard, although this is not the reason why the town carries his name. The association was made by the Norman John de Courcy, a Cheshire knight who was granted the counties of Antrim and Down by Henry II in 1176, and who established himself here at this centre of St Patrick's veneration by promoting the Irish saint. De Courcy donated some relics of Sts Patrick, Columba and Brigid to his Foundation; and gave the town its name, adding Patrick to *Dundalethglas*, as it was previously called. During the Middle Ages Downpatrick suffered at the hands of the Scots: in 1316 it was burnt by Edward Bruce, and, later, it was destroyed by the English during the Tudor wars. In the early 18th century, stability returned to the town under the influence of an English family called Southwell who acquired the Manor of Downpatrick through marriage. They built a quay on the River Quoile and encouraged markets and building. The cathedral, which had lain in ruins between 1538 and 1790, reopened in 1818. It is very fine inside, with impressive stained-glass windows. The **Southwell Charity School and Almshouse** in English Street near Down Cathedral is a handsome early-Georgian building in the Irish Palladian style, now an old people's home. Nearby, in the old county jail in the Mall, is the **Down County Museum** and the **St Patrick Heritage Centre** (*open all year, Tues–Fri 11–5, Sat 2–5; June–Aug, also on Mon 11–5 and Sun 2–5; © (028) 4461 5218; adm free*). There are very interesting exhibits of Stone Age artefacts and local history, as well as a rewarding survey of St

Patrick's life and work; it's also a useful starting point for leads on relics associated with the saint which you might find elsewhere in the county.

Other Places Associated with St Patrick

Just a mile and a half north east of Downpatrick at the mouth of the Slaney is **St Patrick's Church**, in Saul, on the spot where St Patrick founded his first church after deciding to return to Ireland to convert the people. A memorial church of Mourne granite was built here in the 1930s to commemorate this. On Slieve Patrick nearby is a giant statue of the saint also made of granite. Another place of association with St Patrick is the 6th-century Raholp Church, between Downpatrick and Strangford village on the A25. It was founded by Tassach, a disciple of St Patrick, who gave him the last rites and carried his body to its burial place.

To the east of the town, off the B1 some 2 miles (3km) outside, are the **Struell Wells** (*always accessible; adm free*). There must have been worshippers at this pagan shrine long before the arrival of St Patrick, who is thought to be closely associated with them; in all events, the waters are still well-known for their curative properties.

To the west of Downpatrick on the A24 is the little village of **Seaforde**. In the grounds of the big house here is an attractive **butterfly house**, (*open April–Sept, Mon–Sat 10–5, Sun 1–6; adm; ℗ (028) 4481 1225*). It also has a hornbeam maze and specialist nursery. It is fun to climb the newly built Moghul Tower and look down on the richly coloured and patterned walled garden, shop and tea-room. The area is rich in bird and plant life.

Cloughy Rocks Nature Reserve on the coast, south of Strangford village, is particularly rich in inter-tidal plants, and has an ever-changing variety of seabirds and wildfowl. Common seals can often be seen basking on the rocks at low tide. Near Downpatrick, just off the A25 and guarded by Castle Ward at its southeastern end, is the **Quoile Pondage Nature Reserve**. This was formed as the result of a barrage at Castle Island to prevent flooding caused by the tidal inrush of the sea from Strangford Lough into the river. The freshwater vegetation which has established itself here as a result is of great interest to the botanist. And for the ornithologist, a great variety of indigenous and immigrant birds feed and nest here. In springtime you can see great crested grebes preening and displaying their crests. (*Wildlife Centre open April–Sept, daily 11–5; Oct–March, Sat and Sun 1–5; ℗ (028) 4461 5520*). **Inch Abbey** (*open April–Sept, Tues–Sat 10–7; Oct–March, Sat 10–4, Sun 2–4; adm; off the A7*) is a very beautiful ruined Cistercian abbey on an island in the Quoile Marshes. It was founded in the 1180s by John de Courcy.

Going on the A25 in an easterly direction, 1 mile west of Strangford village, you will pass by **Castleward** (*open daily May–Aug exc Thurs 1–6; April and Sept–Oct, Sat and Sun 1–6; grounds open all year round until dusk; adm, car park fee; ℗ (028) 4488 1204*). The character and aspect of this house are worth a detour: it is a compromise between husband and wife, expressed in architecture. Built in the 1760s by Bernard Ward, afterwards Lord Bangor, and his wife Lady Anne, it has a neoclassical façade and a Gothic castellated garden front. The interior echoes this curious divergence of tastes: the reception rooms are gracefully classical, following his Lordship, and the library and her Ladyship's rooms are elaborately neo-Gothic in the Strawberry Hill manner conceived by Horace Walpole. The ceiling in the boudoir caused the poet John Betjeman to exclaim that it was like 'standing beneath a cow'. The property is in the hands of the National Trust and there are a number of other attractions: a Palladian-style temple which overlooks an early 18th-century lake, an early tower house and lovely grounds. A goldsmith's studio provides souvenirs for those who are looking for more valuable mementoes than snapshots. In June the rooms of this gracious house are full of music during the **Castleward Opera Festival**. Close by and just off the A25 is **Loughmoney Dolmen**, which is probably over four thousand years old. It is typical of dolmens scattered round this district.

Strangford village, which can be reached by a coastal footpath, is a few miles on. This is where you can catch the ferry across to the Ards village of Portaferry. No less than five small castles are within reach of Strangford, testifying to its strategic importance: Strangford Castle, Old Castle Ward, Audley's Castle, Walshestown and Kilclief. The nicest way to see them is from the lough, when the ferry is in mid-stream. **Kilclief Castle** (*open April–Sept, Tues–Sat 10–7, Sun 2–7; adm*), which is easy to find on the A2 between Strangford and Ardglass, is very well preserved and in state care. It was built before 1440 and is a stately grey-stone tower house. More castles can be seen round the fishing village of **Ardglass**, an important port in medieval times and now a centre for herring fleets. The best-preserved among them is **Jordan's Castle** (*open July–Aug, Tues–Sat 10–7, Sun 2–7; adm*), a 15th-century tower house with four storeys.

Also in the Strangford area is an 18-hole golf course, and there is good sea-angling off the coast here. The tree-lined village of **Killough**, about 1 mile (1.6km) from Ardglass, was developed as a grain port by the Ward family in the 18th century. There is a good beach and, further down, at St Johns Point, an old ruined church. There are also some very good **strands**, notably Tyrella on the Dundrum Bay. Interesting prehistoric monuments in this area are **Ballynoe Stone Circle** and **Rathmullen Mote**. They are both within easy reach of Downpatrick, situated amongst the maze of little roads in the triangle between the A25, A2 and B176.

Houses in Killough

South Down

South Down is a mainly mountainous area, and extends across to the south Armagh border, girded to the south and east by a beautiful coastline. The rather splendid fjord-like inlet, Carlingford Lough (a name of Scandinavian origin), cuts through the middle of the upland area. It follows a fault line forming the Gap of the North, the main north–south throughfare since ancient times. In this trough, astride the ancient road from Armagh to Tara, lies the town of **Newry.**

Within a 25-mile (40km) circle, some 48 peaks rise in a purple mass of rounded summits. The scenery around the **Mourne Mountains** is not wild or rugged (Bignian and Bearnagh are the only two craggy peaks); their gentle undulations inspire peace and solitude. Few roads cross the Mournes, so this is a walker's paradise: endless paths up and down through bracken and heather, unspoilt lakes and tumbling streams, the wild flowers of moor and heath, birds and birdsong, all under an ever-changing sky.

Of the many walks possible, perhaps the loveliest are up to **Silent Valley** and to **Lough Shannagh** from above Kilkeel, to the glittering crystals of **Diamond Rocks**, to the summits above Spelga Dam, and of course **Slieve Donard** itself, where on a fine clear day you can see across the water to England. For the benefit of the more hearty, it is worth mentioning the 20-mile (32km) boundary wall that links the main peaks. Quite a constructional feat in itself, it used to be followed on the Annual Mourne Wall Walk, until erosion by thousands of pairs of feet caused the event to be cancelled.

Perhaps the best place to start from when visiting this area is **Newcastle**, one of Ulster's more lively seaside resorts, though its popularity has sadly destroyed some of its charm. It has a lovely long sandy beach, and behind it there is the **Royal County Down Golf Course** (*✆ (028) 4372 3314*), a fine championship course. Near Newcastle lies the magnificent forest park of **Tullymore** (*open daily 10–sunset; ✆ (028) 4372 2428*). It has many lovely, though rather well-trodden, forest trails and nature walks on the lower wooded slopes and along the River Shimna.

Before following the coast round, it is well worth heading northwards to visit one or two places. **Castlewellan** has two marketplaces: one oval, one square. This neatly laid out town is surrounded by well-wooded demesnes, one of which is **Castlewellan Park** (*with café and visitor centre; open daily 10–dusk; ✆ (028) 4377 8664*), now a forest park and renowned for its arboretum and lovely gardens. The arboretum was begun in 1740, and there are some magnificent trees. A sculpture trail created from natural materials from the park and lake makes a lovely walk. Due north of Newcastle, about 2 miles (3km) away, is **Murlough Nature Reserve** (*always open; car park free*) where you can explore the sand dunes. Exposed to the wind, the dunes are a wonderfully peaceful haven for waders, waterbirds and shore-birds. Sweet-smelling wild flowers grow unhindered and in the summer delicious wild strawberries weave across the sand-dunes. **Dundrum** is not far beyond. On the outskirts of this once flourishing fishing port, now more of a coal quay, ½ mile (1km) northwest of Dundrum on a wooded hill, are the extensive ruins of a Norman motte and bailey **castle**, enclosing a magnificent partly ruined stone castle with a circular keep (*grounds accessible at all times; keep open April–Sept, Tues–Sat 10–7, Sun 2–7; adm*). Staircases, parapets, towers and a massive gatehouse make this an ideal picnic spot and adventure playground for children. It was built in about 1177 as one of John de Courcy's coastal castles.

Newcastle to Rostrevor

Now travel along the coast from Newcastle to Rostrevor on the A2. From here there's a fine view of the Mournes, with Slieve Donard rising majestically up as the centrepiece. Heading south out of Newcastle, past the now quiet harbour, you come to the National Trust Mourne Coastal Path, which runs for 4 miles (6km) from the very popular Bloody Bridge picnic site, along the rocky shoreline to Dunmore Head. The mountain path beside the Blood Bridge River is a starting point for hillwalkers into the Mournes. Here are the splendid mountains of Slieve Donard (2,796ft/850m) and Slieve Commedagh which face each other, and the rockier peaks of Slieve Bignian and Slieve Bearnagh between which lie Silent Valley and its reservoir of water for Belfast. A network of by-roads runs deep into the foothills behind Annalong and Kilkeel. Here is the unspoilt, undisturbed Mourne way of life—stone cottages, men and women at work in their pocket-handkerchief fields, the elderly passing the time of day, children playing. It is not hard to imagine it all in the days before roads were made. Then, the prosperous economy was based on granite quarries and fishing, and the intensively farmed land was enriched from the wrack beds of Killowen. It has changed little since then; only the coastline has become, sadly, rather built up.

Back again on the coast road: round the corner lies the little village of **Annalong**, set against a backcloth of mountains. The little old harbour still flourishes: boats are being repainted, nets repaired; everyone is doing something, no one hurries. You can visit the working corn mill (*only during Feb–Nov, Tues–Sat 11–5; adm*), which overlooks the harbour and has a herb garden and café. **Kilkeel** is a surprisingly busy, prosperous town, home of the coast's main fishing fleet. It is on the site of an ancient *rath*, and the ruins of a 14th-century church still stand in the square. Just to the northeast of the town is a fine **dolmen**, whose capstone measures over 10ft by 8ft (3m by 2.5m). The B27 road climbs up and across the Spelga Pass towards Hilltown. It has many vantage points for viewing both the mountains and the coastal scenery. The B27 branches right about 4 miles out of Kilkeel; this unnumbered road, known as The Head Road, will take you to the Silent Valley and Ben Crom reservoirs. There is a visitor centre, craft shop and café here, and it is busy in the summer.

Continuing on round the coast, the land levels out quite a bit. Leave the A2 and explore the peninsula of Cranfield Point and Greencastle, reached by narrow little roads. Down to the left lies the long strand of **Cranfield**. Greencastle, the ancient capital of the 9th-century Kingdom of Mourne, is visible on the horizon strategically sited at the entrance of Carlingford Lough. Its position was recognized by the Anglo-Normans who built a strong castle here (**Greencastle Fort**; *grounds accessible at all times; adm free; keep is open April–Sept, Tues–Sat 10–7, Sun 2–7; adm*). The tall, rectangular, turreted keep and some of the out-works are all that remain of this impressive 13th-century stronghold. From the topmost turret of the castle are splendid views across the lough to the Republic.

The road swings round still more, ever twisting and turning as it makes its way along the indented coast. The houses are larger, their gardens bigger and better kept. Clearly this was, and still is, a prosperous area. Sheltered by high hills and set against a purple and green backcloth of pine forests, the town of **Rostrevor** enjoys a mild and sunny climate, hence the profusion of brightly coloured flowers in the gardens, many of them of Mediterranean origin. It has a lovely long seafront and superb views across the lough, but sadly no sandy beach. It is a quiet place to use as a base for walking in the Mourne Mountains or in the pine-scented Rostrevor Forest. A mountain road climbs up northwards, passing the little old church of Kilbroney with its ancient cross, and levelling out to follow the valley of the Bann and emerge at Hilltown. The many tumbling little streams, stony paths and patches of woodland make for excellent picnic sites en route.

Not far from Rostrevor is **Warrenpoint**, a lively and popular resort. It is spacious and well planned, with a very big square and a promenade over half a mile (800m) long, the town being bounded by the sea on two sides. There is a well-equipped marina, golf and tennis facilities, and lots of live music in the pubs. Prior to the mid-18th century there was little here save a rabbit warren—hence its name. The Heritage Centre in Bridge Road (*open April–Oct, daily exc Mon*) has items of local historical interest. A little to the north, on a spur of rock jutting out into the estuary, lies the square, battlemented tower house of **Narrow Water Castle**, which is privately owned. It was built in the 17th century on the site of a much earlier fortification.

From here the road improves dramatically and before long you reach **Newry**, an old and prosperous town sited where St Patrick planted a yew at the head of the strand—hence its name, which in Gaelic is *An Hir*: yew. It enjoys a strategic site astride the Clanrye River. Newry has been a busy mercantile town for centuries, and trade was boosted in 1741 when the Newry Canal—believed to be the oldest canal constructed in the British Isles—connected Newry to Lough Neagh and Carlingford Lough. Today, the canal is stocked with fish, and plans are afoot to open it up to boats, but a huge amount of work has to be done first. The long prosperity of this old town is clearly reflected in its large and imposing town houses and public buildings, though many are now rather dilapidated.

St Patrick's Parish Church is possibly the earliest Protestant church in Ireland. The 19th-century **Cathedral of St Colman** boasts some beautiful stained-glass windows. The town hall is impressively sited astride the Clanrye River, which forms the county boundary. There is much Georgian architecture, and many shops with small-paned windows and slate-hung gables. Some of Newry's oldest houses are to be found in Market Street. Remnants of far earlier centuries are the monastery, the castle and the Cistercian abbey. In the **Arts Centre**, Bank Parade, is a small museum (*open all year, daily exc Sun*) with many varied and interesting exhibits.

Two miles (3km) north of the town, near Crown Bridge, there is a very fine motte and bailey, giving rise to a crown-shaped mound. And at **Donaghmore** 3 miles (5km) on, in the parish graveyard, there is a fine 10th-century carved cross on the site of an earlier monastery under which lies a souterrain. **Slieve Gullion Forest Park**, 4 miles (6.4km) west of Newry in County Armagh, has a lovely 7-mile (11km) drive with wonderful views of lakes, which takes you nearly to the top of Slieve Gullion itself. A path continues upwards to 1,900ft (580m), and you can explore two Stone Age cairns.

Inland around Hilltown

Heading from Newry back across to Newcastle you pass just north of the Mournes. The view across to the mountains is superb and ever-changing. The road is very twisty so it is nice to stop and appreciate the many panoramic vantage points. There are two towns worth visiting. The first, **Hilltown**, the more southerly where the mountain roads from Kilkeel and Rostrevor converge, is a small angling village located at a crossroads on top of a hill. The views are breathtaking. Just over 2 miles (3.2km) northeast of Hilltown, in Cloughmore on Goward Hill, is a huge dolmen known as **Cloughmore Cromlech**. Underneath its three massive upright supports and 50-ton granite capstone, there is a double burial chamber in which traces of bones were found. The road to Kilkeel (B27) passes close to the Silent Valley reservoir—a deep valley between the peaks of the Mournes. The road, known as the Spelga Pass, demands careful driving as it rises and twists amongst the spectacular scenery. However, if you decide to go north on the B25 you will come to a less dramatic landscape.

Easily spotted in the distance by its distinctive mushroom-shaped water tower lies **Rathfriland**—a flourishing market town set high on a hill, and commanding a wide view of the Mournes and the surrounding countryside. This area from Loughbrickland to Rathfriland is called Brontë country because here lived the aunts, uncles and, when he was young, the father of novelists Charlotte, Emily and Anne. Emily is supposed to have modelled Heathcliff in *Wuthering Heights* on her wild great-uncle Welsh, who travelled to London with a big stick to silence the critics of his nieces' books. **Drumballyroney school** and **church** near Rathfriland houses a small interpretative centre (*open March–Oct, Tues–Fri 11–5, Sat–Sun 2–6; adm*) on the Brontës. Patrick Brontë, the father of the girls, was the parish schoolmaster here. The family homestead is at Emdale.

Further north again, heading back for Belfast on the A25/A1, is the town of **Hillsborough**. The Anglo-Irish Agreement was reached here. It is one of the most English-looking villages in Ulster, with fine Georgian architecture, several excellent antiques shops in the Main Street, tasteful craft shops and numerous restaurants. 'Ulster says No' is painted on posters and flags, and a multitude of Union Jacks decorate the streets. To the south of the town in parkland is a massive **fort** built by Sir Arthur Hill, an English settler, in the 17th century (*open all year, Mon–Sat 10–7, Sun 2–7; in winter closes at 4 and also closed Mon*). **Hillsborough Castle**, which was the official residence of the Governor of Northern Ireland until 1973 and mostly houses various diplomats, stands in the parkland too. The wrought-iron gates which bar one's approach from the town are exquisite. St Malachy's, the Church of Ireland parish church, is in handsome planter's-style Gothic, and was built by the Hill family in 1774. If you are lucky enough to get inside, it is typical of the cool unadorned churches of that style with box pews and 18th- and 19th-century wall tablets. It has a well-cared-for atmosphere; very different from the fate of so many Church of Ireland buildings in the Republic which have become redundant because of dwindling congregations.

The **linen homelands**—Banbridge, Craigvaron and Lisburn—is a convenient tag which describes an area of immense economic importance in the history of Northern Ireland. Nearly everybody in Ulster was involved in some way in the 19th and early 20th century in the growing and manufacture of linen, and especially so around the Upper Bann and Lagan River. The **Irish Linen Centre and Museum** (*open all year Mon–Sat 9.30–5, plus April–Sept Sun 2–5; © (028) 9266 3377*) in Lisburn, with its exhibition 'Flax to Fabric', is well worth a visit. If you have time, take the Linen Homelands Tour which visits a water-powered scutching mill, a working linen factory, and the Linen Centre itself (*for the tour contact Banbridge Tourist Office, © (028) 4062 3322*). The Ulster Folk and Transport Museum at Cultra, Holywood, and the Somme Heritage Centre, both extremely worthwhile places to visit, are described under 'The Suburbs of Belfast'.

Shopping

Crafts: The National Trust shops at Castleward, Strangford and Mount Stewart, Newtownards. The Bay Tree, Audley Court, Holywood. Iona, 27 Church Road, Holywood. Lovely craft shop which also sells organic vegetables. Cowdy Crafts, Main Street, Hillsborough. Loch Ruray House, 8 Main Street, Dundrum. Showcase for local crafts. Discovery Glass workshop, High Street, Comber.

Pottery: Parrot Lodge Pottery, 131 Ballyward Road, Castlewellan. Fish, birds of paradise, objects functional and surreal. Eden Pottery, 39a South Street, Comber. Handthrown tableware and garden pots.

Antiques: shops in the Main Street, Greyabbey; at Balloo House, Killinchy; and in Killinchy Street, Comber. Also, The Gallery, Gilford Castle, Gilford, and Main Street, Hillsborough.

Delicacies: excellent bread and cake shops throughout the county. In particular try Adelboden Lodge, Groomsport. For delicious wholemeal loaf and barmbrack, go to the Victoria Bakery, Castle Street, Newry. For excellent wines in an elegant shop, James Nicholson, 27a Killyleagh Street, Crossgar. Italian delicatessen, Panini, at 25 Church Road, Holywood, for the makings of a picnic. Sausages at McCartney's, 56 Main Street. Moira. Champion sausage maker.

Where to Stay

See also **Belfast**, 'Where to Stay'.

North Down

Clandeboye Lodge, Clandeboye, near Bangor, ✆ (028) 9185 2500 (*expensive*). Luxury hotel on the Clandeboye Estate with 18-hole golf course.

Burrendale House, 49 Castlewellan Road, Newcastle, ✆ (028) 4372 2599, ✉ 4372 2328 (*moderate*). Modern, popular with bus tours. **Portaferry Hotel**, 10 The Strand, Portaferry, ✆ (028) 4272 8231, ✉ 4272 8999 (*moderate*). Old-fashioned, yet well-appointed, in a lovely situation. **The Narrows**, 8 Shore Road, Portaferry, ✆ (028) 4272 8148, ✉ 4272 8105 (*moderate*). Recent development with sea-views, walled garden and restaurant. **Old Schoolhouse Inn**, 100 Ballydrain Road, Comber, ✆ (028) 9754 1182, ✉ 9754 2583 (*moderate*). All rooms en-suite, dinner available. **Edenvale Country House**, 130 Portaferry Road, Newtownards, ✆ (028) 9181 4881, ✉ 9182 6192 (*moderate*). Pretty Georgian house in the country with comfortable period bedrooms. **Beech Hill Country House**, 23 Ballymoney Road, Craigantlet, Holywood, ✆ (028) 9042 5892 (*moderate*). Georgian-style bungalow in peaceful extension. **Dufferin Arms**, Killyleagh, ✆ (028) 4482 8229, ✉ 4482 8755 (*moderate*). Comfortable B&B option.

Mrs Coburn, **Sylvan Hill House**, Dromore, ✆/✉ (028) 9269 2321 (*inexpensive*). 18th-century house and delicious food. Mrs Muldoon, **The Cottage**, 377 Comber Road, Dundonald, ✆ (028) 9187 8189 (*inexpensive*). This cosy 200-year-old cottage has turf fires. Mrs W. Mark, **The Maggi Minn**, 11 Bishops Well Road, Dromore, ✆ (028) 9269 3520 (*moderate*). Delicious Ulster fry for breakfast, dinner also available.

South Down

Glassdrumman Lodge, 85 Mill Road, Annalong, ✆ (028) 4376 8451, ✉ 4376 7041 (*expensive*). A superb place to spend the night, though on the pricey side. Next door at the Glassdrumman Lodge Restaurant you can have a delicious meal, with vegetables from the garden and organic meat. **Slieve Donard Hotel**, Downs Road, Newcastle, ✆ (028) 4372 3681, ✉ 4372 4830(*expensive*). Close to golf links. **Rayanne House**, 60 Demesne Road, Holywood, ✆ (028) 9042 5859, ✉ 9042 3364 (*expensive*). Grade A Guest House, comfortable bedrooms with delicious breakfast and an award-winning restaurant.

Mr and Mrs Corbett, **Tyrella House**, Clanmaghery Rd, Tyrella, Downpatrick, ✆/✉ (028) 4485 1422 (*moderate*). Georgian country house with private sandy beach. Riding and grass-court tennis.

Mr and Mrs Adair, 22 The Square, Portaferry, ✆ (028) 4272 8412 (*inexpensive*). A very simple and clean place to stay. Mrs Maginn, **Rathglen Villa**, 7 Hilltown Road, Rathfriland, ✆ (028) 4063 8090 (*inexpensive*). **Ryan's**, 19 Milltown Street, Burren, Warrenpoint, ✆/✉ (028) 4177 2506 (*inexpensive*). 3 rooms en suite. **Drumgooland House**, 29 Dunnanew Road, Seaforde, ✆ (028) 4481 1956, ✉ 4481 1265 (*inexpensive*). Comfortable and friendly. **Pheasants Hill**, 37 Killyleagh Road, Downpatrick, ✆/✉ (028) 4461 7246 (*inexpensive*). Modern farmhouse on small-holding, surrounded by nature reserve. **Forestbrook House**, 11 Forestbrook Road, Rostrevor, ✆ (028) 4173 8105 (*inexpensive*). 18th-century house at the top of a pretty glen. Mrs Macauley, **Havine Farm House**, 51 Ballydonnell Road, Downpatrick, ✆ (028) 4485 1242 (*inexpensive*). Comfortable farmhouse with pretty beamed ceilings in the bedrooms. Great home-made cakes.

self-catering

The following are all attractive old buildings: **Potter's Cottage**, Castleward, Strangford. Sleeps 4, from £160 a week (low season) to $305 high season. **Terenichol flats**, Castleward Estate. Each sleeps 8, £185/405 high/low season. Bookings through the National Trust, ✆ (028) 4488 1204 or ✆ (01225) 791199. **Henry John's Clachan**, 104 Clanvaraghan Road, Castlewellan. Cluster of traditional cottages in quiet mountain valley, ✆/✉ (028) 4377 0050. £360 high season, sleeps 5–7. **Mountains of Mourne Country Cottages**, Kilkeel. Six traditional cottages in country lane. Wonderful views. £355 high season; ✆ (028) 4176 5999.

Youth Hostels

Newcastle Youth Hostel, 30 Downs Road, Newcastle, ✆ (028) 4372 2133. **Hillyard House**, 1 Castle Avenue, Castlewellan, ✆ (028) 4377 0141. Meals available. **Barholm**, 11 The Strand, Portaferry, ✆ (028) 4272 9598, ✉ 4272 9784.

Eating Out

See also **Belfast**, 'Eating Out'.

North Down

Portaferry Hotel, 10 The Strand, ✆ (028) 4272 8231 (*moderate*). Excellent seafood delivered straight from the fishing boats of Portavogie. **Yellow Door**, 1 Bridge Street, Gilford, ✆ (028) 3883 1543 (*expensive*). Roasted wild boar. Cheaper set lunches. **Shanks Restaurant**, Blackwood Golf Club, Crawfordsburn Road, Bangor, ✆ (028) 9185 3313 (*expensive*). Rich, varied menu.

The Lobster Pot, 11 The Square, Strangford, ✆ (028) 4488 1288 (*moderate*). Very good set meals and pub grub. Oysters and other shellfish a speciality. The **Back Street Café**, 14 Queens Parade, Bangor, ✆ (028) 9145 3990 (*moderate*). Good atmosphere and imaginative food down a little lane. **The Grange**, Mill Hill, Main Street,

Waringstown, ℘ (028) 3888 1989 (*moderate*). Delicious baked salmon. **Bay Café**, Station Square, Helen's Bay, ℘ (028) 9185 2841 (*moderate*). Mediterranean-style food. *Must book.* **Adelboden Lodge**, Groomsport (*inexpensive*). Bar snacks and main meals. Good plain cooking. **Villa Toscana**, Toscana Park, West Circular Road, Bangor, ℘ (028) 9147 3737 (*moderate*). Superb Italian food. **The Baytree Coffee House**, Audley Court, High St, Holywood, ℘ (028) 9042 1419 (*moderate*). Friendly place; light lunches and cakes. Salads, steaks. **Plough Inn**, 3 The Square, Hillsborough, ℘ (028) 9268 2985 (*moderate*). Pub grub and steak/seafood bistro. **Cuan Bar and Restaurant**, 6 The Square, Strangford, ℘ (028) 4488 1222 (*moderate*). Venison, quail, plus hot & cold buffet.

Mount Stewart House, National Trust Tearooms (*inexpensive*). On the Strangford Shore, a place for light lunch and high tea May–Sept. **Hillside Bar**, 21 Main Street, Hillsborough (*moderate*). Salad bar, soups, plus oysters in season.

O'Reilly's, 7 Rathfriland Rd, Dromara, ℘ (028) 9753 2209 (*moderate*). Excellent seafood. **Grace Neill's**, 33 High Street, Donaghadee. ℘ (028) 9188 2553 (*inexpensive*). Traditional Irish food served with sophistication in historic pub. **Bow Bells**, Bow Street, Donaghadee (*inexpensive*). Coffee shop with good baking. **Primrose Bar**, Ballynahinch (*inexpensive*). Good sandwiches.

Heatherlea Tea Rooms, 94 Main Street, Bangor (*inexpensive*). Good quiche, pies, salads. **Roma's**, 4 Regent Street, Newtownards, ℘ (028) 9181 2841 (*inexpensive*). Italian food. **Scullery Moyrah**, 101 Main Street, Moira (*inexpensive*). Café in craft shop. Home-made soups, salads, scones. **Daft Eddys**, Sketrick Island, Whiterock, Killinchy, ℘ (028) 9754 1615 (*inexpensive*). Pub on island reached by a causeway. Good soups and steaks.

South Down

Glassdrumman Lodge, 85 Mill Road, Annalong, ℘ (028) 4376 8451 (*expensive*). Memorable food, especially the steak and fish dishes. The family who run it grow their own vegetables and keep their animals in free-range conditions.

Bucks Head, 77 Main Street, Dundrum, ℘ (028) 4375 1868 (*moderate*). Seafood and steaks. **Aylesforte House**, 44 Newry Road, Warrenpoint, ℘ (028) 4177 2255 (*moderate*). Exotic eastern-style menu. **Brass Monkey**, 1 Sandy Street, Newry, ℘ (028) 3026 3176 (*moderate*). Opens at 10.30 for coffee, then good steak, chicken and fish dishes for lunch and dinner. **Seaforde Inn**, 24 Main Street, Seaforde, ℘ (028) 4481 1232 (*moderate*). Venison sausages, mussels. **Deli Lites**, 12 Monaghan Street, Newry (*inexpensive*). Lots of breakfast options, soups, salads and even fair coffee.

The Public Library, Armagh

County Armagh

The smallest county in Ulster, Armagh's scenery is nevertheless varied: from the gentle southern drumlins, to wild open moorland, and the grander mountains and rocky glens further east. The Gaelic tradition of splitting land between all the family gives a familar pattern to the landscape. Here, an intricate network of dry-stone walls gathers what fertility may be had into fields with barely enough room for a cow to turn in. As you travel north towards the reclaimed wetlands on the shore of Lough Neagh, the orchards and dairy pastures become more extensive, and are dotted with small lakes and the rivers that once turned the wheels of the flax mills.

In general, the people are fairly prosperous farmers, although the Troubles of the last twenty years have taken their toll of misery and death. People here feel very strongly about politics, and there is very little middle ground, so you may find it easier to avoid political discussions.

Highlights of the county include Ardress House and The Argory, both National Trust properties which give great insight into the more settled times of the 18th and 19th centuries. For the fisherman there are tremendous catches of bream in the Blackwater River, and walkers can enjoy the quiet tranquillity of Clare Glen. You might be lucky and see a game of road bowls, an old Irish sport that is played here and in County Cork. The area has the reputation for being very rainy, but if you time your visit during May you will see the country at its prettiest, especially around Loughall with its apple orchards in full blossom. Ulsterbus transport is excellent throughout the county, and the main Belfast to Dublin railway line passes along its eastern border, stopping along the way.

History

One of the most fascinating aspects of County Armagh is its history. On the outskirts of Armagh City is the legendary *Emain Macha*, also known as Navan Fort. This was the crowning place of the Sovereigns of Ulster (350 BC to AD 332), and it was from here that the legendary Red Branch Knights sallied out to display their prowess and do great deeds of chivalry. The greatest of these knights was Cú Chulainn, who is supposed to have received his training at the fort (*see* **Old Gods and Heroes**, p.245). Of course, this ancient history is clouded with mystery and legend; it is part of Ulster's mythology and identity, just as Fionn MacCumhail and the *Fianna* are part of that of the rest of Ireland. Legends aside, we do know that when Fergus was King of Ulster in the 4th century, *Emain Macha* was burned and pillaged by forces from Tara, County Meath, and was never restored.

After the decline of *Emain Macha*, the then small city of Armagh established itself as the ecclesiastical capital of Ireland. Here, in the 5th century, St Patrick built his first stone church, around which grew up other churches, colleges and schools. The city developed into a great centre of religion and learning, until the 9th and 10th centuries with the incursion of the Vikings. Today, it is a fine city of attractive 18th-century buildings, built in settled, prosperous days, with an excellent museum.

Getting There and Around

By air: Dublin International Airport is approximately 78 miles (124km) away. Belfast International airport is approximately 39 miles (62km) away.

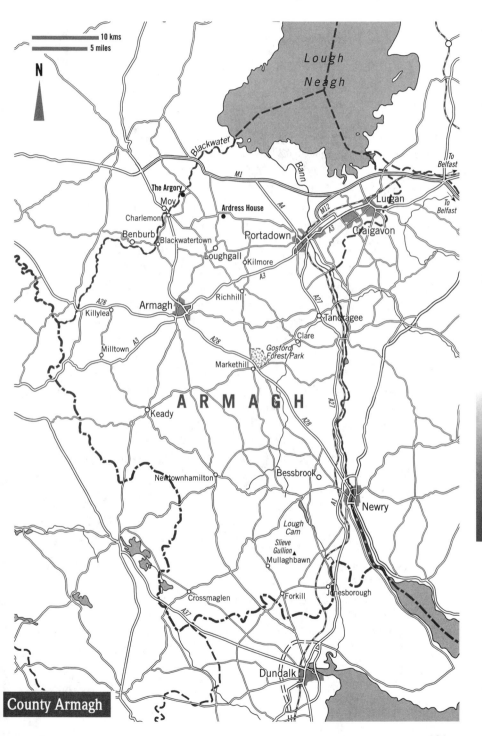

County Armagh

Sports and Activities

Planetarium and Hall of Astronomy: Star shows are put on more frequently in the summer. It is advisable to ring and book for these, ℗ (028) 3752 3689. *http://www. armagh-planetarium.co.uk. Open all year Mon–Fri 10–4.45, Sat and Sun 1.15–4.45.*

Fishing: Between Benburb and Blackwater town an extensive river park makes fishing and water sports of all kinds possible. Contact the Armagh Tourist Office, ℗ (028) 3752 1800. Fishing on the Cusher and Callan Rivers, which are tributaries of the Blackwater River. The local representative for angling, who knows all the rivers and trout lakes hereabouts, is Mr T. Toner, ℗ (028) 3752 6998.

Water sports: Of all types through Craigavon Water Sports Centre, ℗ (028) 3834 2669.

Walking: Carnagh and Slieve Gullion Forest Park planned walks. *Open 10–dusk.* The Ulster Way, a sign-posted trail which traverses the mountains and coastline of Ulster, goes through Armagh. A large stretch along the Newry Canal between Newry and Portadown is very scenic. Details from the Tourist Office in Armagh. For more information phone the Sports Council for Northern Ireland to get details on the Ulster Way, ℗ (028) 9038 1222.

Cycling: Craigavon Borough Council is developing cycle routes on traffic-free paths and minor roads. Contact Lough Neagh Discovery Centre, Oxford Island, ℗ (028) 3832 2205.

Gardens and open farms: Tannaghmore Gardens and Farm, Silverwood, Craigavon, ℗ (028) 3834 3244. Victorian rose garden and rare breeds. Forkhill Open Farm, ℗ (028) 3088 8203.

Golf: 18-hole golf course in Palace Demesne, Armagh, ℗ (028) 3752 5861. Craigavon Golf and Ski Centre, ℗ Lurgan (028) 3832 6606. Tandragee Golf Club, Markethill Road, 18-hole course, ℗ (028) 3884 1272.

Boat trips: From Kinnego Bay, Lough Neagh; also sailing courses. Contact Paddy Prunty, Harbour Master, ℗ (028) 3832 7573.

Birdwatching: Oxford Island: Lough Neagh Discovery Centre, birdwatching and walks, ℗ (028) 3832 2205.

Coney Island: For birdlife and fishing. There is no ferry service: you have to hire a boat from Kinnego Bay or Maghery Country Park; ℗ (028) 3832 2205.

By train: Frequent service between Dublin and Belfast stopping at Portadown and Newry. (The express service does not stop at all).

By bus: Eight Ulsterbus expresses run daily from Belfast. Local buses from Armagh City Bus Station, ℗ (028) 3752 2266.

By bike: Raleigh Rent-a-Bike Centre at Raymonds, 65 Bridge Street, Portadown, ℗ (028) 3835 2828. **The Cyclery**, Grant House, 56 Edward Street, Lurgan, ℗ (028) 3834 8627.

Tourist Information

Armagh, St Patrick's Trian Centre, 40 English St, ℗ (028) 3752 1800, ✉ 3752 8329.

Craigavon Civic Centre, Lakeview Road, ✆ (028) 3834 1199.

Crossmaglen Community Centre, The Square, ✆ (028) 3086 8900.

Portadown, Cascades Leisure Complex, Thomas Street, ✆ (028) 3833 2802.

Lurgan, Lough Neagh Discovery Centre, Oxford Island, ✆ (028) 3832 2906.

Festivals

May: Apple blossom festival.

Early August: All Ireland Intermediate Road Bowls Festival, on roads around Armagh City.

Armagh City

The city of **Armagh**, (*Ard Macha*), now sprawled over seven hills, used to be a centre of Christian learning and tranquillity when Rome was in ruins and London glowed with endless fires started by the Barbarians. Today, there is little to show of the ancient city; its appearance is distinctly Georgian, especially in the Mall, yet it is still the ecclesiastical centre of Ireland. Armagh is a lovely city to walk around with its fine buildings especially in the Mall and in Beresford Row. The Courthouse dates from 1809 and is the work of Francis Johnston, as are many buildings here; he was a local architect who later achieved fame in Dublin. The Courthouse was bombed in 1993, but has since been completely restored. Many of the most interesting places to visit, such as the Armagh Planetarium on College Hill and the Palace Stables Heritage Centre off Friary Road, are a brisk walk away. A visit to the **County Museum** in the Mall East (*open Mon–Fri 10–5, Sat 10–1 and 2–5; adm free*) helps to fill in the city's background. Here, a 17th-century painting shows the old wide streets, space for markets and the prominence of the early hill-top Cathedral of St Patrick. There is also a wide range of regional archaeological exhibits, a local natural history section, and an art gallery which has works by the Irish mystic poet and artist George Russell (1867–1935), better known as A. E. Russell. The **Royal Irish Fusiliers Museum** (*open Mon–Fri 10–4; adm; ✆ (028) 3752 2911*), with displays of old uniforms as well as weapons and medals, is also in the Mall.

The city has recently developed an ambitious project in support of the arts in Northern Ireland: a brand new Arts Centre scheduled to open in 2000, with workshop space for drama, music and dance, two theatres, an exhibition gallery, as well as restaurants and bars. A new 4-screen cinema has opened beside it, ✆ (028) 3751 1033.

The two cathedral churches are unmistakable features of the city's skyline, for they each crown neighbouring hills. Founded by St Patrick, the ancient **Church of Ireland Cathedral** is in the perpendicular style with a massive central tower. Its present appearance dates mainly from the 18th century, but its core is medieval. Before medieval times the city suffered terribly from the Viking raids, and the cathedral and town were sacked at least twenty times in five hundred years. Inside the cathedral is a memorial to Brian Boru, the most famous high king of all Ireland, who visited Armagh in 1004 and was received with great state. The precious *Book of Armagh* (*c.* AD 807), which is now in Trinity College, Dublin, was placed in his hands and his visit noted in the book. He presented 20 ounces of pure gold to the church. Ten years later he hammered the Vikings at the battle of Clontarf in 1014, which put a stop to their encroachment into inland areas (*see* **History**, p.40), but Brian Boru was killed in his tent after the

The Observatory, Armagh

battle was won. His body and that of his son were brought back to be buried here and the memorial to them is in the west wall.

The other heirloom of those ancient days is St Patrick's Bell, which is enclosed in a cover dating from the 12th century; it can be seen at the National Museum in Dublin. The moulding on the west door is very fine, and there is a good stained-glass window in the choir. Notice the carved medieval stone heads high up on the cathedral's exterior and the mysterious statues in the crypt. The surrounding streets run true to the rings of the Celtic *rath* or fort in which St Patrick (directed, so it is said, by a flight of angels) built his church. On the corner of Abbey Street is **Armagh Public Library** (✆ *(028) 3752 3142*), also known as Robinson's Library, which contains some rare books, maps and a first edition of *Gulliver's Travels*, annotated by Jonathan Swift himself. Richard Robinson, Archbishop of Armagh, was a very influential figure in the building of 18th-century Armagh. An **exhibition and historical centre** (*open all year; adm for exhibitions*) has opened in English Street. It is known as St Patrick's Trian (pronounced 'Tree-an') and derives this name from an ancient division of the city. 'The Armagh Story' is illustrated through the ages by an audio visual show, an exhibition on the life and work of St Patrick and his connections with Armagh. The Land of Lilliput is a child-orientated exhibition, which has a giant model of Gulliver as the centrepiece. The Centre also has art exhibitions, tourist information, and is home to Armagh Ancestry (*open Mon–Sat 9–5*), a central source for chasing up ancestors in Armagh county.

Across the valley are the twin spires of the Catholic **Cathedral of St Patrick**. This is a complete contrast to its more sombre Protestant neighbour with its profusion of magnificent internal gilding, marbles, mosaics and stained glass. The building was started in 1849 and finished in 1873; the passing of the years is marked by a collection of cardinals' red hats suspended in the Lady Chapel.

Armagh has the most advanced facilities for astronomical studies in the British Isles. The institution owes its pre-eminence to Primate Robinson, who founded and endowed Armagh's **Observatory** in 1790; it is complemented by a **Planetarium** (*open year-round Mon–Fri 10–4.45, Sat–Sun 1.15–4.45*), which has Ireland's largest public telescope, and also hosts presentations in its **star theatre**. The Observatory was designed by Francis Johnston, who is also responsible for the **Court House** and the Georgian terrace on the east side of the Mall. On the south side of the city is the Palace demesne. The **Palace Stables Heritage Centre** (*open daily all year; adm*) is a restored 18th-century building in the demesne of the Bishop's Palace. The 'Day in the Life' exhibition features typical scenes of life here in 1776 in the time of Primate Robinson. It holds craft exhibitions, fairs, lectures, art shows, music, dance and storytelling.

Around Armagh

The ancient fort of *Emain Macha*, now called **Navan Fort**, dates from 600 BC and is about 2 miles (3km) west of Armagh City on the A28. The fort was a centre of pagan power and culture, and is famous for its association with the Red Branch Knights. When Fergus was King of Ulster in the 4th century, Emain Macha was burned, its timber structures completely destroyed. By the time St Patrick came to *Ard Macha* (Armagh) this Bronze Age centre of power had lain in ruins for over a hundred years. Today, the grassy *rath* extends over about 12 acres (5ha). It is easy to walk or take a bus there from town, and you are rewarded with a pleasant view over the city when you arrive. Once in danger of being destroyed to make way for a quarry, the site has become a chief tourist attraction, and an excellent **Interpretative Centre** (*open all year; adm; © (028) 3752 5550*) has opened close by with a restaurant and shop. The centre is in the shape of a Bronze Age fort, and very unobtrusive; it is definitely worth a detour. The no.73 bus from Mall West Armagh will drop you outside.

To the northeast is the industrial part of County Armagh, with the old linen town of **Portadown** and the new town of **Craigavon**. Though lacking in beauty they do benefit from their proximity to Lough Neagh and the River Bann with man-made lakes, boating ponds and a dry ski-slope. Craigavon's two large artificial lakes are used for water sports and trout fishing. There are two golf courses. An interesting trip can be made to **Moneypenny's Lockhouse** (*open April–Sept, Sat–Sun 2–5*), Newry Canal, Portadown. It contains an exhibition on the history of this 18th-century canal, and the lifestyle of the Lockhouse keeper. It is a peaceful walk from Portadown, along the banks of the canal from Shillington's Quay car park, Castle Street. Near Portadown a network of little roads runs through a charming district covered with fruit trees and bushes, and in May and June the gentle little hills are a mass of pink and white apple and damson flowers. There is an apple blossom festival in May with fairs, concerts, and exhibitions in Keady, Richhill, Tandragee and Loughgall. The orchards were a part of the old Irish agricultural economy long before the English settlers came here, though many of the fruit farmers are descended from Kent and Somerset families, well-used to growing fruit; their main crop are Bramley apples. The retreating glaciers many millions of years ago left behind deposits of clay and gravel which form little hills known as drumlins, of which there are many in this part. The teardrop drumlin country is intersected by trout-filled lakes and streams, high hedges and twisting lanes. In **Richhill** you will find some furniture workshops and a fine **Jacobean manor** with curling Dutch gables. It is not open to the public but the sight it makes within the pretty well-kept village is worth stopping for.

The village of **Kilmore** has what is probably the oldest church in Ireland. In the heart of the present little parish church stands the lower half of a round tower dating from the first half of the 3rd century. Right in the centre of this fertile district is the quaint village of **Loughgall**, which is strung out along the main road, many of its little houses painted in the soft shades of blossom and their gardens bursting with colour. The little **museum** in the main street contains mementoes commemorating the founding of the Orange Order here in 1795 (*open in the summer; key is next door with Mrs Vallary*). Ireland in the late 18th century was a place of localised secret societies, mostly made up of poor agrarian Catholics, mobilised by land hunger, tithes and local issues. The ferment caused by the concessions of Grattan's Parliament towards Catholics in 1793, giving them the vote and more civil liberties, made sectarian tension in this part of Ulster particularly acute. There was a confrontation between the Protestant 'Peep o' Day Boys' and the Catholic 'Defenders' at Diamond Hill outside Loughgall. This led to the founding of the Orange Order which has played such a large part in modern Ulster politics. The Dan Winter Ancestral Home (*call at farmhouse for the key; voluntary donation; 9 The Diamond Derryloughan Road, Loughgall, © (028) 3885 1344*) houses maps and relics of the Battle of the Diamond, and is furnished in the vernacular style.

Not far away is **Ardress House** (*open April–June and Sept, Sat, Sun and bank holidays 2–6; July–Aug daily exc Tues; adm for house and farmyard; © (028) 3885 1236*). This is a 17th-century manor much altered by George Ensor (who married the owner of this once simple farmhouse) so that it is now Georgian in character. It is on the Portadown–May road (B28), 3 miles (5km) from Loughgall. Its elegant drawing room has one of the most beautiful decorative plasterwork ceilings in Ireland. The work is Adam in style and both the ceiling and the mural medallions have been carefully restored and sympathetically painted. Set in lovely parkland, it is now in the care of the National Trust. There is a farmyard display, picnic area, woodland walks and a small formal garden.

Coney Island, one of the few islands in Lough Neagh, is also a National Trust property. It lies to the north, not far from the mouth of the Blackwater, and can be reached by boat from Maghery. Apart from the excellent fishing, this thickly wooded, reedy island of 8½ acres (3.5ha) is also worth visiting for its huge and varied birdlife. St Patrick used the island as a retreat and there is also a rather overgrown holy well. Be prepared for the Lough Neagh flies, which are food for the pollan, a fish unique to these waters and absolutely delicious fried in butter.

Peatlands Park (*park open 9–dusk, visitor centre open April–Sept, Sat & Sun 2–6, also June–Aug, Mon–Fri 2–6*), with its narrow-gauge railway, is close by on the Lough Neagh basin. Educational video and outdoor exhibits on peat ecology. Further east again is the **Lough Neagh Discovery Centre** (*open April–Sept, daily 10–7; Oct–March, Wed–Sun 10–5. Exit 10 off the M1 at Oxford Island*), which explains the geology and natural history of the area; it is possible to go birdwatching in the hides and go on guided nature walks. There are picnic areas, a café and a shop.

Returning southwards along the River Blackwater, which forms the county boundary, 2½ miles (4km) from Charlemont on a tiny little road off the B28 is **The Argory** (*open April–June and Sept, Sat–Sun and holidays 2–6; July–Aug daily exc Tues; adm; ©(028) 8778 4753*). Standing in woodland and parkland, this rather lovely early 19th-century neoclassical house overlooks the river. It is of particular interest in that its contents have remained almost completely undisturbed since the turn of the century. It is much more of a home than a museum, full of treasures gathered over the years from all corners of the earth. The large cabinet organ at the top of the grand cantilevered staircase is quite unique. So is the acetylene gas plant which still lights the house; every room has its own ingenious old light-fittings. Outside you can wander through the stable buildings, semi-formal gardens and woodland, and along river walks.

The village of **Charlemont**, once an important parliamentary borough, is 2.5 miles (4km) upstream. It has an 18th-century cut-stone bridge and a 17th-century ruined fort with star-shaped walls typical of that period, built by Lord Mountjoy, Lord Deputy of Ireland in 1602.

Flax-milling has ceased but flour-milling still thrives in nearby **Tandragee**, a pretty, well-kept town with brightly painted houses. It is of considerable age and was founded by the O'Hanlons, chieftains of these parts before the plantations of James I. The old castle and the town were destroyed in the Civil War of 1641. The present castle is barely more than a century old and now houses the factory of Ulster's foremost crisp, *Tayto*. It is possible to go on an intriguing tour of the crisp factory (*open daily; adm free*).

Clare Glen, one of the prettiest glens in the country, is 4 miles (6km) away to the east of Armagh City. A fine trout stream winds under old bridges and past a now-silent mill. There are lovely walks around here and it is on such country lanes as these that you might come across a game of 'bullets' or road bowls. This game is played with 28oz (795g) balls made of iron, which are thrown along a quiet winding road. The aim is to cover several miles in the fewest shots. Children are stationed along the course to warn motorists, and the betting and excitement amongst the watchers is infectious.

On the Newry road (A28) you pass the village of **Markethill** on the right, and **Gosford Castle**, a huge early 19th-century mock-Norman castle, on the left (*open all year 10–dusk; pedestrians adm, car park fee*). The magnificent grounds are now open to the public and owned by the Forestry Commission. The walled cherry garden, the arboretum, unusual breeds of poultry, nature trails and forest parks make it an enjoyable place to while away some time. Further south and keeping to the more attractive minor roads, you come across the village of **Bessbrook**. This is a model linen manufacturing town, neatly laid out in the 19th century by a Quaker; it still has neither pub nor pawn house. The design of the model town of Bournville near Birmingham, famous for its chocolate industry, is based entirely on Bessbrook. Remains of the huge old mill, dams, weirs and sluices stand deserted, and nearby the impressive cut-stone Craigmore Viaduct still carries the main railway line to Dublin.

Just outside Bessbrook is **Derrymore House** (*open daily 10–14 April and May–August, Thurs–Sat 2–5; adm; ✆ (028) 3083 0353*), a small, thatched manor house set in parkland. Built in 1776, it was witness to the signing of the Act of Union in 1801, and is now in the care of the National Trust.

Travelling south from Bessbrook, the land becomes poorer, the fields smaller, the hedges higher and the roads have more of a twist to them. Soon the hills of south Armagh appear in the distance dominated by the peak of **Slieve Gullion**. This rugged group of hills is steeped in history and legend. Described as the mountains of mystery, the average tourist never hears of them, which is a pity as the whole region has magnificent scenery, beautiful lakes, streams and unspoilt little villages. There have been several bloody incidents in this area, labelled 'Bandit Country'; the population is predominantly Catholic, and the situation here before the ceasefire was extremely tense.

Crossmaglen has a dicey reputation, but with the ceasefire holding the situation has improved. In general, you can enjoy exploring this delightfully unkept area, so different from the tamer country in the north. Caught between Camlough Mountain and Slieve Gullion lies the beautiful ribbon-like Lough Cam. The surrounding hedges and shorelines are the homes of many flowers and birds and there is good fishing on the Fane River, Lough Cam and Lough Ross.

From the other side of Lough Cam, the road climbs up through the trees to the extensive, recently developed **Slieve Gullion Forest Park**. From the top of Slieve Gullion, wonderful panoramic views of the encircling mountains that make up the Ring of Gullion, and the distant hills of Belfast and Dublin, spread before you. Slieve Gullion (*Sliabh gCuillin*: Mountain of the Steep Slope), is often shrouded in mist, and according to local folklore it is magical. Legend tells us that Chulainn was a chief who owned a fierce watchdog which was slain by a boy of 15. The young hero was afterwards called *Cú Chulainn* ('Hound of Chulainn'). On the southern slopes there is an ancient church known as **Killevy Church**. There are the remains of two churches here, each from different periods, whilst this holy place was founded as a nunnery as far back as AD 450. Close by is a holy well and prehistoric passage grave. Close to the County Louth border, just off the N1, about 1.5 miles (2.4km) south of **Jonesborough** east of the bridge, is one of the earliest datable Christian monuments in Ireland. The inscribed **Kilnasaggart Pillar Stone** is early 8th century, and carved with crosses. It commemorates a local dignatory, and the inscription is in Gaelic. **Moyry Castle**, a three-storey ruin nearby, dates from 1601. It was built by Lord Mountjoy, and was ruined in the struggle between the English forces under Mountjoy and the Irish forces under Hugh O'Neill, during the Elizabethan wars.

Both the villages of **Forkhill**, with its trout stream, and **Mullaghban**, with its tiny folk museum, furnished as a south Armagh farmhouse, are picturesquely situated in their own valleys between the hills. On the B30, a short distance from Crossmaglen, a very interesting stop can be made at the old church of **Creggan.** It dates from 1731, and the tower was added in 1799. The O'Neill vault contains over seventy skulls of this ancient family, whose present clan leader is Don Carlos O'Neill of Seville. In the church grounds is a visitor centre with an exhibition on the poets and people of Creggan. Three 18th-century Gaelic poets are buried in the graveyard, one of whom, Art McCumhaigh (1738–1773), wrote a very poignant *aisling*, or vision poem, entitled *The Churchyard of Creagán*, in which the poet encounters the vision of a woman. They bemoan the decline of the Gaels of Tír Eoghain, and the ascendency of John Bull, whilst the poet's last wish is to be buried with Creagan's sweet Gaels. (*Guided tours are available every Sunday June–Sept 2.30–5.30 and at other times by prior arrangement; contact Rev. Mervyn Kingston who lives over the border, ✆ (00 353) 42 71921.*) North of Creggan is **Cullyhanna**, the Cardinal O Fiaich Heritage Centre (*open daily exc Sat; ✆ (028) 3086 8757*). This powerful and strong-minded prelate played his part in the recent history of Ulster, and there is an exhibition of his life, as well as a collection of songs and poems of south Armagh which you can listen to, and a research library. This region is famous for its traditional music, and one place you can be sure to find some is at Hearty's Folk Cottage, Glassdrummond, open on Sunday afternoons for tea and music.

Southeast of Monaghan town is **Crossmaglen**, with its staggeringly large market square. The town is the centre of the recently revived cottage industry of lacemaking. Again, there are earthen works to explore: a superb example of a treble-ringed fort, remains of stone cairns, and a *crannog* (artificial island) on Lough Ross. You are now actually following the old coach road from Dublin to Armagh, itself the ancient link between Emain Macha and Tara (another ancient centre of power), in County Meath. At Dorsey to the east of the town there is the largest entrenched enclosure of its kind in Ireland. Constructed as a defensive outpost for Emain Macha, this huge earthwork encloses over 300 acres (121ha) and lies astride the route. Some of the earth ramparts still remain. It is part of the ancient earth dyke known as the **Black Pig's Dyke**, which extends over most of the borders of Ulster.

Leaving behind the mountains of south Armagh, you enter the attractive upland country known as the **Fews**. The isolated village of **Newtownhamilton** was founded in 1770, but the neighbourhood is associated with the legendary story of Lir, for it was here that the ocean-god King Lir had his palace. Do not go straight back to Armagh, but branch off to the west and climb **Carrigatuke Hill**. From the top an outstanding view of the area as far as Meath to the south, and even Roscommon to the southwest, lies before you. This small area across and down to the border is a miniature Lake District with lots of little irregular lakes caught between tiny hills, vestiges of glacial movement and deposition. Many of the lakes are studded with islands. **Lake Tullnawood** is particularly picturesque. Just north of boot-shaped Clay Lake is the small market town of **Keady**. It was once a very important linen centre, hence the number of derelict watermills in the district. Nearby at **Nassagh Glen** there is a mill, and a huge viaduct that spans the wide valley. Under the viaduct's arches you can picnic among wild flowers, rose briars and red-berried rowan. From here it is only about 6 miles (10km) back to the city of Armagh.

To the west of Armagh, beyond the little hill-top village of Killylea, lies the pretty village of **Tynan**. In the middle of the main street stands a fine sculptured stone cross, over 13ft (4m) high and dating from the 10th century. There are other ancient crosses in the nearby extensive demesne of **Tynan Abbey**; enquire at the estate if you wish to see them.

Shopping

Antiques: Quinn's Antiques, 27 Dobbin Street, Armagh. Huey's Antique Shop, 45 Main Street, Loughgall. Charles Gardiner, 48 High Street, Lurgan.

Crafts: The National Trust Shop, The Argory, Moy. Cloud Cuckoo, Ogle Street, Armagh. Hearty's Folk Cottage, Glassdrummond. Handmade quilts, jewellery, pine furniture. St Patrick's Trian, 40 English Street, Armagh. Mullaghbawn Folk Museum. Tullylish Pottery, Banbridge Road, Tullylish, Portadown; functional and decorative structures in earthy colours. Peatland Park; handcarved figures made from compressed peat.

Market Days: Variety Market in Market Street, Armagh, every Tuesday and Friday; in Shambles Yard every Tuesday and Friday. Livestock market on alternate Saturdays in Newtownhamilton.

Where to Stay

Armagh City

The **Charlemont Arms Hotel**, 63 English Street, ✆ (028) 3752 2028, ✉ 3752 6979 (*moderate*). **Drumsill House**, 35 Moy Road, ✆ (028) 3752 2009, ✉ 3752 5624 (*moderate*). Modern and bland but comfortable. **De Averell House**, English Street, ✆ (028) 3751 1213, ✉ 3751 1221 (*moderate*). Georgian town house, with basement restaurant.

Hillview Lodge, 33 Newtownhamilton Rd, ✆ (028) 3752 2000, ✉ 3752 8276 (*inexpensive*). Reliable B&B with 6 en suite rooms. Mrs Armstrong, **Deans Hill**, ✆ (028) 3752 4923, ✉ 3752 2186 (*inexpensive*). Pretty 18th-century house with lovely gardens, close to Observatory. Two en suite rooms (one four-poster). Short lets for self-catering accommodation. Sleeps 4. **McDees**, Blackwatertown Road,

Drumcullen, Benburb, ℰ (028) 3752 6088 (*moderate*). B&B a few minutes' drive out of town, notably modern interior, and attention to detail in everyhting from bed-linen to breakfast.

Elsewhere in County Armagh

Planter's Tavern, 4 Banbridge Road, Waringstown, ℰ (028) 3888 1510 (*expensive*). Modern motel-style hotel. Mrs Kee, **Ballinahinch House**, 47 Ballygroobany Road, Richhill, ℰ/✉ (028) 3887 0081 (*inexpensive*). Victorian famhouse with spacious rooms, old world ambience. **Lima Country House**, 16 Drumalt Road, Ummerican, Silverbridge, ℰ (028) 3086 1944 (*inexpensive*). **Drumcree House**, 38 Ashgrove Road, Portadown. ℰ (028) 3833 8655 (*inexpensive*). Four rooms; two en suite.

self catering

The Chalet, Dean's Hill, 34 College Hill, ℰ (028) 3752 2099. Sleeps 4, £190 high season. **Benbree**, Forkhill, ℰ (028) 3088 8394. Sleeps 6; from £200. **Mountain View**, Mullaghbawn, ℰ (028) 3088 8410. Sleeps 4/6; from £180.

hostels

Armagh City Hostel, 36 Abbey Street, ℰ (028) 3751 1800, ✉ 3751 1801. New purpose-built hostel with high security and an impressive range of facilities, but utterly sterile. **Waterside House**, Lurgan, Craigavon, ℰ (028) 3832 7573. Hostel located in the conservation area overlooking Lough Neagh; wide range of watersports/activities.

Eating Out

Armagh City

Navan Centre, Killylea Road, (*inexpensive*). Hot meals, snacks, and coffee. **Calvert Tavern**, 3 Scotch Street (*inexpensive*). Good open sand-wiches and grills. Pub grub. **Hester's Place**, 12 Upper English Street (*inexpensive*). Irish stew, great Ulster fry. *Open daytime, closed Wed.* **Jodie's**, 37 Scotch Street (*inexpensive*). Cheerful surrounds, usually has some veg options. **The Darby Byrne**, Palace Demesne, ℰ (028) 3752 9629 (*moderate*). Unique to the county for its dinner shows, murder-mystery nights and the like.

Elsewhere in County Armagh

The **Famous Grouse**, 6 Ballyhagan Rd, Loughgall, ℰ (028) 3889 1778 (*moderate*). Reasonably priced and cosy restaurant. Try the pub grub at lunchtime or *à la carte* menu in the evening. **Seagoe Hotel**, Upper Church Lane, Portadown, ℰ (028) 3833 3076 (*moderate*). Beef and Irish stews. **Denachi Thai**, 72 West Street, Portadown, ℰ (028) 3839 1319 (*moderate*). Thai and European. *Open Tues–Sun evenings.* **Lough Neagh Lodge**, Dungannon Rd, Maghery, Craigavon, ℰ (028) 3885 1901 (*moderate*). Eels, wild trout, steaks. **Old Thatch**, 3 Keady St, Markethill (*inexpensive*). Good cakes and coffee. **Ardress House**, 64 Ardress Rd, Portadown, ℰ (028) 3885 1236 (*inexpensive*). Picnic teas are available on Sundays in summer. **The Argory**, Moy (*inexpensive*). A good tearoom June–Aug. **Hearty's Folk Cottage**, Glassdrummond, near Crossmaglen (*inexpensive*). Sunday afternoons only. Good afternoon teas, arts and crafts and traditional music. **Cafolla**, 2 Carnegie Street, Lurgan (*inexpensive*). Fish and chips. **Hobbs Café**, 10 Market St, Portadown (*inexpensive*). Baked potato, sandwiches.

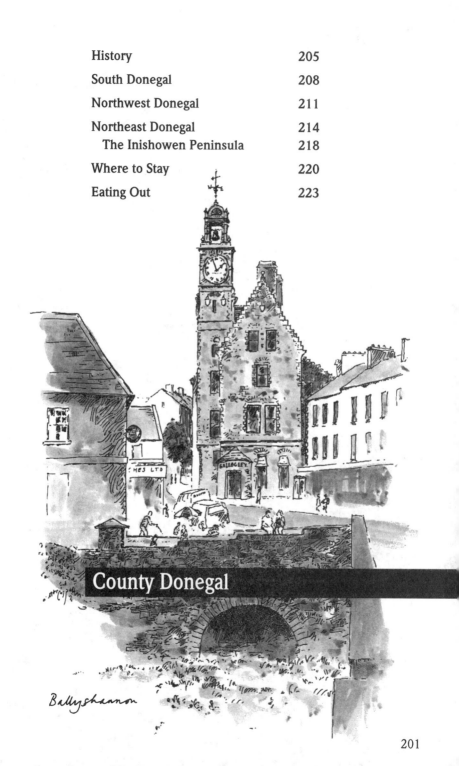

County Donegal

Ballyshannon

County Donegal

10 kms
5 miles

N

Tory Island

Horn Head

Dunfanaghy

Marblehi

Bloody Foreland Head

Falcarragh
Gortahork

Ards Fores
Park

Creesloug

Gola Island

Muckish Mt.

Owey Island

Bunbeg

N56

Altan
Lough

Cruit
Island

Errigal Mt

Derryveagh Mts

Aranmore Island

Burtonport

Glenveagh
National
Park

Glendowan
Mts

Church

Dunglow

N56

Doochary

Gweebarra

Fintown

Portnoo

Narin

Maas

Glenties

Blue Stack Mountains

Barnesmore Gap

N1

Maghera

N56

Ardara

Glencolmcille

Glengesh
Pass

Esk

N15

Malin Beg

Slieve League

Teelin

Kilcar

Killybegs

N56

Dunkineely

Mountcharles

Donegal

Laghy

Lough
Derg

Rossnowlagh

N15

Donegal Bay

Ballyshannon

Bundoran

Donegal (*Dun na nGall* : fort of the foreigner) is a microcosm of all Ireland and the fourth largest county. In the west is the Gaeltacht, with its mountains, heathery moors and boglands, home of the dispossessed Celt. In the east, there are rich pasturelands, plantation towns, and long-settled families which were originally Scottish or English. Set northwest against the Atlantic, much of its beauty comes from its promixity to the sea: from the sweep of Donegal Bay, the maritime cliffs around Slieve League, the intricate indentations of the coast up to Bloody Foreland, and the northern peninsulas formed by long sea loughs, around 200 miles (320km) of coast in all. Donegal is a county of beautiful coun-tryside; the ancient mountain ranges are older than any others in Ireland, and the light of Donegal brings alive the subtle greens and browns of the landscape, and the strength of blue in the sky and sea. There are some exciting walks and climbs for the experienced. Because of the mountains in central Donegal, the weather is often quite different in the southwest quarter.

Each part of Donegal has its own charm and beauty: the rocky flats of the Rosses studded with tiny lakes, the varied scenery of Inishowen, the curved beaches and mountains of Tirconnell, and the rich cattle lands which border the River Foyle. Compared to many of the urban parts of Ireland, Donegal is still a land of wilderness and rock, where a lone farmhouse hugs the hill, and its resident sheepdog hurtles out onto the road to chase the car which dares intrude into his little kingdom.

Yet increasingly, as in other coastal parts of Ireland, there has been an increase in homes and holiday chalets, often built right along the coast. County Donegal has traditionally been the holiday destination of urban Northerners from Belfast and its surrounds; many leave their caravans in Donegal, and as prosperity grows, they are buying into the new developments. The uglier by-products of Ireland's more general prosperity and industrial development is apparent around **Letterkenny**, which grows rapidly every year. The baby boom in Ireland has been experienced in this county more than anywhere else, which (almost) makes up for the rural depopulation which has scourged the countryside since the famine of 1845–49. Of course, the new generation is not being brought up on the old homesteads in lonely picturesque valleys, but in the numerous bungalows and housing estates which line the roads near the factories that the Irish Government has enticed in with substantial financial assistance.

Tourist attractions are being developed with the restoration of buildings of architectural or historical interest such as Lifford Old Courthouse and the Corn and Flax Mill at Newmills new Letterkenny. The archeological and early Christian remains of County Donegal are numerous. St Colmcille, Ireland's most famous native saint, was born here at Gartan, whilst Glencolmcille is closely associated with him.

Some people say that Donegal is the 26th county in a 25-county state, meaning that there is an individuality and independence up here which Dublin likes to ignore. This Ulster county has the largest number of Irish native speakers of any county in Ireland, though, curiously enough, 'Official Irish' is based on the

Leinster dialect. The Ulster dialect has more in common with Highland Gaelic than with the southern strain. There are strong links with Scotland; many districts of Glasgow are reputed to be like parishes of west Donegal, and you will see buses going from places like Annagary all the way to Glasgow. Part of Donegal is officially Irish speaking, (the Gaeltacht).

History

The county has a large proportion of Neolithic and Early Bronze Age remains. The main monument which survives from prehistoric times is Grianan of Aileach, near Burt, a superb structure dating in parts back to the Iron Age 1700 BC and perhaps earlier. The Northern Ui Neill Kings occupied it as their royal seat *c.* AD 700. In Donegal the two important branches of this clan were the O'Neills and the O'Donnells, who became great rivals. The chief of the O'Donnells was known as the Prince of Tirconnell. In about 850, the Vikings settled in Inishowen and along the northwest coast, hence the name of the county, *Dun na n Gall*, Fort of the foreigners. The main County Donegal clans clashed endlessly and the Norman warlords also laid waste to Inishowen, and built Greencastle on Lough Swilly. The wars between the O'Donnells, the O'Dohertys and other Irish *septs* continued for centuries, but towards the end of the 16th century two chiefs, Red Hugh O'Donnell and Hugh O'Neill, combined their powers in an effort to prevent the English from taking over. They were defeated at the battle of Kinsale in 1601 and made their way to the Continent in what is known as the 'Flight of the Earls'. This took place from the shores of Lough Swilly, near Rathmullen, in 1607. The Plantation began with Scots and English 'undertakers' being given land and founding towns. Between 1632 and 1636, the *Annals of the Four Masters* were compiled by Franciscan monks at Bundrowes, near Bundoran. These annals are a valuable source of Irish history. In 1841, the population of Donegal was at its height of 196,448. Then disaster struck with the Great Famine, which affected the west and north of Donegal very badly. In 1921, Ulster was partitioned, and Donegal was cut off from its natural hinterland of Derry by the border.

Getting There and Around

By air: Daily services from Glasgow and Manchester to Eglinton Airport, near Derry, about 40 minutes' drive from Letterkenny, ✆ (028) 7181 0784, with connections to Paris and Brussels. Daily flights from Dublin to Sligo Airport, about 40 minutes' drive from Bundoran. Numerous flights from Glasgow and daily flights from Dublin to Donegal Airport, Carrickfinn, ✆ (075) 48232/48284.

By rail: Daily services from Belfast to Derry, and Dublin to Sligo.

By bus: Express bus services from Dublin to Letterkenny. Local buses: the Lough Swilly Railway Company and CIE link the various towns such as Ballyshannon, Burdoran, Donegal, Killybegs and Letterkenny, ✆ (074) 21309. O'Donnell Coaches daily to Galway and Belfast airport, ✆ (075) 48114. North West Busways link Buncrana and Letterkenny, ✆ (077) 82619. John McGinley, between Irishowen, Letterkenny and Dublin, Glasgow and Donegal, ✆ (0174) 35201. McGeehan's run from Donegal town to Dublin, and have regular services to Glencolmcille and Dungloe, ✆ (075) 46150.

By bike: The Raleigh Rent-a-Bike network operates here. Your local dealers are C. J. Doherty, Main Street, Donegal Town, ✆ (073) 21119; Vincent Carton, Falcarragh, ✆ (074) 35150; Church Street Cycles, Letterkenny, ✆ (074) 26204.

Sports and Activities

Walking: Hill-walking on Slieve League, Muckish, Errigal, Scalp. Details about walking the Ulster Way, a signposted route, can be obtained from the Planning Department, DCC, Lifford, or the Long-distance Walking Route Committee, Cospair, 11th floor, Hawkings House, Dublin 2.

Walking on the Ulster Way has to be well-organized as the landowners must be asked for permission first; they are very anxious about insurance claims against them. Walk with a ranger or by yourself on Glenveagh Estate; or take walking holidays organized by Oideas Gael, Glencolmcille, ✆ (073) 30248, ✆ (073) 30348, *oidgael @ oil.ie*.

Co. Donegal now has mountain rescue teams (plenty of hikers get into trouble). Teams are based at Gortahork, Gweedore and Falcarragh; emergencies ✆ 999.

Sea fishing: In most parts of County Donegal, especially in the Killybegs region, Rathmullan and Inishowen. For deep-sea fishing boat hire, contact Pat Robinson, Kill, Dunfanaghy, ✆ (074) 36290.

Sea angling charter, Inishowen Boating Co., Malin, ✆ (077) 70605, ✆ (077) 70764. Ballyshannon Marine Ltd, ✆ (072) 52960. Bundoran Sea Angling, ✆ (072) 41526. Killybegs, ✆ (073) 31288.

Boats also available for hire in Falcarragh, Ardara, Dungloe, Portnoo.

Game fishing: There are many salmon and trout rivers and loughs in Donegal. For information, contact Foyle Fisheries, Derry, ✆ (028) 7134 2100, who cover northeast and northwest Donegal. For the south and southwest, contact The Northern Regional Fisheries Board, Ballyshannon, ✆ (072) 51435.

Pony-trekking: Stracomer Riding School, Bundoran. Trail-riding holidays arranged, ✆ (072) 41787, *Homfield @ indigo.ie*. Inch Island Stables, ✆ (077) 60335. Lenamore Stables, Muff, ✆ (077) 84022. Little Acorn Farm, Coast Road, Carrick, ✆ (073) 39386. Greenacres Lodge, Rosskey Upper, Convoy, ✆/✆ (074) 47541.

Finn Farm Hostel and Trekking Centre. Cappry, Ballybofey, ✆ (074) 32261. Dunfanaghy Riding Stables, Arnold's Hotel, Dunfanaghy, ✆ (074) 36208. Black Horse Stables, Cashelshannaghan, Letterkenny, ✆ (074) 51327.

Golf: At Bundoran, Portsalon, Rosapenna, and Fahan. The course at Bundoran is over 100 years old, and is one of the best in the country. It runs along the high cliffs above Bundoran

getting to Tory Island

Turasmara Teo operates daily between Tory and Bunbeg, Magheraroarty (and Portnablagh Wednesday only), ✆ (075) 31320. Sailing subject to the weather and tide. Approximately 75 mins from Bunbeg and 40 mins from Magheraroarty.

getting to Arranmore Island

There is a regular ferry that takes approximately 25 minutes; approx. 6 sailings per day, year-round, ✆ (075) 20532.

beach, ✆ (072) 41302. The Portsalon course runs above the beautiful Ballymastocker Bay, ✆ (074) 59459. At Rosapenna the best part of this championship links course runs in a low valley along the ocean, ✆ (074) 55301. Fahan is a gently rolling, sandy course overlooking the Swilly, ✆ (074) 61715.

Otway, near Rathmullen, ✆ (074) 58319, is a fun 9-hole course on the edge of the Swilly. Ballyliffen, ✆ (077) 76672, is the most northerly golf club in Ireland with lovely views over the Atlantic; 18 holes.

Genealogy centre: Donegal Ancestry, Ramelton, ✆ (074) 51266, *donances@indigo. ie.*

Waterbus cruises on Donegal Bay, ✆ (073) 23666. One-hour cruise; sailing times posted on Donegal Pier.

Beaches: Blue flag beaches: Bundoran, Rossnalagh, Nairn/Portnoo, Marble Hill, Portsalon, Culdaff.

Bathing: Silver Strand, Malin Beg, Glencolmcille.

Pottery and art weekends: Mrs O'Kane, Cavanacor House, Ballindrait, Lifford, ✆/✉ (074) 41143. Art Studio, Anghnahoo, Pettigo, ✆ (072) 61788. Weekend drawing and painting courses.

Swimming: Leisureland, Redcastle, ✆ (077) 82306; Waterworld, Bundoran, ✆ (072) 41172.

Malinmore Adventure Centre, Malin Bay, Glencolmcille, ✆ (073) 30123. Scuba-diving, canoeing, boat trips. Gartan Outdoor Education Centre, Churchhill, ✆ (074) 37032. Courses in canoeing, rock climbing, windsurfing.

Gaelic language and culture: Glencolmcille also offers courses in dancing, bodhran playing, archeology, hill walking, ✆ (073) 30248, ✉ (073) 30348, *oidsgael @ iol.ie.*

The Donegal Railway Heritage Centre: The old station house, Donegal Town, ✆ (073) 22655. Nostalgic look back at Donegal's narrow-gauge railways.

Lough Derg Pilgrimage: St Patrick's Purgatory, Pettigo, ✆ (072) 61518.

Franciscan Friary: In Rossnowlagh: offers guesthouse accommodation, ✆ (072) 51342. Opened as a centre for peace and reconciliation, a quiet reflective place where you can join in a retreat if you want to.

Donegal Town, ✆ (073) 21148; open April–Sept.

Letterkenny, Derry Road, ✆ (074) 21160, ✉ (074) 25180; open all year.

Inishowen, Carndonagh, ✆ (077) 74933; open Mon–Fri all year, daily mid-June–Aug.

Festivals

All festival dates vary from year to year. For details of all these contact the Letterkenny tourist office, ✆ (074) 21160. For details of festivals in the Inishowen district, call ✆ (077) 74933.

Early June: Lough Swilly Angling Festival, Rathmullen.

Mid-June: Mary from Dungloe Festival, a family festival of music and song.

Late June: Buncrana Folk Festival, Inishowen.

July: Ramelton Festival, Rathmullen Regatta

12 July: Orange Procession, Rossnowlagh.

August: Letterkenny Folk Festival. Fiddle festival in Glencolmcille.

July/August: Ballyshannon Folk and Traditional Music Festival.

September: Oyster Festival, Moville and Greencastle.

South Donegal

Bundoran to Donegal Town

If you come up from Sligo along the superb sweep of Donegal Bay you will encounter one of Ireland's older seaside resorts, **Bundoran**. On the long main street there is a typically uninspiring hotchpotch of hotels, amusements and souvenir shops. Nearby are wonderful beaches and the Bundoran Golf Course, one of the best-known golf courses in Ireland.

For those who are avoiding populous resorts, **Ballyshannon**, 2.5 miles (4km) up the coast from Bundoran, is ideal. It is said to have been founded in 1500 BC when the Scythians settled a colony on a little island in the Erne estuary. The Scythians were an off-shoot of the Phoenician peoples who were supposed, in one version of the early history of Ireland, (there are many), to have colonized areas of the north. It has its own poet, the bard of Ballyshannon, William Allingham, whose lines,

> *Up the airy mountain,*
> *Down the rushy glen,*
> *We daren't go a hunting*
> *For fear of little men.*

must have been chanted by many generations of children. **The Lakeside Centre**, Belleek Road on the shore of Assaroe Lough, provides lots of watersports and during the summer months a waterbus (✆ *(072) 52555*) plies its way up and down the lough; the trip lasts about one hour. The **Abbey Assaroe Mill** just outside the town (*off the R231 Rossnowlagh road*) was built by the Cistercians many centuries ago, and has now been restored by local enthusiasts and houses a local craft gallery, a coffee shop and interpretative centre.

Nearby are the sands of **Rossnowlagh**. If you are here around 12 July you may witness the last-remaining Orange procession this side of the border from Northern Ireland. Otherwise, Rossnowlagh is known for its surfing. At the **Franciscan friary**, before you reach the pretty little town of Ballintra, you will find the diminutive **Donegal Museum** (*open daily 10–6*), which has a few interesting items, including a piece of Muckish glass made from mica mined in the Muckish Mountains, which you will see as you go further north.

Donegal Town is the meeting point of roads which travel into the heart of Donegal, to the north and to the west. Situated on the River Eske, with a long history of habitation for its strategic site, it is a crowded, busy place even without the tourist buses which congregate near the hotels on the Diamond. (A diamond—or square to most visitors—is an area where fairs and gatherings were held, and in the Plantation period it was placed in the shadow of the

Donegal town

castle so as to guard against the fighting that was the accompanying feature of these occasions.) **Donegal Castle** (*open May–Oct, daily 9.30–5.45; adm*), once a stronghold of the O'Donnells, the Princes of Tirconnell, and then taken over by the planter Brooke family, is a handsome stone ruin built in 1474. It incorporates a square tower and turrets built by the O'Donnells in 1505, and the Jacobean house built by Sir Basil Brooke in 1610. Also of interest is the monument in the Diamond to the Four Masters. *The Annals of the Four Masters* is a history of old Ireland, written by three brothers called O'Clery and O'Mulconry, scholars and monks. The brothers were tutors to the O'Donnells and stayed for a while at the nearby abbey, situated where the River Eske and the sea meet. They wrote this great work between 1623 and 1626. It records an Irish society which was fast disappearing as the English and Scottish were settled in Ireland. Nowadays, Donegal Town is one of the best places to buy tweed. Try Magee's shop in the Diamond and the craft village on the Ballyshannon Road.

Further inland lies the pilgrim's shrine of Lough Derg. Although most holy tradition in Donegal is associated with St Columba (or *Colmcille*), this is known as St Patrick's Purgatory, and between June and August is the scene of one of the most rigorous Christian pilgrimages. People come here from all over the world to do penance, just as they did hundreds of years ago. The pilgrims stay on a small island on Lough Derg for 36 hours. They eat and drink only bread and water, stay up all night praying, and wear no shoes whilst making the Stations of the Cross. Information can be obtained from the Priory, St Patrick's Purgatory, Lough Derg, Pettigo, © (072) 81518. You can't actually visit St. Patrick's Purgatory unless you are a pilgrim, but it's quite a sight from the lough shore and certainly worth stopping for a look. Closer at hand is the lovely Lough Eske which gives good fishing for trout and it is close to beautiful walks in the low range of hills called **The Blue Stack Mountains.** Overlooking Lough Eske is a superb rhodedendron garden at Ardnamona House, best seen from April to mid-June. Ardnamona is also a very good guest house, amongst the most memorable of places to stay in Ireland. There is an admission charge for the gardens.

Donegal Town is a few miles away from the Gaeltacht, which begins after Killybegs. The Gaeltacht forms the officially recognized Irish-speaking area where government grants encourage the local people to stay put. Here you can walk into a shop or bar and catch fragments of true Irish, the oldest recorded Aryan language. It is a strange language: rich, almost soft, but shot through with harsher, guttural tones. It is poignant, moving, but not melodious. The spoken English of Gaelic-speakers is, on the other hand, soft and poetic, as though through translation they have made a second language of it.

Killybegs to Portnoo and Ardara

Follow the N56 through **Mountcharles**, with its splendid view of Donegal Bay, **Bruckless** and **Dunkineely**. These were all centres of the now-defunct lace industry, and are still good places to buy hand-embroidered linen and the subtle patterned Donegal jumpers and rugs. There is a fine collection of early Irish portraits at Ballyloughan House, Bruckless (*contact Mrs Tindal;* © *(073) 31507*). The narrow, winding and climbing road leads you to **Killybegs**. In the summer, bordering hedgerows bloom with honeysuckle and fuchsia, and as you get further west the sweet acrid peat smell on the damp soft air becomes all-pervading. At Killybegs you reach the most important fishing port in Ireland, which is set to expand even further to the tune of forty million pounds so it can accommodate even bigger fishing vessels. There are plenty of sea angling boats for hire here, and in July the place is full for the Sea Angling Festival. In the Catholic Church there is a fine sculptured medieval grave slab of Neall More MacSwyne, which was found near St John's Point (this, by the way, is a lovely peninsula with a pretty beach and beautiful views, signposted left from Dunkineely). The highly paid fishing and processing industry has brought great prosperity. It is quite a sight to watch the catches of haddock, plaice and sole being unloaded. The famous Donegal Carpet Factory started up here in the 1890s, headed by a Scots weaver, Alexander Morton. The hand-knotted carpets were often designed for palaces and embassies all over the world. The factory (*on the Kilcar road out of Killybegs,* © *(073) 31688*) has re-opened, and is producing the original designs in pure wool; the showroom is worth visiting.

Beyond this town you encounter some of the grandest scenery in Donegal; the great cliffs of Bunglass, Scregeigther and **Slieve League** are amongst the highest in Europe, rising to 1,972ft (601m). If you walk along the cliffs from Bunglass along One Man's Pass, a jaggedy ridge, you will see on a clear day fantastic views right down to County Mayo. The determined bird-watcher should be able to see puffins and cormorants, and the botantist should be able to find alpine Arctic species on the back slopes of Slieve League. The village of **Teelin**, under Slieve League, is popular with students on Irish language courses, whilst **Kilcar** is the site of the *Gaelterra Eireann* factory of fabrics and yarns. The wools are hard-wearing and flecked with soft colours. You can buy them here in the craftshop and in craftshops all over County Donegal. This is also a centre for handwoven tweed.

Glencolmcille should be visited next. A local priest called Father McDyer established a rural co-operative here to try to combat the flight of youth from the village through emigration. He helped the local economy greatly and there is a craftshop where you can buy handmade products such as jams, soaps and wines made from gorse and bluebells. A walk along the valley here is a 3.5mile (5km) pilgrimage around 15 cross slabs and pillars known as the Stations of the Cross. It is interesting to follow it as it includes many of the ancient sites of the area, starting off with a Stone Age court-grave in the churchyard of the Church of Ireland. There are some attractively carved grave stones here too. The Stations of the Cross are still performed on 9 June, the saint day of Columba. Notice the beautifully built stone and turf sheds with their thatched roofs which abound in this area. Glencolmcille also has a **folk village**: three cottages representing three different periods of Irish life (*open Easter–Oct; adm; ℂ (073) 30017*). The countryside is full of prehistoric antiquities, dolmens, cairns (including a famous horned cairn called Clochanmore), and ruins of churches connected with St Columba. From the village, an expedition can be made along a winding, narrow road to the tiny bay and long-deserted village of **Port**. The sea cliffs have been fashioned into wonderful shapes, including a hugh sea-stack of 148 metres. For Ireland's most beautiful beach, however, it's 5miles (8km) along the road southwest following the clifftops to the Silver Strand at **Malin Beg**. This gorgeous bay is sheltered by high cliffs all around, and the water is as clear as Waterford crystal. Glencolmcille has also become one of the most important centres for Irish culture and music, with its wealth of visitors who come in search of the best traditional pub 'session' in Ulster. On the other side of the mountain, through the spectacular Glengesh Pass, you arrive at **Ardara**, another centre for Donegal tweed and Aran sweaters; some lovely sweaters at very reasonable prices can be bought here or at Glencolmcille. The new **heritage centre** (*open Easter–Oct, daily 10–6; ℂ (075) 41262*), on the Main Street, tells the history of tweed in the area. Nancy's Bar, also on Main Street, is famous for its atmosphere and oysters.

If you follow the road to Maghera Caves, signposted just outside Ardara on the road to Donegal Town (N56), you will come to another of the most beautiful **beaches** in Ireland; the single-track road from here unfolds a series of wonderful views of mountains, the sea inlet of Loughros Beg Bay, traditional farms, and near the end, a waterfall. The walk to the caves and beach takes you through someone's farm and over sand-dunes so don't overload the picnic baskets.

If you travel a few miles on to the next little peninsula of Dunmore Head you will come to **Portnoo** and **Narin**, two popular beach places for holidaymakers from Northern Ireland. At Narin, you can park or hire caravans. There is a fascinating fort near here, built on an island in Doon Lough (beside Narin). It is over two thousand years old and is a very impressive sight—a circular stone fort which spreads over most of the island. It can be seen easily from the lough shore. At the neck of this peninsula you go from **Maas**, a small fishing resort, to **Glenties** (*Na Gleannta*: the valley—so called because of its position at the junction of glens), which is a good place for knitwear. There is a striking **church** designed by the innovative contemporary Irish architect, Liam McCormick, who is responsible for many fine churches in County Donegal. This one was built in the 1970s. Patrick McGill (1891–1963) the novelist and poet was born here; his semi-autobiographical novel *Children of the Dead End* sold very well in England, but was considered anti-clerical in Ireland.

Northwest Donegal

Fintown to Gortahork

All along the northwest coast you will see mountain ranges broken by long river valleys which reach into the hinterland. Any route along these valleys brings you across the harsh mountainous areas where beauty is bleak and the cost of wresting a living from the poor soil is no longer acceptable.

There is a rather zig-zag road from Fintown to Doocharry which brings you into the **Gweebarra Glen**. Northeast of this, between the Derryveagh and Glendowan Mountains, the valley extends into **Glenveagh**, which is now part of a National Park. However, you should keep heading out towards the sea on the road to Dungloe (do not pronounce the 'g') if you want to see 'The Rosses', as this area is called. The Irish name is *naRosa*, meaning 'headlands', and is a good clue to the landscape. Although this area is going through a housing boom, it is still one of the most charming routes you can take to the north coast; loughs and loughlets are scattered through hilly country and the beaches are lovely. If you make your way to **Burtonport**, an attractive fishing port, there is a regular ferry to **Arranmore Island**. You can have a good day's tramp around the island; there is good cliff scenery in the northwest. It has a rainbow trout lake, Lough Shure. **Cruit Island** can be reached from the mainland by a connecting bridge. From here you can look out at Owey Island, and across at Gola Island with their deserted cottages. Despite the difficulties the islanders had to face, such as hard weather, no services and bureaucratic indifference to their needs, most of them did not want to leave their homes, and many return for the summer or for fishing. (Several are being restored as holiday homes.) Boat hire must be negotiated with the local fishermen; none of them likes to be tied down to taking people out on a regular basis. Try the pubs and ask around. **Bunbeg** has an attractive 19th-century harbour and, close by at **Carrickfinn**, is Donegal airport, with daily flights to Glasgow and Dublin. The locals speak Irish and it is a favourite area for Irish summer schools. Further north past Bloody Foreland in the heart of *Gaeltacht* is **Gortahork** (meaning 'garden of oats'), a small town on one arm of Ballyness Bay. It has a great strand which curves out into the sea, nearly locking the shallow bay in from the ocean. If you are here in the evening you can see cattle fording the waters back to the home farms.

Tory Island

There's a regular ferry to **Tory Island** from the pier at Magheraroarty and from Downings. Bad weather often makes the 7-mile (11km) journey impossible in winter, but if you have time to go there this windswept and barren island is endlessly fascinating. The island has two villages, called East Town and West Town. **East Town** is laid out in the traditional clochan or family grouping pattern of settlement. Close to the shore in **West Town** is the remanants of St Colmcille's **early-Christian monastery**. Here you can see a decapitated round tower, and a T-shaped cross known as a **Tau Cross**. There is only one other in Ireland, which is displayed in the Burren Centre, County Clare. On a sunny day it feels rather like a Greek island with its whitewashed cottages and bright blue and red doors. At the eastern end of the island is **Balor's Fort**, a great rock sticking out into the sea. Balor is the god of darkness with one eye in the middle of his forehead. Mythology says he was one of the Formorii leaders (*see* pp.245 and 247). In the summer you can buy snacks at a tea-room and the café close to the island's only public bar. There is a small hotel, a hostel and several B&Bs. The population is about 130 and thriving with a school and simple Catholic church. The island has become well-known for its fishermen artists who mostly use house paints to create their naïve-style paintings of seascapes and birds. They have been promoted by the landscape artist and portrait painter Derek Hill, whose house and collection of pictures is open to the public at the Glebe Gallery, Churchill. You can buy their work at a small exhibition gallery on the island, although some of the more famous of the island painters exhibit and sell in Belfast and London.

The Mountains Errigal to Muckish

Looking inland from Gortahork you cannot help but notice the glorious outlines of the mountains. Errigal is cone-shaped, and Aghla More and Aghla Beg form a spaced double peak. Muckish means 'pig's back' in Irish, and you will see it is aptly named. You can approach these mountains from this angle, or you could take the road from Bunbeg, past the secret **Dunlewy**

Lough, overlooked by a roofless white church. The **Lakeside Centre** at Dunlewey (*open daily Easter–Oct*) has a fine craft shop and tea room, a farm museum, animals and demonstrations in carding, spinning and weaving wool. You can go on a storytelling trip on the lough surrounded by its beautiful glens. Traditional music sessions are held in June, July and August. Hidden behind this is the **Poisoned Glen**, so called either because the water in the lough is unfit to drink because of certain poisonous plants at the water's edge, or, so another story goes, because of the name some French travellers gave it, having caught some fish there. The hill and mountain climbs in this part are quite strenuous, although a fit pensioner could tackle them.

Climb Errigal from the roadside, and after about an hour's climb you will reach a narrow ridge of 2,400ft (731m), from which you will see Dunlewy Lough on one side and Altan Lough on the other side. Climb Muckish from the Gap or the western end. If you go straight for it from the Falcarragh side you may find yourself going up by the old mine-works, for the mountain was worked for its mica to be used in glass-making; this is quite a dangerous but interesting ascent. The people who lived in the cottages in these lonely sheep glens used to weave Donegal tweed in the evenings, and pass the time singing and composing poetry. The old weaver poets had a good phrase for Muckish, calling it 'an oul turf stack'. And so it is: flat-topped with its flat outline broken only by the remains of a cross. Looking across to Tory, you will see a huge hole, which is supposed to have been made when St Columba threw his staff from the top of Muckish.

Falcarragh to Doe Castle

Back to the coast between Falcarragh and Dunfanaghy is the great granite promontory of **Horn Head**. From a Falcarragh viewpoint it does indeed look like a horn or rock. You can do a complete circuit taking the little road signposted 'Horn Head Coastal Drive' by the bridge at the top of the main street in **Dunfanaghy**, an attractive village overlooking Sheep Haven Bay, which is experiencing a rash of building as moneyed folk from Northern Ireland build new holiday homes. The road leads you past old Hornhead House (*not open to the public*), which was drowned by sand when the bent grass was cut. The road climbs round the rocky farms giving you dazzling views across Sheephaven Bay to Melmore Head to the east and back towards Bloody Foreland. The road passes a 1940s military lookout post, and from here it is possible to walk to the **Little Horn**, which plunges down into the sea with magnificent cliff scenery. From here there is a good walk ahead of you to an old tower. It will take about 40 minutes and you will need waterproof boots. You can peer over the 300ft (91m) cliff to see if the puffin population is in residence; there are some caves and blow holes. **Dunfanaghy** itself has a couple of good family hotels and, on the outskirts, the Workhouse Heritage Centre and Art Gallery (*March–Oct, Mon–Fri 10–5, Sat & Sun 12–5; adm*), which tells the Famine story and exhibits local artists.

Sheephaven Bay is a complicated indentation with beautiful golden sands and a wooded shore. **Marblehill**, with its special provision for caravans, is a favourite place for holidaymakers. The mystic poet-politician George Russell (A. E.) used to stay here in **Marblehill House**. It is possible to rent apartments in the house and stableyard which overlooks the marvellous long curving beach. Further on, the **Forest of Ards** provides some scenic walks and splendid views. At **Creeslough** you can admire another modern church designed by Liam McCormick. Its shape echoes the view of Muckish that you have from there. Otherwise it's a busy village with good shopping and pubs. On the road to **Carrigart** is one of the most romantic castles in Ireland, set on the water's edge—**Doe Castle** (*always accessible*). It belonged to the

MacSwineys (or MacSwynes), who came over from Scotland in the 15th century. They came to help the O'Donnells fight the encroaching Normans, and in the constant small battles which took place with the O'Neill clan. They were part of the influx of mercenary soldiers known as gallowglasses (*see* p.41). The castle was occupied right up until 1890. It had been taken by the English in 1650, and changed hands several times. In 1798 General George Vaughan Harte purchased it; he had been a hero in the Indian Wars, and his initials are carved over the main door. Scramble up the defensive walls for a superb view, on one side looking over Sheephaven Bay and on the other the pretty bridge and waterfall of Duntally.

Northeast Donegal

Downings to Portsalon

To get to the **Rosguill Peninsula** you cross a neck of sand similar to the causeway at Horn Head, and arrive at the fishing village of **Downings**, which is in the 'holidaymakers' zone' of **Rosapenna**, a long-established resort, with a good golf course and harbour. You can sail out to the islands of Tory and Inishbofin from Downings. Ask about boats in the local post office down by the harbour. Very good tweed is made in this area; try McNutt's shop above the harbour. The beach beside the golf course is huge and unspoilt, ideal for a long walk and a swim, if you are hardy. The coastal ciruit (R245) leads to the spectacular **Atlantic Drive**. A branch road off this takes you past the Tra Na Rossen Youth Hostel, the only house designed by Lutyens in Ulster, and up to the wilder beaches of **Melmore Head**. There are several beaches along this road.

Leaving **Carrigart**, another centre for local crafts, the loughside road takes you down to **Mulroy Bay**, a narrow-necked lough bordered by the Fanad Peninsula on the opposite side and strewn with wooded islands. Behind Carrigart rises the Salt Mountain. A little moor-bound road crosses this range and comes out near Cranford. High in these mountains is the deepest lough in Ireland, **Lough Salt**. To take advantage of the panorama you should go up to the lough from the Letterkenny–Creeslough road (N56) and look out to the bays stretching from Horn Head to Fanad.

Down the road is **Milford**, a pretty town on a hill near some good fishing at Lough Fern. From Milford you can explore the **Fanad Peninsula** on the old road, which takes you past the Knockalla range by Kerrykeel and into the hidden reaches of Mulroy by Tamney. In this secluded land there survives a very idiosyncratic Gaelic—although it was not untouched by the

Gypsy caravan

settlements of the 17th century. Even in their isolation the Irish and the Scottish settlers remained distinct. At the far eastern point you can see Fanad Lighthouse which guards the entrance of Lough Swilly and looks across to the Inishowen hills.

Portsalon is beautifully situated over **Ballymastocker Bay**, an immense curve of strand, and, like all the towns on the Swilly, it is curiously linked by the water in its landscape to the opposite view on Inishowen. It is a little like the Greek idea of the sea being a bridge. Rita's Bar with a blazing fire is a famous place to retire to after a walk along the beach. The golf course here is well worth playing, and the views are wonderful. Unfortunately the tiny village of Portsalon is being spoilt by a profusion of holiday houses and caravans. Just a little way north of Portsalon, along the pretty road to Fanad Head, is the garden of **Ballydaheen** (*open May–Sept, Thurs and Sat 10–3; adm*). Protected by sheltering belts of trees, the garden's various 'rooms' and styles have flourished, and the views out to the Swilly are lovely. A planted walk leads down to The Seven Arches, a series of interconnecting caves on a tiny rocky beach. The house at the centre of the garden is Japanese in inspiration, and some of the plantings and design reflects this influence.

Knockalla Mountain to Letterkenny

A terrific coastal drive, which joins the R247, has been built with fabulous views over Lough Swilly and the Urris Hills. This brings you to Rathmullan, nestling in a sheltered plain which borders the Swilly as far as Letterkenny. The whole of **Lough Swilly** has played an important role in many of history's famous episodes. It is deep enough to accommodate modern war-fleets, as indeed it did in the First World War. It has also been the departure route for the Gaelic aristocracy: in 1607 the Earls of Tirconnell and Tyrone took their leave for France from here. Lough Swilly has been called 'the Lake of the Shadows', an apt enough description, although from the Irish it means Lake of Eyes or Eddies (Loch Suilagh).

Rathmullan (meaning: Maolán's ring-fort) is a charming town with sandy beaches and lovely views across Lough Swilly. There are often fishing boats moored here, as well as leisure craft, and, in the summer, little boys diving off the barnacled sides of the pier. Unfortunately, it is being rapidly spoilt with tightly packed holiday houses built close to the beach. Kinnego Bay which carries on from Rathmullan Beach is losing its charm, and the Blue Flag status of the beach has been lost because of water pollution.

The ruined **Carmelite friary** in the town has a romantic air, borne out by the story behind it. In 1587 the MacSwiney clan from Fanad had a castle here where Red Hugh O'Donnell was staying. An ordinary wine merchant's ship was lying in the bay and the reputation of its cargo enticed the young reveller onto the ship. Treachery was soon apparent, as the ship slipped its mooring and carried young O'Donnell off to Dublin Castle as a prisoner of Queen Elizabeth I. He was a great hostage to have captured, for his father was the Lord of Tirconnell, the powerful Sir Hugh O'Donnell, and the son could be used to keep the father loyal to the English rulers. More information is available from the excellent **heritage centre** (*open daily Easter–mid-Sept; adm; © (074) 58229*) in the Martello tower by the pier.

One of the most lovely routes in Ireland is the road between Rathmullan and its neighbour, **Ramelton**. It is often spelt on maps as Rathmelton, which translates as Mealtan's fort, but the town you will see is a relatively unspoilt Plantation town built by the Stewart family, one of the so-called undertakers of the Plantation, meaning that they undertook to supply fighting men and build fortified dwellings to subdue and keep the wild Irish at bay. It developed as a prosperous market town with goods coming up the Lennon estuary from as far away as Tory

Island. Ramelton was nearly self-sufficient in those 18th-century days, with locally made whiskey, linen and leather goods, and other small industries. The Ramelton merchants built themselves fine houses in the Mall. However, Letterkenny stole a march on the town fathers when the railway came. Now it is the boom town. Ramelton is famous for its annual **festival** in July, with its cheerful floats and Queen of the Lennon competition, and for its **pantomime** in February. It is also famous for its thriving bottling industry, and a soft drink of cloying sweetness called McDaid's Football Special. The bottling plant, which is in a fine 19th-century warehouse overlooking the River Lennan, was used for a recent film 'The Hanging Gale' set in famine times. The foundations of the building date back to the original O'Donnell Castle. **The House on the Brae** on the Tank road has been restored by the local Georgian society. It is sometimes used for temporary art exhibitions. American Presbyterians will be interested in the old **meeting house** in the Back Lane which is early 18th century. It is here that the Reverend Francis Makemie (1658–1708) used to worship. He was ordained in 1682 and emigrated to America where he founded the first Presbytery in 1706. It has been restored and houses temporary exhibitions, Donegal's genealogy centre and a library.

Letterkenny is a thriving town, with factories on the outskirts and new housing enclaves; yet it still manages to maintain a country town appearance, with one long main street that loops round into the Swilly Valley. You can use this town as a centre for expeditions east and west. Folk-music lovers might time their visit for the **Letterkenny Folk Festival**, which hosts folk dance and music groups from all over Europe in the middle of August. The **Donegal County Museum** on the High Road (*open Tues–Fri 11–4.30, Sat 1–4.30*) has a very interesting permanent collection of artefacts from early history and folk life, as well as travelling exhibitions. In **Newmills**, 6km north west of Letterkenny, just off the N56, an old flax and corn mill has been restored with a visitor centre (*open June–Sept, daily 10–6.30; adm*), and a riverside walk to a scutcher's cottage and forge.

The Swilly Valley to Doon Well

If you go through Letterkenny up the Swilly Valley you reach the countryside where St Columba spent his first years. (St Columba or Colmcille was the great Irish missionary who founded a church at Iona.) He was born about AD 521 on a height overlooking the two Gartan Loughs. A large cross just on Glenveagh Estate marks the spot. Gartan Clay (which can only be lifted by a family who claim descent from the followers of Columba), has powerful protective properties; soldiers fighting in the First World War carried it. You should follow the road around the lough; if you take one of the forest trails on the Churchill side a glorious prospect awaits you. The long glen which begins at Doochary on the southwest coast penetrates this far along the Derryveagh Mountains and into the scenic Glenveagh, parallel to the Valley of Gartan.

Glenveagh (meaning: the valley of the birch), is beautiful and isolated with a 19th-century fairy-tale castle figured against the mountains on the loughside (*open Easter–Oct, daily, 10–6; closed Fri Oct–Nov. Last admission 45mins before closing; adm for castle and grounds; restaurant, castle tearooms and visitor centre; ✆ (074) 37088*). The gardens here have been developed by Henry McIlhenny, a millionaire whose grandparents came from these parts, and a visit is recommended. It would be difficult to find another such garden which combines the exotic and natural with such ease. Henry McIlhenny gave the wild, heathery acres of Glenveagh to be used as a National Park. Deer roam the glen and peregrine falcons nest in the rocky ledges.

Close by in **Churchill**, the artist Derek Hill has given his house and art possessions to the nation. It is signposted from the village and is known as **Glebe House** (*open May–Sept, daily except Fri 11–6.30; adm*). This plain Georgian house is packed with exquisite and curious *objets d'art*; it also has a fine gallery, the Glebe Gallery, with a collection of Irish interest, besides paintings by Basil Blackshaw, Annigoni, and Victor Pasmore. The gardens are beautifully laid out with shrubs and trees down to the lough's edge. It would be a great pity to miss Glenveagh, and St Columb's and the Glebe Gallery, so make it a full day's outing. If you feel that a surfeit of castles, galleries and gardens may ensue, just make sure you tour the gardens of Glenveagh and skip the castle. Close to Churchill is the Colmcille Heritage Centre (beside the Youth Hostel), which has a very informative display of days gone by.

On the way back from Glenveagh to Letterkenny you pass through **Kilmacrenan** (meaning: church of the son of Enan), called after one of St Columba's nephews. There are some ruins of a 15th-century friary, but the fame of the place rests on the claim that it was here Columba received his education. You can have tea at the traditional thatched cottage of Lurgyvale with its displays of old rural implements. Near here, at **Doon Rock**, about 2 miles (3.2km) on the road to Creeslough, the Princes of Tirconnell were inaugurated. At the curious **Doon Well**, those hopeful of being cured have left tokens; rags mostly, although there is a story that a visiting film star left her lipstick.

Raphoe to Fahan

If you are travelling east from Letterkenny bound for the North, you will pass through the more prosperous midlands of Donegal whose centre is **Raphoe**, an ancient town with a venerable cathedral, ruined Bishop's Palace and a pretty village green. Your fellow passengers on the road will probably be bound for the mart, the key of most Irish farmers' lives, and another indication of the importance of Raphoe. St Adomnan who lived in the 7th century founded an early monastery here. He was an O'Donnell like his ancestor St Colmcille. He wrote a life of Colmcille which reveals a lot about early Christian society; at one synod they passed a law exempting women from regular military service. At **Beltany**, between Raphoe and Lifford, just beyond the River Deele, is a stone circle which has some mystic alignment. Archaeologists who examined the site in 1921 suggested the building had an astronomical purpose because the standing stone in the southwest is an almost perfect equilateral triangle. Its circumference measures 450ft (140m). There are 64 out of a possible 80 stones still standing, and a pleasant view from the top.

Lifford is the administrative centre of the county. The 18th-century courthouse (*open Mon–Sat 10–6, Sun 2–6; © (074) 41228*) is attractive. It is open to the public and houses a genealogical centre as well as a country kitchen where you can have a meal, and a clan centre which traces the importance of Lifford in the history of the county and the role of the dominant clans in the history of Donegal. If you find it open, go inside the **Clonleigh Parish Church** in the middle of the town. Here, in an attitude of prayer, are the Jacobean stone figures of Sir Richard Hansard and his wife, who gave money for the church to be built.

Outside Lifford, just off the Letterkenny Road, at **Ballindrait**, is **Cavanacor Historic House and Craft Centre** (*open Easter–Sept, other times by appointment, © (074) 411 43*). This 17th-century house with a fortified yard was the ancestral home of James Knox Polk, the 11th President of America. The house contains late 17th- and 18th-century furniture, and it is possible to tour some rooms and the small museum. Its exhibits are associated with the American Connection; and with the historic visit of James II, who dined under the sycamore at the front of the house during the seige of Derry in 1689. Enjoy a splendid home-made tea and browse among the attractive crafts, pottery and watercolour paintings—all for sale (*open Easter–Sept, daily exc Mon 12–6; adm; pottery studio open all year*).

The Inishowen Peninsula

Inishowen (*Inis Eoghain*: Eoghain's island) reaches out to the Atlantic between Loughs Swilly and Foyle, a kingdom of its own. Indeed, as its name conveys, it forms a different territory to the rest of Donegal which is part of Tirconnell. This is O'Doherty country. After leaving Letterkenny you pass through the rolling plains round Manor and Newtowncunningham to the neck of the peninsula at **Burt**. An unforgettable sight of this unexplored, almost islanded land can be obtained from the **Grianan of Aileach**, an ancient stone hill-fort. Turn right by an unusually roofed modern Catholic church, another of Liam McCormick's, and climb the unclassified mountain road which gives you views onto the Swilly. Why the Grianan of Aileach is not as well known as Tara in County Meath, considering its spectacular position and its associations, must be one of the curious twists in the recording of history. Besides the circular stone fort and its terraces, there are three stone and earth ramparts, and underneath the Hill of Aileach there are said to be underground passages connecting the hill-top with Scalp Mountain which overlooks the village of Fahan, about 6 miles (7.6km) further down the peninsula. There is an old story that the sleeping heroes of the past lie within the hill, to be wakened at Ireland's hour of need. The fort dates from about 1700 BC, and according to the *Annals of the Four Masters* it was the seat of power for the Northern O'Neill kings from the 5th to the 12th centuries. It was destroyed by their enemies in AD 675 and 1101. The fort guards all approaches, which is why it affords such good views over the Foyle and the Swilly. At the foot of the hill, in the disused church of Ireland, is the Grianan of Aileach visitor's centre (*open daily June–Aug 10–6, Sept–May 12–6; adm*) with a good restaurant and interesting exhibits.

Inch Island, signposted off the main Buncrana–Londonderry Road, is a beautiful place. At the crossroads by the local shop, take the right turn to **Inch Fort** and **Brown's Bay** and look across the limpid water to Fahan, or go for a swim. There is an O'Doherty Clan Centre here (℗ *(077) 60488*).

Fahan is famous for its St Mura's Cross in the Church of Ireland graveyard. This 7th-century two-faced cross with mythological birds and ecclesiastical figures is all that remains of the rich Abbey of St Mura. Here in the rectory, looking across to Inch Top Hill, Mrs Alexander wrote 'There is a Green Hill Far Away', in 1848. There is a beautiful beach with lovely views all around which stretches up to **Buncrana**, a standard seaside resort, with the usual run of amusement arcades. You might stop at the **Vintage**

Traction engine rally

Car and Carriage Museum (*open daily in summer 10am–10pm;* ✆ *(077) 61130*). The Crana River is noted for salmon fishing and there are some pretty walks which lead close to the dilapidated early 17th-century Buncrana Castle and the O'Doherty keep. Just outside Buncrana, at Lisfannen, on the Derry road, is the **World Knitting Centre** (✆ *(077) 62365*), which traces the history of traditional patterns. Also of interest is the restored **Tullyarvan Mill** (✆ *(077) 61613*), on the Crana River; it is the base for Artlink, a community art group, and provides a space for temporary art exhibitions and traditional music functions. It is to be found off the scenic coast route signposted 'Inis Eoghain 100'; the mill is signposted on the right after the bridge. Close by at **Dunree** is **Fort Dunree Military Museum** (*open June–Sept, Mon–Sat 10–6, Sun 1–6; adm*), a restored coastal defence battery depicting 200 years of coastal and military history. It has a wonderful view and a fascinating account of Wolfe Tone's plans to land with French help and take Derry in 1798.

Buncrana to Muff

Take the R238 through the mountains to the spectacular **Mamore Gap**, and gaze at the return view of the Fanad Peninsula. There are plenty of good beaches on the way if you go the longer coastal road, such as **Linsfort** and **Dunree**; and on the other side of the Gap, past Clonmany, are the beaches around the Isle of Doagh. This is unspoiled country, full of fuchsia hedges and little whitewashed cottages. In the Church of Ireland graveyard in **Carndonagh** are some interesting monuments, including the Marigold Stone which has the same ornamentations as St Mura's Cross, and by the roadside opposite the church is one of the most far-famed crosses in Ireland, said to be the oldest low-relief cross in the country (AD 650). This richly decorated and well-preserved cross must have been erected by a prosperous and settled community in those far off times. The most northerly village in Ireland, **Malin**, has a pretty green and has twice been named 'Ireland's tidiest town'. It is a good example of a well-preserved 17th-century Plantation village, with a fine church. Nearby is lovely **Five Fingers Strand**. If you want to see the most northerly tip of Ireland, **Malin Head**, familiar to those of you who listen to radio shipping forecasts, take a road passing extensive sand dunes, after which you come to a pebbly cove where you can pick up semi-precious stones. The old signal tower at Banba's Crown, at the very tip of Malin Head, was the last sight of Ireland for many of the emigrants as they left by ship. From Malin Head you can see lighthouse islands. From here to Glengad Head are cliffs rising to over 800ft (246m). To the east of **Culdaff** are some fine sandy beaches.

All this area is fine walking country; the cliff scenery is interspersed with great stretches of sandhills. You can choose whether to walk around Malin Head itself, or southwards towards **Inishowen Head**. Or visit yet another cross, 2 miles (3.2km) to the south of Culdaff in Clonca. This impressive shaft, called St Boden's Cross, is almost 12ft (4m) in height and is carved with a scene depicting the miracle of the loaves and the fishes. On the road from Culdaff to Moville, in **Carrowblagh**, is an example of an ancient sweathouse—the Irish form of a sauna. The almost enclosed room was heated like an oven and, having heated yourself thoroughly, you were immersed in cold water. This was said to be the cure for aching bones and temporary madness. **Greencastle** is a beach resort with the remains of a 14th-century castle built by Richard de Burgh, the Red Earl of Ulster in 1305, who needed it as a strategic base from which to try and dominate the O'Donnells of Tirconnell (most of Donegal) and the O'Doherty's of Inishowen. The Maritime Museum (*open daily June–Sept 10–6; adm;* ✆ *(077) 81036*) in the old coastguard house is full of interest with a room on the Armada and Emigration.

Further down the coast you come to **Moville**, formerly a point of departure for many emigrants to the New World. It is now a leisure resort with a well-planted green, lined with seats from which you can comfortably gaze at the sea, or have a picnic. At **Cooley**, 1½ miles (3km) to the northwest, is a 9ft- (3m-) high cross and the remains of a chapel with a corbelled stone roof. The area between Moville and Muff has many planter castles. They are known as castles, but are actually big houses, and you get glimpses of them through the trees as you pass by. One of them, Redcastle, is now a luxury hotel; some would consider it ruined with all its modern embellishment. Behind them rise rather forbidding mountains, though if you venture on the mountain roads you come across lost clochans and megalithic monuments, and in July yellow raspberries cluster beneath the hedges.

Shopping

Tweeds and knitwear: McNutts of Downings; tweeds, knitwear and crafts. Magee & Co of Donegal Town. Jean's Craft Shop, Mountcharles. Bonners, Kennedy's and also John Molloy, Ardara, for knitwear. Studio Donegal Handwoven Tweed, Kilcar. Gaeltarra Yarns and Wools, Kilcar. World Knitting Centre, Lisfannon, traces the history of traditional patterns. J. F. Hernon, Ardara, for fine handknit sweaters. Falcarragh Knitwear, Falcarragh. Cindy Graham Handweaver, Craft Village, Donegal Town. Subtle blends of colours inspired by the Donegal landscape.

Crafts: Cottage Linens of Donegal. Bruckless, table linens and handkerchiefs. Mary Barr, Main Street, Buncrana. Donegal tweed, woodwork, batik and pottery at the Donegal Town Craft Village (just outside the town on the road to Sligo). The Gallery, Dunfanaghy, for paintings, antiques and knitwear. Glencolmcille Folk Village Shop for soaps, flower wines, St Brigid's crosses and honey. Lakeside Centre, Dunlewy. The Fish House, Ramelton. Tullyarvan Mill, Buncrana. Artworks, Port Road, Letterkenny. Avalon Craft Shop, Oliver Plunkett Road, Letterkenny.

Jewellery: Handcrafted by Niall Bruton, Donegal Craft Village. Geraldine Hannigan, Goldsmith, Port Road, Letterkenny.

Crystal: Derryveagh Crystal, Falcarragh. Handcut hand blown crystal. Donegal Crystal, The Diamond, Donegal Town.

Books: Four Masters Bookshop, The Diamond, Donegal Town.

Tapestry: Taipeis Gael, Glencolmcille. Naturally dyed, spun and woven tapestry (week-long tapestry courses also available; ✆/☎ (073) 30325).

Pottery: Cavanacor Studios, Cavanacor House, Ballindrait, Lifford. Joanna O'Kane creates delicate off-white bowls, plates and scultures; also watercolours by her husband, Eddie O'Kane.

Where to Stay

North Donegal

Rathmullan House, Rathmullan, ✆ (074) 58188, ☎ 58200, *rathhse@iol.ie* (*expensive*). This top country-house hotel is a lovely 18th-century house set on the edge of Lough Swilly. There are beautiful gardens, and excellent food is served in the dining room or the charcoal grill. It has a very cosy bar with a turf fire in the old cellars, an attractive indoor heated swimming-pool, and a sauna. **Ostan Thoraighe Hotel**, Tory Island, ✆ (074) 35920 (*expensive*). Cosy hotel on this wonderful island.

Arnold's Hotel, Dunfanaghy, ✆ (074) 36208 (*moderate*). This is a fine, old-fashioned hotel, set in a pretty village overlooking Sheephaven Bay. Nearby is the splendid scenery of Horn Head. **Fort Royal Hotel**, Rathmullan, ✆ (074) 58100 (*moderate*). It is another fine period house, with more of a 'family atmosphere' than Rathmullan House.

Mrs Scott, **The Manse**, Ramelton, ✆ (074) 51047 (*inexpensive*). This house is caught in a time-warp of old-fashioned hospitality. You can be sure of stimulating conversation with your hostess, who is well-informed on local history. Mrs Grier, **Crofton Farmhouse**, Aughnish, Ramelton, ✆ (074) 51048 (*inexpensive*). You will get a fine northern welcome in this farmhouse, which is set on the edge of Lough Swilly. Mrs Campbell, **Magheraclogher**, Derrybeg, ✆ (075) 31545 (*inexpensive*). In the middle of the Gaelic-speaking area, this modern house is set on the edge of the pounding Atlantic. Excellent home-made food. Mrs Borland, **Avalon**, Tamney, ✆ (074) 59031 (*inexpensive*). This traditional-style house in the centre of the village has good home-cooked meals. Mrs Taylor, **Gortfad**, Castlefinn, Lifford, ✆ (074) 46135 (*inexpensive*). Very old farmhouse full of antique furniture. Lovely food. **The Pier Hotel**, Rathmullan, ✆ (074) 58115 (*inexpensive*). A favourite with the locals and foreign fishermen. Plenty of atmosphere. **Fernhill House**, Kilmacrennan, ✆ (074) 53575, ✉ (074) 53575, *fernhill@ indigo.ie* (*inexpensive*). Georgian house overlooking Lough Fern with lovely gardens. John and Kay Deane, **Croaghcross Cottage**, Portsalon, ✆/✉ (074) 59548, *jkdeane@iol.ie* (*inexpensive*). Elegant, comfortable, modern country house overlooking Ballymastocka Strand. Six rooms; 1 en suite room suitable for disabled person. Good cooking. Mrs Campbell, **Ardeen**, Ramelton, ✆ (074) 51243 (*inexpensive*). Comfortable, friendly house. **Grania O'Neill**, Baileant Sleibhe, Downings, ✆ (074) 55661 (*inexpensive*). One of the rooms bosts a four-poster bed. **Grace Duffy**, EastTown, Tory Island, ✆ (074) 35136 (*inexpensive*). **Glen Hotel**, Arranmore Island, ✆ (075) 20505 (*inexpensive*). Family-run and friendly.

Castlegrove House, Castlegrove, Letterkenny, ✆ (074) 51118, ✉ (074) 51384 (*moderate*). Marvellous Georgian house in wooded grounds overlooking Lough Swilly. Well-appointed rooms and good food.

South Donegal

St Ernans House Hotel, St Ernans Island, Donegal Town, ✆ (073) 21065, ✉ (073) 22098 (*expensive*). Charming situation on a wooded tidal island. The décor is rather too colour co-ordinated, but it is still a lovely place to stay.

The Sand House, Rossnowlagh, ✆ (072) 51777, ✉ (072) 52100 (*moderate*). Excellent modern hotel, friendly, comfortable, with delicious food and lots of sports available, especially surfing. **Castle Murray House Hotel**, St John's Point, Dunkineely, ✆ (073) 37022 (*moderate*). Comfortable small hotel with fine French food and lovely views. Mr and Mrs Kieran Clark, **Ardnamona House**, Lough Eske, near Donegal Town, ✆ (073) 22650, ✉ (073) 22819, *ardnamona@tempoweb.com* (*moderate*). Magical views, wonderful food and hospitality, small functions and parties catered for. Famous for its rhododendrons, which flower between April and June. **Viking House Hotel**, Belcruit, Kincasslagh, ✆ (075) 43295 (*moderate*). Modern, family-run hotel owned by Daniel O'Donnell, the famous country singer. Mr and Mrs Evans, **Bruckless House**, Bruckless, ✆ (073) 37071, *bruc@iol.ie* (*moderate*). Charming 18th-century house overlooking Donegal Bay, run by a couple who will head you in the right direction whether your interest is walking, prehistoric monuments or just exploring the beaches and countryside. There are simple but comfortable rooms and a mature garden in which to wander about. **Portnason House**, Ballyshannon, ✆ (072) 52016, ✆ (072) 31739 (*moderate*). Georgian house, close to the sea. **Rhu Gorse**, Lough Eske, near Donegal Town, ✆/✆ (073) 21685, *RHUGORSE@iol.ie* (*inexpensive*). Modern country house, overlooking Lough Eske.

Inishowen

Redcastle County Hotel, Redcastle, Inishowen, ✆ (072) 82073 (*expensive*). Heavy, bad-taste décor has rather ruined the charm of this old Plantation house. Lovely setting, however, and popular with the Northern Irish.

Malin Hotel, Malin, ✆ (077) 70606 (*moderate*). Comfortable, small, family-run hotel. Mr and Mrs McGonagle, **Greencastle Fort**, Greencastle, ✆ (077) 81044. Napoleonic fort, with bars, a seafood restaurant and nightclub.

Culdaff House, Culdaff, ✆ (077) 79103 (*inexpensive*). Georgian farmhouse with wonderful views of beach. Mrs Doyle, **Barracin**, Malin Head, ✆ (077) 70184 (*inexpensive*). On the untouched and beautiful Inishowen Peninsula, about 4 miles (6.4km) from Malin village, this modern bungalow overlooks the sea. There are lots of country pursuits, and your hostess produces excellent home-cooked food. Mrs Grant, **Pollin House**, Carndonagh Road, Ballyliffen, Clonmany, ✆ (077) 76203 (*inexpensive*). Also near Malin; here you will find equally good food and a friendly welcome.

self-catering

Mrs Clarke, **Ardnamona**, Lough Eske, ✆ (073) 22650. Pretty cottage in traditional yard, surrounded by lovely arboretum and scenery. **The Cottage**, Croaghross, Portsalon, ✆/✆ (074) 59548, *jkdeane@iol.ie*. New holiday cottage in lovely location; sleeps 6. **Rock Cottage**, Goorey Rocks, Malin, Inishowen, ✆ (077) 70612. Sleeps 2–4; from IR£120 a week low season. **Mamore Cottage**, Clonmany, ✆ (077) 76710 Traditional Irish cottage with open fire. Sleeps 7; IR£220 low season.

hostels

Sandrock Holiday Hostel, Malin Head, ✆ (077) 70289. Overlooking strand, bunk beds in en suite dormitory. **Gallagher's Farm Hostel**, Bruckless, ✆ (073) 37057. Converted farm buildings. **Dooey Hostel**, Glencolmcille, ✆ (073) 30130. Large friendly hostel. **Campbell's Holiday Hostel**, Ardara, ✆ (075) 51491. **Finn Farm Hostel**, near Ballybofey, ✆ (074) 32261. Well-run and clean. **Manse Hostel**, Letterkenny, ✆ (074) 25238. **Greene's Hostel**, Carnmore Road, Dungloe, ✆ (075) 21021. **Screagan Iolair Hostel**, Crolly, Near Gweedore, ✆ (075) 48593. Remote, but free pick-up service from the N56. **Radharc na Mara Hostel**, Tory Island, ✆ (074) 65145. **Malin Head Hostel**, Malin, Inishowen, ✆ (077) 70309. Clean and comfortable. Organic garden and orchard. **Tra na Rosann Youth Hostel**, Downings, ✆ (074) 55374. **Errigal Hostel**, Dunlewy, ✆ (075) 31180. **Corcreggan Mill Hostel**, Dunfanaghy, ✆ (074) 36409. Basic facilities, but in an atmospheric old renovated mill 3km out of town.

North Donegal

Rathmullan House Hotel, Rathmullan, ✆ (074) 58188 (*expensive*). Fresh, original cooking with vegetables from their walled garden. Sunday lunch is good value. **Castlegrove Country House**, Ramelton Road, near Letterkenny, ✆ (074) 51118 (*expensive*). First-rate ingredients and cooking.

Jackson's Hotel, Ballybofey, ✆ (074) 31021 (*moderate*). Excellent salmon and ham. Also good bar lunches. **Kee's Hotel**, Stanorlar, ✆ (074) 31018 (*moderate*). Wholesome food, good service and cheaper bar food. **An Bonnan Bui**, Pier Road, Rathmullan, ✆ (074) 58453 (*moderate*). Small bistro serving excellent food with a South American flavour. **Mirabeau Steak House**, Ramelton. Georgian town house with unpretentious cooking. **The Silver Tassie**, Ramelton Road, Letterkenny, ✆ (074) 25619 (*moderate*). Good value, large helpings, cheap lunches. **The Pier Hotel**, Rathmullan, ✆ (074) 58188 (*moderate*). **Bunbeg House**, The Harbour, Bunbeg, ✆ (075) 31305 (*moderate*). Cosy family-run restaurant, where you can also stay. Healthy snacks and simple vegetarian meals, as well as heartier food. **Danny Minnies**, Teach Killindarra, Annagry, ✆ (075) 48201 (*moderate*). Near Dungloe. Fish platters and *à la carte*. **Danann's Restaurant**, Main Street, Dunfanaghy, ✆ (074) 36150 (*moderate*). Seafood a speciality. **Collins Bar and Restaurant**, Main Street, Dunfanaghy, ✆ (074) 36205 (*moderate*). **Bayview Hotel**, Killybegs, ✆ (073) 31950 (*moderate*). Mainly a seafood restaurant.

Glencolmcille Folk Village Tearoom, ✆ (073) 30017 (*inexpensive*). Home-made scones and bread, and soups. **Lobster Pot**, Burtonport, ✆ (075) 42012 (*inexpensive*). **Iggy's**, Kincasslagh, ✆ (075) 43112 (*inexpensive*). Bar food at lunchtime, oysters, crab. **Cavanacor Tea Room**, Rossgier, Lifford, ✆ (074) 41143 (*inexpensive*). Excellent home-made scones and jam. **China Tower**, Main Street, Ballybofey, ✆ (074) 31468 (*inexpensive*). Chinese and European food. **Bakersville**, Church Street, Letterkenny (*inexpensive*). Delicious croissants, cakes, bread and sandwiches. **Pat's Pizza**, Market Square, Letterkenny (*inexpensive*). Cheap and good. **Lurgyvale Thatched Cottage**, Kilmacrenan. Home-made bread and scones for tea, ✆ (074) 39216 (*inexpensive*). **Galfees**, U33 Courtyard Street, Letterkenny, ✆ (074) 27173 (*inexpensive*). Cheaper menu during the day and early evening. **Dunfanaghy Workhouse**, ✆ (074) 36540 (*inexpensive*). Coffee shop, wine bar in evening with traditional music (seasonal). **An Chistin**, Ulster Cultural Foundation, Glencolmcille, ✆ (073) 30213/30248 (*inexpensive*). Specializes in seafood. Salads, soups. *Open for lunch and dinner March–Oct.* **Grianan of Aileach Visitor's Centre**, Inishowen. Restaurant and snacks, ✆ (077) 68000 (*inexpensive*). Good value lunches in converted church. **McCroy's of Culdaff**, Inishowen, ✆ (077) 79104 (*inexpensive*). Bar food (and traditional music on Tues and Thurs).

South Donegal

Castle Murray House Hotel, St John's Point, Dunkineely, ✆ (073) 37022 (*expensive*). Superb French cooking in lovely hotel. **The Smuggler's Creek**, Rossnowlagh, ✆ (072) 52366 (*expensive*). Dinner menu includes fish and duck. Sunday lunch cheaper. **Le Chateaubrianne**, Sligo Road, Bundoran, ✆ (072) 42160 (*expensive*). Seafood, steak, poultry. Sunday lunch menu cheaper.

Harvey's Point, Lough Eske, Donegal Town, ✆ (073) 22208 (*moderate*). Continental food in beautiful surroundings. **McGroarty's Pub**, The Diamond, Donegal Town. Good pub food. **The Harbour Quay**, Quay Street, Donegal Town, ✆ (073) 21702 (*moderate*). Seafood, lasagne. **Nancy's Bar**, Ardara, ✆ (075) 41187 (*inexpensive*). Delicious oysters. **Maggie's Bar**, Ballyshannon, ✆ (072) 52449 (*inexpensive*). **The Blueberry Tearoom**, Castle St, Donegal Town. Some good vegetarian choices including quiches and lasagne, and makes a fair attempt at real coffee. **Kitty Kelly's**, the Killybegs Road, Kilcar. Friendly welcome in this cottage restaurant that does tasty variations on Irish standards like lamb stew.

Inishowen

Kealy's Seafood Restaurant, Greencastle, Inishowen, ✆ (077) 81010 (*expensive*). Award-winning seafood. Cheaper lunches. **The Corncrake**, Malin St, Carndonagh, Inishowen, ✆ (077) 74534 (*moderate*). Dinner only. **St John's Restaurant**, Fahan, Inishowen, ✆ (077) 60289 (*moderate*). You can be sure of a feeling of well-being in this comfortable Georgian house. Beautifully cooked seafood and vegetables, including the famous seafood pancakes, and the owner is urbane and welcoming. A welcome spot in the middle of the mountain wildness.

Entertainment and Nightlife

music

Look in the local newspapers for traditional and popular music sessions, which change venue all the time. *Ceili* (traditional) music in the pubs in Falcarragh, in Nancy's Bar and Oliver's in Ardara. . Teach Ceoil, Ballyliffen, a house of music and traditional entertainment during July and August on Tuesday and Thursday evenings. Leo's Bar, Crolly, is famous for its traditional music; various members of Clannad, the popular folk group, learnt their skills here.

Lurgyvale Thatched Cottage, Kilmacrenan, Thursday evenings, ✆ (074) 39216. The Bridge Bar, Ramelton. The Irish Music Hostel, Finn Farm, Cappry, Ballybofey, ✆ (074) 32261. Lakeside Centre, Dunlewy. Mount Errigal Hotel, Ballyraine, Letterkenny, ✆ (074) 22700. Venue for dances and music. Thatch Pub, Bridge Street, Ballyshannon. Central Bar, Main Street, Letterkenny. Talk of the Town, Upper Main Street, Donegal Town. The Flough, Muff, ✆ (077) 84024. Songs, dances, poems, homebaking (mainly in summer). McGrory's, Culdaff, ✆ (077) 79104. Well-known music venue (and guest house) on Tuesdays and Thursdays. The Claddagh, Ballybofey. An Teach Ceoil, Fintown. Glen Tavern, Glenties. Tábhairne Hudi Beag, Bunbeg, ✆ (075) 31016. The Scotsman, Donegal Town. Piper's Rest, Kilcar. Biddy's and Hroarty's, Glencolmcille, take turns most evenings to host a traditional session; Fridays are best, when the Oideas Gael students are out and about.

theatre and cinema

Balor Theatre, Ballybofey, ✆ (074) 31840. Theatre planned for Letterkenny in the near future. Cinema in Port Road, Letterkenny, ✆ (074) 21976.

Porches in Virginia

County Cavan

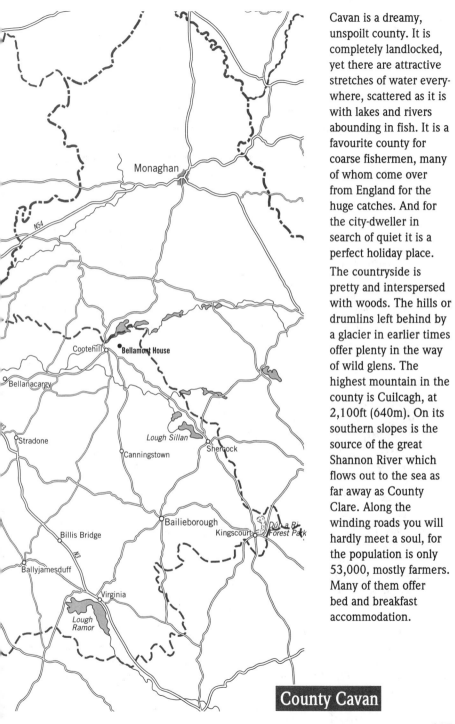

Cavan is a dreamy, unspoilt county. It is completely landlocked, yet there are attractive stretches of water everywhere, scattered as it is with lakes and rivers abounding in fish. It is a favourite county for coarse fishermen, many of whom come over from England for the huge catches. And for the city-dweller in search of quiet it is a perfect holiday place.

The countryside is pretty and interspersed with woods. The hills or drumlins left behind by a glacier in earlier times offer plenty in the way of wild glens. The highest mountain in the county is Cuilcagh, at 2,100ft (640m). On its southern slopes is the source of the great Shannon River which flows out to the sea as far away as County Clare. Along the winding roads you will hardly meet a soul, for the population is only 53,000, mostly farmers. Many of them offer bed and breakfast accommodation.

County Cavan

227

Cavan is an undiscovered county to those who are not in the angling league, and this is undeserved. The ancient history of the county lingers on in the form of charming ruined castles and abbeys, and mysterious stone monuments from the Bronze and Iron Ages. Being in the lakelands, there are a number of *crannog* sites (early lakeland dwellings), and figures left over from pagan times. One of the most curious finds from west Cavan is the three-faced Corleck Head, now in the National Museum, Dublin. It is a rare example of a pagan Trinity figure. Christianity percolated slowly through this lakeland maze, and even up to the 17th century some recorded devotions to saints had a pagan flavour. A principal shrine of the Celtic gods in Ireland was at Magh Sleacht near Ballyconnell, but there is nothing left of it now.

History

Cavan, as it is defined today, is a fairly young county, made in 1584 by the British Lord Deputy. Previously, it was part of the ancient Kingdom of Breffni, and its Gaelic rulers were the O'Reillys. The O'Reillys managed to hold on to power until the division of the county amongst Scottish and English settlers in the 1600s.

In the 19th century the county suffered greatly from the Famine, and the consequent mass emigration. It did have a small linen industry, now defunct, as elsewhere in the North. Along with County Donegal and County Monaghan it is separated politically from the rest of Ulster. This happened in 1921 with the division of Ireland into the 26-county state and the continuing allegiance of the other six Ulster counties to Britain.

Getting There and Around

By rail: No train service in County Cavan.

By bus: Expressway buses stop in Cavan en route between Belfast, Enniskillen, Galway and Dublin. The small towns are served by local buses. Cavan Bus Depot, ☎ (049) 433 1353.

By bike: Ciaran's, Cavan, ☎ (049) 433 2017; Michael's, Belturbet, ☎ (049) 436 1260.

Tourist Information

Cavan, Farnham Street, ☎ (049) 433 1942; open Mon–Fri 9–5, Sat 9–1.

Festivals

February/March: Cavan International Song Contest.

March: Cavan Drama Festival, ☎ (049) 433 1063.

May: County Cavan Fleadh Cheoil; festival of traditional music and dance.

June: Festival of the Lakes, Killeshandra. Music, dance, children's entertainment, powerboat racing and angling competitions. Killinkere Whit Jamboree, Killinkere; car races, concerts and a busking competition. Bailieborough Community Festival. Mountnugent Fáile Abhaile Festival, music races and other sports, including the 'great Mountnugent duck race'.

Sports and Activities

Coarse fishing: In most of the loughs, of which there are hundreds. Particularly good are Loughs Gowna, Bunn, Inchin and Oughter. The Annalee and Woodford Rivers are excellent fisheries. Local tackle shops are the best source of information on hire boats, bait and coarse and pike fishing licences. Try International Fishing Centre, Loughdooley, Belturbet, ✆ (049) 952 2616; the Breffni Arms Hotel, Arva, ✆ (049) 433 5217; Patricia Mundy, in Butlersbridge, Cavan, ✆ (049) 433 1427; Erne Boat Hire in Ballyturbet, ✆ (049) 952 2637. Look out for Hugh Cough's excellent book on coarse fishing in County Cavan. Available in bookshops all over the county.

Walking: The Cavan Way is a 15-mile (24km) marked trail which runs from Blacklion to Dowra, roughly northeast to southwest through hills, forest and limestone scenery, passing on the way prehistoric monuments, a sweat-house near Legeelan, and wonderful views. It also goes close to the Shannon Pot (350yds/300m south of the trail), the source of the Shannon. Information and leaflets from West Cavan Community Council, Blacklion, and Bord Fáilte. There are less strenuous walks in Dún a Rí Forest Park; in Killykeen Forest Park, 2 miles (3km) north of Killashandra on the R201; at Mulrick, 1½ miles (2.5km) southwest of Lough Gowna village on the edge of the lough; and at Castle Lake, a mile (1.6km) north of Bailiesborough on the R178.

Riding: Cavan Equestrian Centre, Shalom Stables, Lath, Cavan, ✆ (049) 433 2017; Redhills Equestrian, Killynure, Redhills, ✆ (049) 435 5042; Killykeen Equestrian Centre, Killykeen, ✆ (049) 433 2541.

Golf: Slieve Russell Hotel championship golf course, Ballyconnell, ✆ (049) 952 6444. Virginia Golf Club, ✆ (042) 966 5766. Blacklion Golf Club, ✆ (072) 53024. County Cavan Golf Club, Cavan Town, specializes in golf tuition, ✆ (049) 433 1283.

Boat trips: Turbet Tours, Belturbet, ✆ (049) 952 2360, for boat trips on Lough Erne. The opening of the Shannon Erne waterway has been a boon for tourism and no doubt new restaurants and bars will appear in the next few years to cater for the canal traffic.

July: Crosskeys Midsummer Festival.

Late July/early August: Belturbet Festival of the Erne.

August: Muff Festival, one of the oldest and largest country fairs in Ireland. Bunnoe Festival, Ballyconnell Community Festival.

October: Cootehill Arts Festival.

Cavan Town and Around

Cavan (*An Cabhan*: the hollow), the county town, is an inconspicuous place. Once it was important as an O'Reilly stronghold in the ancient kingdom of East Breffni. Their castle, **Clough Oughter** (pronounced 'ooter') is a well-preserved example of an Irish circular tower castle and is situated about 3 miles (5km) outside Cavan on an island in Lough Oughter. You approach it from the Crossdoney–Killeshandra road, and the wooded splendour of Killykeen

Forest Park. It is possible to get out to the island if you hire a boat. This 13th-century tower is built over a *crannog* and looks very romantic, viewed from the lakeside. Its history is more sinister. It was used as a prison by the Confederates in the 1641 rebellion, and Eoghan Roe O'Neill, the great leader of the Confederates, died here in 1649, poisoned, it is thought, by his Cromwellian opponents.

North of Cavan Town, **Lough Oughter** is the name given to an entire region of small- to medium-sized lakes, an offshoot of the River Erne complex. This is a well known coarse fishing area. **Lough Inchin**, on the eastern side of the Oughter water system, is noted for pike fishing, though recently roach have been introduced. The **Killykeen Forest Park** is a good access point to the loughs.

There are some worthwhile diversions around Cavan, including a private folk museum called the **Pighouse Collection** (*open at the whim of the owner;*

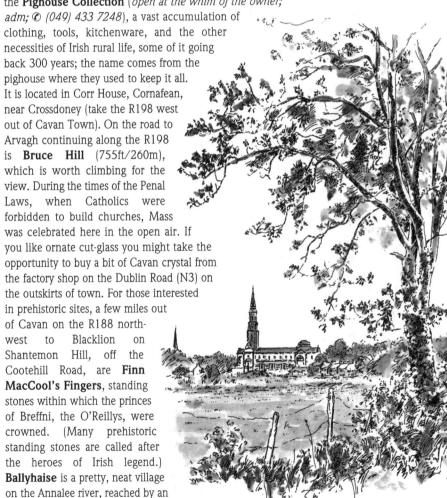

adm; © *(049) 433 7248)*, a vast accumulation of clothing, tools, kitchenware, and the other necessities of Irish rural life, some of it going back 300 years; the name comes from the pighouse where they used to keep it all. It is located in Corr House, Cornafean, near Crossdoney (take the R198 west out of Cavan Town). On the road to Arvagh continuing along the R198 is **Bruce Hill** (755ft/260m), which is worth climbing for the view. During the times of the Penal Laws, when Catholics were forbidden to build churches, Mass was celebrated here in the open air. If you like ornate cut-glass you might take the opportunity to buy a bit of Cavan crystal from the factory shop on the Dublin Road (N3) on the outskirts of town. For those interested in prehistoric sites, a few miles out of Cavan on the R188 north-west to Blacklion on Shantemon Hill, off the Cootehill Road, are **Finn MacCool's Fingers**, standing stones within which the princes of Breffni, the O'Reillys, were crowned. (Many prehistoric standing stones are called after the heroes of Irish legend.) **Ballyhaise** is a pretty, neat village on the Annalee river, reached by an

Cavan town

unclassified road off the R198 going north out of Cavan Town. It has a rather grand arcaded market hall. Nearby is **Ballyhaise House**, built in 1733 and designed by Richard Cassels, who also designed Leinster House in Dublin. It is worth asking to go around it (it is now an agricultural college) to see the lovely oval saloon and plasterwork. It is also worth stopping in **Butlersbridge**, another pleasant village on the River Annalee, to lunch at Derragarra Inn. The fishing is reputed to be good here too.

North Cavan

Another lakeland town is **Belturbet** on the N3 north of Cavan. It is now a thriving angling and boating centre, and was once a depot for the traffic on the Ulster Canal, which might be somewhat revived now the canal has been reopened. A boat trip along here is like driving on Irish roads fifty years ago, it is so unspoilt; you will barely even see a house. At **Milltown**, on the north end of the loughs, is a site associated with the 6th-century St Maodhóg; the site later became an Augustinian monastery, though today little remains but the ruined **Drumlane Church** and a truncated round tower. Look out for the faint carving, on the north side, of a cock and a hen. The church has a lovely Romanesque doorway. Going northwest along the R200 you reach **Ballyconnell**, which is now a stopping place on the Shannon Erne waterway, set on Woodford River. The 17th-century Protestant church here has a carved stone with a human head which came from a medieval monastery. In the grounds of the church are the outlines of two diamond-shaped fortifications dating from the Williamite Wars. The village is a pleasant base for fishing or hill-walking. Three miles (5km) southwest at **Killycluggin** is a stone circle with the remnant of an ornamental phallic stone.

For walkers, 5 miles (8km) to the west on the R200 is the tiny hamlet of **Bawnboy**, which is on the way to some pretty glens and mountains. You can climb 1,148ft (350m) to **Glen Gap** between the peaks of Cuilcagh and Benbrack. For a panoramic view of the neighbouring counties, take the R200 to Glangevlin (also known as Glengevlin), and go through Glen Gap to the summit of the Cuilcagh Mountains. **Blacklion**, a small village on the Fermanagh border, is delightfully situated between Upper and Lower Lough MacNean in the limestone foothills of the Cuilcagh Mountains. It has a frontier post into Northern Ireland but, more importantly for walkers, from here you can walk up to **Lough Garvagh**, **Giant's Cave**, and **Giant's Leap**. These names refer to legendary figures whose origins are lost in the mists of time. For instance, nobody knows who built the fine ring-fort, or *cashel*, 3 miles (5km) away at Moneygashel Post Office near **Burren**, south of Blacklion. It consists of three beautifully built stone walls. The central *cashel* is 82ft (25m) in circumference and has a rampart 10ft (3m) thick, with internal and external stairways. Inside the south *cashel* is a beehive-shaped sweat-house—a kind of Irish sauna that was still popular a century ago. Burren was an important Neolithic centre, and if you have the time to seek them out there are numerous dolmens, including the aforementioned 'Giant's Cave', and a 'rocking stone' in the neighbourhood.

The **Cavan Way**, a signposted trail, passes prehistoric monuments, a sweat-house near Legeelan, and wonderful views. It also goes close to the **Shannon Pot** (350yds/300m south of the trail), the 'eye' where an underground river surfaces to become the source of the mighty River Shannon. Just over the border from Blacklion in County Fermanagh are the famous **Marble Arch Caves** (*see* 'County Fermanagh', p.102). **Swanlinbar**, further to the southeast of this hilly country, is another frontier village. It was once known as the Harrogate of Ireland because of its sulphur baths. **Dowra**, at the western tip of Cavan, sits beside the Shannon at a point where the great river is still barely a stream; to the east of it you can inspect another long surviving section of the the the great ancient earthwork called the **Black Pig's Dyke** that stretches across much of northern Ireland.

Eastern Cavan: Cootehill to Ballyjamesduff

Cootehill, on the county border about 15 miles (24km) northeast of Cavan Town, is a market town named after the Coote family who 'planted' the area with their followers in the 17th century. The Church of Ireland church at the end of its long main street is in the attractive planters' Gothic style. Nearby, to the north of the town in Bellamont Forest, is **Bellamont House**, built by Thomas Coote and designed by the famous Irish architect Sir Edward Lovett Pearce in 1730. It is a beautiful Palladian mansion which fell into decay and was lovingly restored by an Englishman. It has been claimed by an Australian descendant, but at the moment its future is uncertain and it is not open to the public, a great pity as the interiors are spectacular.

The village next-door, **Sherlock**, is rather pretty, with a fine plain Presbyterian meeting house set on the shores of **Lough Sillan**—a good lake for coarse fishing. This is wooded and lake-studded country. Seven and a half miles (12km) away to the southeast is **Kingscourt**. Look in the Catholic church for the delightful stained-glass windows designed by the Dublin artist Evie Hone (1894–1955). Just over a mile (2km) away is **Dún a Ró Forest Park**, where you can picnic by the pretty Cabra River. There are planned walks here, and nature trails. You might see a wild deer amongst the trees. It was the former demesne of the Pratts of Cabra—their castle home is now a hotel.

Beautifully situated on the edge of Lough Ramor is **Virginia**, a village founded in the reign of King James I but named after his aunt, Queen Elizabeth I. It is the most southerly of the Ulster Plantation villages. Dramatist Richard Brinsley Sheridan lived here, often visited by his friend Jonathan Swift, and so did the parents of the other famous Sheridan, General Philip Sheridan of the American Civil War. Although the Protestant population has dwindled since Elizabethan times, the centrepiece of the village is still the Protestant church, which is approached down a straight avenue of clipped yews. There are some pretty rusticated cottages in the main street. It is a very attractive and well-planned town, with graceful trees and traditional painted shop-signs. The lough is beautiful, and full of little islands.

To the northwest is **Ballyjamesduff**, home of the **County Cavan Museum** (*open Tues–Sat 10–5, Sun 2–6; adm*), with historical displays, medieval carvings, and some of the clutter from the Pighouse Collection. Ballyjamesduff was made famous by the song written by the humorous writer and singer Percy French in the early years of last century. At one time French worked as Inspector of Drains with the Cavan County Council. His songs are beloved of Irish emigrant communities all over the world:

> *There are tones that are tender, and tones that are gruff,*
> *And whispering over the sea*
> *Come back, Paddy Reilly, to Ballyjamesduff,*
> *Come back, Paddy Reilly, to me.*

Crafts: Carraig Crafts, Mountnugent. Celtic Crafts, Ballyconnell.

Crystal: Cavan Crystal, Dublin Road, Cavan, ✆ (049) 433 1800; factory tours Mon–Fri.

Delicacies: Goats' cheese from Corleggy Farmhouse, Belturbet, ✆ (049) 952 2219. Besides buying this delicious cheese flavoured with herbs and peppers, you will also enjoy seeing this old-style farm, where pigs wander about the yard, unlike the majority of porkers in Ireland. Another farmhouse cheese is Dun a Ró, a Gouda-type cheese found in the Main Street, Kingscourt. Good picnic supplies available from Back to Nature Health Food Shop, Cavan. At the Lifeforce Mill on Bridge Street in Cavan (*open daily May–Sept, 10–5*), you can make a loaf of bread from stone-ground flour yourself as part of the tour.

Where to Stay

Cavan Town and North Cavan

Slieve Russell Hotel, Ballyconnell, ✆ (049) 952 6444, ◉ 952 6474 (*expensive*). Built by a local millionaire, it has marble columns, fountains and jacuzzis as well as a championship golf-course.

Mrs B. Neill, **Lisnamandra Farmhouse**, Crossdoney, just west of Cavan town, ✆ (049) 433 2577 (*inexpensive*). Ten minutes' drive from Lough Oughter, this award-winning traditional-style farmhouse has comfortable rooms, home-cooking and a very restful atmosphere.

Una Smith, **Riverside House**, Cootehill, ✆ (049) 555 2150 (*inexpensive*). This old farmhouse overlooks the tree-lined River Annalee. It has elegant high ceilings and plasterwork, and open fires in the main rooms. Your host is an expert on all fishing matters, and there is a boat with engine available. Mrs Smith cooks delicious five-course meals in the evenings.

East and South Cavan

The **Park Hotel**, Virginia, ✆ (049) 854 7235 (*expensive–moderate*). Attractive old hunting lodge beside Lough Ramor with a nine-hole golf-course. **Cabra Castle Hotel**, Kingscourt, ✆ (042) 67030, ◉ 67039 (*expensive*). 15th-century pile, with landscaped gardens and a golf course. Self-catering units available. **Sunnyside House**, Lough Gowna, ✆ (043) 83285. A friendly, well-run B&B; a lot of fishing folk stay here. Mrs Bernie O'Reilly, **St Kyran's**, Dublin Road, Virginia, ✆ (049) 854 7084 (*inexpensive*); simple B&B in a lovely setting on the shore of Lough Ramor.

self-catering

Killykeen Forest Chalets, Killykeen Forest Park, ✆ (049) 433 2541. Wooden chalets (IR£195–425) and log cabins (IR£150–320) in Killykeen Forest Park. Mr Kells, **Castlehamilton Courtyard**, Killeshandra, ✆ (049) 433 4840, ◉ 433 4432; attractive 3-bedroom apartments in 17th-century estate outbuildings; IR£140–250. **Doreen**

Clarke, Cornacrea, Cavan, ✆ (049) 433 2023; nice stone house in the country outside Cavan, 4 bedrooms; IR£160.

Eating Out

Cavan Town and North Cavan

MacNean Bistro, Blacklion, ✆ (072) 53022 (*expensive; moderate for lunch*). Imaginative cooking such as fillet of ostrich with rösti; they use mostly locally grown organic produce. The desserts are much lauded.

The Olde Priory, Main Street, Cavan, ✆ (049) 436 1898 (*moderate–inexpensive*). Good atmosphere and plentiful flavoursome helpings; wide menu choice from seafood to pizza.

East and South Cavan

The Old Post Inn, Cloverhill, ✆ (047) 55266 (*moderate*). Renovated old post-house with atmospheric gas lamps. The pork is always good; the pigs are fed on the whey of Corleggy cheese. **The Park Hotel**, Virginia, ✆ (049) 854 7235 (*moderate*). Imaginative and ambitious cooking. **Casey's Steak Bar**, Ballinagh, ✆ (049) 433 7105 (*moderate*). 'The best steaks in Ireland' according to some. **Derragarra Inn**, Butlersbridge (*inexpensive*). Attractive pub by the river. Lots of seafood and traditional music on Fridays during the summer.

Entertainment and Nightlife

Music: McGinty's Corner Bar, Dublin Road, Cavan for traditional music; a winner of the Regional Pub of the Year Award. Louis Blessing's pub, 92 Main Street, Cavan, sometimes has jazz.

County Monaghan

This pleasant, sheltered county is caught at the top betweeen the counties of Armagh and Fermanagh. There are no really high hills, just lots of little ones forming a gently rolling countryside. To the north lies a small fringe of mountains. The central area is hillocky with fairly rich farming land, in many ways reminiscent of County Down. Set among the hills to the south, at almost every bend of the road, lie small well-wooded lakes and sedgy bogholes. The little cultivated fields, trim hedges, tiny lakes, the profusion of wild flowers and the hordes of dragonflies, green and red, make it a land of satisfying detail. In contrast to the smallness of scale, there still remain a few large estates, with their landscaped parks, lakes, formal gardens and age-old trees. You get glimpses of these 'big houses', and the forgotten ones which are crumbling into ruins. Copper beech trees seem to have gone wild everywhere in Monaghan, quite a rarity in Ireland. A native of the place swore that this was the last retreat of the Fir Bolgs, who were squeezed out of the rest of Ireland by the Dé Danaan and the Celts.

County Monaghan is well known to coarse fishermen because of the wealth of lakes; otherwise it has been little visited by tourists. The locals are hoping to change this, and quite a few attractions have been developed. Lough Muckno, near Castleblaney, offers many sporting activities and accommodation. In the southwest the Rural and Literary Resource Centre in Innishkeen is a magnet for admirers of the poet Patrick Kavanagh. To the northeast of the county, the pretty village of Glaslough has an excellent equestrian centre. Close by is Castle Leslie, a Victorian pile overlooking the lough and surrounded by beautiful trees. The castle is open for tours and elaborate dinners. After dinner, the cloaked mistress of the house will guide you by candlelight around its haunted rooms, a performance of fun and drama. This northeastern corner of county Monaghan, bounded by the Blackwater River and the N2, known as the Parish of Truagh, is one of the most untouched areas in the county. The roads are so unused that the grass grows up the middle; many of these little roads would have led into County Tyrone or County Armagh before the Troubles began, and it is hoped that the area will now begin to open up. You will find some pretty mountain scenery and views which stretch over Ulster and beyond.

History

County Monaghan as it is now is a 16th-century creation. As the English conquered territory, they shired it, hoping to make it easier to manage and more anglicized. Here, they joined the territories of the two ruling families, the MacMahons and the McKennas. Other powerful families were the Duffys, O'Carrolls and the Connollys, whose power was finally broken after the 1642 rebellion, when the lands of the Irish chieftains were divided between the English and Scottish 'undertakers', so called because in return for a grant of land they undertook certain duties to keep Monaghan loyal to the English crown. The descendants of those Gaelic families still live in the region today, whilst the undertaker families have disappeared or married into the local population. For over two hundred years, a smouldering resentment over land ownership made the relationship of peasants and landlord very uneasy, but this largely

County Monaghan

Sports and Activities

Fishing: Good coarse fishing in the numerous lakes especially Lough Ooney, Muckno, and the lakes beside Ballybay. Game fishing on the Finn, Fane and Monaghan Blackwater Rivers. Contact Jimmy McMahon, Carrick Sports Shop, Carrickmacross, ✆ (042) 61714, for advice and bait. Talbot Duffy (Ballybay area), ✆ (042) 41692.

Riding: Greystone Equestrian Centre, Castle Leslie, Glaslough, ✆ (047) 88100. Castleblaney Equitation Centre, Castleblaney, ✆ (042) 40418.

Golf: Nuremore Golf Club, Carrickmacross, ✆ (042) 61438. Rossmore Park, ✆ (047) 81316; both 18 holes.

Leisure park: Lough Muckno Leisure Park, Castleblaney, is open to day visitors. Sailing, canoeing, tennis, swimming, fishing, and windsurfing, ✆ (042) 46356.

Walking: The Ulster Way, a signposted track for walkers, joins up here. Certainly County Monaghan is a peaceful place for a fishing or walking holiday. Hilton Park near Scotshouse is the perfect place to stay in style and comfort, and for those on tighter budgets there are plenty of hospitable bed-and-breakfast establishments.

disappeared with the land acts of 1881 when the British government put up money for tenants to buy their own holdings.

In the 19th century County Monaghan benefited from the linen industry, and it was famous for its trade in horses, many of which were exported to Russia for the use of the Imperial army. Now both the linen and the horse trade have gone, along with the old rail and canal links. However, the county is well served by express buses going to and from Dublin and County Donegal, there is a good local bus network, and Monaghan is now noted for its furniture-making, poultry, and mushroom production. The locals are mostly involved in farming activities. Many of the country's chickens, ducks and even the rather exotic quail are produced for the table in County Monaghan. The people are fairly prosperous, and agriculture has been boosted tremendously by membership of the EU. The moist and mild climate produces good grass for cattle rearing, and there are many small mixed farms. The population is about 51,000.

Getting There and Around

By rail: No rail service in County Monaghan.

By bus: Frequent Bus Eireann express buses from Dublin, Donegal, Armagh, Belfast and Derry. Monaghan Bus Station, ✆ (047) 82377. Try also the private operators such as McConnons, ✆ (047) 82020. There are excellent local bus services to the smaller villages.

By bike: Clerkin Cycles, Park Street, Monaghan, ✆ (047) 81113; Paddy McQuaid, Emydale, ✆ (047) 88108.

Tourist Information

Monaghan (Market House), ✆ (047) 81122; open April–Dec.

August: Festival of the Lakes, week-long festival in Ballybay.

September: Jazz and Blues Festival, Monaghan.

October: County Monaghan Arts Festival.

Monaghan Town

Monaghan Town is a good place from which to start one's tour of the county. Built on an old monastic site, this market town has some very fine urban architecture, especially round the market square, called the Diamond. The large **Market House** dates from 1792. There is also a surprising amount of red brick in the smaller streets off the square. It is a very busy, prosperous town with lots of shops and a good restaurant in the square. The small **Monaghan County Museum** (*open Tues–Sat, 11–5; ✆ (047) 82928*) on Hill Street, on the west side of Market Street, founded in 1974, won the EEC museum award in 1980. The museum has amongst its treasures the Clogher Cross, a fine example of Early-Christian metalwork, with its highly decorative detail. There are objects collected from the nearby lake dwellings, including sandals and glass beads. There are also displays dealing with everything from lace-making to railways. The pedimented Market House holds the tourist office and a gallery with varying exhibitions. The 1860s Roman Catholic **St Macartan's Cathedral**, on the N2 to Dundalk, was designed by J. J. McCarthy, whose work is in the Gothic Revival style of Pugin—though sadly a modern improvement has been to remove the original altarpiece. The **Heritage Centre** in the St Louis Convent (*open daily exc Wed, 10–12 and 2.30–4.30; Sat & Sun 2.30–4.30*) traces the fascinating history of the order throughout the world. The building itself is beautiful, and there is a *crannog* on the grounds.

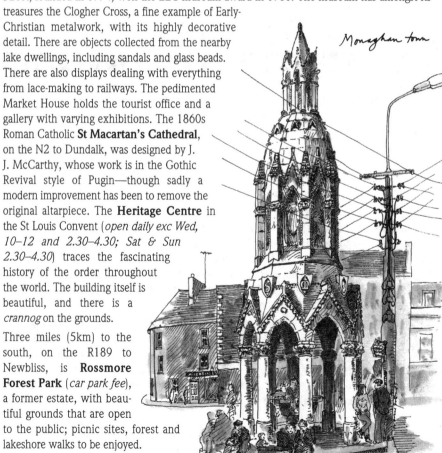

Monaghan town

Three miles (5km) to the south, on the R189 to Newbliss, is **Rossmore Forest Park** (*car park fee*), a former estate, with beautiful grounds that are open to the public; picnic sites, forest and lakeshore walks to be enjoyed.

North Monaghan

Only a small part of the county lies to the north of Monaghan town. It gently rises up from the flood plain of the Blackwater, to the high moorland of Slieve Beagh. Near the village of Glaslough, on the shores of a small grey lake, is the **Castle Leslie** demesne. Sir Shane Leslie wrote superb ghost stories in the early decades of this century. The house, which is still lived in by the Leslie family, is Italianate and full of art treasures. It is possible to tour the house (*open May–Sept, daily 12–7; adm*), or spend the night there (*see* below). Nice tea-room in the conservatory.

To explore the tangle of little roads in this area known as Truagh Parish you will need a detailed local map. To the west of Emyvale is the pretty **Lough More** with good stocks of brown trout and the mountain scenery of Bragan where the local people go to cut their turf. Northeast of here is the townland of **Mullanacross**, and in the graveyard of the ruined and ancient Errigal church are some superbly carved 18th-century gravestones. They depict the stag, emblem of the McKennas, and biblical animals. Just across the road is a holy well, sacred to St Mellan, the patron saint of these parts. Further to the southeast you come across the deserted village of Mullan, which has some fine stone houses.

South Monaghan

To the southeast of Monaghan town lies **Castleblaney**, on a narrow strip of land at the head of Lough Muckno. This is the county's largest stretch of water with perhaps the best coarse fishing there is, though all the lakes around here vie for that award. Founded in the reign of James I, Castleblaney is now a prosperous town. The plain Georgian Court House is rather fine, and in the wooded demesne of **Hope Castle** there are nature trails and picnic sites (*car park fee*). The castle once belonged to the 17th-century Blayneys, who developed the town, but was bought in the 1870s by Henry Hope, who is remembered as the owner of the Hope diamond—the largest blue diamond in the world, but reputed to bring ill-luck to its owner. The Hopes sold up in 1916.

Heading west from Castleblaney on the R183, meandering between the hills and fish-filled lakes, you come down to the town of **Ballybay**, on the shore of Lough Major. It is attractive with the Catholic and Church of Ireland churches rising up, each on its own hill overlooking the grassy lakes and farmland. Ballybay was noted for its horse fair, which sadly has become defunct with the age of the tractor. Flax-growing and tanning used to be very important industries here, but now they too have virtually disappeared.

Fifteen miles (24km) south of Ballybay is **Carrickmacross**, a market town famous for its handmade lace, a cottage industry which was established at the beginning of the century. The very fine lace, appliqué work on tulle is much sought after. Examples can be seen in the Lace Co-operative, in Market Place (✆ *(042) 62506*) and in the Clones Lace Gallery, Ulster Canal Stores, Cara St (✆ *(047) 52125*). The **Roman Catholic church** here has ten splendid windows by the stained-glass artist Harry Clarke, whose work was inspired by the Pre-Raphaelite style.

About 3 miles (5km) north on the Castleblaney Road at Donaghmoyne is **Mannan Castle**, a great hilltop motte and bailey (*free access*). It was constructed in the 12th century, and in 1224 it was encased in stone, some of which can still be seen. Southwest of here, close to

Kingscourt is Dun a Ró Forest Park (*see* p.232), a great place for walks. The hilltop car park gives good views towards the Mourne Mountains.

About 5 miles (8km) to the southeast of Carrickmacross, near the border with County Louth, is the small village of **Inishkeen**. St Dega founded a monastery here in the 6th century, and you can see the remains of the old abbey and its 40ft- (12m-) high round tower with a raised doorway. The **Folk Museum** (*open by arrangement;* ✆ *(042) 78102*) deals with local history, folklife, and the old Great Northern Railway which ran through the village. Patrick Kavanagh was born here in 1904 and is buried in the graveyard of St Mary's church, which features **The Patrick Kavanagh Rural and Literary Resource Centre** (*open Mon–Fri 11–5, Sat & Sun 2–7; adm*). His masterly poem 'The Great Hunger' is a very sad and ironic evocation of rural life in Ireland.

Rockcorry to Clones

To the west of the county there are hundreds of small roads and lanes to explore, with lakes caught between, like a spider's web in the morning dew. Quite near the County Cavan border on the R188 lies the small village of **Rockcorry**, which has some fine 19th-century stone dwellings built for destitute widows. Here too, on the southwestern edge of the village, is the **Dartry Estate** with its open parkland, little lakes and much woodland, now all in the care of the Forestry Commission. It was once a beautiful estate but is less attractive now with massive scars from tree-felling and an air of neglect. There are picnic sites and forest walks, but the big house is a ruin. Nearby, lakes with names like Coragh, Mullanary and Drumlona are full of fish. Further west is the pretty riverside village of Newbliss, and 5 miles (8km) to the northeast again is the town of Clones. Between the two towns, near Kileevan, lies the country church of **Drumswords**. Dating from AD 750, it has now sadly fallen into disrepair, but one window still has the remains of fine basket tracery. South of Newbliss, just off the R189, is **Annaghmakerrigh House**, which was once the home of Sir Tyrone Guthrie (1900–71). Sir Tyrone, a famous theatre, television and radio producer, left his estate to the nation on condition it be used as a house for those who lived by the arts. Many artists and writers come to spend some time in such a congenial place. You may walk through the forest near the house, and down to the lake. It is very peaceful with pretty parkland and trees.

Clones was once linked to Monaghan by the old Ulster railway and Ulster canal. In the days before the First World War it was a thriving town, but it is now rather run-down, although it is still an important agricultural centre. Built on an ancient site, it has some fine remains, many of which have been whisked away to the National Museum. However, it retains an overgrown *rath* with three concentric earthworks, an abbey, a well-preserved 75ft (23m) round tower, and a finely carved Early-Christian sarcophagus, which is probably a MacMahon family tomb. In the graveyard are some fine 18th-century gravestones carved with skulls and crossbones. The key is available from Pattons pub nearby. Presiding over the triangular marketplace, perversely called the Diamond, stands an ancient, much-inscribed cross. It is carved with scenes from the Bible, and is probably 12th century. There are many fine old houses, particularly the imposing market house, now the library. Clones is the main centre of traditional hand-crocheted lace; you will be able to buy some in the local shops, although lace-making is very much on the decline. Charles Gavan Duffy (1816–1903), one of the leaders of the Young Ireland movement of the 1840s and later Prime Minister of Victoria in Australia, was born here. So too was Barry McGuigan, the former world champion featherweight boxer.

Lace: Crochet lace in Clones, at Clones Lace Guild, Fermanagh Street, where there is also a display of antique lace, and a coffee shop. Carrickmacross Lace Co-operative, with a gallery on Market Square, Carrickmacross.

Delicacies: Quail from Emyvale, County Monaghan.

Where to Stay

North Monaghan

Castle Leslie, Glaslough, ✆ (047) 88109 (*expensive*). Elegant rooms furnished with antiques in Monaghan's most notable historic home (*see* above); dinner also available, upon request.

Mr and Mrs Madden, **Hilton Park Country House**, Scotshouse, Clones, ✆ (047) 56007, ✆ 56033 (*expensive*). This stately house set in the middle of luxuriant parkland is a superb place to stay if you are feeling extravagant. The rooms are furnished in keeping with the period of the house, and the food has a reputation for quality. Fishing and shooting in season, golf and lake-swimming are all available to the guests.

Pillar House, Glaslough, ✆ (047) 88125, ✆ 88269 (*inexpensive*). Simple hotel. **The Hillgrove**, Monaghan, ✆ (047) 81288 (*moderate*). Of the same stable as the Slieve Russell in Cavan. **Ashleigh House**, 37 Dublin Street, Monaghan, ✆ (047) 81227 (*inexpensive*). Centrally located B&B.

Mrs O'Grady, **Glynch House**, Newbliss, Clones, ✆ (047) 54045, ✆ 54321 (*moderate*); comfortable rooms in an 18th-century home designed by Richard Harrison. **Creighton Hotel**, Fermanagh St, Clones, ✆ (047) 51284 (*moderate*). Family-run traditional-style hotel.

South Monaghan

Nuremore Hotel, Carrickmacross, ✆ (042) 61438, ✆ 61853 (*luxury*). Posh modern hotel in spacious grounds. Caters especially to golfers, with a fine 18-hole course; also a gym and big indoor pool. **Shirley Arms**, Main Street, Carrickmacross, ✆ (042) 61209 (*inexpensive*). Hotel in the town centre.

Eating Out

Hilton Park Country House (*see* above). **The Four Seasons Hotel**, Coolshannagh, near Monaghan, ✆ (047) 81888 (*moderate*). Comfortable and friendly. **Andy's Restaurant**, 12 Market Street, Monaghan, ✆ (047) 82277 (*inexpensive, moderate for dinner*). All manner of foods (including ostrich) cooked well. **Mamo's Tea Shop**, The Diamond, Clones (*inexpensive*). **The Hillgrove Hotel**, Old Armagh Road, Monaghan. Traditional dinner roast and carvery. **Castle Leslie**, Glaslough (*see* above) ✆ (047) 88109 (*expensive*). An old-world dining experience in truly opulent surrounds; one to consider as a special treat during your visit to Ireland. By advance booking only.

In south Monaghan: **The Nuremore Hotel**, Carrickmacross, ✆ (042) 61438 (*expensive*). Showy food.

The Giant's Ring

Old Gods and Heroes

The Celts

Nobody knows exactly when the first Celts arrived in Ireland; it was some time before 1000 BC, with the last wave of people coming around the 3rd century BC. The Greek chroniclers were the first to name these people, calling them Keltori. Celt means 'act of concealment', and it has been suggested that they were called 'hidden people' because of their reluctance to commit their great store of scholarship and knowledge to written records. Kilt, the short male skirt of traditional Celtic dress, may also come from this word!

The Celtic civilization was quite sophisticated, and much of the road-building attributed to the Romans has been found to have been started by the Celts. The Romans often built on their foundations. In Ireland, ancient roads are quite often discovered when bog is being cleared.

The Irish language, and its ancient and rich epic stories, is predated only by Greek and Latin. But the tradition was strictly oral until the Christian era. Even then, it was well into the 7th century before the bulk of it was written down by scribes, who often added to or changed the story to make some moral Christian interpretation. The reluctance of the Celts to commit their knowledge to writing is directly related to the Druids and their power, for the Druidic religion was the cornerstone of the Celtic world, which stretched from Ireland to the Continent and as far south as Turkey. Irish mythology is therefore concerned with the rest of that Celtic world: there are relationships with the gods and heroes of Wales, Scotland, Spain and middle Europe.

The *Book of the Dun Cow* and the *Book of Leinster*, the main surviving manuscript sources, date from the late 11th century. Many earlier books were destroyed by the Viking raids and entire libraries lost. The various sagas and romances which survived have been categorized by scholars into four cycles. First, the **mythological cycle**: the stories which tell of the various invasions of Ireland, from Cesair to the Sons of Milesius. These are largely concerned with the activities of the Túatha Dé Danaan, the pagan gods of Ireland. Next there is the **Ulster Cycle**, or deeds of the Red Branch Knights, which include the tales of Cú Chulainn and the *Táin Bó Cuailgne*. Then there is the **Cycle of Kings**, mainly stories about semi-mythical rulers. And finally, the **Fenian Cycle** which relates the adventures of Fionn MacCumhail (Finn MacCool) and the warriors of the Fianna. Only qualified story-tellers could relate these sagas and tales under Brehon (Celtic) laws, and they were held in great respect. Several qualities emerge from these sagas and tell us a great deal about the society of Iron Age Ireland, and indeed Europe. The stories are always optimistic, and the Celts had evolved a doctrine of immortality of the soul.

The heroes and gods were interchangeable—there were no hard and fast divisions between gods and mortals. Both had the ability to shape change, and often reappear after the most grue-some deaths. The gods of the Dé Danaan were tall, beautiful and fair, although, later, in the popular imagination, they became fairies or the 'little people'. They were intellectual as well as beautiful, and as gullible as mortals with all our virtues and vices. They loved pleasure, art, nature, games, feasting and heroic single combat. It is difficult to know whether they are heroes and heroines made into gods by their ancestors. In the 11th century, Cú Chulainn was the most admired hero, particularly by the élite of society. Then Fionn MacCumhail took over. He and his band of warriors became very popular with the ordinary people right up to the early 20th century. The English conquests in the 17th century and the resulting destruction and exile of the Irish intelligentsia meant that much knowledge was lost, though the peasantry kept it alive in folklore recited by the *seanachie* or village story-teller. Then, with the famines and vast emigration of the 19th century, the Irish language came under great threat and, with it, the folklore.

It was anglicized by antiquarians and scholars at the end of the 18th century, and later in the 19th century, who did much to record and translate the Irish epic stories into English, and to preserve the Gaelic; many were Ulster Presbyterians. Other names which should be remembered with honour are William Carleton, Lady Wylde, T. Crofton-Croker, Standish James O'Grady, Lady Gregory and Douglas Hyde. Their writings and records of Irish peasant culture have become standard works.

The question of where Irish myth ends and history begins is impossible to define. Historical accounts are shot through with allegory, supernatural happenings and fantasy. Nothing has changed, for a similar mythical process is applied to modern history.

Directory of the Gods

Amergin: a Son of Milesius. The first Druid of Ireland. There are three poems credited to him in *The Book of Invasions*.

Aonghus Óg: the God of Love, son of Dagda. His palace was by the River Boyne at Newgrange. Also known as Aengus.

Ard Rí: the title of high king.

Badhbha or *Badh*: goddess of battles.

Balor: a god of death, and one of the most formidable Fomorii. His one eye destroyed everything it gazed on. Destroyed by his own grandson, Lugh.

Banba, Fotla and Eire Dé Danaan: sister goddesses who represent the spirit of Ireland, particularly in Irish literature and poetry. It is from the goddess Eire that Ireland takes its modern name.

Bilé: god of life and death. He appears as Cymbeline in Shakespeare's play.

Bran: 'Voyage of Bran'. The earliest voyage poem, which describes through beautiful imagery the Island of Joy and the Island of Women. Also, the hound of Fionn MacCumhail.

Brigid: goddess of healing, fertility and poetry. Her festival is one of the four great festivals of the Celtic world. Also a Christian saint who has become confused in popular folklore with the goddess.

Caílte: cousin of Fionn MacCumhail. One of the chief Warriors of the Fianna, and a poet. A Christian addition to his story has returned him from the Otherworld to recount to St Patrick the adventures of the Fianna.

Conall Cearnach: son of Amergin, a warrior of the Red Branch, and foster brother and blood cousin of Cú Chulainn. He avenged Cú Chulainn's death by slaying his killers.

Conchobhar MacNessa: king of Ulster during the Red Branch Cycle. He fell in love with Deidre (*see* below) and died from a magic 'brain ball' which had been lodged in his head seven years before by the Connacht warrior, Cet.

Conn: one of the Sons of Lir, the ocean god, changed into a swan by his jealous stepmother, Aoife. Also, Conn of the hundred battles, high king from AD 177 to 212.

Cormac MacArt: high king from AD 254 to 277 and patron of the Fianna, who reigned during the period of Fionn MacCumhail and his adventures. His daughter was betrothed to Fionn MacCumhail but eloped with one of Fionn's warriors, Diarmuid. His son succeeded him and destroyed the Fianna.

Cú Chulainn: the hound of Culann, also called the Hound of Ulster. He has similarities with the Greek hero, Achilles. He was actually called Sétanta until he killed the hound belonging to Culann, a smith god from the Otherworld. He promised to take its place and guarded his fortress at night. He became a great warrior whose battle frenzy was incredible. Women were always falling in love with him, but Emer, his wife, managed to keep him. He is chiefly famous for his single-handed defence of Ulster during the War of the Tain (Bull of Cuailgne) when Ailill and Medb of Connacht invaded (*see* Medb). He was acknowledged as champion of all Ireland, and forced to slay his best friend, Ferdia, during a combat at a crucial ford. Later Cú Chulainn rejected the love of the goddess of battles, Mórrigan, and his doom was sealed; his enemies finally slew him. During the fatal fight he strapped his body to a pillar stone because he was too weak to stand. But such was his reputation that no one dared to come near him until Mórrigan, in the form of a crow, perched on his shoulder, and finally an otter drank his blood.

Dagha: father of the Gods and patron god of the Druids.

Diarmuid: foster son of the love god, Aonghas Óg, and a member of the Fianna. The goddess of youth put her love spot on him, so that no woman could resist loving him. He eloped with Grainne, who was betrothed to Fionn MacCumhail, and the Fianna pursued them for 16 years. Eventually the couple made an uneasy peace with Fionn, who went out hunting with Diarmuid on Ben Bulben, where Diarmuid was gored by an enchanted boar who was also his own stepbrother. Fionn had the power to heal him with some enchanted water, but he let it slip through his fingers. Aoughas Óg, the god of love, took Diarmuid's body to his palace and, although he did not restore him to life, sent a soul into his body so that he could talk to him each day.

Deidre: Deidre of the Sorrows was the daughter of an Ulster chieftain. When she was born it was forecast by a Druid that she would be the most beautiful woman in the land, but that, because of her, Ulster would suffer great ruin and death. Her father wanted to put her to death at once but Conchobhar, the Ulster king, took pity on her and said he would marry her when she grew up. When the time came she did not want to marry such an old man, particularly as she had fallen in love with Naoise, a hero of the Red Branch. They eloped to Scotland. Conchohbar lured them back with false promises, and Naoise and his brothers were killed by Eoghan MacDuracht. Deidre was forced to become Conchobhar's wife. She did not smile for a year, which infuriated her husband. When he asked her who she hated most in the world, she replied, 'you and Eoghan MacDuracht'. The furious Conchobhar then said she must be Eoghan's wife for a year. When she was put in Eoghan's chariot with her hands bound, she somehow mangaged to fling herself out and dash her head against a rock. A pine tree grew from her grave and touched another pine growing from Naoise's grave, and the two intertwined.

Donn: king of the other world, where the dead go.

Emain Macha: the capital of the kings of Ulster for six centuries, which attained great glory during the time of King Conchobhar and the Red Branch Knights.

Emer: wife of Cú Chulainn. She had the six gifts of womanhood: beauty, chastity, eloquence, needlework, sweet voice and wisdom.

Female champions: in ancient Irish society women had equal rights with men. They could be elected to any office, inherit wealth and hold full ownership under law. Cú Chulainn was instructed in the martial arts by Scáthach, and there was another female warrior in the Fianna called Creidue. Battlefields were always presided over by goddesses of war. Nessa, Queen of Ulster, and Queen Medb of Connacht were great warriors and leaders. Boadicea of Britain was a Celtic warrior queen who died in AD 62, and this tradition survived with Grace O'Malley of County Mayo into the 16th century.

Ferdia: the best friend of Cú Chulainn, killed by him in a great and tragic combat in the battle over the Brown Bull of Cuailgne (or Cooley).

Fergus MacRoth: stepfather of Conchobhar, used by him to deceive Deidre and Naoise and his brothers. He went into voluntary exile to Connacht in a great fury with the king, and fought against Conchobhar and the Red Branch. But he refused to fight against Cú Chulainn, which meant the ultimate defeat of Queen Medb and her armies.

The Fianna: known as the Fenians. A band of warriors guarding the high king of Ireland. Said to have been founded in about 300 BC, they were perhaps a caste of the military élite. Fionn MacCumhail was their greatest leader. In the time of Oscar, his grandson, they destroyed themselves through a conflict between the clans Bascna and Morna. In the 19th century the term was revived as a synonym for Irish Republican

Brotherhood, and today it is used as the title for one of the main Irish political parties, Fianna Fail, which means 'Soldiers of Destiny'.

Fintan: the husband of Cesair, the first invader of Ireland. He abandoned her and survived the Great Deluge of the Bible story by turning into a salmon. Also, the Salmon of Knowledge who ate the Nuts of Knowledge before swimming to a pool in the River Boyne, where he was caught by the Druid Finegas. He was given to Fionn MacCumhail to cook. Fionn burnt his finger on the flesh of the fish as he was turning the spit, sucked his thumb, and acquired the knowledge for himself.

Fionn MacCumhaill: anglicized as Finn MacCool. He was brought up by two wise women, then sent to study under Finegas, the Druid. After acquiring the Knowledge of the Salmon, Fintan, he became known as Fionn, the Fair One. He was appointed head of the Fianna by Cormac MacArt, the high king at the time, in place of Goll MacMorna who had killed his father. His exploits are many and magical. His two famous hunting hounds were Bran and Sceolan, who were actually his own nephews, the children of his bewitched sister. His son, Oísín, was the child of the goddess Sadb, but he suffered unrequited love for Grainne. In the story of the Battle of Ventry, Fionn overcomes Daire Donn, the King of the World. He is said not to be dead, but sleeping in a cave, waiting for the call to help Ireland in her hour of need.

Dé Fionnbharr and **Oonagh:** gods of the Dé Danaan who have degenerated into the King and Queen of the Fairies in folklore.

Fionnuala: the daughter of Lir. She and her brothers were transformed into swans by her jealous step-mother, Aoife. The spell was broken with the coming of Christianity, but they were old and senile by then.

Fir Bolg: 'Bagmen'. A race who came to Ireland before the Dé Danaan. They do not take much part in the myths.

Fomorii: a misshapen and violent people, the evil gods of Irish myth. Their headquarters seems to have been Tory Island, off the coast of County Donegal. Their leaders include Balor of the Evil Eye, and their power was broken for ever by the Dé Danaan at the second Battle of Moytura, in County Sligo.

Gaul: Celt. Gaulish territory extended over France, Belgium, parts of Switzerland, Bohemia, parts of modern Turkey and parts of Spain.

Geis: a taboo or bond which was usually used by Druids and placed on someone to compel them to obey. Grainne put one on Diarmuid.

Goibhnin: smith god, and god of handicraft and artistry.

Goll MacMorna: leader of the Fianna before Fionn MacCumhail.

Grainne: anglicized as Grania. Daughter of Cormac MacArt, the high king. She was betrothed to Fionn MacCumhail but thought him very old, so she put a *geis* on Diarmuid to compel him to elope with her. Eventually he fell in love with her (*see* Diarmuid). After Diarmuid's death, although she had sworn vengeance on Fionn, she allowed herself to be wooed by him and became his wife. The Fianna despised her for this.

Laeg: charioteer to Cú Chulainn.

Lir: ocean god.

Lugh: sun god who slew his grandfather, Balor, and the father of Cú Chulainn by a mortal woman. His godly status was diminished into that of a fairy craftsman, Lugh Chromain, a leprechaun.

Macha: a mysterious woman who put a curse called *cest nóiden* on all Ulstermen, so that they would suffer from the pangs of childbirth for five days and four nights in times of Ulster's greatest need. This curse would last nine times nine generations. She did this because her husband boasted to King Conchobhar that she could race and win against the king's horses, even though she was pregnant. She died in agony as a result.

Medb: anglicized as Maeve. Queen of Connacht, and wife of Ailill. She was famous for her role in the epic tale of the cattle raid of Cuailgne (Cooley), which she started when she found that her possessions were not as great as her husband's. She wanted the Brown Bull of Cuailgne which was in Ulster, to outdo her husband's bull, the White-Horned Bull of Connacht. This had actually started off as a calf in her herd, but had declined to stay in the herd of a woman! She persuaded her husband to join her in the great battle that resulted. The men of the Red Branch were hit by the curse of the *nóiden* (*see* Macha), and none could fight except Cú Chulainn, who was free of the weakness the curse induced and single-handedly fought the Connacht champions. Mebh was killed by Forbai, son of Conchobhar, whilst bathing in a lake. The bulls over which the great battle had been fought eventually tore each other to pieces.

Milesians: the last group of invaders of Ireland before the historical period. Milesius was their leader, a Spanish soldier, but his sons actually carried out the Conquest of Ireland.

Nessa: mother of Conchobhar. A strong-minded and powerful woman who secured the throne of Ulster for her son.

Niall of the Nine Hostages: high king from AD 379 to 405, and progenitor of the Uí Neill dynasty. There is a confusion of myth and history surrounding him.

Niamh: of the golden hair. A daughter of the sea god Manannán Mac Lir. She asked Oísín to accompany her to the Land of Promise and live there as her lover. After three weeks, he discovered three hundred years had passed.

Nuada of the Silver Hand: the leader of the Dé Danaan gods, who had his hand cut off in the great battle with the Fomorii. It was replaced by the god of healing.

Ogma: god of eloquence and literature, from whom Ogham Stones were named. These are upright pillars carved with incised lines which read as an alphabet from the bottom upwards. They probably date from AD 300.

Oísín: son of Fionn and Sadh, the daughter of a god, and leading champion of the Fianna. He refused to help his father exact vengeance on Grainne (to whom Fionn was betrothed) and Diarmuid (with whom Grainne eloped), and went with Niamh of the Golden Hair to the Land of Promise. Oísín longed to go back to Ireland, so Niamh gave him a magic horse on which to return, but warned him not to set foot on land, as three hundred years had passed since he was there. He fell from his horse by accident and turned into an old, blind man. A Christian embellishment is that he met St Patrick, and Oísín told him the stories of the Fianna, and they had long debates about the merits of Christianity. Oísín refused to agree that his Ireland was better off for it. The spirit of his mood comes through in this anonymous verse from a 16th-century poem translated by Frank O'Connor.

> *Patrick you chatter too loud*
> *And lift your crozier too high*
> *Your stick would be kindling soon*
> *If my son Osgar stood by.*

Oscar or **Osgar:** son of Oísín. He also refused to help Fionn, his grandfather, against Diarmuid and Grainne. The high king of the time wished to weaken the Fianna and allowed the two clans in it, Morna and Bascna, to quarrel. They fought at the battle of Gabhra. Oscar was killed and the Fianna destroyed.

Partholón: the leader of the third mythical invasion of Ireland. He is supposed to have introduced agriculture to Ireland.

Red Branch: a body of warriors who were the guardians of Ulster during the reign of Conchobhar MacNessa. Their headquarters were at Emain *(Eamhain)* Macha. The Red Branch cycle of tales has been compared to the Iliad in theme. The main stories are made up of the *Táin Bó* Cuailgne (the Brown Bull of Cuailgne or Cooley). Scholars accept that the cycle of stories must have been transmitted orally for nearly a thousand years, providing wonderfully accurate descriptions of the remote past.

Dunluce Castle

From Stone Circles to Castles

Ireland is fascinatingly rich in monuments, and you cannot fail to be struck by the number and variety of archaeological remains. They crown the tops of hills or stand out, grey and mysterious, in the green fields. Myths and stories surround them, handed down by word of mouth. Archaeologists too have their theories, and they are as varied and unprovable as the myths.

Man is known to have lived in this country since Middle Stone Age times (roughly from about 6000 BC). There are no structures left from these times but, after the coming of Neolithic or New Stone Age peoples, some of the most spectacular of the Irish monuments were built.

Here is a brief description of the types to be seen in order of age.

Stone Circles

The stone circles served as prehistoric temples and go back to Early Bronze Age times. Impressive examples may be seen on Beltany Hill, near Lifford, County Donegal. Earthen circles probably served a similar purpose: for example, the Giant's Ring at Drumbo near Belfast, which surrounds a megalith. They have been variously interpreted as ritual sites and astronomical calendars. They are mainly found in the southwest and north of the country. Associated with them are standing stones.

Megalithic Tombs

Neolithic colonisers came with a knowledge of agriculture to Ireland between 3000 and 2000 BC and erected the earliest megalithic chambered tombs. They are called the court cairns, because the tombs are made up of a covered gallery for burial with one or more unroofed courts or forecourts for ritual. Pottery has been found in these tombs. Court cairns are mainly found in the northern part of the country.

Linked to the court cairns is the simple and imposing type of megalith—the dolmen or portal dolmen. This consists of a large, sometimes enormous, capstone and three or more supporting uprights. The distribution of the dolmen is more widespread but tends to be eastern. Most excavated wedges belong to the Early Bronze Age—2000 to 1500 BC. They are now largely bare of the cairns or mounds which covered them. The people who built them advanced from being hunters to growing crops and keeping domestic animals.

The most spectacular of the great stone tombs are the passage graves. Unchambered burial mounds also occur throughout the country. They date largely from the Bronze Age, but earlier and later examples are known.

Standing Stones

Also known as gallauns. Single pillar stones which also have a ritual significance, and occasionally mark grave sites. Others carry inscriptions in ogham characters.

Ring-forts

The most numerous type of monument to be seen in Ireland is the ring-fort, known also as *rath*, *lios*, *dun*, *caher*, and *cashel*. There are about 30,000 in the country. These originated as early as the Bronze Age and continued to be built until the Norman invasion. The circular ramparts, varying in number from one to four, enclosed a homestead with houses of wood, wattle-and-daub, or partly stone construction. The royal site at Grianan of Aileach, near Derry, is a well-preserved example of a stone fort. Collections of earthworks identify the royal seats at Tara, County Meath, and Emain Macha, County Armagh, where earthen banks are now the only reminders of the timber halls of kings. They lie at the centre of a complex tangle of myth and tradition in the ancient Celtic sagas.

Hill-forts

Larger and more defensive in purpose are the hill-forts, whose ramparts follow contour lines to encircle hill-tops. To this class belongs the large green enclosure at Emain Macha known as Navan Fort, County Armagh.

Crannógs

Crannógs, or artificial islands, found in lakes and marshy places, are defensive dwelling sites used by farmers, with even earlier origins than the forts, which continued in use sometimes until the 17th century.

Early Irish Architecture

Before the Norman invasion most buildings in Ireland were of wood. None of these has survived. In the treeless west, however, tiny corbelled stone buildings shaped like beehives and called **clochans** were constructed. They were used as oratories by holy men. Some, possibly dating from the 7th century, still exist.

Most of the early mortared **churches** were modelled on wooden prototypes. They were very small, and already were built with stylistic features which are characteristic of Irish buildings: steeply pitched roofs, inclined jambs to door and window-openings. Many of these small churches would have been roofed with wood, or tiled or thatched, but some were roofed with stone. The problem of providing a pitched roof of stone over a rectangular structure was solved by inserting a relieving semi-circular arch below the roof. The small space over the arch forms a croft. These buildings lack features by which they can be accurately dated; a conservative dating would be from the beginning of the 9th century onwards.

Round Towers

Contemporary with these early Irish churches, and very characteristically Irish, are round towers, of which about 120 are known to have existed in Ireland. They are tall, gracefully tapering buildings of stone, with conical stone roofs, which were built as monastic belfries, with the door approximately 12ft (3.5m) from the ground. This is a clue to their use as places of refuge or watch-towers during the period of Viking raids between the 9th and 11th centuries. Food, precious objects and manuscripts were stored in them. The ladder could then be drawn up. There are about seventy surviving examples in varying degrees of preservation.

The monk who wrote these beautiful lines expresses the tensions of those days:

Bitter the wind tonight,
Combing the sea's hair white:
From the North, no need to fear
the proud sea coursing warrior.

version by John Montague

High Crosses

These carved stone crosses, usually in the typical 'Celtic' ringed form, contain a great variety of biblical scenes and ornament. They are found in most parts of the country in early monastic sites. The earliest type are simple crosses carved on standing stones. They are most common in the west and in the Dingle Peninsula, County Kerry. The development of low-relief carving began in the 7th century, gradually becoming more complex, for example the cruciform slab at Carndonagh, County Donegal. It is carved with scenes of the Crucifixion, and interlaced ornament. The ringed high cross first appears at a later date; the earliest group of high crosses date from the 8th century. In this group the cross-shafts and heads are magnificently carved in sandstone with spirals and other decorative forms derived from metalwork, with figure-carvings on the bases. To the north, in the Barrow valley, is another group, later in date and more roughly carved in granite. The Barrow group has an interesting innovation: the faces of the shafts and heads are divided into panels, in which a scene, usually biblical, is portrayed.

Sandstone was used again for these crosses in the 10th century; they still grace monastic ruins scattered across the Central Plain. Favourite subjects for the carver were the Crucifixion; the Last Judgment; Adam and Eve; Cain and Abel; and the arrest of Christ. Later elaborate crosses may be seen at Clones, County Monaghan, Ardboe, County Tyrone and Donaghmore, County Down.

By the end of the 11th century the cross was changed; the ring was often left off, and the whole length of the shaft was taken up with a single figure of the crucified Christ. Ecclesiastical figures often appear on the opposite face and on the base, and the decoration of the north and south faces usually consists of animal-interlacing. Crosses of this style were carved up until the mid-12th century.

Romanesque Architecture

Characteristics of this decorative style appear in Irish buildings of the 12th century. While remaining structurally simple, the Irish churches of the period have carved doorways, chancel-arches or windows, with ornament in an Irish variation of the style. Many of the characteristic features of the early churches, such as antae and sloping jambs, were kept throughout the Romanesque period. The use of the chevron, an ornamental moulding, is common in Irish-Romanesque work, and it is nearly always combined with rows of beading. Carved human heads were sometimes used as capitals to the shafts in the orders of the doorways.

Gothic Architecture

With the coming of the Normans and changes they wrought, the native tradition in building declined, and Gothic architecture was introduced in the 13th century. The Irish

Gothic cathedrals were on a smaller scale than their English and Continental counter-parts and the grouping of lancets in the east window and south choir wall are typical of the Irish buildings.

Because of the turbulent times during the 14th century there was very little building done in Ireland, but this changed in the 15th and 16th centuries and a native Gothic style began to emerge, particularly in the west. It is best seen in the Franciscan friaries and the rebuilt Cistercian abbeys of the period. Features of the Franciscan style include a narrow church, a tall tapering tower, carved cloister and small window openings. The Cistercian style had a larger church, a huge square tower topped by stepped battlements, and a large carved cloister.

Castles

Although the Normans had built many castles before they came to Ireland, in the first years of the invasion they built fortifications of wood, usually taking over the sites of ancient Irish forts. The remains of these can be seen all over the eastern half of the country in the form of mottes and baileys. At the end of the 12th century the construction of stone fortifications on a large scale began. The early Norman castle, an example of which you can find at Carrickfergus, County Antrim, had a great square keep in a large bailey, and was defended by a high embattled wall, with turrets and barbicans. A very attractive feature of the Irish countryside is the ruined 15th- or 16th-century tower house. From about 1420 these buildings became common fortified farms consisting of a tall, square tower which usually had a small walled *bawn* or courtyard. In most cases the *bawn* has disappeared, but well-preserved examples can be seen at Doe Castle near Creeslough, County Donegal.

Glossary of Archaeological, Architectural and Associated Terms

Anglo-Norman: the name commonly given to the 12th-century invaders of Ireland, who came in the main from southwest Britain, and also their descendants, because they were of Norman origin.

Bailey: the space enclosed by the walls of a castle, or the outer defences of a motte (*see* Motte-and-bailey).

Barrel-vaulting: simple vaulting of semi-circular form.

Bastion: a projecting feature of the outer parts of a fortification, designed to command the approaches to the main wall.

Battlement: a parapet pierced with gaps to enable the defenders to discharge missiles.

Bawn: a walled enclosure forming the outer defences of a castle or tower-house. Besides being an outer defence it provided a safe enclosure for cattle.

Beehive hut: a prehistoric circular building, of wood or stone, with a dome-shaped roof, called a *clochan*.

Bronze Age: the earliest metal-using period from the end of the Stone Age until the coming of the Iron Age in Ireland, 2500 BC.

Caher: a stone fort.

Cairn: a mound of stones over a prehistoric grave; they frequently cover chambered tombs.

Cashel: a stone fort, surrounded by a rampart of dry stone walling, usually of late Iron Age date (*see* Ring-fort).

Chancel or choir: the east end of a church, reserved for the clergy and choir, and containing the high altar.

Chapter house: the chamber in which the chapter, or governing body of a cathedral or monastery met.

Chevaux-de-frise: a stone or stake defence work set upright and spaced.

Cist: A box-like grave of stone slabs to contain an inhumed or cremated burial, often accompanied by pottery. Usually Bronze Age or Iron Age in date.

Clochans (I): little groups of cottages, too small to be villages, grouped in straggly clusters according to land tenure and the ties of kinship between families. The land around the *clochan* forms the district known as a townland. A familiar sight is deserted or ruined *clochans* in mountain and moorland areas where huge numbers of people left with the land-clearances and famine during the 19th century.

Clochan (clochaun) (II): a small stone building, circular in plan, with its roof corbelled inwards in the form of a beehive. There are many examples in the west, especially in County Kerry. The word *clochan* is from the Irish *cloch*, a stone. The structures were early monks' cells. Nowadays they are used for storing things.

Cloisters: a square or rectangular open space, surrounded by a covered passage, which gives access to the various parts of a monastery. Many medieval cloisters survive.

Columbarium: a dovecote.

Corbel: a projecting stone in a building, usually intended to carry a beam or other structural member.

Corbelled vault: a 'false dome', constructed by laying horizontal rings of stones which overlap on each course until finally a single stone can close the gap at the centre. It is a feature of prehistoric tombs.

Corinthian: the third order of Greek and Roman architecture, a development of the Ionic. The capital has acanthus-leaf ornamentation.

Court cairn: a variety of megalithic tomb consisting of a covered gallery for burials and one or more open courts or forecourts for ritual purposes. Very common in the North of Ireland.

Crannóg: (from crann: a tree) an artificial island constructed in a lake or marsh to provide a dwelling-place in an easily defended position for isolated farming families. They would have been in use until the 17th century.

Curragh or currach: a light canoe consisting of skins, or in more recent times tarred canvas, stretched over a wickerwork frame.

Curtain wall: the high wall constructed around a castle and its bailey, usually provided at intervals with towers.

Demesne: land/estate surrounding a house which the owner has retained for his own use.

Dolmen: the simplest form of megalithic tomb, consisting of a large capstone and three or more supporting uprights. Some appear to have had forecourts.

Doric: the first order of Greek and Roman architecture, simple and robust in style. The column had no base and the capital was quite plain.

Dun: a fort, usually of stone and often with formidable defences.

Early English: the earliest Gothic architecture of England and Ireland, where it flourished in the 13th century. It is characterized by narrow lancet windows, high pointed arches and the use of rib-vaulting.

Esker: a bank or ridge of gravel and sand, formed by sub-glacial streams.

Folly: a structure set up by a landlord to provide work for poor tenants in the 19th century, and to amuse himself.

Fosse: a defensive ditch or moat around a castle or fort.

Gallaun: *see* Standing Stone.

Gallowglass: Scottish mercenary soldier hired by Irish clan leaders to fight their enemies.

Hill-fort: a large fort whose defences follow a contour round a hill to enclose the hilltop. Hill-forts are usually Early Iron Age.

Hospital: in medieval times, an alms-house or house of hospitality with provision for spiritual as well as bodily welfare, usually established to cater for a specific class of people.

Ionic: the second order of Greek and Roman architecture. The fluted column was tall and graceful in proportion and the capital had volutes (spiral scrolls in stone) at the top.

Irish-Romanesque: the Irish variety of the Romanesque style in architecture. *See* Romanesque.

Iron Age: the Early Iron Age is the term applied to the earliest iron-using period: in Ireland, from the end of the Bronze Age, *c.* 500 BC, to the coming of Christianity in the 5th century.

Jamb: the side of a doorway, window or fireplace. Early Irish churches have characteristic jambs inclined inwards towards the top. The incline is called the batter.

Keep: the main tower of a castle, serving as the innermost stronghold. There is a fine rectangular one at Carrickfergus, County Antrim. Castles with keeps date from the late 12th century until about 1260.

Kerne: an Irish foot-soldier of Tudor times.

Kitchen-midden: a prehistoric refuse-heap, in which articles of bronze, iron, flint and stone have been found; also shellfish debris, which indicate what our ancestors ate.

Lancet: a tall, narrow window ending in a pointed arch, characteristic of Early-English style. Often occur in groups of three, five or seven.

La Tène: a pre-Christian Irish classic ornamental style, which is linked to ornamental designs found in France.

Lunula: a crescent-shaped, thin, beaten gold ornament, of Early Bronze Age date—an Irish speciality.

Megalithic tomb: a tomb built of large stones for collective burial, Neolithic or Early Bronze Age in date.

Misericord or miserere: a carved projection on the underside of a hinged folding seat which, when the seat was raised, gave support to the infirm during the parts of a church service when they had to stand.

Motte-and-bailey: the first Norman fortresses which were made of earth. The motte was a flat-topped mound, shaped like a truncated cone, surrounded by a fosse and surmounted by a wooden keep. An enclosure, the bailey, bounded by ditch, bank and palisade, adjoined it. The bailey served as a refuge for cattle and in it were the sheds and huts of the retainers. This type of stronghold continued to be built until the early 13th century.

Nave: the main body of the church, sometimes seperated from the choir by a screen.

Neolithic: applied to objects from the New Stone Age which was characterized by the practice of agriculture, in Ireland, between 3000 and 2000 BC.

Ogham stones: early Irish writing, usually cut on stone. The characters consist of strokes above, below or across a stem-line. The key to the alphabet may be seen in the Book of Ballymote, now in the library of the Royal Irish Academy, Dublin. Ogham inscriptions occur mainly on standing stones. The inscription is usually commemorative in character. They probably date from AD 300.

Pale: the district around Dublin, of varying extent at different periods, where English rule was effective for some four centuries after the Norman invasion of 1169.

Passage grave: a type of megalithic tomb consisting of a burial-chamber approached by a long passage, and covered by a round mound or cairn.

Pattern: the festival of a saint, held on the traditional day of his death.

Plantation castles: a name given to defensive buildings erected by English and Scottish settlers under the plantation scheme between 1610 and 1620, which were very common in Ulster.

Portcullis: a heavy grating in a gateway, sliding up and down in slots in the jambs, which could be used to close the entrance quickly.

Rath: the rampart of an earthen ring-fort. The name is often used for the whole structure.

Rib-vaulting: roofing or ceiling in which the weight of the superstructure is carried on comparatively slender intersecting 'ribs' or arches of stone, the spaces between the ribs being a light stone filling without structural function.

Ring-fort, rath or **lis:** one or more banks and ditches enclosing an area, usually circular, within which were dwellings. It was the typical homestead of Early-Christian Ireland, but examples are known from *c.* 1000 BC to *c.* AD 1000. The bank sometimes had a timber palisade. Some elaborate examples were defensive in purpose.

Romanesque: the style of architecture, based on late Classical forms, with round arches and vaulting, which prevailed in Europe until the emergence of Gothic in the 12th century. *See* Irish-Romanesque.

Round towers: slender stone belfries, also used as refuges. Built between the 9th and 12th centuries.

Rundale: a system of holding land in strips or detached portions. The system has survived in parts of County Donegal.

Sedilia: seats recessed in the south wall of the chancel, near the altar, for the use of the clergy.

Sept: in the old Irish system, those ruling families who traced their descent from a common ancestor.

Sheila-na-Gig: a cult symbol or female fertility figure, carved in stone on churches or castles. No one is sure of their origin.

Souterrain: artificial underground chambers of wood, stone, earth, or cut into rock. They served as refuges or stores and in some cases even as dwellings. They occur commonly in ring-forts and, like these, date from the Bronze Age to at least Early-Christian times.

Standing stone: an upright stone set in the ground These may be of various dates and served various purposes, marking burial places or boundaries, or serving as cult objects.

Stone fort: a ring-fort built of dry-stone walling.

Sweat houses: an ancient form of sauna. Sometimes the mentally ill were incarcerated in them for a while in an attempt to cure them.

Teampull: a church.

Torc: a gold ornament from the Middle to Late Bronze Age, made of a ribbon or bar of gold twisted like a rope and bent around to form a complete loop. They are of Middle to Late Bronze Age date.

Tracery: the open-work pattern formed by the stone in the upper part of a Middle- or Late-Gothic window.

Transepts: the 'arms' of a church, extending at right-angles to the north and south from the junction of nave and choir.

Tumulus: a mound of earth over a grave; usually the mound over an earth-covered passage grave.

Undertaker: one of the English or Scottish planters who were given confiscated land in Ireland in the 16th century. They 'undertook' certain obligations designed to prevent the dispossessed owners from reacquiring their land.

Vaulting: a roof or ceiling formed by arching over a space. Among the many methods, three main types were used: barrel-vaulting, groin-vaulting and rib-vaulting. Rib-vaulting lent itself to great elaboration of ornament.

Zoomorphic: describing decoration based on the forms of animals.

The Irish language is the purest of all the Celtic languages, and Ireland is one of the last homes of the oral tradition of prehistoric and medieval Europe. Preserved by the isolated farming communities, there are also many expressions from the dialects of early English settlers. Irish was spoken by the Norman aristocracy and they patronized the Gaelic poets and bards. But with the establishment of an English system of land tenure and an English-speaking nobility Gaelic became scarce, except in the poorer farming areas. The potato famine in the 1840s hit the people who lived in such areas, thousands died and emigrated, and Gaelic speaking was severely reduced.The Gaelic League, founded in 1870, initiated a new interest and pride in the language and became identified with the rise of nationalism. In 1921 its survival became part of the the new State's policy. It was decided that the only way to preserve Gaelic was to protect and stimulate it where it was still a living language.

Language

The areas where it is spoken today are mostly in the west, and around the mountainous coast and islands. They form the Gaeltacht. Here everything is done to promote Irish-speaking in industry and at home. Centres have been set up for students to learn amongst these native speakers. There are special grants for people living in Irish-speaking areas but the boundaries are rather arbitrary. In Galway there's a boundary line through a built-up area so there's a certain amount of animosity towards those living on one side of the line, Irish speakers or no! There is also the problem of standardizing Irish, for the different dialects are quite distinct. The modern media tend to iron out these with the adoption of one region's form of words in preference to others. County Donegal seems to get the worst deal, being so much further from the centre of administration, although it has the largest number of native speakers.

You can appreciate all the reasons for promoting Irish, but it is only in the last few generations that the language has become popular. Before, it was left to Douglas Hyde and Lady Gregory to demonstrate the richness of Irish language and myth, and they had the advantage of being far away from the grim realities of hunger and poverty that the Irish-speakers knew. Gaelic, like certain foods (usually vegetables), had associations with hunger and poverty, and belonged to a hard past. The cultural co-ersion of the 1930s had a negative effect on most Irish people. It was only in Ulster that Gaelic speaking and culture kept its appeal in the face of protestant and official antipathy. Even now, people prefer to use English rather than stay in the Gaeltacht existing on grants and other government hand-outs. Gaelic is a compulsory subject in schools in the Republic, and there is a certain amount in the newspapers, on television, radio, signposts and street names (with English translations!). The use of Gaelic amongst the more intellectual middle classes is now on the increase, and this is being reinforced by the establishment of Gaelic speaking primary schools throughout the country. Irish Gaelic is one of the official languages of the European Union.

The carrying over of Irish idiom into English is very attractive and expressive. J. M. Synge captured this in his play Riders to the Sea. In fact, English as spoken by the Irish is in a class of its own. Joyce talked of 'the sacred eloquence of Ireland', and it is true that you could hardly find a more articulate people. Their poetry and prose is superb, and the emotions which their ballads can release is legendary. Hardship and poverty, have not killed the instinctive desire within to explain life away with words. The monks who scribbled in the margin of their psalters wrote with oriental simplicity this poem entitled 'Winter'.

> *My tiding for you: The stag bells*
> *Winter snows, summer is gone.*
> *Wind is high and cold, low the sun,*
> *Short his course, sea running high.*
> *Deep red the bracken, its shape all gone,*
> *The wild goose has raised his wonted cry.*
> *Cold has caught the wings of birds;*
> *season of ice–these are my tidings.*

9th century, translation by Kuno Meyer

That hardship brings forth great poetry is a theory strengthened by the school of contemporary northern Irish poets who have become known all over the world: Seamus Heaney, James Simmons, Derek Mahon, Medbh McGuckian. The cutting criticisms of Brian O'Nolan (known as Flann O'Brien), the gentle irony of Frank O'Connor and the furious passion of Sean O'Casey, Patrick Kavanagh and Liam O'Flaherty and John McGahern to name only a few, have become part of our perception of the Irish spirit since Independence. The list of recent writers could go on and on. One can only urge you to read them. There is a particularly good anthology of short stories edited by Benedict Kiely (Penguin), and an anthology of Irish verse, edited by John Montague (Faber & Faber).

Even though the disciplined cadences of the Gaelic bardic order was broken by the imposition of an English nobility in the 17th and 18th centuries, the Irish skill with words has survived, and is as strong as ever. As a visitor to Ireland you will notice this way with words when you have a conversation in a pub, or ask the way at a crossroads, or simply chat to the owners of the farmhouse where you spend the night.

The Meaning of Irish Place Names

The original Gaelic place names have been complicated by attempts to give them an English spelling. In the following examples, the Gaelic versions of the prefixes come first, followed by the English meaning.

Some Ulster and Other Expressions

Gaelic	English	Gaelic	English
agh, augh, achadh	a field	doo, du, duv, duf, dubh	black
aglish, eaglais	a church	dun, dún	a fort
ah, atha, áth	a ford	dysert, disert	hermitage
all, ail, aill	a cliff	glas, glen, gleann	a valley
anna, canna, éanarch	a marsh	illaun, oileán	an island
ard, ar, ard	a height	knock, cnoc	a hill
as, ess, eas	a waterfall	ken, kin, can, ceann	a headland
aw, ow, atha	a river	kil, kill, cill	a church
bal, bel, béal	the mouth (of a river or valley)	lis, liss, lios	a fort
		lough, loch	a lake or sea inlet
bal, balli, bally, baile	a town	ma, may, moy, magh	a plain
ballagh, balla bealach	a way or path	mone, mona, móna	turf or bog
bawn, bane, bán	white	monaster, mainistir	a monastery
barn, bearna	a gap	more, mór, mor	big or great
beg, beag	small	owen, avon, abhainn	a river
boola, booley, buaile, booleying	the movement of cattle from lowland to high pastures	rath	a ring-fort
		rinn, reen	a point
		roe, ruadh	red
		ross, ros	a peninsula, a wood
boy, buidhe	yellow	see, suidhe	a seat, e.g. Ossian's seat
bun	the foot (of a valley) or the mouth (of a river)	shan, shane, sean	old
		slieve, sliabh	a mountain
caher, cahir, cathair, carraig	a rock	tir, tyr, tír	country
cashel, caiseal, caislean	a castle	tubber, tobrid, tubbrid, tobar	a well
clogh, cloich, cloch	a stone	tra, traw, tráigh, trá	a strand or beach
clon, clun, cluain	a meadow		
derg, dearg	red		

Proverbs and Sayings

an oul sceach	crosspatch
assay	calling attention, as in Hi!
auld flutter guts	fussy person
balls of malt	whiskey
ballyhooley	a telling off (in Cork)
blow-in	stranger to the area
boreen	country lane
brave	commendable, worthy, e.g. a brave wee sort of a girl
bravely	could be worse, e.g. business is doing bravely
caution	(as in 'He's a caution'), a devil-may-care-type
chawing the rag	bickering couple
chick	child
cleg	horsefly
clever	neat, tight-fitting, usually refers to a garment
coul	wintry, cold
crack	fun, lively chat
cranky	bad-tempered
craw thumper	a 'holy Mary' or hypocrite
cut	insulted, hurt
dead on	exactly right
deed	passed away, dead
destroyed	exhausted
dingle	dent, mark with an impression
dip	bread fried in a pan
dither	slow
doley little fella	he's lovely
dulse	edible seaweed
eejit	fool
fairly	excellent, e.g. that wee lad can fairly sing
feed	meal
fern	foreign
in fiddler's green	you're in a big mess
fierce	unacceptable, extreme, e.g. it's fierce dear (expensive)
figuresome	good at sums
fog feed	lavish meal
foostering around	fiddling about
guff	impertinence, cheek
half sir	landlord's son

harp six	tumble
he hasn't a titter of wit	no sense at all
jar	a couple of drinks
lashins	plenty
mended	improved in health
mizzlin	raining gently
mullarkey	man
neb	nose
nettle	drive someone barmy
ni	now, this moment
not the full shilling	half-witted
oul or auld	not young, but can be used about something useful, e.g. my oul car
owlip	verbal abuse
palsie walsie	great friends
paraletic	intoxicated
plamas	sweet words
playboy	conceited fellow
poless	police
put the caibosh on it	mess things up
quare	memorable, unusual
qurrier or cowboy	bad type, rogue
rare	to bring up, educate
rightly	prospering, e.g. he's doing rightly now
scalded	bothered, vexed, badly burned
she's like a corncrake	chatterbox
skedaddled	ran quickly
skiff	slight shower or rain
slainte	drinking toast
soft	rainy, e.g. it's a grand soft day
spalpeen	agricultural labourer
spittin'	starting to rain
terrible	same use as 'fierce'
themins	those persons
thick as a ditch	stupid
thundergub	loud-voiced person
village bicycle	loose woman
wean	pronounced *wain*, child
wee	little; also in the north means with, e.g. did I see you wee that man?
you could trot a mouse on it	strong tea

Wise, and beautifully expressed with a delightful wry humour, these sayings and proverbs have passed into the English language. They highlight the usual Irish preoccupations with land, God, love, words and drinking, as well as every other subject under the sun. These are just a few examples; for a comprehensive collection read *Gems of Irish Wisdom*, by Padraic O'Farrell.

On God

It's a blessing to be in the Lord's hand as long as he doesn't close his fist.

Fear of God is the beginning of wisdom.

God never closes the door without opening another.

Man proposes, God disposes.

On the Irish Character

The wrath of God has nothing on the wrath of an Irishman outbid for land, horse or woman.

The best way to get an Irishman to refuse to do something is by ordering it.

The Irish forgive their great men when they are safely buried.

It is not that the Ulsterman lives in the past ... it is rather that the past lives in him.

Advice

No property–no friends, no rearing–no manners, no health–no hope!

Never give cherries to pigs, nor advice to a fool.

Bigots and begrudgers will never bid the past farewell.

When everybody else is running, that's the time for you to walk.

You won't be stepped on if you're a live wire.

If you get the name of an early riser you can sleep till dinner time.

There are finer fish in the sea than have ever been caught.

You'll never plough a field by turning it over in your mind.

Don't make a bid till you walk the land.

A man with humour will keep ten men working.

Do not visit too often or too long.

If you don't own a mount, don't hunt with the gentry.

You can take a man out of the bog but you cannot take the bog out of the man.

What is got badly, goes badly.

A watched pot never boils.

Enough is as good as plenty.

Beware of the horse's hoof, the bull's horn and the Saxon's smile.

Time is the best story-teller.

On Marriage and Love

Play with a woman that has looks, talk marriage with a woman that has property.

After the settlement comes love.

A lad's best friend is his mother until he's the best friend of a lassie.

A pot was never boiled by beauty.

There is no love sincerer than the love of food. (G. B. Shaw)

It's a great thing to turn up laughing having been turned down crying.

Though the marriage bed be rusty, the death bed is still colder.

On Argument and Fighting

Argument is the worst sort of conversation. (Dean Swift)

There is no war as bitter as a war amongst friends.

Whisper into the glass when ill is spoken.

If we fought temptation the way we fight each other we'd be a nation of saints again.

We fought every nation's battles, and the only ones we did not win were our own.

On Women

It takes a woman to outwit the Devil.

A cranky women, an infant, or a grievance, should never be nursed.

A women in the house is a treasure, a woman with humour in the house is a blessing.

She who kisses in public, often kicks in private.

If she is mean at the table, she will be mean in bed.

On Drinking

If Holy Water was porter he'd be at Mass every morning.

It's the first drop that destroys you; there's no harm at all in the last.

Thirst is a shameless disease, so here's to a shameless cure.

On the Family

Greed in a family is worse than need.

Poets write about their mothers, undertakers about their fathers.

A son's stool in his father's home is as steady as a gable; a father's in his son's, bad luck, is shaky and unstable.

On Old Age

The older the fiddle, the sweeter the tune.

There is no fool like an old fool.

On Loneliness

The loneliest man is the man who is lonely in a crowd.

On Bravery

A man who is not afraid of the sea will soon be drowned. (J. M. Synge)

On Flattery

Soft words butter no turnips, but they won't harden the heart of a cabbage either.

On Experience

Experience is the name everyone gives to their mistakes. (Oscar Wilde)

c. 8000 BC	Humans arrive in Ireland, travelling across the land bridge with Scotland.
c. 3000 BC	New Stone Age race build Newgrange in County Meath.
c. 2000 BC	Arrival of Beaker people.
c. 100 BC	Arrival of one wave of Gaelic (Celtic) peoples.
AD 200	The Kingdom of Meath is founded, and the high kingship at Tara, County Meath begins.
AD 432	St Patrick starts his Mission.
AD C7–8	Gaelic Christian Golden Age.
795	Viking raids begin.
1014	Battle of Clontarf and death of Brian Boru, the high king who won this decisive battle over the Vikings.
1170	The Anglo-Norman conquest begins with the arrival of Richard, Earl of Pembroke, called 'Strongbow'.
1171	Henry II visits Ireland, and secures the submission of many Irish leaders and that of his own Norman barons.
1314	The Bruce Invasion, which failed, under Edward Bruce.
1366	Statutes of Kilkenny which forbade the English settler to speak the Gaelic language, adopt an Irish name, wear Irish apparel, or marry an Irishwoman.
1394–99	Irish leaders war with Richard II.
1534–35	Rebellion of Silken Thomas, known as the 'Kildare Rebellion'.
1541	Irish Parliament accepts Henry VIII as King of Ireland.
1558	Accession of Elizabeth I. The Reformation does not succeed in Ireland.
1562 on	Elizabethan Conquest and settlement of various counties.
1569–73	The first Desmond Revolt.
1579–83	Final Desmond Revolt and suppression.
1592–1603	Rebellion of the Northern Lords, known as the Tyrone War.
1601	Battle of Kinsale—a defeat for Hugh O'Neill, Earl of Tyrone and his Ulster chiefs.
1607	Flight of the Earls of Tyrone and Tyrconnell to the Continent.
1608	Plantation of Ulster with Scots begins in Derry and Down.
1641	Irish Rising begins. At this time, 59 per cent of land in Ireland is held by Catholics.
1642–49	Catholic Confederation of Kilkenny.
1649	Cromwell arrives in Ireland.
1650	Catholic landowners exiled to Connacht.
1652	Cromwellian Act of Settlement.
1660	Restoration of Charles II.
1680	Accession of James II.
1689	April to July, Siege of Derry.
1690	July, The Battle of the Boyne. A great victory for William of Orange.
1691	September to October, Siege of Limerick.

Chronology

1691	October, Treaty of Limerick.
1695	Beginning of Penal Laws. Catholics now own 14 per cent of land.
1699	Irish woollen industry destroyed by English trade laws.
1704	Protestant non-conformists excluded from public office by Test Act.
1714	Catholics own 7 per cent of land.
1772	Rise of the Patriot Party in parliament, known as Grattan's parliament.
1778	Organization of Irish Volunteers.
1778	Gardiner's Relief Act for Catholics eases the Penal Laws.
1779	English concessions on trade and the repeal of most of the restrictive laws.
1782	Establishment of Irish Parliamentary independence.
1791	The Society of United Irishmen founded.
1795	Orange Order founded.
1798	Rebellion of '98.
1801	Act of Union.
1829	Catholic Emancipation Bill passed.
1842–48	The Young Ireland Movement.
1845–49	The Great Famine which began with the blight of the potato harvest.
1840s on	Emigration of thousands to the New World.
1848	Abortive rising led by Smith O'Brien.
1867	Fenian Rising.
1869	Disestablishment of the Church of Ireland.
1875	Charles Parnell elected Member of Parliament for County Meath.
1877	Parnell becomes Chairman of the Home Rule Confederation.
1879–82	Land war.
1886	Gladstone's first Home Rule Bill for Ireland defeated.
1890	Parnell cited in divorce case and he loses the leadership of the Irish Party in the House of Commons.
1892	Gladstone's second Home Rule Bill defeated.
1893	Gaelic League founded.
1899	The beginning of the Sinn Fein movement.
1903	Wyndham's Land Act.
1912	Third Home Rule Bill introduced.
1913	Ulster Volunteer Force founded.
1914	The outbreak of the First World War. The third Home Rule Bill receives Royal assent, but is deferred until the end of the war.
1916	The Easter Uprising.
1918–21	The Anglo-Irish War.
1920	Amendment Act to the Home Rule Bill which allows the Six Counties in Ulster to vote themselves out and remain with the rest of Britain.

1920–21	Heavy fighting between the Auxiliaries (known as the Black and Tans) and the Irish Nationalist forces.
1921	July, King George V officially opens the Stormont Parliament in the Six Counties.
1921	December, the Anglo-Irish treaty signed.
1922	January, the treaty is ratified in Dail Eireann. The start of the Irish Civil War between pro-treaty majority and anti-treaty forces.
1922	November, executions of anti-treaty leaders by Free State in Dublin.
1923	End of Civil War.
1926	De Valera founds Fianna Fail.
1932	General Election. Fianna Fail win.
1937	Constitution of Eire.
1938	Agreement with Britain; economic disputes are ended. Britain gives up tributary and naval rights in 'Treaty' ports.
1939	IRA bombing campaign in Britain. Outbreak of Second World War; Eire is neutral.
1945	End of Second World War.
1948	General Election in Ireland. Defeat of Fianna Fail, and de Valera is out of office for first time in 16 years.
1952	Republic of Ireland declared and accepted by Britain, with a qualifying guarantee of support to the Six Counties.
1956–62	IRA campaign in the North.
1968	First Civil Rights march.
1969	January, people's democracy march from Belfast to Derry. Marchers attacked at Burntollet Bridge.
1969	August, British troops sent to Derry.
1971	February, first British soldier killed by IRA. August, internment of IRA suspects. Reforms to the RUC, and electoral system.
1972	Direct Rule imposed from Westminster: the Stormont Government and Irish Parliament are suspended.
1973	The Sunningdale Agreement. An Assembly established with power-sharing between different political leaders.
1974	Ulster Worker's Strike brings down Assembly. Direct Rule reimposed.
1981	Bobby Sands dies after 60-day hunger strike.
1985	Anglo-Irish Agreement.
1993	Downing Street Initiative.
1994	August–IRA cease-fire.
1996	Canary Wharf bombing in London. IRA declares cease-fire over.
1997	IRA cease-fire renewed.
1998	Good Friday Agreement.
	May, Referendum Agreement. June, New Assembly elections by proportional representation.
1999	Assembly set up; end of Direct Rule. Decommissioning talks continue.

Further Reading

Archaeology, Architecture and Art

An Archaeological Survey of Co. Down (HMSO, 1966).

Bardon, Jonathan, *Belfast, An Illustrated History* (Blackstaff Press).

Beckett, J.C. et al, *Belfast, The Making of a City* (Appletree).

Benn, George, *Vol I—A History of the Town of Belfast, from the earliest times to the close of the 18th century* (London, Marcus Ward & Co 1877); *Vol II—A History of the Town of Belfast, from 1799 till 1810, together with some incidental notices on local topics, and biographies of many well-known families* (London, Marcus Ward & Co 1880).

Brett, C. E., *Buildings of Belfast 1700–1914* (Friar's Bush Press, Belfast 1985).

Brett, C. E., *Court Houses and Market Houses of the Province of Ulster* (1973).

Buildings of Armagh, Ulster Architectural Heritage Society (UAHS) (1992).

Craig, Maurice, *Classical Irish Houses of the Middle Size: Lost Demesnes* (Architectural Press).

Crookshank, Anne and The Knight of Glin: *Painters of Ireland* c. *1660–1920* (Barrie & Jenkins).

Dean, J. A. K., *Gate Lodges of Ulster. A Gazetteer* (UHAS).

de Breffny and Folliott: *Houses of Ireland* (Thames & Hudson), *Castles of Ireland* (Thames & Hudson), *Churches and Abbeys of Ireland* (Thames & Hudson).

Dixon, Hugh, *An Introduction to Ulster Architecture* (1975).

Estyn Evans, E., *Prehistoric Ireland* (Batsford).

Evans, David, *An Introduction to Modern Ulster Architecture* (Thames & Hudson).

Fallon, Brian, *Irish Art 1830–1990* (Appletree Press).

Guinness, Desmond, *Great Irish Houses and Castles* (Weidenfeld & Nicholson).

Harbison, P.; Potterton H. and Sheehy J.: *Irish Art and Architecture* (Thames & Hudson).

Henry, Françoise, *Early Christian Irish Art* (Mercier).

Kennedy, Brian, *Irish Art and Modernism* (Institute of Irish Studies).

Larmour, Paul, *Belfast: An Illustrated Architectural Guide* (Friars Bush Press, Belfast).

Maire de Paor, *Early Irish Art* (Aspect of Ireland Series).

Malone and Stranmillis—Belfast (UHAS) (1991).

McCracken, Eileen, *The Palm House and Botanic Garden, Belfast* (UHAS).

McCutcheon, W. A., *The Industrial Archaeology of Northern Ireland* (HMSO).

O'Brien, Jacqueline and Guinness, Desmond, *A Grand Tour* (Weidenfeld & Nicholson).

O'Byrne, Cathal, *As I Roved Out* (Irish News Belfast repr Blackstaff Press).

O'Hanlon, Rev W. M., *Walks Among the Poor of Belfast, and Suggestions for their Improvement* (Belfast 1853 repr SR Publishers 1971).

Open, Michael, *Fading Light, Silver Screens: A History of Belfast Cinemas* (Greystone Books).

O'Riordain, S. P. O., *Antiquities of the Irish Countryside* (Methuen).

Patton, Marcus, *Central Belfast: A Historical Gazetteer* (1993 UHAS).

Rankin, Peter, *Irish Building Ventures of the Earl Bishop of Derry* (UHAS).

Thackeray, W. M., *The Irish Sketch Book, 1842* (repr Blackstaff Press 1985).

Tohill, J. J., *Pubs of the North*, 1990.

Walker, Brian (ed), *Frank Matcham, Theatre Architect* (Blackstaff Press). All about the restoration of the Opera House in Belfast.

White, *John Butler Yeats and the Irish Renaissance* (Dolmen).
Burkes Guide to Country Houses: Ireland (Burkes).
Historic Monuments of Northern Ireland (HMSO 1983).

Guides and Topographical

Blair, May, *Once Upon the Lagan: Story of the Lagan Canal* (Blackstaff Press).
Craig, Maurice and Knight of Glin, *Ireland Observed* (Mercier).
Day, A. and McWilliams, P. (ed), *The Ordnance Survey Memoirs of Ireland* (Ulster series).
Harbison, Peter, *Guide to the National Monuments of Ireland* (Gill & Macmillan).
Hayward, R., *In Praise of Ulster* (out of print).
Morton, H. V., *In Search of Ireland* (Methuen).
Murphy, Dervla, *A Place Apart* (Penguin).
Pepper, John, *Ulster Phrasebook* (Appletree Press)
Rowan, Alistair, *North West Ulster* (Pevsners).

Irish Walk Guides

Simon, Patrick and Foley, Gerard, *No. 3 North West* (Gill & Macmillan).
Warner, Alan, *Walking the Ulster Way* (Appletree Press).
Wright, Peter, *Ulster Rambles* (Greystone Press).

Maps

Historical Map (Bartholomew).
Northern Ireland Map, by Bord Fáilte (Ordnance Survey).
Irish Family Names Map (Johnson & Bacon)—divided into North, East, South and West.
Ordnance Survey maps, 1:126720 (half-inch). (Sheet 5 covering Belfast no longer available.)
Ireland North Holiday map, 1:250,000 (Ordnance Survey).

Folklore, Music and Tradition

Danaher, *Folktales of the Irish Countryside* (Mercier).
Estyn Evans, E., *Irish Folk Ways* (Routledge).
Feldman, Allan and O'Doherty, *The Northern Fiddler: Music and Musicians of Donegal and Tyrone* (Blackstaff).
Flanagan, Laurence (ed), *The Darling of My Heart.* Two thousand years of Irish love writing (Gill & Martin).
Flower, R., *The Irish Tradition* (Clarendon Press).
Gaffney S. and Cashman, S., *Proverbs and Sayings of Ireland* (Wolfhound).
Gregory, Lady Isabella Augusta, *Gods and Fighting Men* (Smythe).
Healy, J. N., *Love Songs of the Irish* (Mercier).
Healy, J. N., *Percy French and his Songs* (Mercier).
Hyde, Douglas, *The Stone of Truth and other Irish Folktales* (Irish Academic Press).
O'Boyle, Sean, *The Irish Song Tradition* (Gilbert Dalton).
O'Connell, James, *The Meaning of the Irish Coast* (Blackstaff).
O'Faolain, S., *Short Stories* (Mercier).
O'Farrell, P., *Folktales of the Irish Coast* (Mercier).
O'Flaherty, Gerald, *A Book of Slang, Idiom and Wit* (O'Brien).
O'Keeffe D. and Healy, J. N., *Book of Irish Ballads* (Mercier).

O'Sullivan, Sean, *Folklore of Ireland* (Batsford).

Wilde, William, *Irish Popular Superstitions* (Irish Academic Press).

Photography

Estyn Evans, E. and Turner, B. S., *Ireland's Eye: The Photographs of Robert John Welch* (Blackstaff).

Friars Bush Press publish a series of historic photographs, covering tours of different parts of Ulster.

Hill & Pollock, *Images and Experience—Photographs of Irishwomen 1880–1920* (Blackstaff Press).

Hogg, Alexander, *Photographs of Belfast 1870–1939* (Friars Bush).

Johnstone and Kirk, *Images of Belfast* (Blackstaff).

Maguire, W. A., *Caught in Time* (Belfast).

Walker, Brian & Dixon, Hugh (ed), *No Mean City. Belfast 1880–1914 Photographs of Robert French* (Friars Bush); also by French *In Belfast Town*.

Walker, B. M.; O'Brien, A. and McMahon, S., *Faces of Ireland* (Appletree Press).

Politics, History and Literary History

Bardon, Jonathan, *A History of Ulster* (Blackstaff Press).

Beckett, J. C., *The Making of Modern Ireland* (Faber).

Brady, O'Dowd, Walker (ed), *Ulster: An Illustrated History* (Batsford).

Campbell, Brian et al (ed), *Nor Meekly Serve My Time—The H-Block Struggle 1976–81* (Beyond the Pale).

Carr, Peter, Dundonald, *The Most Unpretending of Places—A History of Dundonald, Co. Down* (White Row Press).

Cruise O'Brien, M. and C., *Concise History of Ireland* (Thames & Hudson).

Cruise O'Brien, Conor, *States of Ireland* (Hutchinson).

Edwards, R. Dudley, *A New History of Ireland* (Gill & Macmillan).

Edwards, R. Dudley, *An Atlas of Irish History* (Methuen).

Foster, R. F. (ed), *The Oxford History of Ireland* (OUP)

Foster, R. F., *Modern Ireland 1600, 1972* (OUP)

Kee, Robert, *The Green Flag* (Sphere).

Kelly, Mary Pat, *Home Away from Home—the Yanks in Ireland* (Appletree Press).

Leslie, Shane, *The Irish Tangle for English Readers.*

Lyons, F. S. L., *Ireland Since the Famine* (Fontana).

McCavery, *Newtown: A History of Newtownards* (White Row Press).

MacLysaght, E., *Surnames of Ireland* (Irish Academic Press).

MacLysaght, E., *Irish Families: Their Names and Origins* (Figgins).

Maxwell, Constancia, *Country and Town under the Georges* (Dundalgan Press).

Millar, David, *Don't Mention the War—Northern Ireland Propaganda and Media* (Pluto Press).

O'Brien, G. & Roebuck, P. (ed), *Nine Ulster Lives* (Ulster Historical Foundation).

O'Farrell, P., *How the Irish Speak English* (Mercier).

Stewart, A. T. Q., *The Narrow Ground* (Faber).

Wallace, M., *A Short History of Ireland* (David & Charles).

Woodham Smith, Cecil, *The Great Hunger (History).(Penguin)*

Walker, B. M., *Sentry Hill: An Ulster Farm and Family* (Friars Bush Press).

Biography and Memoirs

Bence Jones, Mark, *Twilight of the Ascendancy* (Constable).

Day, Angelique (ed), *Letters from Georgian Ireland* (Friars Bush Press).

Doyle, Lynn, *An Ulster Childhood* (Blackstaff Press).

Draper, Vivienne, *The Children of Dunseverick* (Brandon).

Hunt, Hugh, *The Abbey, Ireland's National Theatre 1904–79* (Gill & Macmillan).

Kavanagh, Patrick, *The Green Fool* (Penguin).

McAughtrey, Sam, *Hillman Street Blues—Tales from a Belfast Boyhood* (Appletree Press).

Ormsby, Frank (ed), *Northern Windows: An Anthology of Ulster Autobiography* (Blackstaff Press).

Parke, William K., *A Fermanagh Childhood* (Friars Bush Press).

Toibin, Colm, *Walking Along the Border* (Macdonald).

Fiction, Poetry and Plays

Bell, Sam Hanna, *December Bride* and other novels (Blackstaff Press, BBC and others).

Birmingham, George, any novels (Blackstaff, BBC and others).

Bolger, Dermot (ed), *The Picador Book of Contemporary Irish Fiction* (Pan).

Carleton, William, *The Black Prophet* (Irish University Press).

Carleton, William, *Traits and Stories of the Irish Peasantry* (Colin Smythe).

Crone, Anne, *Bridie Steen* (Blackstaff Press).

Durcan, Paul; Yeats, W. B., Heaney, Seamus; Simmons, James and Clarke, Austin, *The Faber Book of Irish Verse*.

Fallon, Peter & Mahon, Derek (ed), *The Penguin Book of Contemporary Irish Poetry*.

Friel, Brian, stories and plays (Penguin and others).

Hewitt, John, any poetry.

Irvine, Alexander, *My Lady of the Chimney Corner* (out of print).

Moore, Brian, any novels.

O'Brien, Flann, *The Poor Mouth* (Picador).

The Penguin Book of Irish Verse and *The Penguin Book of Irish Short Stories*.

Cooking, Crafts, Flora, Fauna and Fishing

Bridgestones Guides to Where to Stay and Eat in Ireland (Estragon Press).

Gill & Macmillan do a series of fishing guides on Game, Coarse and Sea Angling.

Fitzgibbon, Theodora, any cookbooks.

Hackney, Paul (ed), *Flora of the Northeast of Ireland* (Institute of Irish Studies).

Heron, Marianne, *The Hidden Gardens of Ireland* (Gill & Macmillan).

Irvine, Florence, *The Cookin' Woman—Irish Country Recipes* (Blackstaff Press).

Lewis, C. A., *Hunting in Ireland* (J.A. Allen).

O'Brien, Louise, *Crafts of Ireland* (Gilbert Dillon).

O'Reilly, Peter, *Trout & Salmonn Loughs of Ireland* (Harper Collins).

O'Reilly, Peter, *Trout & Salmon Rivers of Ireland* (Merlin Unwin Books).

Reeves-Smyth, Terence, *Irish Gardens, Irish Country Houses, Irish Castles* (3 separate titles) (Appletree Press).

Traditional Irish Recipes (Appletree Press).

Webb, D. A., *An Irish Flora* (Dundalgan).

Index

Glenarm 145–6, 154, 155
Glencolmcille 204, 208, **210–11**, 220, 222, 223, 224
Glenelly, River 110, 112, 114
Glenoe 143
Glens of Antrim 76, 138, 142, 144–9
Glenties 211, 224
Glenveagh 77, 78, 91, 206, **217**
gliding 125
Glynn 143
gods **244–8**
  Co. Antrim 140, 145, 146, 147
  Co. Armagh 198–9
  Co. Donegal 218
gold 110
golf 17–18
  Belfast 162
  Co. Antrim 141, 152
  Co. Armagh 192, 195
  Co. Cavan 229
  Co. Donegal 206–7, 208, 215
  Co. Down 175, 182
  Co. Fermanagh 97
  Co. Londonderry 125
  Co. Monaghan 238, 242
  Co. Tyrone 110, 113
Good Friday Agreement 56, 62
Gortahork 212
Gortin Glen Forest Park 112, 114
Gosford Castle 197
Gothic architecture **252–3**
Gothic Revival architecture 81, 239
Gothick architecture 81
government 56–63
Gowna, Lough 229, 233
Gracehill 152
Grattan, Henry 46, 117
gravestones 103, 210, 240, 241
Great Copeland 85
Greek Revival architecture 133
Green Island 175
Greencastle 205, 208, **219**, 222, 224
Greencastle Fort 183
Greyabbey 177, 186
Grianan of Aileach 205, 218, 251
Griffith, Arthur 55
Groomsport 186, 188
guest houses 34
Guinness, Hon. Desmond 80–1
Guinness 16
Guthrie, Sir Tyrone 241

Hamilton, Malcolm 102
Hamilton, Captain William 111
hang-gliding 27
Hanging Rock 95, 102
Hansard, Sir Richard 217
Harper, Catherine 92
Harrison, Richard 242
Harte, General George Vaughan 214
Healy, Michael Joseph 99
Heaney, Seamus 92, 128, 170
Helen's Bay 166, 188
Helen's Tower 166

Henry, T. W. 179
Hervey, Frederick Augustus 78, 127, 128
Hewitt, John 92
Hezlett House 76, 127
Hibernio-Romanesque architecture 81
Hidden Ireland 45
Hill, Derek 77, 83, 92, 212, 217
hill-forts 218, **251**
Hillsborough 185, 186, 188
Hilltown 174, 184
hill-walking 28
historic houses and gardens 76–82
history **37–64**
hitch-hiking 10, 36
holy wells **67**, 102, 180, 196, 217, 240
Holyrood 185, 186
Holywood 86, 186, 188
Home Rule 52–3
Hone, Evie 232
Hope, Henry 240
Hope Castle 240
Horn Head 213
horse riding see pony-trekking
horses 238, 240
hotels 33
Hughes, Archbishop John 115
Huguenots 67, 152
Humbert, General 47–8
Hume, John 60
hunting 27
hurling 27
Hyde, Douglas 53, 245

Inch Abbey 180
Inch Island 218
Inchin, Lough 229, 230
Inishkeen 103, 236, 241
Inishowen 204, 205, 206, 207, 208, **218–19**
inland waterways see canals
insurance 20
internment 58
Ireland, Republic of 55–6, 61, 62–3
  see also Cavan, County; Donegal, County; Monaghan, County
Irish coffee 16
Irish Georgian Society 80–1
Irish Land League 50–1
Irish language see Gaelic
Irish Republican Army (IRA) 55, 56, 64, 132
  ceasefire 61–2
  Northern Ireland 57, 58, 59, 60
  origins 54
Iron Age 118, 205, 255
  see also Celts

Jackson, Andrew 143
James I 42, 117, 123, 232
James II 44–5, 130, 217–18
Janus figures 100, 101
John, King 142
Johnston, Francis 81, 82, 193, 194
Jordan's Castle 181

Kavanagh, Patrick 92, 236, 241
Keady 79, 199
Keats, John 176
Kesh 101, 104
Kevin of Glendalough, Saint **72**
Kieran, St (Ciaran) **72**
Kilcar 210, 224
Kilclief Castle 181
Kilkeel 174, 183, 187
Killadeas 100
Killeshandra 228, 233
Killevy Church 198
Killinchy 186, 188
Killinkere 228
Killough 181
Killybegs 206, 210, 223
Killycluggin 231
Killykeen Forest Park 229, 230, 233
Killyleagh 179, 186
Killymoon Castle 82, 110, 116
Kilmacrenan **217**, 221, 223, 224
Kilmore 195
Kilnasaggart Pillar Stone 198
Kilroot 143
Kinbane Head 149
Kincasslagh 221–2, 223
Kingscourt 232, 233
Knight Ride (Carrickfergus) 90, 143
knitwear 25, 210, 211, 219, 224
Knockmany Chambered Cairn 118

Labour Party (Republic of Ireland) 63
lacemaking 24, 198, 210, 240, 241, 242
Lagan, River 162, 165
language see Gaelic
Lanyon, Sir Charles 82, 163
Larne 142, **143–4**, 155
Lavery, Sir James 164
Layde Church 147
leanhaun shee 92
leprechauns 91
Leslie, Sir Shane 240
Leslie Hill Heritage Farm Park 141, 152
Letterkenny 204, 207, 208, **216**, 220, 221, 222, 223, 224
Lever, Charles 151
Lewis, C.S. 178
Liamvady 135, 136
licensing hours 17
Lifford 204, 217, 220, 221, 223
Lighthouse Island 85
lighthouses 215, 219
Limavady 79, 125, 126
Limerick 24, 44–5
linen 25, **85–6**
  Belfast 167
  Co. Antrim 90, 152, 153, 185
  Co. Armagh 197, 199
  Co. Cavan 228
  Co. Donegal 204, 216
  Co. Down 185
  Co. Monaghan 238
  Co. Tyrone 76, 110, 113, 116
Lir 199, 247

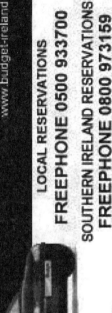